Performance, Subjectivity, and Experimentation

PERFORMANCE, SUBJECTIVITY, AND EXPERIMENTATION

Edited by Catherine Laws

Leuven University Press

Table of Contents

Introduction

Catherine Laws

The study of music across cultures and practices often explores how subjectivity acts in and through music: how individual, felt experience is mediated by compositions, by performances, and in listening to music. The question of what it is to be a musical "subject" then leads to that of how the perceptions of individuals and groups become constituted, socio-musically, into identities. And this, in turn, leads to the understanding that music reflects identity, an understanding that is now deeply engrained in both musicology and popular media commentary. However, there is more to it than this. It is now over twenty years since Simon Frith, developing comments made by Kofi Agawu, took studies of popular music to task for their one-sidedness: their failure to consider subjectivity and identity as processes formed (and continually reformed) through performance, not just expressed by it. As Frith says, subjectivity is "*mobile*, a process not a thing," with "our experience of music . . . best understood as an experience of this *self-in-process*" (1996, 109). These words resonate with ideas prevalent in contemporaneous (and subsequent) research in performance studies, particularly in theatre, live art, and dance, research predicated on the understanding that subjectivity is *performative*. Following Judith Butler (1988) and others, subjectivity is understood as an emergent process, *constituted* (not merely expressed) by what we say and do.

These concerns are still very much with us, evidenced in ongoing preoccupations with questions of selfhood, identity, and difference—not just in arts practices and theory, but also everyday life and, of course, politics.[1] The present book contends that musical practices are hugely important in this regard but that insufficient attention has been paid to how and why.

In 2014 a group of musician-researchers at the Orpheus Institute, Ghent, formed a research cluster with the title "Performance, Subjectivity, and Experimentation."[2] The aim was to examine, through forms of composition, improvisation, and performance, along with related critical inquiry, how an impression or idea of a musical self emerges from the complex, distributed practices of music-making, in which a range of different entities always play a part: people, instruments, histories, and contexts. The underlying motivation was a shared sense that questions of agency, subjectivity, and identity have not been adequately addressed in relation to—or through—performance prac-

---

1 Appiah discusses the "modern prevalence of ideas about identities" (2016, xiii).
2 The core members of this group are Catherine Laws, William Brooks, David Gorton, and Stefan Östersjö, but each of the subprojects has involved other collaborators. The research has taken place not just at the Orpheus Institute, but also at the University of York (UK), Malmö Academy of Music, Lund University (Sweden), and the Royal Academy of Music (UK).

tices, and that these things matter not only in themselves but also in relation to wider issues of musical authority, meaning, affect, and empathy. We wanted to move beyond the theoretical perspectives on subjectivity that have emerged in recent decades, first in critical theory and thereafter in musicology, repurposing some of this as appropriate but working, primarily, from a practice-oriented perspective. Instead of simply applying theoretical perspectives to practice, we would use practice-led (artistic) research processes to examine the core questions of how subjectivity emerges through processes of creativity and forms of collaboration.

The theoretical discourse on subjectivity is extensive and widely dispersed across disciplines in the arts, humanities, and social sciences. Increasingly, it is also informed by developments in fields such as neuroscience and embodied cognition. For our research cluster, practice had to be the starting point if we were to explore how subjectivity is instantiated and embodied in performance—how the activities of musical performance both reflect and help shape our understanding of individual, felt experience, and how the dynamic relationships between performer, musical materials, and the context of performance affect the production of subjectivity. The research projects of that cluster have all included creative work specifically designed—conceptualised and planned—to help address those questions. From the start, a key issue was how to experiment with the processes of performance so as to explore, draw out, and foreground subjectivity in action.

Our work led to the production of a range of artistic outputs but also to a substantial study, *Voices, Bodies, Practices: Performing Musical Subjectivities*, published in 2019. However, as part of the wider research process, in 2016 we held a two-day seminar with an open call for interested parties (especially practitioner-researchers) from across Europe and beyond to join us to share their perspectives on this topic. The present book, *Performance, Subjectivity, and Experimentation*—along with the linked examples of musical (or in some cases intermedial) practice—developed out of that event. The first, partner volume, *Voices, Bodies, Practices*, is tightly focused around the four subprojects that formed the Orpheus Institute research cluster and that evolved through a long-term process of shared practice and critical reflection. In this second volume there is a wider range of voices. There is also no common approach, methodology, or theoretical framework. That is deliberate: across these two volumes we hope to open up certain aspects of the debate and to form some starting points for further investigation. Because the topic of subjectivity in performance is huge, however, it seemed important to draw together a wider network of ideas, perspectives, and practices.

Certain threads run through the book. Notably, all the chapters are concerned with contemporary practices, whether in music alone or combined with other arts. This stems partly from the wider tendency towards a degree of reflexivity in Western art music of the second half of the twentieth century and beyond: that is, the tendency to produce musical experiences that invite us into their processes or into considering quite what (or sometimes whom) we are hearing (and seeing, or imagining) as we listen, invoking our embodied, affective, or conceptualised responses as listening subjects. Moreover, since artistic practice can be an important means of understanding the processes by which subjectivity is produced, the research process often entails making new work that self-consciously explores these issues—sometimes explicitly and thematically and sometimes implicitly—in its processes.

Contemporary practices therefore form the basis of this book. Those practices range from work that conforms to the traditional Western classical separation of composer and performer, to work that is more concerned with improvisation or devising. Other instances lie somewhere in between, examining collaborative or otherwise co-creative processes in which individual agency and authority are difficult to unravel, which in itself reveals much about the complexities of subjectivity. Some chapters are concerned with acoustic practices, some with digital and/or electronic forms. Some consider purely music practices; others include the interaction of music and sound with processes of writing and choreography. We have made no attempt to be fully diverse in terms of styles, cultures, or practices, however. This is a relatively small collection, designed to provide a range of perspectives on the core topic, not an overview of how subjectivity operates across musical performance. Indeed, to try to do this would have been problematic, with each individual piece then appearing to "represent" its field or practice, when in fact one of the issues here is the very contingency, practical and social, of subjectivity, and hence the difficulty of extrapolating beyond the specifics of particular embodied interactions in particular contexts. Thus there is no attempt to provide any kind of overarching theory; instead, we seek to evidence some of the diverse ways in which subjectivity, manifested as an individual or collective "voice" or "persona," is always *different*: always multiple, unstable, embodied, and contingent. In today's political climate, it is critical to question how subjectivities are pressed into rigid, essentialist forms of identity; the arts—perhaps especially the performing arts—have an important role to play in refusing simplistic, singular definitions.[3]

The chapters are all, to different extents and in different ways, concerned with forms of intersubjectivity. Indeed, as should by now be clear, underpinning the book is the understanding that subjectivity is always intersubjective, always composite—an idea that is hardly new but that often seems to be forgotten in the tendency, especially in musical practice, to focus on individuals and individuality. Moreover, these chapters *evidence* the ways in which that intersubjectivity is manifest. The first three chapters all offer different ways of approaching this topic quite explicitly and in relation to ensemble practices. Deniz Peters examines the emergence of states of musical togetherness and empathic, shared emotion in musical improvisation. This discussion of the formation of a "we-subject" identifies processes of "tuning in" and relationality, both themes that are central to, but drawn out differently, in Juliana Hodkinson's examination of processes of "affective resonance." Using Bourriaud's theory of

---

3 In *The Lies That Bind: Rethinking Identity* (2018), Kwame Anthony Appiah argues that much present-day thinking about identity is still heavily dependent on primarily (Western) nineteenth-century ideas that are problematically essentialist and dangerously outmoded.

relational aesthetics, Hodkinson examines the production of intersubjectivity from the interactions of composers, performers, listeners, instruments, and other objects, through shared experience of bodies, sound, and space.

In Peters's discussion of intersubjectivity the focus is improvisation. In her own work, discussed in her chapter, Hodkinson retains the role of composer but usually leaves many decisions to the rehearsal (and even the performance): composer and performers work together on the same or similar tasks, sometimes with the audience also participating. A certain distinction of roles is maintained, with different forms of agency in operation, but a relational subjectivity emerges from the shared, embodied experience of a dynamic, affective, and social interaction.

Chapter 3, by David Gorton and Stefan Östersjö, shifts into a more conventional Western classical situation in which composer and performer are relatively distinct entities with relatively discrete roles. However, Gorton and Östersjö have for some time been researching, through the practices of their ongoing collaborations, the nature of the "voice" that emerges in performance. Earlier publications, including a chapter in our partner volume, *Voices, Bodies, Practices*, have analysed the production of this "discursive voice" in Östersjö's solo guitar performances: a composite, intersubjective entity, formed through the interaction of composer, performer, the affordances and resistances of instruments, and the wider context of surrounding cultural practices. Here, they consider how this concept extends into two duo contexts.

The chapter that follows, co-written by Zubin Kanga, Anne Veinberg, Maria Kallionpää, Adrian Hazzard, Chris Greenhalgh, and Steve Benford, ostensibly moves into the territory of solo performance. It is concerned with the processes of subjectivity at work when two different performers realise a new composition for Disklavier, affording comparison of their different responses. The piece, *Climb!* (2016–17) by Kallionpää, consists of a game-like structure embedded within an interactive system: the performer in fact plays in duet with the self-playing Disklavier, with much of the musical material mirrored or exchanged between the electronic and human parts. The chapter therefore opens up questions not only of human intersubjectivity—produced through the interactions of composer, performer, and game system developers (and examined from their different perspectives)—but also of how a pianist trained to be an autonomous, individual performer, behaves when confronted with a distributed network designed precisely to manipulate his or her sense of performative autonomy. This is, then, very different from the kind of interactive network of human and nonhuman agents considered by Hodkinson; yet many of the underlying issues of subjectivity—co-creativity, agency, and interaction—again emerge.

In the chapter by Kanga et al., the performer's sense of agency and musical selfhood is challenged by the interference of the interactive system. Richard Craig's contribution is, on the face of it, far removed from this, concerned with an acoustic solo flute performance. Here, though, the development of a composition through a performer-led process focused on Craig's breathing technique leads to a different kind of blurring of agency: of performer and instrument, mediated by notation. The piece operates at the limits of the incorporation of the instrument into the body schema, pushing this to extremes that both rely upon and also disrupt the integration of body and flute. Craig examines this point of resistance: the boundary point between the instrument is experienced both as a tool of subjective expression—an idea fundamental to musical practice across styles, periods, and cultures—and, conversely, as an entirely external object. Drawing on the phenomenology of illness, Craig also examines the parallel process that takes place within the body, on the boundaries between a transparent sense of the "flow" of bodily action that can occur in performance and its apparent opposite, the phenomenological experiencing of the body as other, as itself an objectified instrument.

Craig's chapter prises open questions of embodied subjectivity that are approached in earlier chapters but further developed in my own. This, again, concerns a solo—for piano—but the performance examined here, of Annea Lockwood's *Ceci n'est pas un piano*, combines instrumental sound, recorded text, and video images in a piece that explicitly thematises the performer's embodied relationship to the instrument. I wrote and recorded the performance text myself, and the chapter draws upon theoretical perspectives on the uses of autobiographical writing in women's performance art. I explore the subjective space opened up between the physically present performer—who forms a version of herself through a particular embodied engagement with the piano as a physical object, sound source, and cultural agent—and the absent performer evoked by the recorded voice. Here the "discursive voice" forms in the space that is explicitly mediated by the interactions of the performing body, the instrument, and the recorded voice, but also implicitly formed by a composer, a past performer, and the wider context of performance production.

The gendered formation of subjectivity remains in the foreground in the next two chapters. Eleanor Roberts shifts the discussion into the interaction between artistic agency, institutional critique, and feminist practice, examining cellist Charlotte Moorman's 1969 collaboration with Nam June Paik and their collection of performances in "Avant-Garde Music" at London's Institute of Contemporary Arts. As Roberts discusses, Moorman's work has previously been characterised as inauthentic and theatrically extravagant. Those accounts are challenged here, reconfiguring Moorman's performances as pleasurable, strategic, and an agent for different subject positions for women artists. This is the only chapter that does not approach its subject through artistic research. Instead, it opens up important related questions about the relationship between the live event and its archival "remains," examining the potential for feminist interpretation to expose, retrospectively, the self-conscious staging of female subjectivity.

Nguyễn Thanh Thủy and Stefan Östersjö continue the examination of gendered subjectivity, but in the context of intercultural collaboration. Drawing on Susan Leigh Foster's examination of gesture and movement in constituting the gendered performance of subjectivity, this chapter examines the choreography of gender in traditional Vietnamese music performance. To explore gesture in instrumental performance in relation to this understanding of cultural and gendered practices, the Vietnamese-Swedish ensemble The Six Tones collaborated with Swedish choreographer Marie Fahlin and British sound artist Matt Wright to develop the installation *Inside/Outside*. Nguyễn and Östersjö discuss the role of the body and the play with gendered identity in this process.

Finally, Jin Hyung Lim extends the arguments for musical performance as a personal, social, political, and cultural act—the embodiment of a performer's multiply formed subjectivity—into her discussion of performing the piano music of Korean composer Isang Yun. Yun's music lies broadly in the field of mid-twentieth-century European modernism; but, despite his turbulent relationship with his homeland, aspects of his Korean musical heritage, and his interests in Eastern philosophy can be detected in his compositions. Typically, musicologists might seek evidence of this diasporic identity in Yun's scores—in this case, his piano works. This chapter, however, takes a different approach, situated in relation to the performer's own, similar position as a Korean pianist, trained in the Western classical tradition, who has lived in Canada and Europe for half her life. How do performer identity and experience intersect with propositional and contextual knowledge of a composition when one is playing an instrument, hearing and feeling sounds? How do the performer's specific forms of understanding and her situated cultural background produce a particular performative response, itself a manifestation of subjectivity?

It is now commonplace to consider subjectivity not as foundational or as an "essence," but rather as produced in and through our interactions with others, with "things," and within structures of discourse and power. In musical contexts, this means production with other performers, composers, and audiences; with instruments, other technologies, and contexts of performance; and with arts funders, producers, theorists, and so on. The various chapters of this book all ask what this means in *practice*: in *musical* practice, as a mode of understanding. It offers the work of diverse practitioners to reveal aspects of this dynamic. We hope that this, in itself but especially in relation to the complementary publication, contributes new perspectives on the ways in which subjectivity is performed in and through musical practices.

*　　*　　*

As in the partner volume, *Voices, Bodies, Practices*, it is necessary, before proceeding, to be clear about the use in this volume of the key terms *subjectivity*, *identity*, and *agency*. All are commonly used, but they often have subtly different meanings in different contexts. Since they are used here as in the first volume, the explanations that follow are reproduced from the introduction to that book.

For the purposes of this book, we understand SUBJECTIVITY simply as the condition of being a subject and the process by which we become or are perceived as such. This means having the capacity to hold beliefs, desires, and a sense of self, but it does not assume that subjectivity and selfhood are the same thing. The question of what a self "is"—whether it exists at all, whether self-awareness necessarily means having an awareness of self, and the relationship between consciousness and self-awareness (as discussed particularly usefully by Zahavi

2006)—continues to be debated in philosophy, phenomenology, and neuroscience. However, that we act *as if* we are at least partially self-determining, on the basis that our "selves" are significant in some way—behaving as if the individual subject experiences the world in particular ways and re-produces or otherwise expresses back to the world that experience—ensures that subjectivity remains significant to culture and creativity. Nevertheless, subjectivity is produced by and also feeds into discourses, structures, and systems; following Judith Butler (2005, 2012, 2015), we understand subjectivity to be constituted as "intelligible," which means that quite how an individual can "be" or act is constituted socially and culturally, not purely individually. We repeatedly perform (act out) modes of subjectivity that become naturalised and feel foundational, but that are produced in and through the constraints of our contexts. As such, the capacity to take up a subject position—and the nature of being a subject—operates within a dynamic process: subjectivity is produced in and through discourse (of any kind, and always embodied, whether linguistic, musical, or whatever), but the subject has the potential to be articulate (in whatever way) within that discourse and to articulate things *differently*, creating new meanings.

The concepts of subjectivity and IDENTITY are closely interwoven. Many writers use them interchangeably, and where a difference is apparent there is no evident consensus as to where it lies. However, for the purposes of this book we use "identity" to refer to the more explicitly socially constituted aspects of subjectivity: subjectivity that involves a question of sameness or difference from others (Weeks 1990, 89) and that hence relates to socially constituted communities, groups, or practices. In that sense identity appears when subjectivity becomes symbolic, when an intersection forms between the sense of self and the characteristics apparent in the ways in which a group identifies itself.[4] Of course, identity is no more fixed than subjectivity; it changes, constantly. Moreover, identity can constitute subjectivity—my sense of myself as a woman can be predicated on my sense of what it is to be identified as a woman—and vice versa: the identity of "woman" can be formed from individual subjective experiences of gender. The relationship is complex and unstable, constantly evolving. Appiah (2018, 12) neatly summarises the social dynamic between subjectivity and identity: "Identities come, first, with labels and ideas about why and to whom they should be applied. Second, your identity shapes your thoughts about how you should behave; and, third, it affects the way other people treat you. Finally, all these dimensions of identity are contestable, always up for dispute: who's in, what they're like, how they should behave and be treated."

Likewise, the relationship between agency and subjectivity is complex. Sally Jane Norman describes agency as designating "potentially innumerable, finely differentiated capacities for action" (2013, 283), and we share that basic understanding of the term. In that sense, subjects certainly can have agency. Nevertheless, as Shaun Gallagher observes (2012, 28), agency "has multiple contributories, some of which are reflectively conscious, some of which are

---

4 The construction of identity, both personal and artistic, has been central to the writings of the latter-day pragmatist Richard Shusterman (2000, 2002).

pre-reflectively conscious, and some of which are non-conscious," and as a result the relationship between agency and intentionality or ownership is not at all straightforward. Examples from the body, particularly with regard to motor control and processes associated with body schema (the preconscious system of motor capacities, abilities, and habits that enables movement) help demonstrate this; Gallagher notes the significant differences between deciding to move a body part in a particular way, to accomplish a defined task, and other aspects of motor control that we feel we "own" but do not consciously think of before (or sometimes even during) their execution: "It is possible to say that I am moving, and therefore that it is *my* movement, and thus have a sense of ownership for it, in cases where there is no sense of agency for the movement, for example in reflex or involuntary movements" (Gallagher 2007, 347).[5] This is, of course, very relevant to musical performance, in which intentionality of movement and matters of bodily agency are often very complex, due to the nature of the physical training at the instrument.

As Gallagher argues (2012, 17), agency is therefore phenomenologically "thin," in that it is often short-lived and tends to lie in the pre-reflective background of experience. Nevertheless, its operation across levels of awareness makes it significant to our attempts to understand the capacity to act in and hence influence the world. In its very ambiguity of intentionality, it is closely interwoven with the problematics of the sense of self: it contributes to the production of subjectivity, and manifestations of subjectivity often carry implications of agency, but the two are not interchangeable. While we might often perceive subjectivity as produced in part by the recognition of agency, subjects can, equally, lack agency. Likewise, following Bruno Latour (2005) and others, since agency is not predicated on intentionality, in a network of action any "actor"—any active entity—can potentially be agential: not just subjects but also non-human objects. In our context, instruments, in particular, certainly often seem to carry agency, powerfully influencing musical activity, behaviours, and meaning. Agency can also be collective, emerging from the interaction of "actors" (whether human or nonhuman). Importantly, also, as Bennett Hogg and Sally Jane Norman write (2013, 116), "agency only has significance in a world that offers resistances; not to be identified with free will, agency is directed negotiation carried out within the limits of physical reality and of the behaviour of persons and things. Agency is emergent rather than given." Again, this becomes important in terms of the ways in which musicians negotiate the affordances and resistances of instruments and the contexts of performance.

---

5 See Gallagher and Cole (1995).

References

Appiah, Kwame Anthony. 2018. *The Lies That Bind: Rethinking Identity; Creed, Country, Colour, Class, Culture*. London: Profile Books.

Butler, Judith. 1988. "Performative Acts and Gender Constitution: An Essay in Phenomenology and Feminist Theory." *Theatre Journal* 40 (4): 519–31.

———. 2005. *Giving an Account of Oneself*. New York: Fordham University Press.

———. 2012. "Can One Lead a Good Life in a Bad Life? Adorno Prize Lecture." *Radical Philosophy* 176 (9): 9–18.

———. 2015. *Senses of the Subject*. New York: Fordham University Press.

Frith, Simon. 1996. "Music and Identity." In *Questions of Cultural Identity*, edited by Stuart Hall and Paul du Gay, 108–27. London: Sage.

Gallagher, Shaun. 2007. "The Natural Philosophy of Agency." *Philosophy Compass* 2 (2): 347–57.

———. 2012. "Multiple Aspects in the Sense of Agency." *New Ideas in Psychology* 30 (1): 15–31.

Gallagher, Shaun, and Jonathan Cole. 1995. "Body Image and Body Schema in a Deafferented Subject." *Journal of Mind and Behavior* 16 (4): 369–90.

Hogg, Bennett, and Sally Jane Norman. 2013. "Editorial Introduction: Resistant Materials in Musical Creativity." *Contemporary Music Review* 32 (2–3): 115–18.

Latour, Bruno. 2005. *Reassembling the Social: An Introduction to Actor–Network Theory*. Oxford: Oxford University Press.

Norman, Sally Jane. 2013. "Contexts of/as Resistance." *Contemporary Music Review* 32 (2–3): 275–88.

Shusterman, Richard. 2000. *Performing Live: Aesthetic Alternatives for the Ends of Art*. Ithaca, NY: Cornell University Press.

———. 2002. "Regarding Oneself and Seeing Double: Fragments of Autobiography." In *The Philosophical I: Personal Reflections on Life in Philosophy*, edited by George Yancy, 1–21. Lanham, MD: Rowman and Littlefield.

Weeks, Jeffery. 1990. "The Value of Difference." In *Identity: Community, Culture, Difference*, edited by Jonathan Rutherford, 88–100. London: Lawrence & Wishart.

Zahavi, Dan. 2006. *Subjectivity and Selfhood: Investigating the First-Person Perspective*. Cambridge, MA: MIT Press.

Between I and You in Music

Shared Emotions, Relational Improvisation, and Artistic Research

Deniz Peters

University of Music and Performing Arts Graz

It is precisely this mutual tuning-in relationship by which the "I" and the "Thou" are experienced by both participants as a "We" in vivid presence.
. . . this precommunicative social relationship comes to the foreground. . . . in . . . dancing together, making love together, or making music together. (Schütz [1951] 1976, 161–62)

An intimate duo between two violins or between violin and piano allegorises [*versinnbildlichen*] the crucial element in romantic love much better than the fusion of two halves into a spherical being, or Virgin Mary and Baby Jesus. (Krebs 2015, 60, my translation)

Imagine an ensemble performance that is brimming with proximity: the players' actions appear to emerge from one mind and one body, no matter how complex or conflict-laden the musical events they create or interpret. This is a highly desirable experience and artistic achievement even for a mature ensemble musician. Alfred Schütz and Angelika Krebs in the initial quotations compare a duo or ensemble in such a state—the state of profound musical togetherness—to that of lovemaking (Schütz) or even to love itself (Krebs). In the inverse case of weak or missing musical togetherness, there is an audible disconnect between the players, even when they manage to play in synchrony or painstakingly reproduce a matching interpretation. A listener will readily notice that, in the latter case, the players "don't click," that there is little or no "chemistry." Musical togetherness is an astonishing interpersonal achievement, yet—despite readily recognising its presence or absence, and despite recent research on ensemble playing—it remains a mystifying phenomenon. What is it that grounds musical togetherness? What kind of state or feeling is it? And how can it be achieved?

These questions show that musical togetherness is both a practical and theoretical problem, a problem of (musical) skills and a problem for our understanding. In this chapter, I address both sides of this problem by way of artistic research. I first give some background to an analysis of musical togetherness, discussing certain key concepts and spotting some shortcomings; I then discuss artistic explorations aimed at deepening our understanding of musical togetherness, and argue that the musical achievements reached and identified reveal the presence of shared feelings (in the particular understanding developed by Angelika Krebs). I conclude that genuine musical togetherness instantiates a state of higher-level subjectivity—a state in which two subjects enter a compound subjectivity *without* losing their individual autonomy—and briefly discuss conditions for musical togetherness in this sense, as well as implications of the insight.

1. Preliminary considerations:
The "tuning in-relationship," the forming of
a "We," musical empathy, and related concepts

Alfred Schütz, in his influential essay "Making Music Together: A Study in Social Relationship" ([1951] 1976), conceives musical togetherness as instantiating a state of shared consciousness: "Both [co-performers] share not only the inner *durée* in which the content of the music played actualizes itself; each, simultaneously, shares in vivid present the Other's stream of consciousness in immediacy" (176). This state extends not only between co-performers, but also, as Schütz claims, between composers and "beholders" (a term with which Schütz refers to both: performers as interpreters and listeners, and listeners in the audience): "Although separated by hundreds of years, the latter [beholder] participates with quasi simultaneity in the former's [composer's] stream of consciousness by performing with him [*sic*] step by step the ongoing articulation of his musical thought. The beholder, thus, is united with the composer by a time dimension common to both, which is nothing other than a derived form of the vivid present shared by the partners in a genuine face-to-face relation" (171–72). Schütz believes this very state (as characteristic of musical experience) to be foundational for communication (173, 177) and mounts his critique of the prevalent sociological models of communication of the day from this vantage point (161). To support his thought on the shared stream of consciousness, Schütz leans on the following definition of music: "For our purposes a piece of music may be defined—very roughly and tentatively, indeed—as a meaningful arrangement of tones in inner time" (170). It turns out that Schütz implies a quasi-formalistic definition of music, because "meaningful" to him refers to "an interplay of recollections, retentions, protentions, and anticipations which interrelate the successive elements" (170)—that is, musically immanent relations between parts. To Schütz, inner time is "the very medium within which the musical flow occurs" and differs from outer time in that it is not measurable (171). In this way, by shifting the place where synchrony is established into an oblique inner realm, Schütz *presupposes* synchrony, without critically assessing whether synchrony really is present, or whether it yields the claimed "immediacy."[1]

Contra Schütz, however, upon replaying and rehearing, performers or listeners do not hear pieces of music as unfolding *identically* in time. Growing acquaintance with a piece or performance alters temporal perception, and attention, distraction, and knowledge will highlight different aspects in different episodes of listening (and different listeners). Thus, the idea of a literal sharing of consciousness—even in inner time—across centuries or even across current co-performers as generated by the organisation of the musical piece seems implausible. While Schütz's classic text indeed presents a nascent understanding of the phenomenon of musical togetherness and of its primary characteristics and conditions (these being a process of "tuning-in," and the forming of a "We"),[2] a more conceptually nuanced, accurate and precise, and musically rich and concrete view is desirable. What else, then, other than a *temporally induced* state of shared consciousness, establishes joint action, and what may go even beyond joint action in musical togetherness?

Instead of thinking of "tuning-in" as an obscure process of temporal alignment in inner time produced by composed musical organisation, I propose it is reached through a reciprocal process of perception geared at *grasping* the other's state—arriving at a developing community of feeling between the performers. The word for the process of grasping another human being's state is *empathy*. Later in this chapter I shall argue that empathy is indeed at play in reaching musical togetherness, and that empathy occurs as a dialogical psychological process. Before I do so, I offer some preparatory thoughts on the concept of empathy as distinct from some other concepts that address related interpersonal human capabilities, and some thoughts on the structure of the "We" referred to by Schütz.

Empathy

Theodor Lipps was one of the Gestalt psychologists who at the turn of the twentieth century began to use the word and concept of empathy (*Einfühlung*). In his *Grundlegung der Ästhetik* (foundations of aesthetics) of 1903, Lipps describes his view that upon hearing someone else's affectively charged vocal utterance resembling a sound oneself would make under a certain affect, we encounter the affect not as connected to the sound, but "within" it—meaning that the affect is not imagined as being the sound's cause, but experienced in its very quality. The experience, to Lipps, is not passively arrived at but actively

---

1   In the subsequent passage (Schütz [1951] 1976, 172), engrossed in the distinction between a "polythetic" character of musical experience and the "monothetic" character of grasping mathematical meaning, Schütz overlooks that musical meaning is not only "polythetic" but to some degree flexible: it *depends* on, for example, the temporal cohesion and distribution of performances, which *vary* from instantiation to instantiation. In poetry too, meaning changes as tempo, emphasis, and tone vary in different recitations.

2   The "living through a vivid present in common, constitutes . . . the mutual tuning-in relationship, the experience of the 'We,' which is at the foundation of all possible communication" (Schütz [1951] 1976, 173).

produced by way of an inner joining in (*inneres Mitmachen*).[3] The perceiving person, according to Lipps, contributes the affective quality of the seen, so the specific quality seen (e.g., in another's eye) becomes, for instance, pride; simultaneously, the pride is no longer only seen, but is also *felt*. The act of projection of the perceiver's feeling into the perceived is what Lipps calls empathy (1903, 111). Empathy, in Lipps's view, then, is an imitation of a perceived affective content via one's own affective capacity. Lipps claims that it is the act of empathy that, in the aesthetic experience of an artwork, thus endows the seen with psychological vitality, and that similarly extends to the realm of human life.

One way in which Lipps's view is problematic is that it overestimates the ease of matching the other's state with one's own; for Lipps, a basic equivalence between the two is a given. However, could not the "experienced" affect sometimes be produced by *misguided* imitation or *misinterpretation*? Could not real joy be projected in imitation of pretended joy, and thus misperceived? Would it not be necessary to continuously correct one's estimation of the other's state to arrive at a more adequate grasp? And would empathy therefore, contra Lipps, not be a projection of an estimated state onto another being, through which one endows their appearance with affectivity, but a (continuously revised) process of (imperfect) perception of another's state as nevertheless *genuinely* hers or his? Both Edith Stein's and Max Scheler's accounts of empathy argue towards this view (see Stein 1989, 10–11, 14, 84–86). To Scheler, the feeling grasped through empathy (Scheler uses the German word *Nachfühlen* instead of *Einfühlen*) is not (necessarily) shared or recreated by the one who empathises; rather, she or he grasps the quality of the other's feeling as the *other's*.[4]

One of the benefits of this latter view is that it accounts for the fact that not everyone who empathises does this out of sympathy. People may suffer through *or* enjoy another's misfortune, the psychological grasp of which they arrive at via empathy. Scheler's remark—that feelings grasped via empathy need not become one's own—thus marks an important difference between empathy and sympathy. This is particularly helpful considering that in everyday conversation and marketing language (and implicit conceptions), empathy and sympathy are often confused. A quick online search for "empathy" in the Corbis image

---

3 My paraphrase abbreviates the following passages: "Wir geben allerlei Affekte, Gemütsbewegungen, Arten der inneren Erregung, etwa Schreck, Freude, Erstaunen, unmittelbar in Lauten kund. . . . Und höre ich nun einen Laut, ähnlich demjenigen, in welchem ich selbst meinen Affekt verlautbarte, so finde ich—nicht damit verbunden, sondern unmittelbar in ihm, diesen Affekt wieder. Dies 'Finden' scheint zunächst ein bloßes unmittelbares *Mitvorstellen*. In der Tat ist es mehr. Ich gewinne nicht nur die Vorstellung, daß dem Laut der Affekt zu Grunde liege, sondern ich *erlebe* diesen. Ich mache ihn innerlich mit [*sic*], um so sicherer und voller, je mehr ich dem Laut innerlich ganz zugewendet bin. Ich bin geneigt, mit dem Jubelnden mich zu freuen, also in seinen Jubel innerlich einzustimmen" (Lipps 1903, 106–7).

4 "Es ist wohl ein *Fühlen* des fremden Gefühls, kein bloßes Wissen um es oder nur ein *Urteil*, der Andere habe das Gefühl; gleichwohl ist es kein Erleben des wirklichen Gefühles als eines Zustandes; wir erfassen im Nachfühlen [*sic*] fühlend noch die *Qualität* des fremden Gefühles—ohne daß es in uns herüberwandert oder ein gleiches reales Gefühl in uns erzeugt wird" (Scheler 1923, 5, as translated in Scheler [1954] 2017, 9; It is indeed a case of feeling the other's feeling, not just knowing of it, nor judging that the other has it; but it is not the same as going through the experience itself. In reproduced feeling we sense the *quality* of the other's feeling, without it being transmitted to us, or evoking a similar real emotion in us). The translation given as "reproduced feeling" slightly misrepresents the meaning of *Nachfühlen*, which literally means to "feel-out-for" rather than to imitate and re-create; however, the rest of the sentence helps establish the correct meaning.

database delivers photos of caring, mild, and compassionate-looking people, extending their hands and gently touching others. As was noted, the dangers of conceptual confusion are not to be taken lightly, as an empathetic person *may* of course be benevolent—just like someone responding with sympathy—but they may just as well be *malevolent*, grasping another's pain and coldly ignoring or cruelly indulging in it.

It makes sense, therefore, to distinguish between empathy and sympathy, and to clarify the relation between the two. In Scheler's classic book *Wesen und Formen der Sympathie* (*The Nature of Sympathy*) of 1913 (see 1923, [1954] 2017), he identifies, describes, and thoroughly distinguishes four forms of sympathy from one another: (1) *Miteinanderfühlen* (lit. feeling together, mutual feeling, shared feelings); (2) "*Mitgefühl an etwas*" (fellow-feeling about something); (3) *Gefühlsansteckung* (contagion); and (4) *Einsfühlen* (feeling of oneness) (1923, 9). Only the first two of these feelings presuppose empathy. Contagion, Scheler's third sympathy category, is altogether different from empathy: rather than naming the attentive and imaginative grasping of another's feeling quality as *the other's* feeling, it names an involuntary process of taking on someone else's feeling quality without becoming aware of its origin, and remaining interested only in one's *own* experience of it. Scheler's fourth category, the feeling of oneness, is an ontological claim about the existence of a subpersonal state of psychological union. Sympathy in this sense refers not to a sameness but to an actual *identity* of a feeling in two or more beings. Feeling together or shared feeling, Scheler's first category of sympathy, names the equality of feeling between two individual beings; and his second form of sympathy, "fellow-feeling about something," or "sympathy with," is, according to him, a feeling *about* a feeling—for example, benevolence or malevolence. Notice that to take on someone else's feeling at which one arrived through empathy is an option for those who sympathise. (Note also that empathy is a process, whereas sympathy is a feeling.)

While Scheler leaves it open whether another's feeling may be taken on in sympathy, Peter Goldie offers another variant: sympathy, to Goldie (2000, 9), "is … best understood as a sort of emotion, involving thought about and feelings towards the difficulties of another, motivations to alleviate those difficulties where possible, and characteristic facial expressions and expressive actions." Concerning *compassion*—yet another related term—Martha Nussbaum, in her *Upheavals of Thought* (2001), offers that it is "a painful emotion occasioned by the awareness of another person's undeserved misfortune" (301). To Nussbaum, *sympathy* simply is a milder version of compassion: "people who are wary of acknowledging strong emotion are more likely to admit to 'sympathy' than to admit that they feel 'compassion'" (302). (And of *pity*, yet another related term, Nussbaum writes: "'pity' has recently come to have nuances of condescension and superiority to the sufferer that it did not have when Rousseau invoked *pitié*" [301].)

Current academic usages of the term empathy in music psychology, the aesthetics of music, or the philosophy of mind often combine (and sometimes conflate) Scheler's *Nachfühlen* with contagion—his third form of sympathy.

Also, when an author uses the word *empathy*, it sometimes implies that the empathising person takes on the feeling of the one who is being empathised with; Jerrold Levinson (1996, 125) and Roger Scruton, in their respective accounts of musical expression, both display this use.[5] Many other authors do not explicitly discuss their understanding of the terms, or use them too liberally, which sometimes obfuscates the growing literature on empathy (and in particular in music). Felicity Laurence (2017), in her opening prologue to Elaine King and Caroline Waddington's *Music and Empathy* points out this state of affairs and dedicates substantial space to clarifying the concept of empathy. While convincingly distinguishing between three diverging elements that are often mixed up in current usages of the term, Laurence's own definition ends up overly inclusive, ultimately conflating empathy with sympathy.

Empathy, in my present understanding, thus names our conscious ability to—imperfectly—grasp another human being's psychological state through the affective character of their appearances and actions. Its use in music affords our turning towards the other not to maintain a face-to-face relationship, as Schütz claims, but an ear-to-ear relationship. That ear-to-ear relationship can, under certain circumstances, lead to the combining of individual musical expressions into joint expressivity. This is a particular quality of togetherness that is filled with mutual understanding and affective correlation beyond synchrony: the state of forming a "We" not just by association under a shared goal or shared values, but on the level of an intimate affective relation—the exquisite state described at the outset of this chapter. What makes it exquisite is its relation to subjectivity. I'll turn to this quality briefly now before discussing its musical exploration.

We-ness (Edith Stein on higher-level subjectivity)

If togetherness to the level of oneness can be achieved in music, how might one figure this oneness? Does it dissolve the subject into a grand unified metaphysical whole? Matthew Rahaim (2017, 176–77, 188–89) points out that the image of full togetherness in the sense of lost individual autonomy appears frequently in some parts of the common discourse on music.[6] Such is also the idea that Lipps and Scheler had of a feeling of oneness, a feeling of complete union between two or any number of people, which they thought to be ontologically prior to feelings of self, and which, importantly, they thought was the basis for all forms of empathy and sympathy.[7]

---

5 Roger Scruton prefers to use *sympathy* (for what to Scheler would be *Nachfühlen*, i.e., empathy), but also uses *empathy*: "If . . . you are afraid of a danger, and I, observing your fear, come to share in it while not being afraid for myself, then my fear is sympathetic feeling. . . . (The special case where the response coincides with the emotion responded to is sometimes called empathy—translating the German *Einfühlung*)" (Scruton 1997, 354).

6 Rahaim argues that the idea that music's unifying powers are based on a metaphysics of unity is a common cliché, arguing instead for a metaphysics of alterity.

7 According to Scheler (1923, 112–15), for example, the feeling of oneness (*Einsfühlung*) grounds empathy (*Nachfühlen*), which in turn grounds fellow-feeling (*Mitgefühl*).

Edith Stein clarifies the shortcomings of Lipps's and Scheler's arguments: "What led Lipps astray in his description was the confusion of self-forgetfulness, through which I can surrender myself to any object, with a dissolution of the 'I' in the object. Thus, strictly speaking, empathy is not a feeling of oneness" (Stein 1989, 17). Stein goes on to locate two potential ways in which a *feeling* of oneness might nevertheless occur: by literally having the same feeling (e.g., in a communal response of relief and joy to the disappearance of a shared threat) and thus combining the others' and one's own experience into *our* experience, that is, into the experience of a "'we' as a subject of a higher level,"[8] and by adjusting one's own feeling by way of empathy to match the others'.[9] We-ness, in this understanding, represents a new subject—a subject of a higher, interpersonal level, encompassing more than one person—rather than representing a return to an ontologically fused state. The shift of attention on the "we" attenuates the experience of "I" and "you," without eliminating it: "But 'I,' 'you,' and 'he' are retained in 'we.' A 'we,' not an 'I,' is the subject of the empathizing" (Stein 1989, 18). Stein notes that even Scheler missed this distinction: "Scheler clearly emphasizes the phenomenon that different people can have strictly the same feeling (*Sympathiegefühle*, pp. 9 and 31) and stresses that the various subjects are thereby retained. However, he does not consider that the unified act does not have the plurality of the individuals for its subject, but a higher unity based on them" (ibid., 122n28).

In what follows, I discuss how in an improvisatory encounter within an artistic research project, Simon Rose and I explored togetherness and evinced *this* kind of unity. Working towards a deeper understanding of the phenomenon of musical togetherness, and of the (intersubjective) structure of its experience and constitution, I shall argue that musical togetherness of the intimate quality sought comes into being when the ensemble manages to move beyond joint actions and into shared feelings. In analysing one example of my experimental practice, I arrive at a notion of dialogical playing that, as I reflect in the subsequent section, fulfils Angelika Krebs's conditions of *Miteinanderfühlen* (shared feelings).

2. Exploring musical togetherness musically

When wanting to learn more about and understand better the qualities of togetherness that occur between musicians when playing together, it might seem self evident to scrutinise performances of classical duo repertoire (recall Goethe's famous passage in a letter to Carl Friedrich Zelter in which

---

8 "I feel my joy while I empathically comprehend the others' and see it as the same. And, seeing this, it seems that the non-primordial character of the foreign joy has vanished. Indeed, this phantom joy coincides in every respect with my real live joy, and theirs is just as live to them as mine is to me. Now I intuitively have before me what they feel. It comes to life in my feeling, and from the 'I' and 'you' arises the 'we' as a subject of a higher level" (Stein 1989, 17).

9 "I empathically arrive at the 'sides' of joyfulness obstructed in my own joy. This ignites my joy, and only now is there complete coincidence with what is empathized. If the same thing happens to the others, we empathically enrich our feeling so that 'we' now feel a different joy from 'I,' 'you,' and 'he' in isolation" (Stein 1989, 18).

he compares listening to a quartet with listening to a conversation between four rational people [Goethe 1892, 369]). However, any duo in the sense of composed and performed art music is intrinsically a curious trio. In a composed work, the musical actions played out by the performers are fairly tightly scripted, by the score, by a composer's implicit oeuvre, and by performance tradition and compositional practice. That is to say, they are largely predetermined, preorganised, and premeditated. Of course there is room for interpretation that turns the score, which is always underdetermined, into a sounding work—and interpretation is for this very reason an art in its own right that balances the composer's voice with the performer's. But importantly for our line of thought, the composition nevertheless already provides the *form* and, thinking in terms of process, the *continuation* along which the shared emotional narrative unfolds. Bruce Ellis Benson, in *The Improvisation of Musical Dialogue* (2003), brilliantly analyses the reciprocity at work when performers navigate the tension between compositional givens, musical traditions, their own expressive voice, and audience expectations, and shows how composers themselves are active—and entangled—in this dialogical situation via *responsibility* (see, especially, 168–76). While a composer thus may well be seen to be setting up and outlining the process of an encounter between performers, the quality of that encounter ultimately depends on the latter. There are many ways and indeed, dimensions in which a performance may still fall short of achieving the dialogical intimacy Angelika Krebs is pointing towards; thus, the duo's challenge is indeed formidable. It is not without reason that ensembles rehearse for years and build a musical life together to achieve the state of playing with shared emotions again and again anew onstage.

Therefore, in trying to grasp the musical challenge and the richness of the musicians' interpersonal and emotional achievement *in performance*, the influence of the composer's contribution complicates matters. This is different in improvisation. While compositionality is no less important in free improvisation (just as much as improvisationality in interpretation), the interpersonal dynamic that occurs in the encounter is not guided by constant influences of pre-existing choices of another's making. An exploration of musical togetherness by way of improvisation in at least this sense gives closer access to the very place where dialogicity is most exposed in its very making.

A note of caution: I am far from thinking that free, or experimental, improvisation, is free from social scripts.[10] While freely improvised music is generally characterised by an encounter between individual voices—voices who, to different degrees, assert their autonomy, or provide a supporting frame for such an act—this very characteristic can easily mislead one to believe that interpersonal encounters in improvisational situations are in any sense more ethical or democratic than elsewhere. I certainly agree with Fischlin, Heble, and Lipsitz who, in *The Fierce Urgency of Now* (2013), discuss the ethical potential of freely improvised music, which they essentially conceive as enabling a coming together in difference, in which voices from underprivileged or marginalised

---

10   I largely concur with Nicholas Cook's view (2017).

backgrounds are heard. But there is no guarantee that any interhuman proximity is reached in concrete terms in any given improvisation. While free improvisation is increasingly viewed as a testing ground for ways and models of ethical social encounter, the actual qualities achieved in encounters are under-researched and undertheorised. While Gillian Siddall and Ellen Waterman (2016, 3) rightly describe subjectivity as "a complex negotiation of lived embodied experience and social forces that work to regulate behavior and therefore shape that experience," authors in improvisation studies too seldom venture into the concrete realm of what it means that "in improvising we experience the immediate relationships between our bodies and others" (ibid.), *beyond* the effect this experience might have for the separate subjects or subjectivities involved. What of the intersubjective level?[11] Of all the contributors to the two-volume *Oxford Handbook of Critical Improvisation Studies* (Lewis and Piekut 2016), only Vijay Iyer, Celia Pearce, and Ed Sarath dedicate short passages to intersubjectivity: Pearce (2016, 2:455–56) introduces the strong idea of intersubjective flow (however, by leaning on Csikszentmihalyi's very broad understanding of flow as "an optimal state of concentration and connectedness that is maintained through a careful balance between boredom and anxiety" [ibid., 2:455]); Sarath's (2016, 2:144) notion of an "intersubjective field of consciousness" drifts steadily into what Matthew Rahaim above called the metaphysics of union; and Iyer (2016, 1:79) expounds an understanding of intersubjectivity in the musical experience as having "a sense of mutual embodiment," though he does not develop this interesting suggestion further. Nevertheless, that is what would be needed for us to more fully address the question: How dialogical is the interpersonal reality that is actually reached? As Bruce Ellis Benson writes (2003, 171): "We usually think of freedom as 'negative freedom'—freedom *from* constraints. But what I have in mind here is 'positive freedom'—freedom *for* genuine dialogue. . . . One needs to be able to *listen* to the other." As much as improvising ensembles indeed achieve an organic unity within their playing that marks their ensemble sound; genuine dialogicity in Benson's sense only lights up on very few occasions and in very few, extraordinary encounters. This is despite the fact that extreme familiarity and musical intimacy are often present in sophisticated improvisatory ensemble practice. And this seems only to be expected in a performance situation that, after all, aims for spontaneous creativity—the first risk taken in these circumstances is, with a nod to Schütz, that of primarily divergent streams of consciousness. How can one attain freedom *for* dialogue amid the various scripts, habits, and egocentric interests that mark an improvised musical encounter, even in the absence of a premeditated composition? And through which of our human faculties does this dialogue unfold?

---

11 It seems an important step in the right direction when Ellen Waterman (2016, 302) describes improvisatory group interaction, after analysing performer's subjective statements, as involving "different conceptions of subjectivity—both the authentic (dialogical) self and the socially constructed (contingent) self—fluidly and even simultaneously in a constant circulation of power."

Case study: artistic experimentation towards a shared voice

I now turn to analysing a freely improvised duo piece by Simon Rose and me—
free in the sense that we did not agree on any specific musical constraints or plan
before playing, other than viewing our performance as an encounter of equals
without foregrounding or being led by a particular style. The encounter took
place within the framework of the "Emotional Improvisation" research project
(FWF/PEEK: AR188). We improvised the piece in question on the third day of
Rose's eleven-day research residency at the project space, a forty-square-metre
room in an old apartment building in Sporgasse 32, within the central historic
district of Graz, Austria. Like many sessions within the complex overall project,
it was recorded as part of the ongoing video and audio documentation, with a
simple stereo microphone setting (two Sennheiser MKH 8020 omnidirectional
microphones going into a Sound Devices USBPre 2). The two microphones
were placed next to the 1970 Bösendorfer 225 grand piano (lid removed) inside
the curve and pointing diagonally towards the centre of its soundboard at the
meeting point between treble and bass bridges; Rose in this piece used his 1932
Conn Transitional baritone saxophone, standing at the tail end of the piano.
A selection of improvisations from that third day—including the piece I am
about to discuss—and from one of the subsequent days were released as *Edith's
Problem* by Leo Records (Peters and Rose 2017) with no cuts or edits except for a
slight attenuation of some street and building noise to which the microphones
were particularly sensitive. The piece is called "between, part one"; its duration
is 6:44 and it is the CD's first track.

Rose and I were of course entering this particular piece primed by about
twenty hours of previous playing and analytical discussions, at a point where
the desire to create a piece made up of fine-grained shared aesthetic decisions
was very present in our minds. Yet to desire something is not the same as being
capable of it (and twenty hours normally offer hardly more than an inkling of a
joint practice). Rose and I had noted that we achieved some unexpectedly stable
and structurally productive aesthetic mutuality in the preceding days, including during the first time we ever played together. On this particular third day,
however, something remarkable happened: at one point, Rose played sounds
that would emerge from the resonances of the sounds that I had played; and I
discovered a way of seamlessly entering Rose's sound, prolonging it or altering
it in numerous ways (instances of this can be heard on tracks 4, "resonance,
part one," and 6, "resonance, part two" of the CD). We were both struck by the
impression that our instruments sounded like a new, compound instrument
on those occasions. We were therefore also listening out with deep attention
for the presence of such instrumental fusion throughout "between, part one."
It stands out during the beginning in particular, in which Rose plays slowly
modulating timbral variations of a single note (actually a multiphonic on B♭)
that enter into the resonance of a fairly small two-handed cluster in the piano's
middle register. We calmly improvise five variants of this. The third variant,
26 seconds into the piece, begins with a soft, toneless blowing by Rose, which,
instead of leading to a sounding tone in the sax, is taken up by a (dynamically

matching) piano cluster as if *turning into* the latter; the sounding tone that then arises played by Rose and the piano cluster's resonance form a single timbral identity. (Even the toneless blowing through which Rose smoothly recedes from his long stretched sounds enters the piano resonance's character, bracketing or opening its identity.) In the fourth variant, this timbral gesture returns; at this point all aesthetic decisions that go into creating the integrated sonic shape are evidently *shared*.

The improvised piece that emerged from this initial shared gesture shows shared decision-making on numerous compositional levels. A structural and formal analysis in hindsight demonstrates (in one possible reading) that we arrived at five highly cohesive sections of slightly contrasting character, in which a prominent sonic event in the second section (marked interval motives in the upper piano register) becomes a restated vibrant shift between two chords within the cluster, first juxtaposed by Rose's slap-tonguing, then interspersed with related shriek-like sounds resonating from the fluttering upper part of a sax multiphonic (e.g., at 4:36) in the fourth section, with a short cadential gesture in the central third section, and a shared return to (an abbreviated version of) the initial section in the closing section 5. Harmonically speaking, the piece has an implicit tonality, moving from E♭ to C and back as referential pitches (for example exposed in single notes in the piano: E♭ at 3:01:18 and C at 4:47:09; and in the sax's initial E♭ multiphonic, its iridescent C/C♯ at 4:28, and its closing E♭ at 5:27:14). And there are further extensive compositional decisions that appear jointly taken: spontaneous joint atmospheric changes; durational correspondences within integrated shapes, within polyphonic events, and within silences (even lengthy silences stretch out between simultaneously ceasing and simultaneously commencing sounds). As a whole, the piece makes evident a large number of shared actions, at micro and macro levels of compositional choices: shared timbres (within each other's resonances, new integral sonorities), shared gestures (within a motive, but also concatenated into *Klangfarbenmelodie*-like gestural developments), shared pitches (unison/octave), shared silences, shared pulse, shared textures and dynamic shifts, shared tonality, shared atmospheres, and shared recurrences of combinations of all the preceding. Going further than establishing a shared instrumental character, then, this piece manifests a shared compositional voice.

3. MUSICAL TOGETHERNESS AS AFFORDING A DIALOGICALLY ESTABLISHED SHARED EMOTIONAL NARRATIVE

One might call the kind of playing that leads to a compositionally complex improvisation rich with relations between the players' actions *dialogical*. The dialogicity here is, of course, a far cry from the echo-like imitational events sometimes exaggeratedly referred to as musical dialogue in casual conversation. It is qualitatively different from mere imitational playing. First, dialogical playing takes up *some* aspects of the heard while transforming others and integrating them into another aesthetic process (and might therefore be called *relating* rather than *imitating*); second, and crucially, genuine dialogue engages with the other not only as a formal producer of structurally and functionally interesting sounds but also as a sentient human being with whom, as Martin Buber says, we are involved.[12] Responsiveness within such dialogical playing therefore is not only quick (i.e., temporally fine-grained) and musically logical; to respond means to hear the other on a psychological level, letting oneself be affected by the heard, and in turn revealing oneself on the psychological level, to be heard and responded to. To listen to each other while playing is easier said than done, particularly if listening means to be sensitive to the character of the played at every moment, as well as to its development in time. To let the heard matter to one's own state raises the bar of listening even further.[13] Empathetic listening means nothing more, and nothing less, than entering a process of grasping the other's affective presence in the unfolding performance, on the level of personal expressivity (realising that the musician chose to make that sound out of an urge to follow up or turn against a particular state he or she is in or perceives). Third, and no less importantly, musical dialogue can (by the very nature of the medium) embrace *simultaneity*. By juxtaposing or integrating two musical actions with each other at the same time, players enter a domain of exchange that largely eludes language or text; it is a domain music shares with dance. The ensuing voice belongs, in such passages of simultaneity, at the same time to each performer, and to *them both*.

Now, if both players mutually, symmetrically engage in this kind of listening and responsive playing, the psychological dynamic obviously becomes rather complicated, but the central process is one in which—as in the case of Rose and I—*we* influence the development and *we* let ourselves be influenced by it; and the development includes *both* our psychological presences, integrating our expressive actions to form a cohesive (rather than fragmented or incongruent) narrative. And if we are in such a state together, we are then exploring unpredictable psychological regions together, and making these heard. The shared compositional and improvising voice is *our* voice.[14]

---

12 "Dieser Mensch ist nicht mein Gegenstand; ich habe mit ihm zu tun bekommen" (Buber 2009, 152, my translation; This human being is not my subject matter; I have come to be involved with him).

13 Cf. Judith Butler's comparable observation that receptivity ("being moved by something in a way that you hadn't planned . . . and letting something emerge as a consequence of that") points towards a relational understanding of agency as "not based on mastery" (Butler and McMullen 2016, 31).

14 Stefan Östersjö and David Gorton, in their chapters "Austerity Measures I: Performing the Discursive Voice" (Gorton and Östersjö 2019), and "Negotiating the Discursive Voice in Chamber Music" in the present volume, give a thorough discussion of a concept closely related to that of *shared voice*—what they call the *discursive voice*. The discursive voice analysed by Gorton and Östersjö (2019) emerges from the relation between composer and performer upon joint work in determining the materials of a composition; it unfolds within a responsiveness to the composer's style as heeded by the performer during the stage of (joint) improvisatory invention of material, and an openness to performer's structural and phrasal decision-making before and during the performance. As they evocatively put it: "It could be said that to an extent David was composing with Stefan's 'voice,' as well as his own. Similarly . . . in performance Stefan . . . also composed with David's 'voice,' as well as his own" (ibid., 55). This remarkable result of research through experimentation brings together the realms of composer and performer, treated separately by both Schütz and Benson as they are usually separated by time and rarely made a topic of joint investigation between composer and performer. The *shared voice* of the present context is a variant that differs in two respects from Östersjö and Gorton: (1) it takes place between the "voices" of two improvisers, who compose and perform *without* a written score and in real time; (2) while the discursive voice concerns "interactions . . . shaped by the respective practices of both" (ibid.), the present concept of a shared voice vitally addresses the simultaneity of psychological events and their *discovered*

We know when this happens. We know it because we experience an impression of deep mutual understanding; of personal intimacy; of having gained and shared a profound knowledge about and with the other; of having left one's musical self and having found an extension to one's voice: an *intersubjectively* shared voice. This is knowledge by acquaintance, knowing what it is like, of the experience of a musical "we" expressed throughout an entire piece. (A side note: The realisation that one is being heard with close attention to detail and expression by the other is deeply satisfying. Feelings of being recognised, of agreement [even in difference], of acceptance, of being attended to, and of the other's tolerance and patience in the subsequently prolonged experience all nurture a feeling of trust [including and beyond the trust in the other's competence and skill]; and that feeling of trust enables one to enter more deeply emotionally into what is currently at hand. Trust is thus not only a *condition* for good ensemble musicking, as Anthony Gritten claims in a thoughtful essay [2017], but beyond this, also a *result* of relational playing.) As one feels increasingly recognised, one takes on more responsibility in paying attention to hearing the other's contribution and investing oneself into the growing joint affective work. As we are playing relationally, we are moving from empathising with each other to a state of sympathetic playing—not as two soloists or leader and supporter, but as a genuine, dialogical duo.[15]

But wait. Could one not be fooled into believing that one is in the presence of genuine shared feeling, when in reality existing musical habits, formulae, simple repetitions, or more complex compositional knowledge provide enough orientation and cohesion to produce that illusion? Yes, indeed—but any action in the direction of fixity or individual rule-based playing comes at the cost of autonomy, or at the cost of mutual integration. Formulaic playing, for one, exposes itself in its very rigidity, and remains bound by this, unable to connect here and now. Conversely, excessive versatility, contrasting, digressing, and risk-taking may lead to distancing and fragmentation between the players. A piece that is experienced as *dialogically* cohesive is cohesive because of the players' success at opening up a space of joint affective exploration that preserves the individual players' autonomy while contributing to a shared narrative.

Another hesitation: Parallel feeling according to Krebs (herself leaning on Scheler) is simply a simultaneity of similar or even equal feeling towards the same intentional object without any relevant awareness of or interest in the other's matching state (Krebs 2015, 114). Rather than experiencing shared feelings, might the duo not simply be experiencing parallel feelings? Musically speaking, any parallel feeling, even were it established at some point, would be accidental and very short-lived in the absence of close and ongoing mutual

---

interrelation in the tightly knit exploration of expression between I and you in music—something resounding in Gorton and Östersjö's suggestion that "we find the coded instances in the stimulated recall of 'finding through playing' to be central for understanding the nature of the development of a 'discursive voice' in chamber music performance" (this volume, 76). My above claim is that such "finding" involves a qualitative shift from the two subjectivities of "I" and "Him/Her" to the level of the "We."

15 I stress this point because the largest part of the literature on ensemble performance research to my knowledge seems only to consider the asymmetrical power relationship between players, analysing performances under the aspect of leadership and role-taking.

interest regarding each player's current contribution. Since the musical experience is what is attended to, and since the music is jointly invented and sounded, parallel feeling could only ensue paradoxically in moments of distraction.

In the remainder of this chapter, I put forward an argument towards the claim that it really is Scheler's first category of sympathy—mutual feeling—that seems to best describe the psychological component behind the intersubjectively shared voice of the case study. For this I draw on Angelika Krebs's profound analysis and understanding of "feeling together." Krebs (2015) extends Edith Stein's concept of *we-intentionality* and combines it with joint action theory, to reach beyond the latter. We-intentionality can mark joint actions. Krebs goes on to show how shared emotions have the same structure of togetherness as joint action. Yet shared feelings imply *joint work on feelings*, not just joint physical actions. In her central analysis, Krebs identifies eleven elements of shared emotions, the following five of which are necessary. Two or more people share an emotion, if:

1. they are similarly emotionally affected by the situation,
2. they recognise each other's emotional affectedness,
3. they jointly evaluate the situation,
4. they act jointly out of the emotion, and
5. they tie the individual emotional components together into a shared emotional narrative. (Krebs 2015, 220, my translation)

Strikingly, Krebs's five necessary elements seem to be fulfilled by what is going on in mutually empathetic improvisation of the described sort. Both improvisers are similarly emotionally affected by the situation; if they weren't, the piece would obviously lack coherence, which it does not despite being a "free" improvisation. Both recognise each other's emotional affectedness—given that they listen empathetically to the affective charge of the other's contribution, which is evident in any sonic proximity or sustained relation between sonic actions, that is, the precision of responsiveness. They jointly evaluate the situation, which becomes apparent when compositional decisions lead to a coherent structure and at points where joint decisions as to material or atmospheric changes are made. The improvisers both act jointly out of the emotion, which is clear whenever they succeed in producing a shared gesture or shared timbre that provides expressive continuity to the current state. And both improvisers tie the individual emotional components, for example, expressive gestures and phrases, together into a shared emotional narrative: they sustain their intimate encounter for the entire duration of the piece, as evident in the compositionality of the improvised action right down to every minute detail.

With "feeling together" being the central component in her understanding of dialogical love, it now seems deeply true that Krebs finds dialogical love best represented in the idea of an "intimate duo" as shown in the initial quotation. My own argument is approaching closure. We have arrived at the main point (obscured by the role of the composer who at some other time and in some other place provided the basic structure) from which interpreters in the case of a *classical* duo might arrive at joint emotions. Their art goes together with the composers' art of anticipating a direction and a predetermined path for the social exploration of the interpersonal. If, however, a free improvisation fulfils Krebs's elements, as it does in *relational improvisation* (with which I name a practice rather than a genre), then the we-subject is genuinely present and embodied in the improvisers—and the improvisation itself in its relational qualities is an evident expression thereof.

Hence, a musical we-subject, if reached, is an achievement. It is an artistic achievement, but also an ethical, interhuman one. And so is the we-subject in a shared emotion. It does not follow from singular agreement; neither does it afford an endless chain of agreements as Krebs points out in her critique of the individualistic approaches as part of the joint action debate (see Krebs 2015, 160–170). When making music together, it lives in those agreements that become possible as the shared emotions emerge, take their courses, deepen, or dissipate, by way of an improvisatory process responsive to the other's states via empathetic listening, and giving away one's own states by expressive playing. For this, the achievement of sharing requires, next to caring, a good measure of daring. What the musical case, in turn, reveals, is how episodes of shared emotions enrich our selves (entering unfamiliar regions of shared experience). When wishing to not just convey but *share* an emotion, it might thus be beneficial to improvise. Advancing our capabilities of entering shared states through shared musical decision-making—in free improvisation, or in improvisation at the moment of joint interpretation—may thus be a good domain for the *furthering* of our very capabilities for shared emotions. Thus, Schütz was, in an important sense, right about music's dialogical power, although my considerations at this point suggest that it is not music that magically creates togetherness. Rather, togetherness eventuates between you and I, as we work to relate via music, with and beyond our subjectivities, as is then expressed in the music.

Acknowledgements

The research for this chapter was supported by the Austrian Science Fund (FWF): AR188 within the artistic research project "Emotional Improvisation" FWF/PEEK:AR188.

References

Benson, Bruce Ellis. 2003. *The Improvisation of Musical Dialogue: A Phenomenology of Music*. Cambridge: Cambridge University Press.

Buber, Martin. 2009. "Ich und Du." In *Das dialogische Prinzip*, 9–136. Gütersloh: Gütersloher Verlagshaus.

Butler, Judith, and Tracy McMullen. 2016. "Improvisation within a Scene of Constraint: An Interview with Judith Butler." In *Negotiated Moments: Improvisation, Sound, and Subjectivity*, edited by Gillian Siddall and Ellen Waterman, 21–36. Durham, NC: Duke University Press.

Cook, Nicholas. 2017. "Scripting Social Interaction: Improvisation, Performance, and Western 'Art' Music." In *Improvisation and Social Aesthetics*, edited by Georgina Born, Eric Lewis, and Will Straw, 59–77. Durham, NC: Duke University Press.

Fischlin, Daniel, Ajay Heble, and George Lipsitz. 2013. *The Fierce Urgency of Now:*

Improvisation, Rights, and the Ethics of Cocreation. Durham, NC: Duke University Press.

Goethe, Johann Wolfgang von. 1892. "Goethe to Zelter, Weimar, 9th November, 1829." In *Goethe's Letters to Zelter, with Extracts from Those of Zelter to Goethe*, edited and translated by A. D. Coleridge, 369–71. London: George Bell.

Goldie, Peter. 2000. *The Emotions: A Philosophical Exploration*. Oxford: Clarendon Press.

Gorton, David, and Stefan Östersjö. 2019. "Austerity Measures I: Performing the Discursive Voice." In *Voices, Bodies, Practices: Performing Musical Subjectivities*, by Catherine Laws, William Brooks, David Gorton, Nguyễn Thanh Thủy, Stefan Östersjö, and Jeremy J. Wells, 29–79. Orpheus Institute Series. Leuven: Leuven University Press.

Gritten, Anthony. 2017. "Developing Trust in Others: or, How to Empathise Like a Performer." In *Music and Empathy*, edited by Elaine King and Caroline Waddington, 248–66. Abingdon, UK: Ashgate.

Iyer, Vijay. 2016. "Improvisation, Action Understanding, and Music Cognition with and without Bodies." In Lewis and Piekut 2016, 1:74–90.

Krebs, Angelika. 2015. *Zwischen Ich und Du: Eine dialogische Philosophie der Liebe*. Berlin: Suhrkamp.

Laurence, Felicity. 2017. "Prologue: Revisiting the Problem of Empathy." In *Music and Empathy*, edited by Elaine King and Caroline Waddington, 11–36. Abingdon, UK: Ashgate.

Levinson, Jerrold. 1996. *The Pleasures of Aesthetics: Philosophical Essays*. Ithaca, NY: Cornell University Press.

Lewis, George E., and Benjamin Piekut, eds. 2016. *The Oxford Handbook of Critical Improvisation Studies*. 2 vols. New York: Oxford University Press.

Lipps, Theodor. 1903. *Grundlegung der Ästhetik. Ästhetik: Psychologie des Schönen und der Kunst 1*. Hamburg: Voss.

Nussbaum, Martha C. 2001. *Upheavals of Thought: The Intelligence of Emotions*. Cambridge: Cambridge University Press.

Pearce, Celia. 2016. "Role-Play, Improvisation, and Emergent Authorship." In Lewis and Piekut 2016, 2:445–68.

Peters, Deniz, and Simon Rose. 2017. *Edith's Problem*. Leo Records, CD LR 812, compact disc.

Rahaim, Matthew. 2017. "Otherwise than Participation: Unity and Alterity in Musical Encounters." In *Music and Empathy*, edited by Elaine King and Caroline Waddington, 175–93. Abingdon, UK: Ashgate.

Sarath, Ed. 2016. "A Consciousness-Based Look at Spontaneous Creativity." In Lewis and Piekut 2016, 2:132–52.

Scheler, Max. 1923. *Wesen und Formen der Sympathie: Der "Phänomenologie der Sympathiegefühle."* 2nd ed. Bonn: F. Cohen. Translated by Peter Heath as Scheler (1954) 2017.

———. (1954) 2017. *The Nature of Sympathy*. Translated by Peter Heath. Abingdon, UK: Routledge. First published as Scheler 1923. This translation first published 1954 (London: Routledge & Kegan Paul). This edition of the translation first published 2008 (Piscataway, NJ: Transaction).

Schütz, Alfred. (1951) 1976. "Making Music Together: A Study in Social Relationship." In *Collected Papers II: Studies in Social Theory*, edited by Arvid Brodersen (ed.), 159–78. The Hague: Martinus Nijhoff. Essay first published 1951 (*Social Research* 18 [1]: 76–97). Volume first published 1964 (The Hague: Martinus Nijhoff).

Scruton, Roger. 1997. *The Aesthetics of Music*. Oxford: Oxford University Press.

Siddall, Gillian, and Ellen Waterman. 2016. "Introduction: Improvising at the Nexus of Discursive and Material Bodies." In *Negotiated Moments: Improvisation, Sound, and Subjectivity*, edited by Gillian Siddall and Ellen Waterman, 1–19. Durham, NC: Duke University Press.

Stein, Edith. 1989. *On the Problem of Empathy*. Translated by Waltraut Stein. 3rd rev. ed. Washington: ICS Publications. First published 1917 as *Zum Problem der Einfühlung* (Halle: Buchdruckerei des Waisenhauses).

Waterman, Ellen. 2016. "Improvisation and the Audibility of Difference: Safa, Canadian Multiculturalism, and the Politics of Recognition." In *Negotiated Moments: Improvisation, Sound, and Subjectivity*, edited by Gillian Siddall and Ellen Waterman, 283–306. Durham, NC: Duke University Press.

Moving and Being Moved

Affective Resonance at Play in Sonic Performances

Juliana Hodkinson

Independent composer; Grieg Academy, University of Bergen;
Royal Danish Academy of Music, Copenhagen

INTRODUCTION

With the notion of affective resonance, I propose here a communicative view of intersubjectivity, according to which we understand one another and understand things together through bodily interactions. Embedded within this social concept is the more abstract sonic trope of resonance. Drawing on the social and sonic aspects of affective resonance together enables the description of a particular way of regarding intersubjectivity in live musical and other sonic performances that binds together different subjects with physical stuff (instruments, objects) in sense-making. Focusing on this interlinked aspect of musical experience releases the perceived effects of sonic artworks from being viewed primarily as coming from the intentions and designs of their composers or artists, simply mediated by performing musicians and passively or contemplatively "received" by audiences. Musical performance can then be more fully acknowledged as a site in which several processes of embodied social interaction run together.

Seen this way, a performance is not only a synchronisation of performers' articulations and expressions, perceived and contemplated by listeners. It is a convergence of many people's experiences of being in the middle of a dynamic, interactive situation, where sense-making is formed at the intersection of moving (expression) and being moved (affect). In every social encounter, two cycles of embodiment—emotion (moving, a centrifugal motion) and affect (being moved, a centripetal motion)—become intertwined, continually modifying each subject's affective affordances and resonance. This complex process may be regarded as the bodily basis of empathy and social understanding. Within a discussion of subjectivity in contemporary music and creative sound-making, this networked way of conceiving performance in music and sound art directs emphasis towards the necessity of acknowledging a larger number of subjects and relations in the process of forming artistic meaning. Not only intention, interpretation, and contemplation are at play, but rather a more complex feedback situation, in which interactions between all kinds of participants resonate in the process of making sense. The success of an artistic moment is constituted not only by composers' and musicians' abilities to express themselves, but also by the permeability of composers, musicians, and listeners, and their mutual resonance within a given situation or system. For the sake of avoiding a noise-based, mechanical phenomenon, I will bypass the temptation to make sonic play on the somewhat binary notion of feedback and stay here with the broader notion of resonance and its implied social and physical components within the body, our physical surroundings, particular vessels (instruments), and their resonant frequencies, and subsequently the associated notions of sympathetic resonance and consensus.

Activating the trope of resonance within the social and sonic paradigm of music performance gives us pause to consider the role of sound as a bundle of physical phenomena, linking matter and objects with our bodies and opening up for consideration the role of instruments, objects, and vibration in processes of sonic artistic communication. At the same time, resonance has become a new paradigm within cultural studies, where this originally acoustical phenomenon has been adopted as a metaphor for interactions between different areas of social reality (Erlmann 2010; Rosa 2016; James 2019).

All this entails an acknowledgement of the participation of a wider field of subjects and objects in making sound and in sense-making than those studied by analysis, interpretation, and reception history; this is also fundamental to *Voices, Bodies, Practices* (the partner volume to this book), with its focus on "the constitution of subjectivity through the interaction of embodied subject, other human agencies, and instrumental technological mediation in the specific site of performance production" (Laws 2019, 21). The topic of expanding participation is here explored from three different angles: first, the influence of musicians and composer on one another in the creation of new work, in processes that may or may not be led by detailed scores; second, the involvement of the active listener as participant at various levels in sonic works; and third, the involvement of objects and instruments as resonating contributors to the relations at play.

Relational aesthetics and art music

While affective resonance as a concept may be relevant to a large number of fields, the interest here is in advancing an expansion in the qualitative terms by which contemporary music and sound art are discussed. Relational aesthetics and networked social interaction have established themselves integrally within many areas of artistic work—the visual arts, architecture, and theatre—becoming a *modus operandi* for artists, curators, and spectators. But they have been slow to occupy a central place within music. Nicolas Bourriaud's *Esthétique relationnelle* (*Relational Aesthetics*) became paradigmatically influential immediately after its publication in 1998. In it, Bourriaud formulated an aspect of visual arts practices that had been evolving since the 1970s, in which interpersonal relations and their social contexts were central to the experience of artworks, rather than independent or imaginary encounters between art objects and individual viewers. In relational art, spectators may be regarded as an interlinked community, with the artwork producing encounters between people who collectively make sense of the work and the encounter as convergent entities.

Given that the formats within which many of the works that Bourriaud discusses—installation, video, sculpture—are ones in which spectators' experiences are not usually synchronous (since visitors stream through galleries at their own pace, spread out over a period of weeks or months), it may seem particularly radical, or simply abstract, to conceive of spectators as not only having interactive relations with an artwork but also forming communities through them. Within the context of a sonic arts discourse, it seems much easier to point to live musical formats—concerts with audiences—as fertile contexts for relational aesthetics. Yet, during the late twentieth century, the reading of musical concerts as social contexts was largely limited to historical musicology and ethnomusicology. Significantly, Philip Bohlman's "Musicology as a Political Act" from 1993 charged musicology with essentialising music by means of a series of exclusions—the social, the political, feminist theory, the body, race, and class. This angle was taken up by Georgina Born in a 2007 lecture calling for a relational musicology that could include popular music studies alongside ethnomusicology, music sociology, and traditional musicology, in order to soften epistemological and ontological borders within music studies (Born 2010). Bohlman's initial focus was on integrating Jewish music into the dominant musical discourse, and Born's on breaking down oppositions between classical and popular musics. However, no one was making the case from within musicology and musical aesthetic theory that work produced under the institutional conditions of contemporary art music was or should be accentuating the mingling of composers', performers', and listeners' agencies.

It was not until 2012 that the term *relational music* gained expediency, employed by philosopher Harry Lehmann. Acknowledging Bourriaud's strategy of including extra-aesthetical relations in definitions of what art can be, Lehmann nevertheless finds Bourriaud's theory of relational aesthetics to have been developed within the context of a narrow and particularly radical group of avant-garde works. In Lehmann's view, this limits the effect of Bourriaud's theory beyond those kinds of pieces. Against Bourriaud's notion that art can create performative situations, in which spontaneous interpersonal relations can arise between makers and spectators, Lehmann (2012, 115) sets an understanding of "relations" in a different sense as applying between music and not-music (images, actions, and words). He situates his discussion of relational music at the "end" of classical modernism in music with the assumption that the pursuit of unheard sounds has run into the sand. What we now need, then, is alternative ways to understand works whose central effect does not depend upon an aesthetics rooted in the terms of absolute music, such as works that integrate extra-musical content at a compositional level.

Lehmann attributes the effects of "the digital revolution" on contemporary music—on which his philosophical theory of music turns—as falling into three important patterns. First, the digitalisation of musical composition and distribution has undermined art music's traditional identification with the aesthetics of absolute music, which had previously refused all conceptual and relational orientations. Second, the use of the computer as an interface for both creating and communicating artworks of all kinds has levelled sound, image, and language within artistic content. Third, these shifts, together with postmodern pluralistic society's lack of common cultural denominators, lead, Lehmann asserts, to a deinstitutionalisation and democratisation of contemporary music, and a corresponding opening up of its structures (2012, 116).

Lehmann has since expounded his definition of relational music in a series of lectures given largely within the same canonising contemporary music institutional structures as those within which the works that he comments on are commissioned and performed[1]—an approach quite opposite to the deinstitutionalising and broadening effect that his definition of relational music assumes. The danger here is a process of canonisation rooted in a circularity of the production of works and their theoretical valorising. This has created a paradigmatic effect within those structures, with the term "relational music" broadly accepted in Lehmann's terms, as referring to a particular group—a new canon—of works, composers, and compositional approaches. This is so not only because of the broad professional interest in the topics that Lehmann addresses, but also due to the nature of Lehmann's theoretical argumentation, by which he ranks individual works as being, categorically, relational or not relational. However, the socially relational expansion of the meaning and affect of contemporary music and sound art has in fact been notoriously slow to evolve, with the institutional structures within these fields arguably remaining typically hierarchical, undiverse, and otherwise resistant to relational ways of thinking.

Interestingly, sound art at the non-cochlear end of the scale, as defined and discussed by Seth Kim-Cohen (2009), is not discussed as part of this. Kim-Cohen's concern, in contrast to Lehmann, is to propose that "sound art, as a discrete practice, is merely the remainder created by music closing off its borders to the extramusical. . . . Sound art is art that posits meaning or value in registers not accounted for by musical systems" (Kim-Cohen 2016, 126). Matthew Shlomowitz (2014), critiquing Lehmann, makes the important addition that contemporary music's ongoing search for novel musical material could be replaced not just by a search for new concepts, but more interestingly by a search for work that engages the material and discursive, the abstract and the relational—that is, retaining the pleasure of sound and joining it with the pleasure of new concepts. In this quest, I would in turn add, contemporary music and sonic art are no different to commercial pop music, in that the joining of familiar musical constructs with new production formats drives a continual development of sound ideals whereby the music of today has a recognisably different sound to that of yesterday. In the broad hermeneutic of affective resonance, there is no opposition between seeing phenomena as occupying both material and discursive planes.

---

1 For example: "The Gehalts-Aesthetic Turn of New Music," lecture held at the Experimentalstudio Academy Matrix, Freiburg, 2013; "Conceptual Music and the Gehalt-Aesthetic Turn," lecture held at the Darmstädter Ferienkurse 2014; "Gehaltsästhetik—Relationale Musik—Konzeptmusik," lecture held at the Universität der Künste Berlin, 2015; "33 Theses on Conceptual Music," lecture and seminar held at the Norwegian Academy of Music, Oslo, 2017; "Experiments in Relational Music," lecture held at the Artistic Research Forum, University of Stavanger, 2016.

The artwork that thrives in the middle of such a set of relations is, however, necessarily open to continual reinterpretation, its meaning and sense being perpetually in flux. Further, it cannot be assumed that all types of relations are directed towards a benevolent and open-minded kind of community thinking. Within the dynamics of curatorial and institutional influence and appropriation, and all the trappings of cultural capital and the finances of the art market, the relational way of evaluating art risks entangling works in the machinery of neo-liberal hegemonic frameworks. We cannot assume that "resonance" will always produce harmonious democracies. However inclusive any given concept may be, its translation into reality will necessarily throw up exclusions, just as the emancipation of the spectator involves not only increased proximity but also alienating distance.

So, putting together Shlomowitz's arguments with the considerable commodification and gentrification of visual artworks in the relational-art seam, I would appeal here for a convergence of embodied interaction between different subjects around sonic and musical live performances as being hopefully a rich entanglement of the pleasure of sound (resonance) and emotional response (affect).

The concept of affective resonance has arisen from combining theories within interactive social cognition theory, developmental psychology, physics, and philosophy (Mühlhoff 2015). It is developed from considerations of meaning as arising through interaction between experience, symbols, and things, and created through subjects participating in their surroundings. I see this emphasis on participation creating not only interaction but also sense as part of an inter-subjective turn that acknowledges a bio-logical understanding of meaning, in which sentient, bodied creatures organise, nurture, mature, and free themselves through lived experience. Resonating—being or coming into resonance, as an affective hermeneutic—follows the ontology of vibrational force. I would connect Erin Manning's politics of touch (2007), Elizabeth Grosz's primordial vibrational philosophy (2008), and Jane Bennett's ecological materialism with this train of thought (2010).

PARTICIPATION

The central concerns of work created along the trajectory of the participatory turn moves away from tensions within the inner material workings of compositional devices under the composer's control towards affective resonance and social interaction. Embodied interaction between composers, musicians, listeners, and objects entails a move towards participation at a number of levels. Relations of agency begin to shift; the role and nature of the musical score, of composition and rehearsal change. This fits with Mühlhoff's observations on aspects of emotional experience that are not only relational but also processural, and constantly dynamic in relation to situational configurations.

If we take first of all the case of devising, in music, a participatory experience—for example, between musicians and composer—then increasing the dynamic sensitivity will entail a process that uses rehearsal time and invested trust in a different way than is the norm with many forms of rehearsing and practising. In this situation, the interaction is between different kinds of music experts, but still questions of professional skill and virtuosity in composition and performance are likely to crop up, as well as the question of what has been composed or performed. Compared with the process by which a composer first writes a score that is then interpreted by musicians, there may be an increase of efficiency in some aspects for the composer, but a decrease of efficiency for the musicians. Composer Carolyn Chen has described her ambivalence concerning the experience of this transition to a participatory way of working: "As a composer without a standard working score, I sometimes felt like an emperor in a self-tailored naked suit. I had ordered a parade, and people were rolled out, but I didn't always know exactly where we were going. There was no extant document to be interpreted as a source of authority, to pass minimum standards of competence, to reassure us that we were all doing our jobs okay" (Chen 2016).

This phase is however simply one to be overcome, and Chen has persisted fruitfully with this way of working. In *Signs of Struggle* (2016), an improvisation piece for four people, objects, castanet (*sic*), bass drum, and room, Chen pursues relations between listening and sound-making within a sphere of attention to perceptual detail and obstruction, where musicians' intentions and behaviour may increasingly diverge. In this process, developed with musicians sympathetic to contact improvisation, bodily movement, and percussion/object performance, "the score is developing from performance as much as performance from score" (Chen 2016).[2]

This was also somewhat my experience with devising a number of pieces in which I committed, for different reasons in each case, to developing composition in rehearsal, and in which I held back from fixing key aspects of the content ahead of the involvement of performers and even listeners.[3] My piece *(something in capitals)* (2017), for six or twelve voices with gadgets, small bells, and two to four instrumentalists, was originally composed during and between rehearsals, with the commissioning vocal ensemble Solistenensemble Phønix16 and instrumental improvisation ensemble S.A.F.T.[4] Attracted by the chance of working with an extremely heterogeneous group of musicians, most of them very experienced in different styles of historical or contemporary performance and improvisation, I devised the piece by providing stimuli for relatively free explorations of sonority, beginning initially with "omm" ("aum," ॐ) and gradually introducing fixed text, electronic gadgets, and broad indications for glissandi, sonority, and dynamics. The explorations in rehearsal convinced me that leaving pitch and duration open to the consensus of any given moment produced more interesting results than if I were to fix as many aspects as possible in the score.

Clearly, the compositional avoidance of specifying, for example, pitch while indicating several singers to fall in with one another around a basic vibrational

---

2 Two separate runs of Carolyn Chen's *Signs of Struggle* can be watched at https://www.youtube.com/watch?v=8YQRVoGcRzo and https://www.youtube.com/watch?v=82SczbfUTps.

3 *(something in capitals)* (2017), for Solistenensemble Phønix16, *Pass* (2018) for Poing, and ♥ *LOVE* (2019), devised in collaboration with Icelandic Love Corporation and Ensemble Adapter.

4 The score and a recording of *(something in capitals)* can be accessed at http://www.julianahodkinson.net/works/something-in-capitals.

gesture such as "omm" guaranteed that if no one singer were allocated to lead the "omm" everyone would enter on different pitches.[5] I left it open to the singers whether they would orient towards a common tone and to what extent. The additional stipulation in the piece—that outside the "omm" vibrations and spoken/half-spoken passages a glissando (in any direction over any range) was to constitute the steady pitch state—was in a way an exploration of finding strong resonances that would be both convergent and divergent, and in any case dynamic. Between rehearsals, I fixed the sung text, to make it different for each part but with some rhyming characteristics in terms of both verbal rhythm and either consonants or vowels. For example, in the following two phrases there are six different lines of three to five words each, spoken simultaneously by six or twelve voices, each of whom adhere throughout the piece to an individual set of colours indicating different subgroupings. Bold type and underlining indicate that the words are to be sung (not spoken) and that the vowels are to be extended: Convergent vowels or consonants produce a kind of rhyming throughout, while meanings are heterogeneous. This combination supports a sense that while the musicians are in a way performing the same thing, or something similar, there is also an essential divergence in what they perform.

I came to the first rehearsal with no fixed notated material—simply some verbal instructions for creating particular sustained resonances; on the back of each rehearsal, I worked on providing additional verbal instructions for the next day, together with writing more text and further refining the range of non-verbal sonic material.[6] In a situation like this, alarm bells of appropriation are going off in the heads of musicians and composer alike all the time, as the working process of all concerned diverges from enculturated norms of composition. I wanted to allow the vocal and instrumental musicians' expertise and responses to flow into the making of the work, without fixing "their" particular motifs, gestures, or solutions into my notation. That is to say, I wanted to create a notation for a composition according to which, not only in the first performance but in every performance, there would be both convergence and divergence in relation to certain fixed elements. This is somewhat different than asking for improvisation, even in a broad understanding of that term. In *(something in capitals)*, the musicians have very specific tasks, and they perform tutti with similar temporal articulations most of the time. But pitch is not fixed at all, and rhythm is either removed entirely or given through the contours of the half-spoken text.

This was not the first time I had worked with a semi-aligned timing that simultaneously made a confidently-cued ensemble entry difficult and yet seemed

---

5 The full score of *(something in capitals)* can be viewed at http://www.julianahodkinson.net/sites/default/files/pdf/Hodkinson_SomethingInCapitals.pdf.

6 *(something in capitals)* was commissioned by the vocal group Solistenensemble Phønix16 and its artistic director Timo Kreuser. It was performed twice by them in 2017 and 2018 in two different formations—first with six voices together with improvisation ensemble S.A.F.T., and then with twelve voices together with duo NoiserKroiser. Phønix16's artistic director Timo Kreuser is a performing member of both these instrumental improvisation formations, and his encouragement from within the instrumental corpus was an important part of the work's development. *(something in capitals)* has additionally been performed by Piteå New Voices with instrumentalists Oriol Pares, Mika Persdotter, James Black, and Jens Peter Møller in 2019, conducted by Sigurdur Arni Jonsson.

contingent on "getting it right," within a certain narrow range of quasi-togetherness. In *some reasons for hesitating* (1999), I wrote for fifteen instruments without providing a score—a strategy that in turn frustrated the possibility of working with a conductor in a conventional way. This chamber music is built on predominantly quiet and precarious timbres that are hard to balance, and many of the attacks and decays are either hard to control or difficult to hear. The musicians are required both to strive for accuracy and precision in relation to the production of timbres and coincidence of entries, and to be accepting of their own and others' inability to get it right every time—implicitly, they are even required to cover up for one another's failures, by carrying on, and sustaining the overall timbral and affective fabric of the piece. This set of circumstances has produced a number of more and less happy performances over the years. Some ensembles have attempted to modify the role of their conductor in order to provide a central point of orientation during rehearsal; others have begun rehearsing with a stopwatch. One ensemble even suggested cutting and pasting all the parts together into a conventional score layout, before realising that this would bring little alleviation to the overall challenge. As I wrote in the preface to each part: "It is a major point that the relatively large ensemble plays without conductor and that there is no score—i.e. a performance demands the highest degree of mutual attentiveness and communication between musicians, and there is no absolute compositional control over the vertical coordination. This practice displaces the interest from music's ideal representation in the score to music as an event and unique experiential opportunity" (Hodkinson 1999).[7]

This use of a verbal explanation in the parts, together with the question of the status of the parts in relation to the missing score, has been discussed from a textual perspective by writer Cynthia Troup, with whom I was collaborating at that time within a larger interdisciplinary artistic team, and who later wrote the libretto to our opera *Turbulence* (2013):

> There is no score. In this collection of booklets, with its sixty-one pages of sparse staves, only two pages are identical for each instrumental part: a sheet of "notes on chronography and the coordination of parts," and a more closely typed sheet of "notes to the musicians." As an inclusive address to the readers of different musical lines, these two pages substitute for the composer's orderly collation and standardisation of parts. Yet they do so only provisionally, as Hodkinson's text both anticipates and embarrasses any desire for a score. (Troup 2000, 1)

> So much contingency in the realisation of parts and ensemble undermines the notion that triumphant fluency must be an attribute of performance; that indeed fluency is a key reason for concert performance, and for composing music. Beyond merely excluding a score, *some reasons for hesitating* works against expectations of self-evident continuity and coherence by the content of its parts, and thus the piece works against a closed narrative, an integrated description. Pursued as an accumulation of booklets and as an audio recording, if not as an irreversible performance experience, it will not answer to any verbal representation that purports to be other than open-ended, partial, and allusive—that is, in a sense, hesitant. (Ibid., 3)

---

7 The performance notes, a sample page from the oboe part, and a recording of *some reasons for hesitating* can be accessed at http://www.julianahodkinson.net/works/some-reasons-for-hesitating.

In the vocal piece *(something in capitals)* (2017) I wanted to mirror the divergence between what the singers say/sing with an asymmetry in the way that would be experienced by listeners. Distributing the singers around the periphery of the audience was one way of ensuring that every listener would experience some voices as more prominent than others, and that this focus would vary throughout the audience, as well as supporting the singers' independence of verbal articulation within the ensemble.

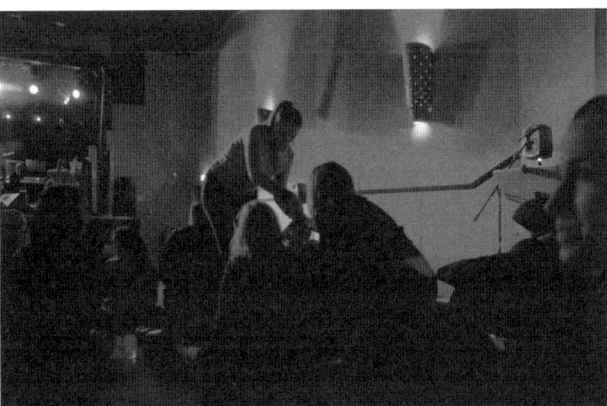 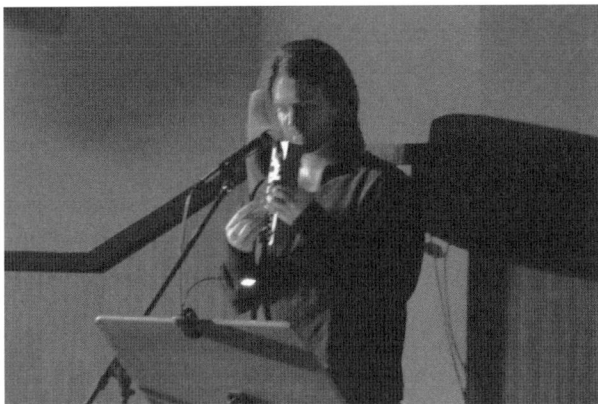

Figure 2.1a–b.

Additionally, I wanted there to be a kind of vibration that would be experienced individually, if at all (or at least, by some but not all listeners). Twice during the piece, some of the singers leave their positions and walk among the audience: The first time, they carry tiny bells that are muted in their cupped hands; they animate them only slightly a couple of centimetres away from individual listeners' ears, so that the movement of the bell is felt as a sensation of quasi-touch rather than heard as a conventional act of hearing vibrating air. The second time the singers walk carrying small battery-powered electronic gadgets with weak in-built speakers (short-wave radios, monotrons, and similar, emitting sounds in a spectrum between white noise and sine tones, switching between square and sawtooth waveforms, and occasionally including radio broadcasts, mechanical arpeggiations or vibrati). These devices have slightly more projection than the miniature bells, but they still do not project across an auditorium and their effect remains a relatively esoteric experience for the listeners closest by. I asked the performers to approach listeners in the manner of offering them a short ear massage.

For pieces devised in this way, such as Chen's *Signs of Struggle* or my *(something in capitals)*, there is additionally the question of how they will be rehearsed and performed by different groups, and which sounding results would be most convergent or divergent in relation to the first performance. What is the role, in subsequent performances, of the composer's and musicians' experiences from the first performance, and what influence do recordings of previous perform-

Figure 2.1a–b. *Left*, singers from Solistenensemble Phønix16 passing through the audience with small bells; *right*, singer from Solistenensemble Phønix16 performing on a small gadget while singing at Columbia Theater Berlin, December 2017. Photo: Torsten Flüh.

ances have on future interpretations? All these issues add up to a significant challenge to enculturated ideas of musical works and the role of the composer, and to the processes of composition and rehearsal as necessarily separate. Peter Kivy (1993) addresses these issues in a philosophical discussion of variant performances of works with some indeterminate attributes, proposing performances as "types" of a given work that is a "token"; furthermore, he contrasts dominant notions of musical composition as creating works with approaches focused on the aspect of discovery in composition. If we are able to view oppositional relations (e.g., between normative views of works, composers, and performers) as being not mutually exclusive, then we can understand the kind of music that consists of both indeterminate and fixed aspects as still upholding subsidiary concepts such as score, composer, and performance. Elements such as non-specific notation systems and the independence of the performers in respect of certain parameters, then, offer not a challenge but an extension to restrictive ideals such as accuracy and compliance.

I would like to move on from this discussion of how musicians complete indeterminate elements of a score through rehearsal and performance, to the case where the listener is styled a participant in a musical performance. The prerequisite of participation and of the use of the audience as a tool of performance in contemporary music is that crucial elements of the work concept have shifted, in the twenty-first century, from being score-based to being sound-based. This is partly due to the general extension of the sphere of performance to include a broader instrumentarium, including historical instruments, instruments from many different cultures, invented and specially constructed instruments, objects, and materials. Parallel to this, the rise of electronic music in many forms, and of hybrid electroacoustic formats and electronic extensions to acoustic instruments, has blurred borders between the digital and the instrumental, between the fixing of works through notation or in audio files, and has even offered opportunities for audio or video files to serve as auditory or visual time-based scores. Furthermore, the blending of genres and cross-fertilisation of styles has brought classical contemporary music into contact with processual influences from jazz, mass mediation from pop, and spontaneous composition from improvisation. All these shifts towards practices of difference, interrelation, and hybridity have undermined the universalising presuppositions of the musical score. With this weakening of the status of the score as a notational ideal appropriate to all and any kinds of instruments, an opening arises not only for a broader range of performers, including artists from other disciplines, experts performing on instruments outside their normal practice, amateurs, non-specialists, and children, but also for performance without rehearsal and practice. More space opens up for spontaneity, including spontaneity of interpretation (as opposed to out-and-out improvisation).

For the purposes of this participatory discourse within music, we may need to distinguish between two senses of the performer—one, the trained musician, the other, the listener drawn into the field of action. This distinction does not assume that the listener is untrained; on the contrary, within a sonic art performance niche, listeners are highly likely to be themselves musicians, composers, or curators with a background and/or current practice within music. Clearly, when audience members are drawn into the performance of the piece, they do not cease to listen. Nevertheless, the distinction between musicians and listeners as performers assumes that the listener is unprepared, unrehearsed for the performance that is being undertaken. So, the collective audience consists of multiple individuals who, when activated as performers, contribute a kind of intersubjective exchange to the events. This intersubjective paradigm is elegantly realised in Huang Ruo's *The Sonic Great Wall* (2016), which not only involves listeners in meditation, recitation, humming, singing, whispering, and moving, but also encapsulates the participatory premise in the metaphorical, historical, and physical model of the wall as something to be softened by contemporary practices, whether political or artistic.[8] If a given wall is regarded by one party as a defence against incursion by another party, then the responsibility lies potentially on both sides to resolve the need for its impermeability and make it porous. This could apply equally to the power relations fixed in modernist contemporary music's reliance on score, composer, and work occupying particular status, and on a stage facing an auditorium, inserting a division between performers and audience (Toelle and Sloboda 2019).

Whether due to the listenership being unprepared or simply untrained and unrehearsed for performance, the involvement of listeners often leans towards the ludic: a mode in which play, experimentation, lack of ritual, and acceptance of mistakes may successfully come together. This element was also present in my piece *Pass* (2018), for three musicians with objects and illuminated environment.[9] In *Pass*, the audience is first collected onstage and required to find coins in their wallets to contribute to the performance, in preparation for the act of sharing and redistribution that the piece's title refers to. Listeners are then asked to hum a sustained tone, and order themselves according to the number of coins they hold, before being dispersed in the auditorium, cleared to serve as an expanded performance area. The audience responds to a series of prompts and invitations, given mainly by me. During the early part of the performance, I address the audience as a group and invite them to interact as such; as things progress, I approach them individually with smaller gestures of invitation, talking to single listeners more quietly in the relative dark. During the course of the performance, the lighting gradually shifts from being first a relatively uncomfortable, over-revealing spotlight shining directly down on the audience from the stage traverse, to finally a wash of black light allowing only pure whites and neon colours to stand out, with all other colours merging into grey/brown tones in the darkness. Building to some extent on my previous participatory piece, *Nothing breaking the losing* (2016), in the use of threads held by audience members with clusters of tiny resonant objects hanging from them (coins, keys, small bells, etc.), *Pass* unfolds through a progression of light and sound

---

8   Excerpts from Huang Ruo's *The Sonic Great Wall* can be watched at https://youtu.be/UUqilXf5EP0.

9   *Pass* was commissioned by the trio Poing with funds from the Norwegian Arts Council, and first performed by them at Sentralen, Oslo, in the Periferien concert series, on 11 March 2018. *Pass* was performed with the intervention or framing of Poing's idiosyncratic arrangement of the four movements of Bach's Brandenburg Concerto No. 1—for saxophones, accordion, double bass, and the musicians' own voices.

throughout a large space, in which the listeners find themselves at the centre of a collective action to which the performance of the three musicians relates at times more or less as a background. Rolling marbles in the dark (heard and possibly felt rather than seen), and engaging with luminous balls of light and table-tennis balls, listeners become busy "fielding" objects and balls, relaunching them into the centre of the room, and energising the activity of the cluster of objects. As the activity throughout the room grows—also involving shaking cans and throwing coins as into a wishing-well—listeners' continual pulling and shaking on the threads leads, literally, to a tangle of converging lines in the centre of the room. Despite all efforts to uphold the central focus, the many small sonic and visual events and movements going on all around make for a diffuse situation in which everyone is looking at everyone else the whole time, searching for cues, connections, and opportunities for interaction.

Mühlhoff (2015, 1002) conceives of social resonance as more than just sharing affective experience: he moves ahead to the notion that through social interaction, people together create affective qualities that were not there before the encounter. The dynamics that Mühlhoff focuses on are "phenomenal qualities of being-in-resonance, experienced as a gripping dynamic force of moving and being-moved in relation" (ibid., 1003). If two dynamical systems (of which two people might be one example) are coupled, their joint behaviour may display aspects of coordination, with their movements becoming synchronised, which may be the result of subtle or even minute vibrations that cause their oscillations to synchronise.

My point in underlining participation is linked also to a desire for a broader social distribution of creativity in contemporary arts and culture. If, traditionally, in Western classical music, composers were male, individual, working alone at the piano or desk on compositions that were performed within hierarchical structures and exclusionary paradigms, today they are of more genders, working also in partnerships and complex collaborations, keenly wanting to be interconnected with musicians, listeners, and contexts, their practices spilling over into a range of different disciplines. So it is for me, in any case. I am interested in the materiality of the artwork and the collaboration with musicians' performative skills, but I am also curious how the artistic and even performative knowledge shared or embodied by the listener influences the way a work unfolds in all its processes of being created and perceived. Insofar as listening may be regarded as a kind of "aural performative"—an action performed by our ears and made sense of through our listening apparatus—all intense listening experiences would represent an embodiment of artistic knowledge.[10]

---

10 I have previously proposed the notion of the *aural performative* as one that makes listening into a reiterative act, or practice (akin to the act of utterance, or simply talking). The aural performative would be the act of appropriating sound through perception and giving aural perception a sense-making role, rather than regarding listening as a passive and mechanical procedure in which sounds pass through our auditory apparatus (Hodkinson 2007, 139).

Resonance

I use the term *resonance* in a broad sense to refer to physical properties of sound coupled with social and imaginative properties, whereby an object or subject emitting a vibration causes another object or subject to vibrate sympathetically. I see a natural role for a focus on resonance to couple with social and cultural diversity and allow us to look both at musical structures (tuning and harmonic systems, acoustic or electronic instruments from different sources or cultures combined in hybrid ensemble forms) and at openings in musical and institutional practice in order to bring a larger and more diverse group of backgrounds into meaningful artistic resonance with one another.

As both a musical and a figurative term, *resonance* may be explored with methodologies centred on listening and experience, and therefore embracing the listener. Such an approach within artistic research would allow us to access the sensing body and its experiences as an active and open form, continually improvising its relation to things and to the world. This is after all one part of what draws us to art—the possibility, for a limited moment in time, of indulging in improvising our own experience and expectations.

According to Christian Grüny, resonance is "mimesis at a distance" (Schäffler 2018). It is neither the collapsing into one another of subject and object, a dissolution of borders, nor an equivalence of the listener and the music (as in ecstatic dance, for example). Nor is it a distanced, if differentiated, reception of music, in which the sensual sphere of experience and being addressed or even affected is excluded. Rather, resonance is there when the space between subject and object starts to be reduced, without them fusing into one. In this condition there is a moment of freedom, a perceptual improvisation, which corresponds, as Schäffler points out, to our dealings, as listeners, with music: in Grüny's words, "what resonates responds to what it encounters in a way that is neither arbitrary, nor [in]determined or -determinable" (quoted in Schäffler 2018, 5, my translation). When a field of resonance is rolled out, an entanglement of sonic relations can take place. Through embodied interaction we are able to attune ourselves to one another in dynamic connections that run simultaneously in various directions, in a rhizome of affective and affinitive connections. Even small actions and minute excitations within a sub-dynamic tangle might amplify a sociality that leads us away from a focus on sound's purely mechanical physical components.

Actor–network theory has similarly pointed up the existence of perpetually shifting networks of relationships between all things natural and social, levelling the hierarchies between objects, ideas, processes, and other factors, and leading to a withdrawal from divisions between the subjective and the objective. When somebody is affected, their agency is likely to be altered in some way, affecting in turn their environment. Being affected makes us change direction or adjust our behaviour or composure, even if only incrementally. This possibly subtle change might seem far removed from the ideas of participation, democracy, and empowerment that pervade many of the more ambitious discourses that link participatory art to political potential. And it is. It is vague and indefinable. That is precisely because this is another kind of participation, but one nevertheless significant to the efficacy of artworks and what art can do. Drawing observers into a sonic space, encouraging them to explore, with awareness of both their own and others' sonic actions, involves often small gestures of exchange, interaction, exploration, and mirroring, such as those we know from conversation or other situations of social adaptation.

This intersubjective turn has a history—it draws on, among others, the works of Fluxus and indeterminacy, and on happenings and other mid-twentieth-century formats that leaned on a historically specific politics and a specific social and artistic framework of expectations and resistances. Arguably, it also extends across the development of much sound art, as a practice set apart from musicking. In a way, the current intersubjective turn is completely different from these historical practices, and in a way there is a continuity, evidenced, for example, in the steadily expanding influence of Pauline Oliveros's practices of deep listening and sonic meditation from the late 1980s onwards, or by a series such as Peter Ablinger's *Chair Projects* (1995–2007), which stage listeners within various environments, such that, as Ablinger says (2014), "not the sound, but the listening is the piece."[11] Looking, today, for compositions that encourage a performative intersubjectivity, we find examples in James Saunders's series of *things to do* (ongoing since 2012), which often call on players to work with materials collected either spontaneously or before performance, reacting in quick succession within game rules that bring virtuosity in decision-making to a head.[12] Some of these pieces also draw on audience volunteers to choose and perform sounds, actions, and interactions, with the aim of both exposing and obstructing personal preferences, as well as testing reaction times and people's overall responsiveness to one another.

For the adventurously inclined, philosopher Aaron Finbloom's series of conversation pieces, such as *Tell Me More About* (2018) and *Deictic Dialectics* (2018), fall into this category of participatory performance pieces, even though they are not explicitly designed with an audience in mind.[13] Like Saunders's *things to do*, Finbloom and Hannah Kaya, co-creators of the piece *Oscillations of One-to-Many* (2017),[14] see this work as being in the tradition of John Zorn's *Cobra* (1984)[15]—presumably in its use of cues designed to encourage players to break out of individual habits in improvisation and allow others' actions to affect one's performance—and of John Cage's chance operations, in the strict use of timing. A number of techniques are deployed in order to intervene in the flow of each person's talking; these include tasks such as humming a note or

---

11 Information on Peter Ablinger's *Chair Projects* can be accessed at https://ablinger.mur.at/docu01.html.

12 Videos of pieces from James Saunders's *things to do* series can be watched at http://www.james-saunders.com/things-2/.

13 A video of Aaron Finbloom's *Tell Me More About* can be watched at https://www.youtube.com/watch?v=Klm2Y_cghBE. The instructions and a video of Aaron Finbloom's *Deictic Dialectics* can be viewed at http://www.finblooming.com/deictic-dialectics.html.

14 The instructions for Hannah Kaya and Aaron Finbloom's *Oscillations of One-to-Many* can be viewed at http://www.finblooming.com/oscillations-of-one-to-many.html.

15 For the score of this work, see Finbloom and Kaya (2017). The score concludes with a section titled "Detailed explanation of artistic and technological paradigms, approach to musical praxis and technological implementation, including personnel needs and qualifications."

taking an audibly affirmative role in relation to what someone else is saying. One of Finbloom's other conversation pieces—*A Few (More) Silences* (2015)—was created in collaboration with composer Sandeep Bhagwati (see Finbloom and Bhagwati 2015). In common with Finbloom's other conversation pieces, *A Few (More) Silences* involves a strict structuring of rules and roles, but also draws on Bhagwati's practice of negotiating relations between and among composers, performers and artists in different disciplines, a composer-led collective endeavour that Bhagwati describes as "comprovising" (Kim 2018).[16] In this way, *A Few (More) Silences* brings Bhagwati's notion of comprovising collaboratively into contact with Finbloom's radical conversation practice.

In Christina Kubisch's performance-installation *Orchestra on a Wire* (2018) for orchestra, electric cables, induction headphones, electromagnetic fields, and string quartet, the listener explores sounds, silent spaces, and interferences by changing body position in relation to a maze of wires hanging down from an overhead truss structure. The dramaturgy of the sound—arising from the pace and intensity at which it is experienced—is controlled by the listener, who to some extent becomes a composer of his or her own experience, as also happened previously in Kubisch's *Electric Walks* (ongoing since 2004).[17] Aside from the shift from urban space to performance space, one main difference between the *Electric Walks* and *Orchestra on a Wire* is that, in the latter, listeners mill around the crowded grid of coordinates and begin to silently anticipate, by sensing subtle body movements, what other listeners might be experiencing, so becoming curious about sounds that are latent in the interaction between hanging cables but are not projected into the space.

Encouraging listeners to act simultaneously in different ways produces not only a potential for cacophony but also an acoustic layering that can develop into a multimodal narrative. Listening while doing combines the act of hearing something with that of witnessing while also being implicated in overall strategies: a polyphonic social mode wherein silences and crowds of sound bookend one another. The previously silently listening "I" becomes audible.

One unique, explicit activation of listeners in the process of creating and perceiving sound is found in Simon Löffler's *c* (2013), for three glockenspiels, "to be heard through the teeth." For the duration of this piece, listeners are required to bite into rods with transducers attached, through which the amplification of three glockenspiels is sent.[18] Each listener (including the performing musicians) wears ear-protecting headphones, and places their teeth on the rods, receiving the vibrations of the instrumental sounds via bone conduction through their teeth.

---

16 The score of Aaron Finbloom and Sandeep Bhagwati's *A Few (More) Silences* can be viewed at http://www.finblooming.com/a-few-more-silences.html.

17 Information about Christina Kubisch's *Electrical Walks* can be found at http://www.christinakubisch.de/en/works/electrical_walks, and an introduction to it can be watched at https://vimeo.com/54846163.

18 Simon Löffler's *c* was commissioned by, and first performed at, Spor Festival, Aarhus, in 2013. I curated that festival, which had the theme "Tacet." The score of Simon Löffler's *c* can be viewed at https://issuu.com/edition-s/docs/c_a4land_/16.

Objects and post-instrumental music

Finally, in this excitation of different relations, we come to the category of things—ubiquitous things from anywhere and everywhere: portable objects, sound-makers, or placeholders for sound. This aspect begs questions of scale, ambience, contingency, commodification, and objecthood in musical and sonic performances. Musical instruments are one obvious category of "things" within this field. However, instruments are so strongly associated with particular musicianly motoric skills and a wealth of historical influences, that our ability to regard them within an object-oriented ontology fades somewhat in the face of stylistic discourse.

These ideas have been in my mind during the years of work on my piece *Lightness*, which falls within a field of non-instrumental or post-instrumental practice. *Lightness* is scored for household matches and matchboxes, and additional related materials such as variously grained sandpaper (emulating the grainy sound of the match head against a rough ignition surface), and water and sand (for extinguishing the matches with controlled movements).[19] In an initial research and development phase with Speak Percussion in 2014, we tested the technical and sensory-motoric opportunities and limits of working with fast-paced striking of matches, and addressed the challenges of working with a potentially flammable situation in pitch black. Through the premiere in 2015 and subsequent performances, I have had the opportunity to revise, tweak, and accompany various different ensembles' encounters with the piece, bringing it to a level of precision and harmonisation between the technical, musical, and visual aspects that would never have been possible following the conventional order of completing composition and notation before the start of rehearsals. Scale, ambience, contingency, and the development of sensory-motoric skills in relation to objects and materials with which we had little musical experience all needed to come together in the workshops and in the changes to the piece after gaining experience of it in concert.[20]

In an earlier series of works with household matches—*Some sounds for L. L.* (1999), *All the time* (2001), and *All that we cannot say* (2002)—I worked within acoustic instrumental-theatre formats. Revisiting the same material with Speak Percussion over a decade later, we saw the possibility of scaling up the sound and making it more robust through amplification, as well as employing technical aids (inverted-script tablets and click tracks) to solve all issues of notation and coordination in the dark while achieving increased rhythmic complexity. All this tightened my grip on the objects and their potential for compositional use, as well as the musicians' ability to demonstrate virtuosity and sensitivity. This process helped us find both the limits and the maximum potential of working with matches, and also brought their material properties, as particular objects, into focus. Additionally, it brought to a head the contingency of the

---

19 The score and a recording of *Lightness* can be accessed at http://www.julianahodkinson.net/works/lightness.

20 *Lightness* has been performed many times by Speak Percussion, Ictus, Drumming Grupo de Percussão, and others.

matches' objecthood as light-makers that might or might not light, differently every time, whose burn may be sustained or not, whose extinguishing might be fast or slow, whose unpredictable spark may even briefly signal danger. During the course of any performance of *Lightness* several hundred matches are struck, sometimes in the quickest succession possible for practised percussionists; thus, inevitably a range of uncontrolled flames and sparks, misfirings, and failed extinguishings occur. The volatility in the behaviour of the match inserts a kind of agency stemming from its objecthood: we recognise that things do not always behave the same way even though they may look the same.

A number of approaches to the understanding of relations between humans and things encourage us to think about objects and things in a different way. Posthumanism, new materialism, actor–network theory, and agential realism are some of the influential schools of thought that extend notions of agency beyond humans, examining situations in which particular objects become the centre of negotiations of power and truth, such that an object may be so important for a given situation that it has a certain agency in that situation, and assembles a social sphere around it. In theatre, people are most often the centre of attention, with props and costumes, lights, and so on relegated to second place. In music performance, this hierarchy has been exacerbated by the imposition of a definition of absolute music that by implication classifies a vast number of significant factors as extra-musical.

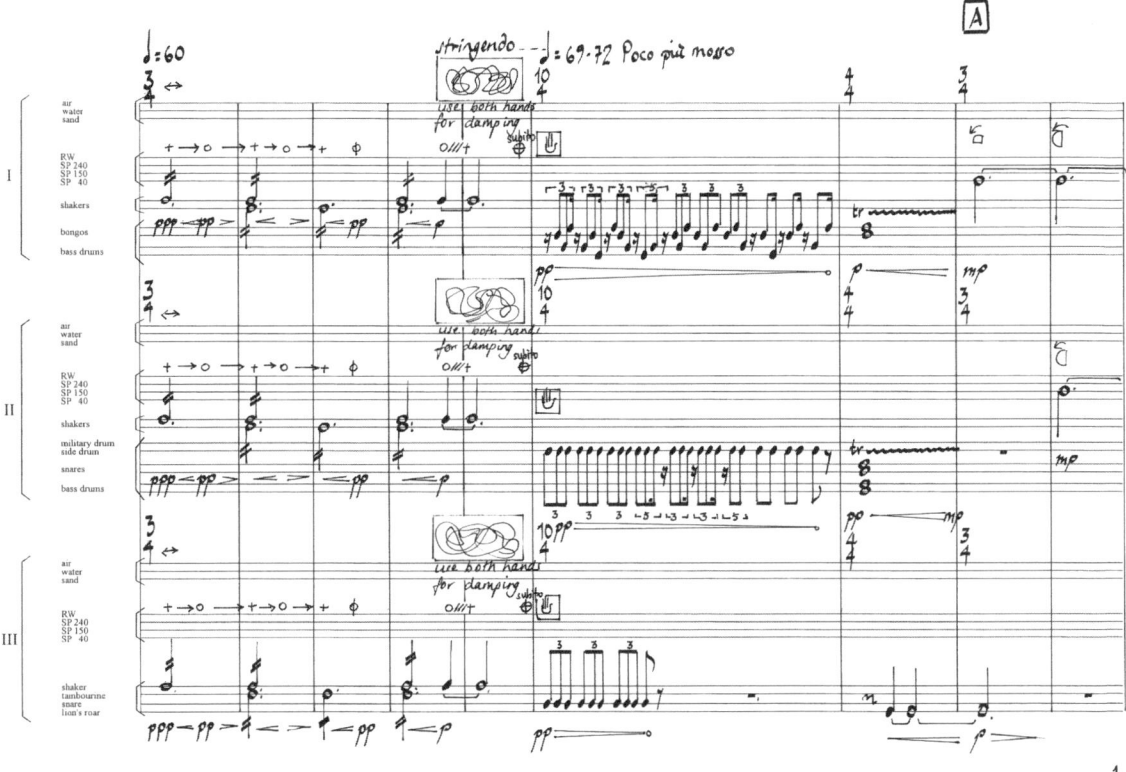

Figure 2.2.

Figure 2.2. Excerpt from the score of *Lightness* (2015).

An extended view of the agency of objects was a defining point of departure for Ashley Fure's opera for objects *The Force of Things* (2017), which takes its title from the first chapter of Jane Bennett's groundbreaking manifesto for a new materialism, *Vibrant Matter*.[21] Bennett's observations are central to my discussion here: "A lot happens to the concept of agency once nonhuman things are figured less as social constructions and more as actors, and once humans themselves are assessed not as autonoms but as vital materialities" (Bennett 2010, 21).

As further explored in later chapters, with respect to the flute (Craig), the piano (Laws), and the *đàn tranh* (Nguyễn and Östersjö), at this crossroads sits the instrument as a powerful agent of meaning: the technology at the heart of the musician's sensory-motoric technique. In several works by Marianthi Papalexandri-Alexandri and Pe Lang, instruments and apparatuses are prepared for particular types of resonance, using electromagnetic motors. In *Untitled II* (2010), *Untitled III* (2011), *Solo for Motors and Resonant Body* (2012), and *Duo for Motor and Sound Panels* (2016), musicians perform by "tending" machinic instrumental constructions, thereby discovering, through small movements, alterations in sustained resonances or drones.[22] Changes in finger pressure, adjustments to motor speeds, and modifications in the tension of threads linked to membranes, for example, together with the musicianly sense of pacing and timing in allowing resonances to establish themselves or gently transform, are all of equal importance to the sounding result and the performance experience. The musician's interaction with these "artmachines," to borrow a term from Anne Sauvagnargues (2016), has a strong affinity with the audience's listening mode—there is a kind of perceptual "doing." Witnessing a performance, here, is as much an experience of hearing the musician listening as seeing him or her playing. At the same time, the sensory-motoric fusion of instrument, objects, musicianly dexterity, and skill seems to produce a unique kind of body language and musicianly behaviour within the kinaesthetic paradigm.

Summary

In summary, I have tried to sketch out the role of resonance and vibration in forming collective and affective intersubjectivities, in a push to incorporate more subjects and objects into the meaningful sphere of live musical and other sonic interactions. I have proposed conceptualising the convergence of connections through sonic material as a process of wide-ranging affective resonance. From the immediate phenomenal experience of being immersed with each other in a short space of time for possible interaction, a small amplification of the intersubjective can in this way create a mode of sensitivity to the murmurings of social and political aspects of theory and artistic practice in conjunction with broader concepts, ideas, and practices.

---

21 Bennett's work is revisited later in this volume (144), in Catherine Laws's discussion of the "thing power" of the piano.

22 Information about Marianthi Papalexandrini-Alexandri and Pe Lang's works can be found at http://marianthi.net/works.html.

References

Ablinger, Peter. 2014. "Peter Ablinger— Stühle / Chairs." Accessed 21 February 2020. http://ablinger.mur.at/docu01. html.

Bennett, Jane. 2010. *Vibrant Matter: A Political Ecology of Things*. Durham, NC: Duke University Press.

Bohlman, Philip V. 1993. "Musicology as a Political Act." *Journal of Musicology* 11 (4): 411–36.

Born, Georgina. 2010. "For a Relational Musicology: Music and Interdisciplinarity, Beyond the Practice Turn." *Journal of the Royal Musical Association* 135 (2): 205–43.

Bourriaud, Nicolas. 1998. *Esthétique relationnelle*. Dijon: Presses du réel. Translated by Simon Pleasance and Fronza Woods with Mathieu Copeland as *Relational Aesthetics* (Dijon: Presses du réel, 2002).

Chen, Carolyn. 2016. "We Should Hang Out More: Some Thoughts on the Devising Process for Signs of Struggle, for 4 Moving People and Objects in a Room." *Experimental Music Yearbook*. Accessed 13 February 2020. http:// experimentalmusicyearbook.com/ Signs-of-struggle.

Erlmann, Veit. 2010. *Reason and Resonance: A History of Modern Aurality*. New York: Zone Books.

Finbloom, Aaron, and Sandeep Bhagwati. 2015. *A Few (More) Silences*. Accessed 14 February 2020. http://www.finblooming. com/a-few-more-silences.html.

Finbloom, Aaron, and Hannah Kaya. 2017. *Oscillations of One-to-Many*. Accessed 14 February 2020. http://www.finblooming. com/oscillations-of-one-to-many.html.

Grosz, Elizabeth A. 2008. *Chaos, Territory, Art: Deleuze and the Framing of the Earth*. New York: Columbia University Press.

Hodkinson, Juliana. 1999. *some reasons for hesitating*. Set of parts with notes to the musicians. Copenhagen: Edition Wilhelm Hansen.

———. 2007. "Presenting Absence: Constitutive Silences in Music and Sound Art Since the 1950s." PhD thesis, University of Copenhagen.

James, Robin. 2019. *The Sonic Episteme: Acoustic Resonance, Neoliberalism, and Biopolitics*. Durham, NC: Duke University Press.

Kim, Jin-ah. 2018. "Thoughts on Sandeep Bhagwati's Comprovisation: Concepts and Practices." *Circuit* 28 (1). Accessed 14 February 2020. http://revuecircuit. ca/articles/28_1/51.04-thoughts-on-sandeep-bhagwatis-comprovisation/.

Kim-Cohen, Seth. 2009. *In the Blink of an Ear: Toward a Non-cochlear Sonic Art*. London: Bloomsbury.

———. 2016. *Against Ambience and Other Essays*. London: Bloomsbury.

Kivy, Peter. 1993. *The Fine Art of Repetition: Essays in the Philosophy of Music*. Cambridge: Cambridge University Press.

Laws, Catherine. 2019. Introduction to *Voices, Bodies, Practices: Performing Musical Subjectivities*, by Catherine Laws, William Brooks, David Gorton, Nguyễn Thanh Thủy, Stefan Östersjö, and Jeremy J. Wells, 13–25. Orpheus Institute Series. Leuven: Leuven University Press.

Lehmann, Harry. 2012. *Die digitale Revolution der Musik: Eine Musikphilosophie*. Mainz: Schott.

Manning, Erin. 2007. *The Politics of Touch: Sense, Movement, Sovereignty*. Minneapolis: University of Minnesota Press.

Mühlhoff, Rainer. 2015. "Affective Resonance and Social Interaction." *Phenomenology and the Cognitive Sciences* 14 (4): 1001–19.

Rosa, Hartmut. 2016. *Resonanz: Eine Soziologie der Weltbeziehung*. Berlin: Suhrkamp. Translated by James C. Wagner as *Resonance: A Sociology of Our Relationship to the World* (Cambridge: Polity Press, 2019).

Sauvagnargues, Anne. 2016. *Artmachines: Deleuze, Guattari, Simondon*. Translated by Suzanne Verderber with Eugene W. Holland. Edinburgh: Edinburgh University Press.

Schäffler, Philipp. 2018. "Im Sog der Resonanz: Zu einem neuen Begriff in Musikwissenscahft, -ästhetik, -soziologie und -pädagogik." *Positionen: Texte zu aktuellen Musik* 115 (May): 2–6.

Shlomowitz, Matthew. 2014. "Real World Sound in Relational Music." Accessed 13 February 2020. https://www.shlom. com/?p=relational.

Toelle, Jutta, and John A. Sloboda. 2019. *The Audience as Artist?* The Audience's Experience of Participatory Music." *Musicae Scientiae* review article, 26 April. https://journals.sagepub.com/doi/abs/10.1177/1029864919844804.

Troup, Cynthia. 2000. "On the Score of (for the Reason of) Juliana Hodkinson's *some reasons for hesitating* (1999)." Accessed 21 February 2020. http://cynthiatroup.com/wordpress/wp-content/uploads/CTroup-On-the-Score-of-October-2000.pdf. Published in Danish translation in *Autograf Tidsskrift for ny musik* 9 (4): 9–11. Citations refer to the online English-language version.

Negotiating the Discursive Voice in Chamber Music

David Gorton

Royal Academy of Music, University of London

Stefan Östersjö

Piteå School of Music, Luleå University of Technology

. . . the last part is going to be a slight, nice, little challenge for all of us, including [the composer], to make it a bit more interesting perhaps?[1]

INTRODUCTION

The context that underlies this chapter is a near decade-long collaboration between the two authors, composer David Gorton and guitarist Stefan Östersjö. Initially established as a research project as well as an artistic collaboration, we[2] have been particularly interested in exploring the ways in which our individual identities combine, and the ways in which these identities can be challenged or reshaped in the emerging compositions and performances. Initially the artistic and written outcomes from this research were concerned with a one-to-one collaborative relationship, and musical outcomes for solo instrument. The focus of this chapter, however, concerns the next logical stage with the introduction of an additional performer into the collaborative system and music written for duo combinations.[3]

The first artistic outcome of our collaboration was *Forlorn Hope* for 11-string alto guitar, a composition that weaves fragments from John Dowland's *Forlorn Hope Fancy* together with material derived from a pre-compositional phase that

---

1 Violinist Mieko Kanno commenting on *Cerro Rico* at the first rehearsal.

2 Throughout this chapter the two authors are referenced in the first-person plural form. While, superficially, some parts of the discussion may privilege compositional or performative concerns, the layer of commentary that this chapter provides should be understood as having been written from the combined perspective of both the authors throughout. In the case studies, the authors and other collaborating practitioners are identified by name.

3 The specific analytical approaches in this chapter relate directly to the concept of *discursive voice* as discussed below and at length in Gorton and Östersjö (2016, 2019), but are situated within the broader research field of performance studies that emerged in the 1990s. José Bowen defined the widening field, which embraced both music psychology and musicology as a study of "how the music sounds, but it also considers performance attitudes, gesture, social context, and audience response" (Bowen 1996, 19). In systematic musicology, research into gesture has contributed substantial further knowledge of the role of embodiment in musical performance (see, for instance, Rink 2002, 2015). The study of ensemble and duo interactions in performance has been taken forward in research in the disciplines mentioned in, for example, McCaleb (2014) and Rink, Gaunt, and Williamon (2017).

constituted collaborative testing of a microtonal tuning system and extended improvisations. A study with Eric Clarke and Mark Doffman, which was part of the AHRC-funded Centre for Musical Performance as Creative Practice, analysed video evidence of these initial explorations and observed that there are moments of fluidity in our respective identities in the generation and selection of musical materials, which contrast with other moments in the longitudinal creative process in which our roles are more solidly recognisable as that of composer and performer. We also identified the importance of various cultural tools, such as instruments, notation, and the music of other composers, in this case Dowland, that shape these oscillations between fluidity and solidification, and that act as filters in the generation and refinement of materials. In the published outcome of the study we comment that "in the phase that precedes what might (perhaps misleadingly) be called the 'private compositional phase' of *Forlorn Hope*'s development, there is an exceptionally fluid and distributed interpenetration of partially dissolved roles, instruments, tuning systems, living and dead composers, and embodied thinking-through-practice" (Clarke et al. 2017, 132–33). In commenting on the project, Nicholas Cook (2018, 61) additionally observes that "we might describe this as a creative assemblage on the model of Deleuze's own example: COMPOSER-PERFORMER-GUITAR."

In an attempt to further analyse the fluidity within practice observed by Clarke et al. (2017), and to expand Cook's Deleuzian assemblage, we have drawn upon the concept of the subjective "voice" as a means to describe the ways in which the cultural and sociological layers of signification interact with the embodied knowledge of a musician. What seems immediately useful about Cook's observation is how it details an understanding of the negotiation of "voice" between a composer and a performer, and how it is mediated through an instrument, and thus we have developed a model that represents the complex entanglement of interconnections that constitute performer and composer "voices" (Gorton and Östersjö 2016, 584). The sociological perspective we analyse from the notion of "habitus" as a means for understanding the situatedness of musical practice, thereby also providing a more substantial understanding of the embodied workings of the relation between a musician and technological and psychological tools like instruments, scores, and compositional systems: this is further discussed in our chapter in the partner volume, *Voices, Bodies, Practices* (Gorton and Östersjö 2019).

In her posthumously published book, *The Sonic Self*, Naomi Cumming sheds light on the subjectivities inherent within musical performance:

> To a musician, it is hardly news that subjectivities may be attributed to music itself: tones of voice, with their emotional connotations, appearing in sound; affective states, suggested by gestural action, heard in the shaping of a melodic segment; aspects of willed direction found in the impetus of tonal harmony. The musician's work is to master these potentialities on a given instrument and to work with them in accordance with the requirements of a style, drawing out the possibilities of a composed musical moment by making his or her choices of sound, emphasis, and tempo. Something of the musician's own "character" will be heard in the choices he

or she makes, in the patterns of emphasis that constitute a performance style. So it is that his or her own "subjectivity" appears. (Cumming 2000, 9)

Cumming describes the finding of her own musical character, her "voice," upon acquiring a new violin as a teenager: "When I began to play it, the sound of this new violin seemed to draw from me something I did not know I possessed. It was as if the violin had the potential to become the voice I lacked. This was quite a discovery, not made fully in a moment of time but over a couple of years" (3). Through her violin lessons she begins to make sense of what this "voice" is, and how it relates to her instrument: "What [my teacher] sought, somehow, was an identification of his students with the sound of the violin as a voice that could be expressive of their own passion, and yet a cultivated distance that would allow them also to draw out the best in the violin's tone, in a critical stance that recognized it as more than a projection of their subjective states" (4). For Cumming, her subjective "voice" is therefore a result of both a bodily and emotional relationship with her instrument, but also something separate, that can be listened to with critical detachment: "a relationship with the violin's sound can include the idea of projecting a 'voice' that is one's own, and also of standing apart to listen to the sound as the 'voice' of another" (5).[4]

We have drawn on this concept of "voice" in relation to the development of *Forlorn Hope* (Gorton 2018b) and of *Austerity Measures I* (Gorton 2018a), the second outcome of our collaboration, observing how "a performer's voice emerges essentially from the concrete listening of performing, and the live, bodily interaction with an instrument" (Gorton and Östersjö 2016, 589); these are processes best described as explorations of the affordances and resistances of different types of musical agent, including instruments, notations, and the particular musical traditions and contexts. In any performance of a scored composition, a negotiation between a performer's voice and the voice of the composer takes place through these explorations, becoming manifest in particular approaches to articulation, shape, contour, sound, timing, and so on. In contrast, we note how "a composer's voice may rather emerge from the inner listening of the writing situation, through the identification of particular ways of shaping music, of solutions to musical problems that have a bearing on form and the physical nature of music as performed" (ibid.).

In a study of the collaborative process that led to the making of *Austerity Measures I*, we drew on the observation that, just like in the interaction between musicians in chamber music playing, or in improvised performance, a negotiation of performer and composer voices leads to the creation of what we call a "discursive voice." Here, the discursive voice can be conceived not simply as a combination of the composer's and performer's voices but rather, we claim, "the discursive voice emerges from the process of collaboration.... What emerges is a negotiation; a coming together of the two voices through the exploration of a situation in the present" (Gorton and Östersjö 2016, 593). The diagram

---

4   This notion of "voice" as simultaneously interior and exterior is further discussed in chapter 6, by Catherine Laws, in relation to the explicit thematisation of self and "voice" in autobiographical performance.

in figure 3.1 attempts to represent the complex relationships that constitute the formation of a collaborative "discursive voice," through which

> performer and composer grant privileged access to the constituent parts of their own "voices." In a collaborative situation this could involve working jointly at an instrument to develop materials and instrumental techniques, overlapping reciprocally with jointly developing notation for such materials. Such interactions would be shaped by the respective practices of both. Over time, the composer's broader compositional practice may become influenced and shaped by the performance practices of the performer to the extent that these affect other work. Similarly, the broader practices of the performer, especially the manner in which they approach other composers' music, may become influenced and shaped by the collaborative interaction. The formation of a "discursive voice" may thus be situated within the shared contexts of practice that is common to both. (Gorton and Östersjö 2019, 54–55)

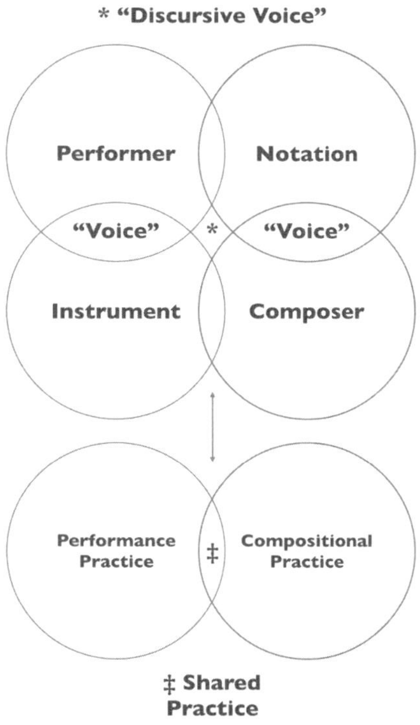

Figure 3.1.

The diagram thus represents an expansion of Cook's Deleuzian assemblage and attempts to identify a space within which the "discursive voice" can be co-produced, between the complex entanglement of the constituent parts of a collaborative relationship: people, instruments, notation, and the contextual practices within which they work.

56

Figure 3.1. Relationships that constitute the formation of a collaborative "discursive voice." Reproduced from Gorton and Östersjö (2019, 55).

In this chapter we will consider a development of this model to include an additional performer in two duo compositions, each of whom bring their own instruments, habitus, and performing contexts to the established collaboration. The compositions that will be discussed are *Cerro Rico* for soprano violin and charango (Gorton 2018c), and *Charon* for two guitars (Gorton 2019).[5] Like *Forlorn Hope*, the former uses borrowed pre-Baroque materials and unusual instruments (the soprano violin is strung an octave higher than the viola, and the charango is a small Andean guitar with five sets of double strings all tuned within an octave), raising questions in performance concerning the identity of the scored materials and the management of an unusual sound combination. Also like *Forlorn Hope*, *Charon* uses instruments that have been microtonally tuned, raising questions in performance concerning the management of resonance and sound. We will look in particular at collaborative negotiations that emerged in the initial rehearsal period for each piece, drawing on analytical methods that are suited to each particular circumstance.

Cerro Rico

From initial discussions about the piece to the first rehearsals, the development of *Cerro Rico* took over six years. Figure 3.2 shows a timeline of events where decisions were made, each of which contributed ingredients to the development of the piece. The choice of instruments was an important constituent. The use of the charango and an unspecified type of violin was the first decision, which in turn led indirectly to the title of the piece, which is named after a Bolivian mountain, with geographical associations with the charango, that is famous for producing vast amounts of silver for the Spanish Empire, and in which, it is said, up to eight million miners have died since the sixteenth century.

A collaborative workshop on the charango between Stefan and David generated some prototype materials for use in the charango part, and the acquisition of the music for Heinrich Isaac's *Fortuna desperata* provided material that was later used in the final section of the piece, and, in a much slowed-down version, contributed most of the melodic outlines for the soprano violin part throughout. The selection of the soprano violin derives from a workshop session with David and violinist Mieko Kanno, in which she demonstrated a number of different violins: the soprano was chosen because it was one of David's and Mieko's favourites, because the open strings were closest in pitch to those of the charango, and because of the clean purity of its sound. These ingredients were collected together some time before any formal composing was carried out, but already they provided programmatic elements, a sound picture, notation, various musical materials, and the sense of restriction often associated with small instruments.

---

5   *Cerro Rico* and *Charon* were both first performed at the Orpheus Institute research festival "Who Is the 'I' That Performs? Enacting Musical Identities," Tinnenpot Theatre, Ghent, 29 November 2019; Stefan Östersjö (guitars), Mieko Kanno (soprano violin), and Jessica Kaiser (guitar). Videos of each piece can be found on the Orpheus Institute YouTube channel, at https://www.youtube.com/playlist?list=PLjE5jh1TKjREEyBWnbSaFefJqHOY63Jdg.

Date	Place	Who	Event
July 2011	Performance Studies Network Conference, Cambridge	David Gorton, Mieko Kanno, Stefan Östersjö	Initial discussion about piece for charango and violin
October 2012	Ghent	DG, SÖ	Further discussion and choice of *Cerro Rico* as title/theme
December 2012	Oxford	DG, SÖ	DG borrows a charango from SÖ
January 2014	Cambridgeshire	DG, SÖ	Workshop with charango, developing types of tremolo and slow-moving counterpoint
February 2016	British Museum, London	DG	DG obtains copy of Isaac's *Fortuna desperata* from harpsichordist Julian Perkins after concert
May 2016	Glasgow	DG, MK	MK shows DG selection of violins; soprano violin is chosen
April 2017	Cambridgeshire	DG	DG composes *Cerro Rico*
October 2017	Malmö	DG, MK, SÖ	Rehearsals of *Cerro Rico*

Figure 3.2.

Cerro Rico is a slow piece, but with the instrumentalists occupying two different conceptions of slowness. On the one hand, the soprano violin plays unusual note lengths but at a tempo that is not unusual: specifically, minim = 60, but playing largely breves and longs. Figure 3.3 shows an extract from the violin part with long notes interspersed with ornamental quicker notes. On the other hand, the charango plays note lengths that might be considered more normal, but at an unusual tempo: specifically, mostly quavers but played at quaver = 15. Figure 3.4 shows an extract from the charango part with quaver patterns interspersed with ornamental demisemiquavers.

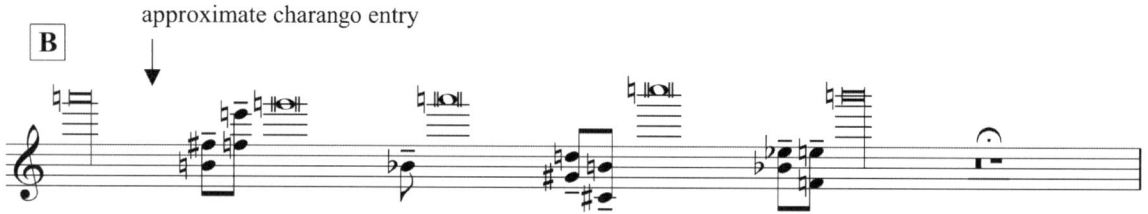

Figure 3.3.

Figure 3.2. Timeline of the development of *Cerro Rico*.

Figure 3.3. Soprano violin part of *Cerro Rico* at rehearsal letter B. Minim = 60 (breve = 15).

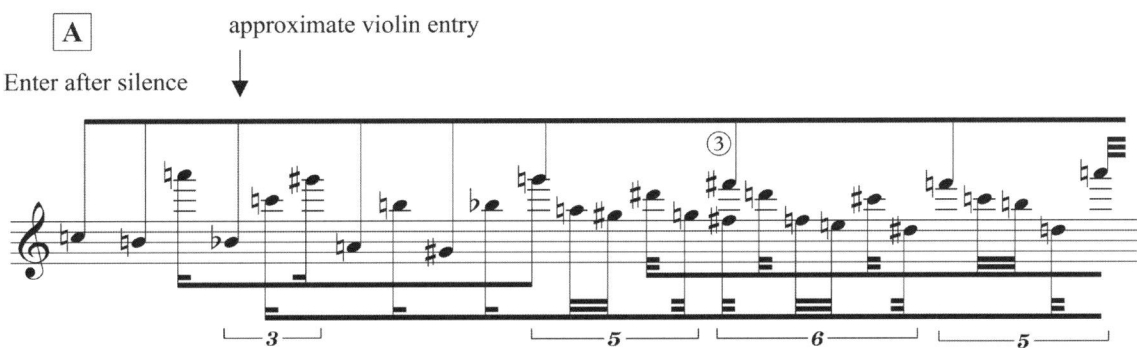

Figure 3.4.

There is no score for *Cerro Rico*, just two independent parts. But it is possible to see from figures 3.3 and 3.4 something of how the two parts are coordinated, with entries at the rehearsal letters cued from one player to the other, and approximate entries marked, respectively. This mechanism extends throughout most of the seventeen-minute duration of the piece, with rehearsal letters B, C, E, G, J, L, and N cued to the charango player by violin entries, and with the other rehearsal letters cued the other way around. As the piece progresses from the sections shown at rehearsal letters A and B in figures 3.4 and 3.3, respectively, the materials gradually increase in speed and density until a climax is reached of fast scalic passages in the soprano violin and rasgueado tremolos in the charango. This climax is short-lived and quickly decays, introducing the final section of the piece from rehearsal letter N. This section constitutes around a quarter of the total duration of the piece and uses material taken from Heinrich Isaac's three-part *Fortuna desperata* with two sets of repeats added. The upper part is placed in the violin, with the two lower parts transposed up an octave, or in some places two octaves, and combined in the charango part. As a result of the quick decay of the charango, its limited range across the five double strings, and the octave transpositions, the two parts often combine into a single line. The contrapuntal relationship between the parts is broken in time as well as in register, with the charango beginning its material at the player's discretion several bars after the violin has started. Figure 3.5 shows how this moment appears in the charango part. The opening of the violin material is displayed as a cue at letter N, with the instructions stating: "match the pulse of the violin . . . enter between six and twelve beats after the violin." It was the first of these instructions that triggered the collaborative negotiation that we will now explore.

Figure 3.4. Charango part of *Cerro Rico* at rehearsal letter A.
Quaver = 15 (demisemiquaver = 60).

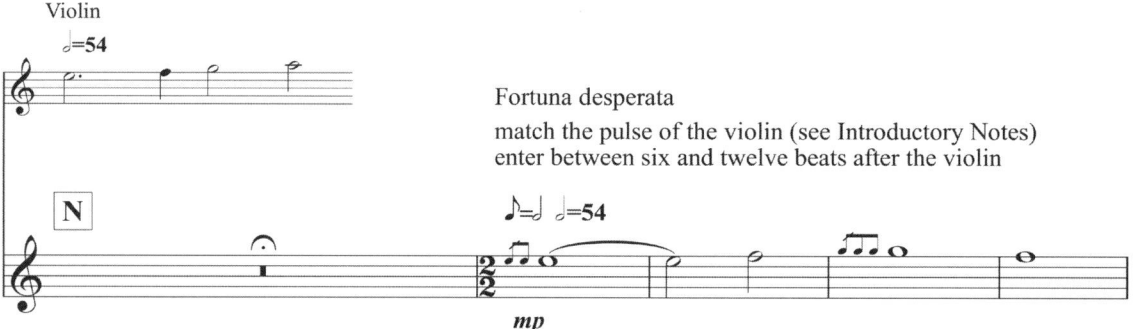

Figure 3.5.

Mieko and Stefan met to rehearse *Cerro Rico* in Malmö on 16 October 2017. David then joined them for further rehearsals on 17 October, and the following day the piece was played through to a small group of colleagues at the Malmö Academy of Music as part of a seminar. Already on the first day, Mieko and Stefan were raising concerns about how they were to approach the final section, with a literal interpretation of the instruction "match the pulse of the violin" causing frustrations in the realisation, as can be seen from this transcription of a discussion at the end of the first rehearsal.

> MK: . . . the last part is going to be a slight, nice, little challenge for all of us, including David, to make it a bit more interesting perhaps?
>
> SÖ: Yes.
>
> MK: So . . . we can start together, but . . . then, no coordinating, or maybe introducing some ornaments, or we don't do the repeat exactly the same. By the way, do you have a repeat too?
>
> SÖ: I do have repeats.
>
> MK: I have two.
>
> SÖ: Two of them, yes.
>
> MK: Or something to have a . . .
>
> SÖ: Something to disintegrate, you know . . . it works nicely when we start, and it's kind of interesting with the strange counterpoint you get. But after a while . . .
>
> MK: . . . and then there are nice canons where we enjoy doing, but then the phrasing is a bit compromised because we have to be so metronomic right now, because when I've got a [sings], but then still have to go tick, tick, tick [indicating a metronome].

Possible explanations for the concern expressed in this transcription lie in the materials from earlier in the piece. The start of the piece is so slow that it feels very restrictive to play, a feeling that is intensified by the small sizes of the two instruments, the limited range of the charango, and the effect of clamping the left hands to the fingerboards. As the piece progresses, faster materials are introduced, freeing up both left and right hands, and creating an increas-

Figure 3.5. Charango part of *Cerro Rico* at rehearsal letter N: the final section.

ing sense of individual freedom and space, something that is enhanced by the lack of bar lines in the parts and the separate and independent conceptions of tempo and pulse. But with the introduction of the *Fortuna desperata* material, and with it, bar lines and a shared pulse, the previously gained sense of freedom and independence is lost. As the above conversation continued, the possible strategies that emerged for making the final section more "interesting" are the free introduction of ornaments, the disruption of pulse, and the reclamation of line, all of which are strategies for regaining the sense of independence from earlier in the piece.

The following day, after David's arrival, the final section was played through four times with discussion in between. For the purpose of analytical comparison, we have selected a short twelve-bar extract from the final section, which can be seen in figure 3.6. The audio from the four run-throughs was cut to these twelve bars from the violin part and then analysed using Sonic Visualiser. As a result of the indeterminate entry of the charango after rehearsal letter N, the charango is playing a different set of twelve bars in each of the four run-throughs. For this reason, the position within the piece is measured using the violin part only, and the questions of alignment considered in the following analysis concern the synchronisation of articulations between the instruments without reference to specific rhythmic patterns.

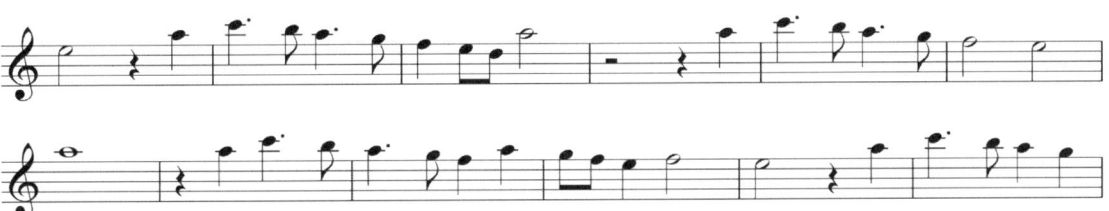

Figure 3.6.

Figure 3.7 is an export from Sonic Visualiser representing the first time that Mieko and Stefan played the piece through to David (example 1). The diagram is split into two systems; at the top of each system, in front of the upper waveform, are a series of vertical lines that represent every articulated note in the violin part. This can be compared with the notation in figure 3.6, with the very start of the diagram aligned to the beginning of the minim E, the second vertical line aligned to the crotchet A, the third vertical line aligned to the dotted crotchet C at the start of the next bar, and so on. Underneath these, at the bottom of each system in front of the lower waveform, are a series of vertical lines that represent each charango note. The charango is playing material with a similar rhythmic profile to that of the soprano violin (i.e., quavers, crotchets, dotted crotchets, minims, and semibreves), but with a variable starting position in relation to the soprano violin. Where ornaments are played it was the initial onset that was annotated in the analysis.

61

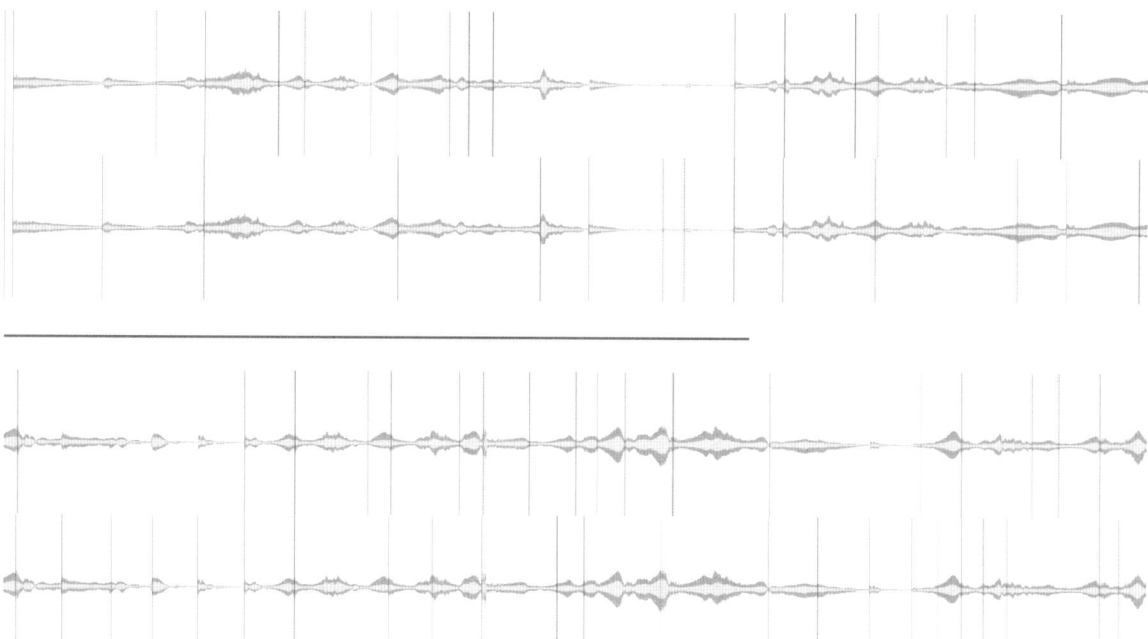

Figure 3.7.

In this example, Mieko and Stefan played metronomically in time with one another with a steady pulse, as they had done the previous evening in their independent rehearsal, and this can be seen in the regular patterns of the vertical lines. There were moments of unevenness that can be seen in the middle of the second system, but otherwise the rhythmic unisons largely match up and the quaver rhythms are evenly spaced.

For the second run-through (example 2) we attempted to implement what had been discussed the previous evening, with the introduction of rubato and a disrupted pulse. Figure 3.8 shows the export of the relevant twelve bars of this attempt, and it can be seen that there was a strategy in the charango for placing anticipated rhythmically unison moments late (shown in figure 3.8 with marker "A"); but also it can be seen that at the start and end of the extract, the charango pre-empts the violin (shown in figure 3.8 with marker "B"). Following this run-through we all agreed that we liked it better than the previous version, but David observed that he thought the dynamic shaping was more successful than the metrical shaping, and asked whether it would be possible to maintain rubato moments, but within a more shared conception of pulse. Mieko pointed out that because the phrasing is not together, following one another's rubato could be difficult, but she agreed to try again with "a little more discipline to the metronomic coordination."

Figure 3.7. Sonic Visualiser export for example 1.

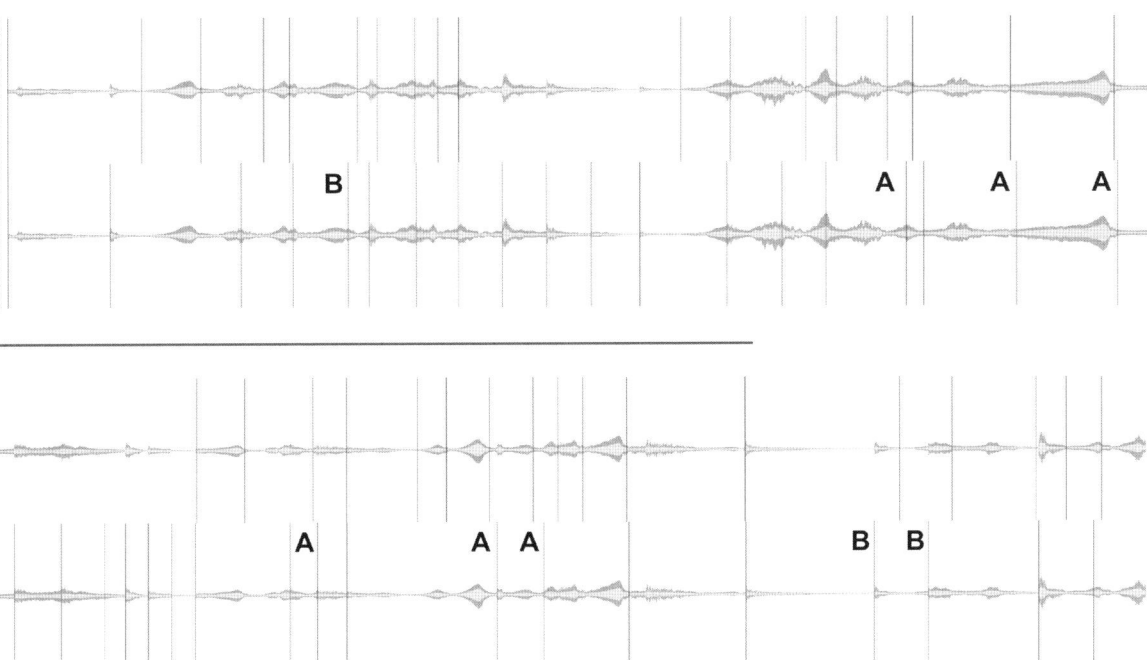

Figure 3.8.

Figure 3.9 shows example 3. This third run-through is more together than the previous one, but significantly it is the starts and ends of the violin phrases where the rhythmic unisons occur (shown in figure 3.9 with marker "A"). There is more rhythmic flexibility through the middle of the phrases than in the first version, and thus, while the sense of disrupted pulse from the second version is lost, what has been gained is a more flexible sense of line.

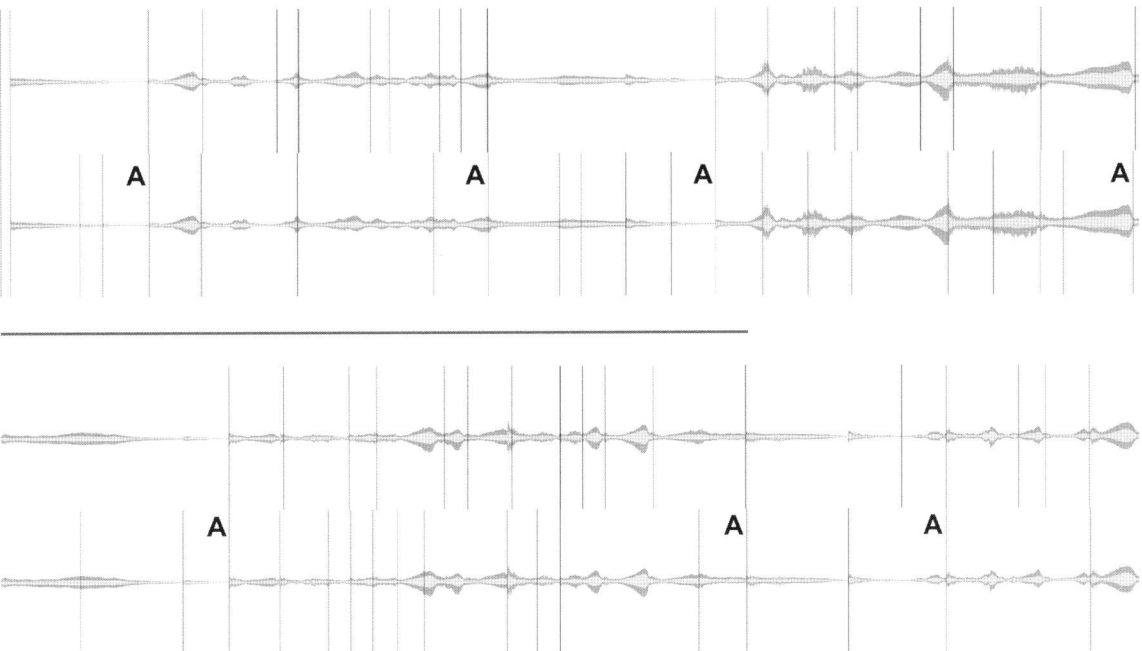

Figure 3.9.

Figure 3.8. Sonic Visualiser export for example 2, with markers.

Figure 3.9. Sonic Visualiser export for example 3, with markers.

Following this run-through we agreed that while we had all enjoyed this version, we preferred the previous one (example 2). The following transcription shows fragments of the discussion surrounding this realisation.

> SÖ: I kind of like this one.
>
> MK: [yes].
>
> SÖ: Do you feel it was too straight?
>
> MK: I quite liked the last one.
>
> SÖ: Previous one, yes.
>
> DG: It was more stretchy ... if you wanted to go ... back towards ... more elasticity. But it's the listening thing that I am interested in triggering: the fact that you listen to one another and respond accordingly.
>
> MK: Well, because if we are not coordinated so strictly, we can sort of get into that mode of listening to each other, but also out of it. It's kind of like being able to move in and out, which is what's happening in the first part [of the piece] ...
>
> DG: Do you want to try another one, where you're now more stretchy?
>
> MK: You mean that ... we are completely on different pulses?
>
> DG: Yes.
>
> SÖ: Because we sort of speculated on that possibility yesterday, whether we should ... actually start more aligned and then just ...
>
> DG: And then just go off ...
>
> SÖ: I'm not sure about that actually, but we could try to see what happens? ... If we disintegrate after a bit.
>
> MK: Yes, on the other hand, completely disintegrate is also quite difficult.
>
> DG: Especially with material like this, which is imitative.
>
> MK: Yes, imitative ... and not being together, is like you know ... I have to shut it off.
>
> SÖ: Yes, I don't know, one could try. But it isn't obvious how to make it work.
>
> MK: It's like trying, it's like phasing isn't it? Trying not to be together, consciously.
>
> SÖ: Well, we could give it a try as an experiment, because it would actually be a process more similar to what's going on in the rest of the piece.

In this discussion the regaining of independent lines and the disruption of pulse, both of which had been discussed the previous day, are considered from the perspective of listening. On the one hand this encompasses a listening between performers that is responsive to each other's freely shaped lines. But in contrast there is also a different kind of listening in which the performers are consciously not together (see also the discussion section below).

Figure 3.10 shows the Sonic Visualiser output for the fourth example. It seems that in this example there is both the dislocated pulse of the second version and the flexibility of line of the third version now combined. There are also some curious moments of togetherness, some of which are carried over, relative to the violin part, from previous versions (shown with marker "A") and some of which are new (shown with marker "B").

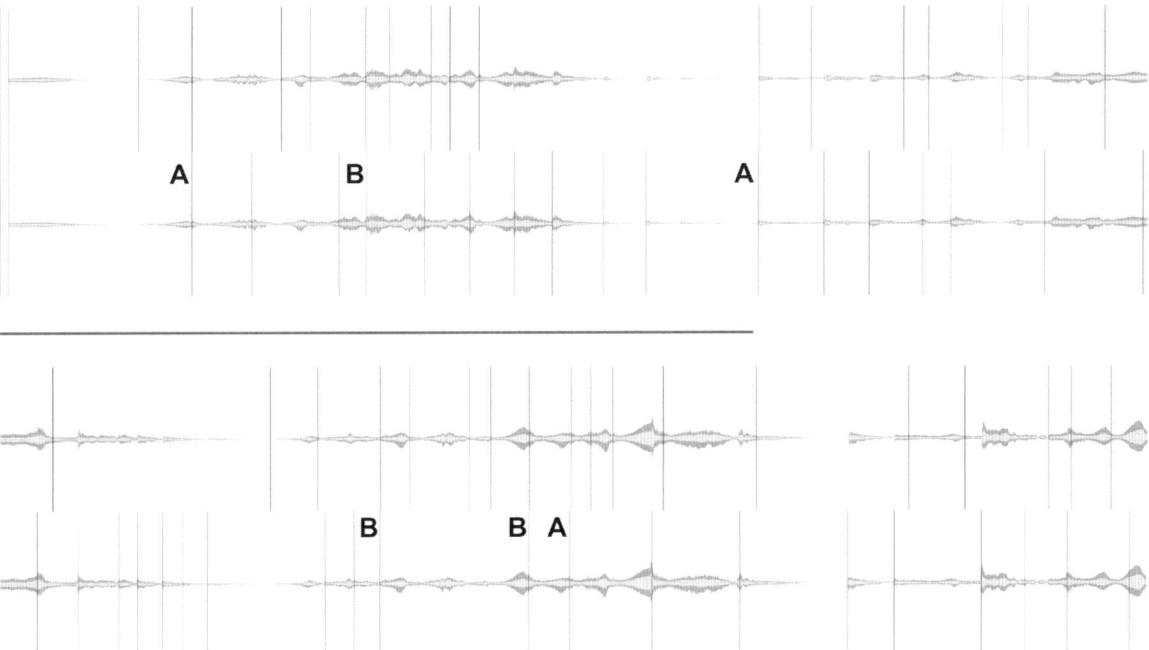

Figure 3.10.

While the dislocation of pulse in the fourth example can be seen clearly in figure 3.10 in the misalignment of vertical lines between the soprano violin and charango annotations, the flexibility of line can be visualised through the uneven distribution of vertical lines within each part. Figure 3.11 attempts to further demonstrate this flexibility of line by comparing the soprano violin part from the "metronomic" first example with that of example 4. Here the top line on each system is the soprano violin part taken from example 1, while the bottom line is the soprano violin from example 4. The two lines have been equalised in length, meaning that one of the examples has been time-stretched to match the duration of the other, resulting in a comparison of relative placements of each note in the soprano violin from the two examples.

In figure 3.11 the "stretchy" character discussed in the above transcription can be seen in the lower line from example 4. While at the opening the phrasing pushes ahead when compared with the "metronomic" first example, there is a significant pulling back of the pulse at the end of the first system and beginning of the second system. A compression of pulse in the middle of the second system brings the two examples back into closer alignment. The "complete disintegration" proposed in the transcription of the rehearsal does not occur in example 4, but instead something arguably more interesting does: where "trying not to be together, consciously" is in evidence from the misalignments in figure 3.10, a different kind of togetherness emerges. If the violin and charango parts from example 4 are dislocated in the analysis and realigned by imitative phrase, it is possible to see that there is a correlation between the areas where

65

Figure 3.10. Sonic Visualiser export for example 4, with markers.

stretching and compression take place, suggesting that while there is a dislocated pulse and a rhythmic flexibility of line, there does seem to be a shared understanding of *how* flexible the line will be, with a mapping of rhythmic contour from the violin part to the charango. This will be further explored in the discussion section below.

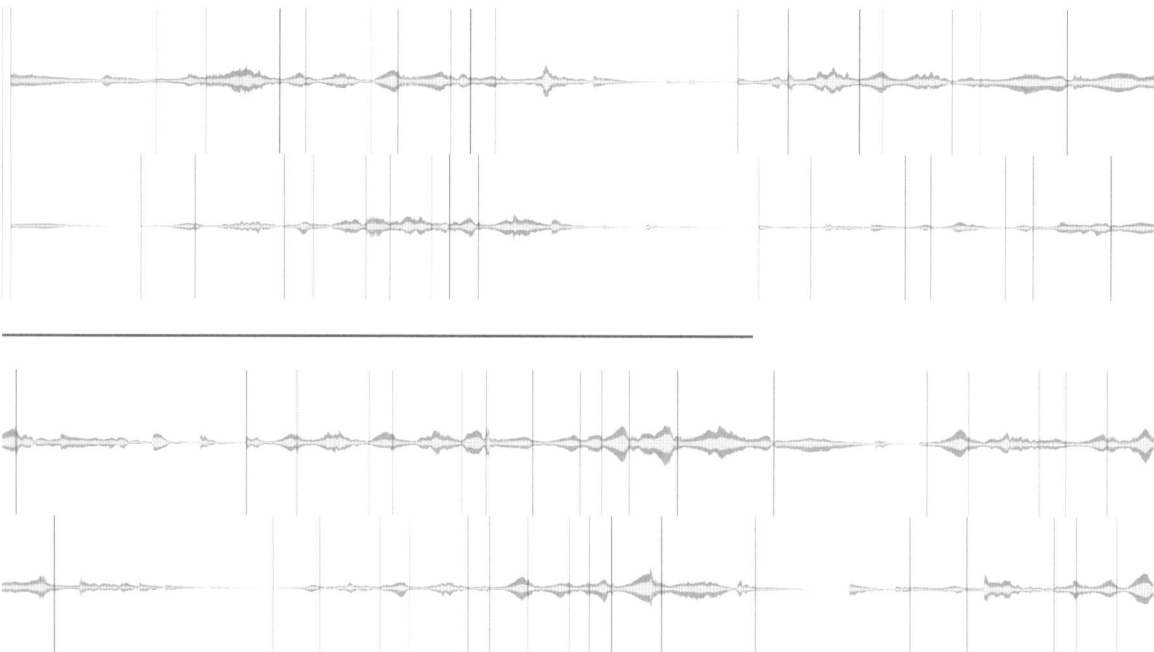

Figure 3.11.

CHARON

Written for two microtonally tuned guitars, *Charon* has a relatively simple structure in which three types of material are stated and repeated, in places with the two parts reversed, before a coda with a sparser texture brings the piece to a close. A short refrain with an interchange of microtonal chords links the sections together. The title of the piece refers to the larger of Pluto's moons, with which it forms a binary system with the barycentre of the orbit positioned outside either body. The first detailed photographs of Charon's surface were taken by the New Horizons space probe in July 2015 at the time that the piece *Charon* was composed, with the character of the binary system acting as a metaphor for duo interaction.

The tuning system for the two guitars had been initially developed five years previously during a series of collaborative working sessions in which Stefan and David tested a number of similar tunings on three different types

66

of guitar.[6] Each of the tuning systems uses the naturally flat seventh harmonic (approximately one sixth of a tone flat) produced on one set of strings as a reference pitch by which to tune another set of strings. Figure 3.12 shows the instructions for implementing the tuning system for *Charon* as it appears in the score. After tuning the guitars conventionally (E–A–D–G–B–E from bottom to the top), the first string should be sharpened so that its third harmonic (B) is in tune with the seventh harmonic of the fourth string (C-sixth-tone-♭). Then the third string should be flattened so that its third harmonic (D) is in tune with the seventh harmonic of the sixth string (D-sixth-tone-♭). Finally, the fifth string should be flattened so that its seventh harmonic (G-sixth-tone-♭) becomes in tune with the third harmonic of string two (F♯). This results in an alternating pattern of strings that are "in tune" and those that have a sixth-tone alteration, as can be seen in figure 3.13.

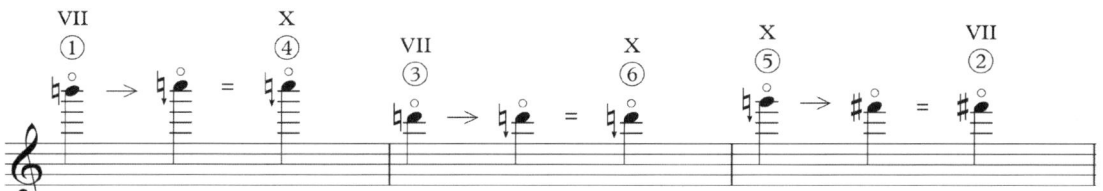

Figure 3.12.

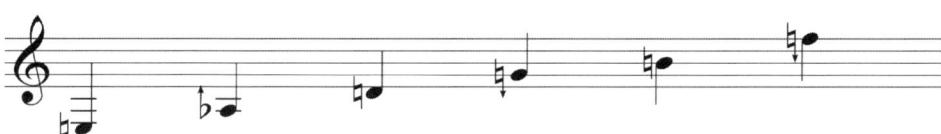

Figure 3.13.

Of the types of material in *Charon* that constitute its structure, only the first two types are of relevance to this chapter. The first page of the piece comprises harmonics played in rhythmic unison of sequential quavers between the two guitars and distributed into phrase groupings. Figure 3.14 shows bars 4 and 5, which are typical of the first page and of later repetitions; this will be referred to as the "first material."

---

6   Elsewhere these collaborative working sessions have been called the "Malmö Sessions." For further details see Gorton and Östersjö (2016), Clarke et al. (2017), and Cook (2018).

Figure 3.12. Instructions for implementing the tuning system for *Charon*.

Figure 3.13. Tuning of the guitars in *Charon*.

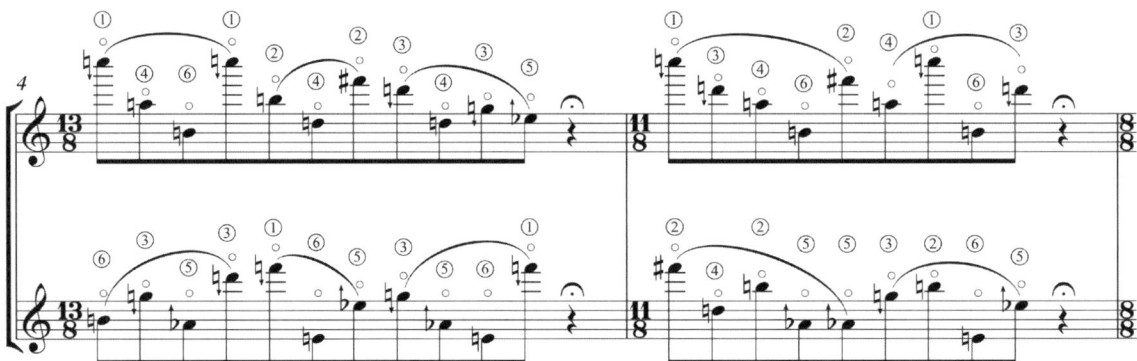

Figure 3.14.

Following a dovetailing effect between materials, the "second material" is first established from bar 11. Here, angular lines marked "espressivo e con molto rubato" are set against one another (see figure 3.15), with short bar lines indicating that precise synchronicity between the two instruments is temporarily suspended.

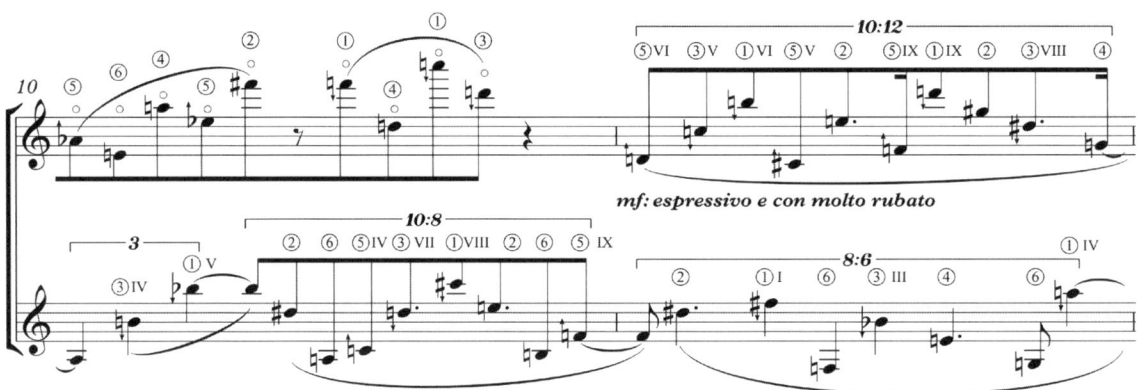

Figure 3.15.

A study using *Charon* was designed to capture the initial negotiations between the two performers, Stefan Östersjö and Jessica Kaiser, and to analyse the encounter between their respective "voices" and that of the composer. The first rehearsals took place in May 2019 and were planned as part of an artistic research residency at the Doctoral School at Kunstuniversität Graz (KUG), which also constituted the first working sessions within a new cluster formed of PhD students and senior researchers at the Piteå School of Music and KUG,

68

Figure 3.14. *Charon*, bars 4–5.

Figure 3.15. *Charon*, bars 10–11.

all looking at duo interactions in musical performance.[7] We were particularly interested in creating an in-depth understanding of the negotiation of "voice": in anticipation of the different kinds of interaction that might emerge, we decided to approach the analysis using stimulated recall.

Stimulated recall is a common qualitative research method used in a variety of disciplinary contexts. The term was originally used by Benjamin Bloom in 1953 in a study using audio recordings of classroom teaching with the aim to enable students to recount their original thought processes. Kagan and Krathwohl (1967) further developed this method by asking subjects to view complete documentation, stopping it mid flow to identify moments that required comment. In music research, stimulated recall has been widely used to study collaborative processes (see for example Bastien and Hostager 1988, 1992, 1996; Bastien and Rose 2014). As part of an international research project, Stefan Östersjö developed a study of collaborative interaction within the Vietnamese-Swedish ensemble The Six Tones (Frisk and Östersjö 2013). There were a number of specific challenges in the study as a result of the intercultural contexts and the need to translate speech and texts between languages.[8]

In 2010, when the two authors began their collaboration, qualitative analysis of video also became a central method. In the first study, which looked at the development of *Forlorn Hope* with a focus on interactions in the early working sessions (the Malmö sessions), the analysis was based on observation and analysis of transcriptions and selected video clips (Clarke et al. 2017). The second study, which analysed four performances of *Austerity Measures I*, used a more structured method of stimulated recall in which we worked together with two musicologists with the aim to identify perceived expressive gesture within the performances (Coorevits et al. 2016; Gorton and Östersjö 2019). Thus, rather than simply reconstructing an original experience, the repeated exposure to the video documentation in each of these studies had two purposes: first, to create a reflexive understanding of the event and, second, to allow the participating researchers to negotiate an intersubjective understanding (Brooks, Östersjö, and Wells 2019).

In May 2019 we began applying some of the same techniques to the video documentation of *Charon*. The rehearsals were recorded with multiple cameras and then compiled by the film-maker Jana Tost. The two guitar players, composer, and an additional observer (Deniz Peters) selected sections of the video documentation that corresponded with parts of the rehearsals that they collectively thought had been the most interesting in relation to the aims of the study. This material was analysed using a method of open coding, an analytical approach drawn from grounded theory (Strauss and Corbin 1990), in which descriptive labels (codes, e.g., [code = DG question]) are applied to the video,

---

7   The first rehearsals of *Charon* also form a study in Jessica Kaiser's doctoral research on duo interaction; the authors are grateful to Jessica for sharing the source materials. The analysis of the rehearsals of *Charon* is drawn from the initial coding sessions made at the KUG Doctoral School by the two authors, Jessica Kaiser, and Deniz Peters, who was hosting the residency.

8   See Brooks, Östersjö, and Wells (2019) for an expanded discussion of stimulated recall. See also Chapter 8 of this volume for a further discussion of the role of qualitative analysis in the work of The Six Tones.

thus identifying patterns of similarity across the rehearsals. The coding was further defined by drafting detailed annotations that provide a layer of description for each coded instance in the video. The creation and gradual refinement of the codes, and their respective annotations, were outcomes of a negotiated, joint understanding between the four researchers, in which each contributed comments and observations from their respective insider and outsider views. The analysis was carried out using the computer-assisted qualitative data analysis software (CAQDAS) Hyper Research, in which annotations and codes are attached by timecode to the original video. The annotations constitute an important reference in the following analysis.

Prior to the first rehearsals, Jessica and Stefan separately recorded their respective parts, and shared them with one another. A comparison of these recordings makes it clear that their initial individual approaches were different in many respects. For instance, the shaping of the second material in the initial recordings is articulated differently both in terms of temporal shaping and in phrasing and sound (see figure 3.15). Here, Stefan approached the material as polyphonically layered, and therefore the fingering structured the material as chordal entities. Jessica, on the other hand, focused on the great leaps in the melodic structure and conceived of it as a singular line. Stefan's approach to rubato was also related to how the phrasing would bring out a quasi-polyphony, while Jessica aimed at a more literal representation of the given rhythmical structure. These differences become apparent in the following analysis of the rehearsal.

Stefan, Jessica, and David met in Graz on 8 May for the first rehearsal, together with Deniz Peters who was hosting the research residency. When Stefan and Jessica sat down to start rehearsing the piece it was the first time that they had played together. We will look at the work in the first rehearsal that was concerned with the first page of the score, in which harmonics are articulated in rhythmic unison across various phrase lengths of repeating quavers (see figure 3.14), described here as the "first material." Following initial play-throughs for around quarter of an hour, detailed discussion is initiated by David who poses a series of open ended questions [code = DG question] "regarding the identity of the guitarists in the opening section," and asking "whether the performers want the sound to be more balanced or more consistent or inconsistent" (this and further annotations are by Gorton, Kaiser, Peters, and Östersjö, 9 and 10 May 2019). The initial response is an agreement [code = joint decision] in which Jessica and Stefan identify a "wish to go for a more inconsistent sonority." David observes that there are rare occasions on the first page where the vertical harmony between the two guitars is an octave and asks [code = DG question] "whether bringing out vertical harmony could be a way to increase inconsistency in the texture." He continues with a further, more rhetorical question in which he expresses a "wish for the notated phrasing groups to be brought out more clearly." In response to the first of these questions, Jessica states that "she finds the dissonant intervals . . . stand out more in the texture by themselves." In contrast, Stefan suggests that "the perceived musical object is not essentially the vertical harmony in a given moment but rather the compound sonority of the sounding harmonics" and suggests that the first page be tried again [code = deferred decision].

Following this play-through [code = observation], "Jessica notes how the bass notes generally come out more in the texture, and that balancing the registers may be a way to achieve a more coherent sonority. David comments that Stefan's playing is already compensating for this by placing more attack on the higher notes," and suggests that they both try [code = DG suggestion] "to play with more attack across the strings in order to give the impression of a more consistent sound." These comments directly contradict the previous agreement of working towards an inconsistent sonority and introduce the idea of working towards a consistency in sound by applying differentiated attacks across the strings of the instruments. This is tried out by Jessica and Stefan, who play through the first page "with more attack in the middle and high register harmonics, creating a different texture to before, which is more resonant" [code = finding through playing]. It was observed that "this approach to right-hand technique is a way of approaching the resistance of the instrument" and that this particular attempt represents "an increased shared sensitivity" that has emerged "as the result of a process of reflection, through the conversation with David as well as through the playing" [code = shared sensitivity].

In discussing this latest attempt, Stefan states that he thought this approach to be "more even" and "workable," but also that he essentially did not agree with it and had imagined playing the section rather differently [code = disclosure]. When prompted by David he described how he had imagined using deliberate contrasts of attack in order to articulate the phrase shaping. Jessica observes that Stefan's suggestion might "create difficulties in the interplay between the two instruments, and she also states that she likes the way the opening was played previously, and in retrospect she thinks this may be related to David's question of whether we think of the opening as one or two instruments playing" [code = observation]. David asks [code = DG question] "whether the qualities of both approaches can be combined, suggesting that this will demand a slower tempo, in order to make the type of shaping that Stefan demonstrated possible." A sequence of playing attempts follows, in which Jessica and Stefan attempt to synthesise the two approaches, using different attacks across the strings in order to produce a consistent sound, but with additional differentiation in attack to delineate the phrase shapes. With a slight slowing of the tempo a different type of phrasing and resonance emerges [code = finding through playing].

Figure 3.16 attempts to portray in an image this sequence of events. Each code described above is represented with a summary of its annotation. Throughout the sequence many of the implications of each code are played out in the code immediately following. But, as shown by the additional arrows, the diagram also shows how implications and consequences cut across the rehearsal time. For example, David's question about phrasing at 17:56 remains largely unaddressed until Stefan's disclosure at 25:36 brings the issue of phrasing back into the conversation about a shared sound. Similarly, the joint decision to work towards an inconsistent sonority at 16:58 is revoked at 21:17 with the move to playing with a consistent sound, but then partially reinstated at the suggestion of a synthesis of approaches at 29:52. The complex series of interactions can be seen as a gradual process of collective understanding, in which diversions, contradictions, and different approaches become reconciled. The mechanism for this collective understanding seems to be a cyclical process of question–model–testing–question, in which "finding through playing" is the means for decision-making. This will be further explored in the discussion section below.

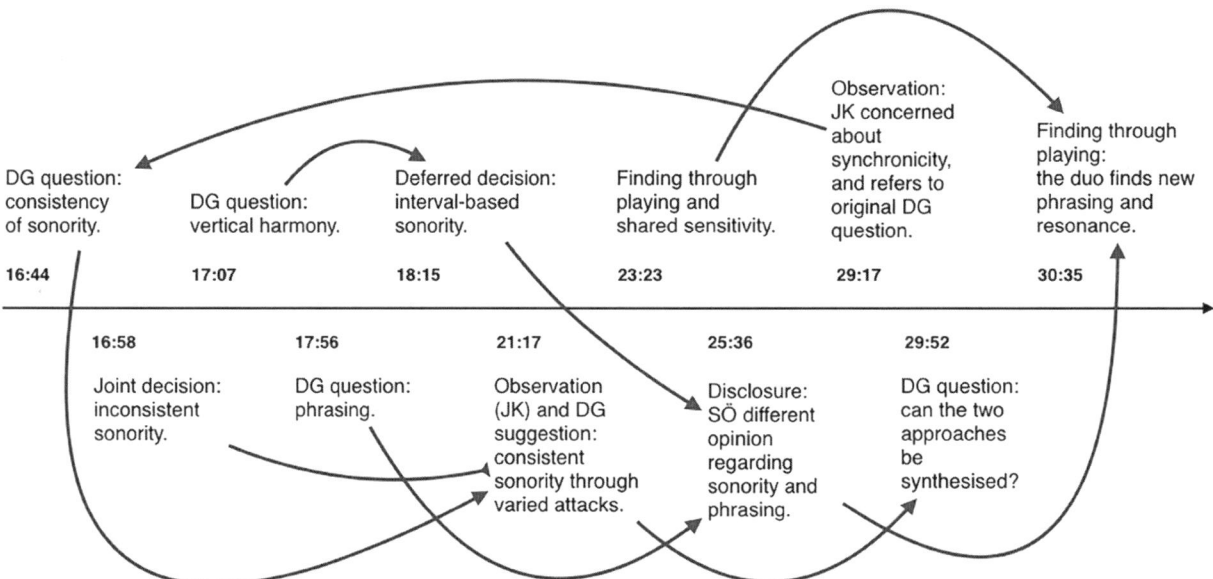

Figure 3.16.

In the second rehearsal on 9 May, David again opens the session by posing a question, which was characterised in the annotation as a "multi-layered question regarding the individual shaping of the music. He starts by observing how in some ways the composition is restrictive but turns the question to the two performers asking how a space for individual shaping can be created" [code = DG question]. Stefan observes [code = observation] that across the piece "material can be divided in two categories, where the material based on natural harmonics ["first material"] is much more restrictive than the other." Jessica follows this by stating that she feels that "the tuning system, and the fact that the location of each note on the fretboard is already indicated in the score, is very restrictive compared to how a guitarist would normally prepare a fingering which reflects a series of interpretive choices. David agrees and points to how a certain limited number of choices are still possible" [code = observation]. Jessica continues by observing that "the two performers have quite different approaches to the passages with more complex rhythmical layering" [code = observation]. Stefan responds to this, describing his interpretative strategies to the "second material" [code = disclosure]. "This entails an interest in drawing out quasi-polyphony and thereby applying a chordal approach to the figurations. He also states that one reason for this approach is his personal distaste for 'dodecaphonic modernist melody with great leaps' and thereby this strategy avoids bringing such melodic lines out of the material." Stefan then demonstrates what he means by this [code = demonstration]. It then becomes Jessica's turn to describe how she approaches the "second material" [code = disclosure], stating that she takes "a more linear approach that is more melodic and legato." These differences in approach had already been observed, albeit tacitly, in the initial recordings made by the two performers.

At this point David asks a series of questions. First, he asks how the two players use vibrato [code = DG question]. "Stefan confirms, as David had assumed, that he doesn't use vibrato at all, and that the fingering he has does not allow for any. On the other hand, Jessica confirms that she does use vibrato." This discussion is followed with a question about "right-hand variations in tone colour, and Stefan responds by showing some examples of how the quasi-polyphony invites him to a play with tone colour." David's third question concerns dynamic shaping [code = DG question]. "Stefan confesses that he does not always follow the given groupings" but in contrast "Jessica confirms that, in principle, she follows the given phrasing, but that she uses dynamic shaping to bring out important notes in the melodic structure." Following a played example from Stefan, Jessica suggests that they play to each other their individual parts to demonstrate their respective strategies for this section of material [code = demonstration]. After several minutes of playing to one another, Jessica comments that she might be "influenced by having heard Stefan play the same material" [code = observation], but David responds by suggesting that by knowing what each other are doing, the duo can push in opposite directions "thereby increasing the inner dynamic in the performance." Stefan and Jessica attempt this differentiated approach [code = finding through playing] and find a "way to combine the individual approaches" [code = shared sensitivity].

The diagram in figure 3.17 attempts to show for the rehearsal work on the "second material" what the previous diagram showed for the "first material." Notable here is that the direction of the rehearsal seems to come from the initial question that David makes about individual shaping, but that there is a cumulative effect towards the final "finding through playing." This seems as much a result of the individual demonstrations as of the supplementary questions posed by David concerning dynamic shaping, rhythmic groups, and vibrato, all of which emerge as part of composite strategies for the duo to exert their individual approaches.

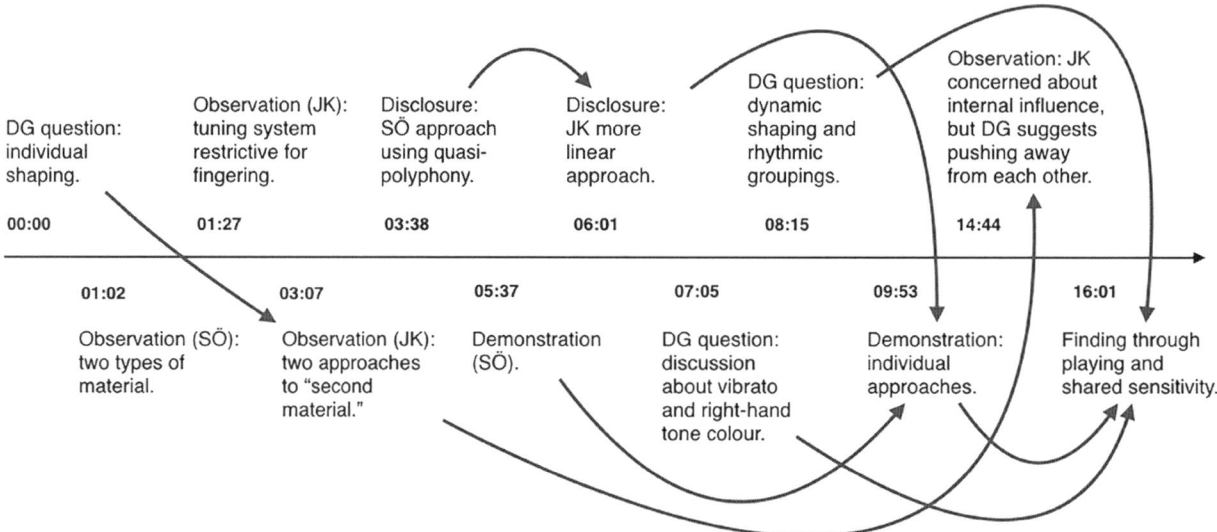

Figure 3.17.

DISCUSSION

The rehearsal processes described above represent the very first interactions between two performers, their instruments, the scores, and the composer of the pieces. In the rehearsals of *Cerro Rico* we observed a series of approaches to the temporal organisation and shaping. The rehearsals of *Charon* represent a contrasting perspective, through which the two performers engaged with aspects of sound, articulation, and phrasing.

We have identified a process that recurs in different shapes in the two case studies, in which the score and the composer have the role of activating questions. In *Cerro Rico* the instruction regarding synchronisation constitutes the initial question through the activation of an enquiring response from the performers, while in *Charon* the composer repeatedly poses verbalised questions from within the rehearsals. The two performers engage with these questions by creating models for how to understand and approach the questions, and then test these models through playing.

An example of such a model is when Jessica observes how "the bass notes generally come out more in the texture, and that balancing the registers may be a way to achieve a more coherent sonority." In doing so, Jessica is responding both to David's earlier question about sonority in the first material, and to the most recent playing in the rehearsal. Such observations are essential in the ongoing communication, since they provide a verbalisation of a musical phenomenon, and thereby make a further analysis possible. Such analysis is evident in David's suggestion "to play with more attack across the strings in order to give the impression of a more consistent sound." This suggestion further refines the model by which the group is collectively coming to address the pre-

74

vious questions, and is tested again in the following playing. A similar moment in the rehearsal of *Cerro Rico* is when Mieko takes the minimalist music process of "phasing" as a descriptor of a performative model for how to consciously not play together. These two stages, of observation and identification of artistic method, are essential in the formation of a model, which is then tested and evaluated. The above timing analysis of *Cerro Rico* shows how this model is appropriated as a means to address the question of matching a pulse while not being together, resulting in a shared understanding of how flexible the lines can be within the overall dislocated pulse.

In *Cerro Rico*, the conditions and parameters of this modelling exist within the musical materials, specifically in the extreme slowness at the outset, the semi-coordinated lack of synchronisation, and the progressive freedom from the restrictiveness of the opening materials. It is the introduction of bar lines and the instruction to match pulses in the final *Fortuna desperata* section that triggered a renegotiation in what the notation could mean, as its literal interpretation proved unacceptably resistant to the freedoms of the previous section. The presence of the composer in this negotiation helps provide licence, as well as challenge, for the increasingly flexible understanding of what "matching the pulse" could mean within this context. Additionally, the shift to the citation of historic materials raises new questions of how to interpret this section, not only in relation to the music that precedes it but also with regard to the consideration of the performance practice of the cited music. Simultaneously it raises provocative questions of where the "voice" of the composer is situated, if not in the production of original materials.

While not so immediately visible in the examples, the co-engagement with instruments is also important in the *Cerro Rico* collaboration, with much of the slow contrapuntal writing and fast tremolo material originating from the charango workshop, and the joint selection of the instruments themselves providing essential ingredients in the development of the piece. While it is true to say that both these instruments are indeed unusual within contemporary classical music, it is also worth observing that they are not unusual to the two performers in question, and neither is the idea of playing unusual instruments. This shared knowledge and experience is an important, although largely invisible, constituent of the overall system. Mieko's reference to the shared experience of "phasing" as a solution to "consciously not playing together" shows how important habitus and tacit knowledge are within the formation of performative models. While the instruments used in *Cerro Rico* are restrictive through their limited size and range, and thus have an agency of restricting the musical discourse, in *Charon* the two classical guitars pose less resistance of this kind. However, Jessica remarks on how she finds the tuning system to be a highly restrictive factor, particularly when shaping the "second material" of the piece, since the microtonal structure makes the choices of where to finger a certain note very limited, while on a guitar with standard tuning, most pitches are found on a number of strings in different positions. The different and contrasting solutions to this restriction that Stefan and Jessica find are central to their eventual shared understanding of the material evident in the "finding through playing."

At the start of this chapter, the concept of a collaborative "discursive voice" was described as a complex entanglement of individuals, and their co-engagement with instruments, notation, and shared contexts and practices. The concept of "voice" builds on an understanding of musical practice as embodied and socio-culturally situated. From this perspective, the embodied interaction with tools such as scores and instruments are central. In the description of this, two such processes demand further discussion. First, the interaction between the composer and the score. The nature of the questions that David poses in the rehearsal we find typical of how a composer's "voice" is formed through the complex entanglement of first composing a piece of music and finalising its notation, and then engaging in the score as a piece of performed music in rehearsal and concert situations. Where notation is often (perhaps mistakenly) thought of as a means for conveying the precisely defined intentions of a composer, its use as a means for activating various kinds of interpretative choice in performance can easily be overlooked.[9] In both *Cerro Rico* and *Charon* there are aspects of the notation that are obtusely paradoxical: the use of short bar lines in the "second material" of *Charon* to denote a suspension of synchronicity coupled with vertically aligned complex rhythms; the instruction to "match the pulse of the violin" in *Cerro Rico*, which is only given in one part, in a scoreless piece, within a context of metrical detachment. These paradoxes demand questions of what they might mean, and what possibilities they might engender. In the rehearsals themselves, David's mode of interaction was by question rather than direction. Like aspects of the notation, these questions provide a guiding framework by requesting that the performers think about specific things while simultaneously opening up possibilities for exploration.

Second, we find the coded instances in the stimulated recall of "finding through playing" to be central for understanding the nature of the development of a "discursive voice" in chamber music performance. Here, the negotiations are embodied and situated in the performative domain of musical creativity. Such negotiation of musical shaping requires a particular openness of listening, through which two musicians bend the ear toward the other (Östersjö and Nguyen 2013). At times, the negotiation rests on a combination of the performer's "voice" and the constellation of two distinctly different voices creating a third and novel voice. At other times, a performer may find ways of transforming their own "voice," as the result of intentional blending with the "voice" of the other. Such a search for novel sonorities can be described through Schaeffer's concept of "musicianly listening."[10] The musical "Other" that demands an openness expressed through the finding of novel

---

9   Brian Ferneyhough observes an extreme example, where a notation that offers a *"practical surfeit of infor-mation"* is the ultimate means for identifying interpretative priorities in performance ([1978] 1995, 4–5).

10   Michel Chion (2009, 39) defines musical listening as referring "back to traditional heritage, to establis-hed and accepted structures and values, which it attempts to rediscover or recreate; whilst *musicianly* hearing or invention seeks rather to locate interesting new phenomena or to innovate in the facture of sound objects. The musical attitude rests on old values; the musicianly attitude actively seeks new ones." But these two modes of listening are not to be understood as opposed; rather, they normally comple-ment each other. Chion continues by suggesting that "by going backwards and forwards, by successive approximations between these two approaches, it might be possible to discover and establish values for a new music" (ibid.).

sonorities can be the other performer or it may very well be the score or indeed the composer. But the sessions also contain moments of verbal engagement with the musical material, and we find these moments of sharing observations and experience important too in the creation of a community of practice in the development of performative models.

While these sessions all took place at the very beginning of a rehearsal period, it appears that the principles through which musical collaboration is shaped by the emergence and negotiation of "voice" come through clearly in the joint analysis. The subtlety of such artistic processes can only be experienced by engaging with the music as performed, and this holds true for composer, performer, and listener, in their attempts to make their music "more interesting."

REFERENCES

Bastien, David T., and Todd J. Hostager. 1988. "Jazz as a Process of Organizational Innovation." *Communication Research* 15 (5): 582–602.

———. 1992. "Cooperation as Communicative Accomplishment: A Symbolic Interaction Analysis of an Improvised Jazz Concert." *Communication Studies* 43 (2): 92–104.

———. 1996. "On Cooperation: A Replication of an Experiment in Jazz and Cooperation." *Comportamento Organizacional e Gestao* 2 (1): 33–46.

Bastien, David T., and Jeremy Rose. 2014. "Cooperative Activity: The Importance of Audiences." In *Revisiting Symbolic Interaction in Music Studies and New Interpretive Works*, edited by Norman K. Denzin, 21–36. Studies in Symbolic Interaction 42. Bingley, UK: Emerald Group.

Bloom, Benjamin S. 1953. "Thought-Processes in Lectures and Discussions." *Journal of General Education* 7 (3): 160–69.

Bowen, José Antonio. 1996. "Performance Practice versus Performance Analysis: Why Should Performers Study Performance." *Performance Practice Review* 9 (1): 16–35.

Brooks, William, Stefan Östersjö, and Jeremy J. Wells. 2019. "Footnotes." In *Voices, Bodies, Practices*, by Catherine Laws, William Brooks, David Gorton, Nguyễn Thanh Thủy, Stefan Östersjö, and Jeremy J. Wells, 169–232. Orpheus Institute Series. Leuven: Leuven University Press.

Chion, Michel. 2009. *Guide to Sound Objects: Pierre Schaeffer and Musical Research*. Translated by John Dack and Christine North. EARS: ElectroAcoustic Resource Site. Accessed 20 February 2020. http://ears.pierrecouprie.fr/spip. php?article3597. First published 1983 as *Guide des objets sonores: Pierre Schaeffer et la recherche musicale* (Paris: Buchet Chastel).

Clarke, Eric F., Mark Doffman, David Gorton, and Stefan Östersjö. 2017. "Fluid Practices, Solid Roles? The Evolution of *Forlorn Hope*." In *Distributed Creativity: Collaboration and Improvisation in Contemporary Music*, edited by Eric F. Clarke and Mark Doffman, 116–35. New York: Oxford University Press.

Cook, Nicholas. 2018. *Music as Creative Practice*. New York: Oxford University Press.

Coorevits, Esther, Dirk Moelants, Stefan Östersjö, and David Gorton. 2016. "Decomposing a Composition: On the Multi-layered Analysis of Expressive Music Performance." In *Music, Mind, and Embodiment: 11th International Symposium, CMMR 2015*, edited by Richard Kronland-Martinet, Mitsuko Aramaic, and Sølvi Ystad, 167–89. Cham, Switzerland: Springer.

Cumming, Naomi. 2000. *The Sonic Self: Musical Subjectivities and Signification*. Bloomington: Indiana University Press.

Ferneyhough, Brian. (1978) 1995. "Aspects of Notational and Compositional Practice." In *Collected Writings*, edited by James Boros and Richard Toop, 2–13. Abingdon, UK: Routledge. Essay first published 1978 in French translation (*Semaine de musique contemporaine*).

Frisk, Henrik, and Stefan Östersjö, eds. 2013. *(Re)thinking Improvisation: Artistic Explorations and Conceptual Writing*. Malmö: Malmö Academy of Music.

Gorton, David. 2018a. *Austerity Measures I* for ten-string guitar (2012). Berlin: Verlag Neue Musik.

———. 2018b. *Forlorn Hope* for eleven-string alto guitar and optional electronics (2011). Berlin: Verlag Neue Musik.

———. 2018c. *Cerro Rico* for violin (or soprano violin) and charango (2017). Berlin: Verlag Neue Musik.

———. 2019. *Charon* for two guitars (2015). Berlin: Verlag Neue Musik.

Gorton, David, and Stefan Östersjö. 2016. "Choose Your Own Adventure Music: On the Emergence of Voice in Musical Collaboration." *Contemporary Music Review* 35 (6): 579–98.

———. 2019. "Austerity Measures I: Performing the Discursive Voice." In *Voices, Bodies, Practices: Performing Musical Subjectivities*, by Catherine Laws, William Brooks, David Gorton, Nguyễn Thanh Thùy, Stefan Östersjö, and Jeremy J. Wells, 29–79. Orpheus Institute Series. Leuven: Leuven University Press.

Kagan, Norman, and David Krathwohl. 1967. *Studies in Human Interaction: Interpersonal Process Recall Stimulated by Videotape*. East Lansing: Michigan State University, College of Education, Educational Publication Services.

McCaleb, J. Murphy. 2014. *Embodied Knowledge in Ensemble Performance*. Farnham, UK: Ashgate.

Östersjö, Stefan, and Nguyễn Thanh Thùy. 2013. "Traditions in Transformation: the Function of Openness in the Interaction between Musicians." In *(Re)thinking Improvisation: Artistic Explorations and Conceptual Writing*, edited by Henrik Frisk and Stefan Östersjö, 184–201. Malmö: Malmö Academy of Music.

Rink, John, ed. 2002. *Musical Performance: A Guide to Understanding*. Cambridge: Cambridge University Press.

———. 2015. "The (F)utility of Performance Analysis." In *Artistic Practice as Research in Music: Theory, Criticism, Practice*, edited by Mine Doğantan-Dack, 127–47. Abingdon, UK: Ashgate.

Rink, John, Helena Gaunt, and Aaron Williamon, eds. 2017. *Musicians in the Making: Pathways to Creative Performance*. New York: Oxford University Press.

Strauss, Anselm L., and Juliet M. Corbin. 1990. *Basics of Qualitative Research: Grounded Theory Procedures and Techniques*. Newbury Park, CA: Sage.

Deus ex Disklavier

Subjectivity and Technological Resistance in the Performance of Maria Kallionpää's *Climb!* for Disklavier and Electronics

Zubin Kanga,[1] Anne Veinberg,[2] Maria Kallionpää,[3]
Adrian Hazzard,[4] Chris Greenhalgh,[4] Steve Benford[4]

[1] Royal Holloway, University of London; Sydney Conservatorium of Music,
the University of Sydney; Royal Academy of Music, London;
[2] Leiden University / docARTES; [3] Aalborg University;
[4] Mixed Reality Laboratory, School of Computer Science, University of Nottingham

INTRODUCTION

No two people who scale Everest climb the same mountain; no two performers who perform a work experience it identically. The subjective experiences of performers change depending on their roles in the work. There are vast differences between the experiences of composer-performers, where the composer and performer are the same person and have the same perspective, to the experience of performers acting as interpreters of composers, where any performer's experience of the composer's perspective is partial and one of many in a distributed network. But what happens if, in a duet, the human performer's partner is an interactive machine? And how does that performer's attitude to and knowledge of a system affect the experience of the work built around it?

This chapter explores the subjective experience of two performers' preparations and performances of the work *Climb!* (2016–17), by Maria Kallionpää, in a single concert at the All Your Bass Festival, Nottingham, in January 2018. Concert films of the performances by the pianists Zubin Kanga and Anne Veinberg can be viewed online at the following URLs: for Zubin Kanga's performance, see https://youtu.be/JwzmmEtAdTU; for Anne Veinberg's performance, see https://youtu.be/wbGCU6QFGr4.

Climb! is constituted by a game-like structure embedded within an interactive system: the pianist plays a duet with a Disklavier (a brand of modern, computer-driven player-piano); through a combination of choice and chance, a particular pathway up the "mountain" is taken.

Using this case study, we explore fundamental differences in the performers' subjective experiences of mobile scores and interactive technologies, raising many questions: how unique is a performer's experience of an interactive system? How do differences in understanding of the "game" aspect of the piece affect a performer's experience? Do different subjective experiences of a system result in wide variations in the performances? And most crucially, how well can the composer and system developers control and manipulate a performer's subjective response to the work, and how can the performers resist and reframe these efforts at control?

This chapter addresses these questions by first exploring the creation and development of *Climb!* before examining a concert that featured two consecutive performances of the work by pianists Anne Veinberg and Zubin Kanga. Both performers have extensive experience in working with interactive technologies, but they have quite different levels of experience with the Disklavier systems used in this piece, and they embrace widely varying technical and interpretative approaches. The two performances (and their preparation) are examined by the performers themselves as well as by the composer and system developers—Adrian Hazzard, Chris Greenhalgh, and Steve Benford—who also analyse feedback surveys from the audience. This pair of performances provides a unique chance to test the variation in the subjective experience of an interactive computer system, providing key insights into many of the above questions.

This research uses a combination of ethnographic and auto-ethnographic methodologies. At different stages of the development, rehearsal, and performance of the work, each of the participants is both an insider to the process and an outsider, with all participants only having a partial perspective on the work as a whole. In examining a case study from multiple viewpoints, we have drawn on some of the ideas of Marc Leman, who differentiates between different types of subjective perspectives (first- and second-person perspectives) and an objective perspective on the same performance (third person) that require different methodologies and skill sets providing uniquely different insights (Leman 2010, 127). We also draw on the ever-growing body of work examining composer–performer collaborations from multiple perspectives. The structure presented by Clarke, Cook, Harrison, and Thomas (2005) is a useful model that allows a composer, performer, and two outside observers to all comment on a single work. There have also been some excellent examples of pairs of composer-performers creating work and documenting and researching the work concurrently. David Gorton and Stefan Östersjö examine a collaboration elsewhere in this book and in a previous article (Gorton and Östersjö 2016); Gorton's paper with Zubin Kanga (2016) also serves as a valuable model.

1. WHAT IS *CLIMB!*?

Climb! is a non-linear composition performed by a pianist with and on a Disklavier and with additional electronics. Composed by Maria Kallionpää, it brings together the concepts of a classical virtuoso piano piece and an interactive computer game (Kallionpää and Gasselseder 2016). The work was realised collaboratively between the composer, the Mixed Reality Laboratory at the University of Nottingham, and the e-Research Centre at the University of Oxford.

Climb! is a direct continuation of Kallionpää's previous research project on hyper-instruments (such as the Disklavier and the magnetic resonator piano), the aim of which was to explore how to enhance and multiply the technical and expressive qualities of the performers (Kallionpää 2014, 1–8). In *Climb!* this multiplication is achieved by the pianist performing together with, as well as against, the Yamaha Disklavier, a combination that enables sonic and instrumental results that a single human pianist could not normally obtain. These include, for example, enabling clusters that sweep through the entire keyboard, playing simultaneously on several octave ranges, or the rendition of complex rhythms and fast tempi that would be otherwise impossible to play.

Compositional structure

Climb! uses a narrative metaphor of a challenging climb up a mountain. The work consists of a set of twenty-six distinct sections scored for both pianist and self-playing Disklavier. These sections are structured into three different "macro compositions" ("paths") and various "micro compositions" ("events") that symbolise different journeys up these paths towards the top of the mountain (see figure 4.1). In this sense, the structure of *Climb!* was inspired by Chadabe's concept of a musical piece as a "process" rather than a "fixed object" (1996, 43).

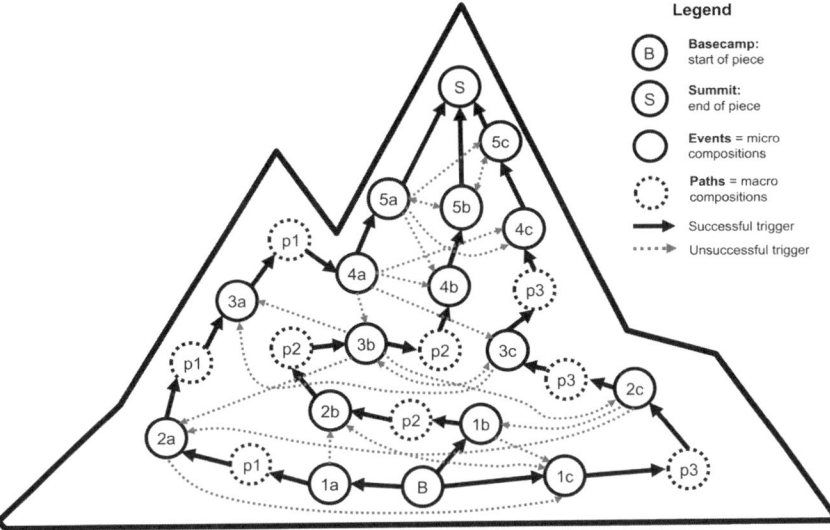

Figure 4.1.

Although not strictly a programmatic work, the events in *Climb!* are descriptively named to represent the avatar's (i.e., the pianist-performer's) challenging journey, which entails encounters with, for example, hallucinations, mystical

Figure 4.1. Structure of *Climb!*

landscapes, falling rocks, animals, and changing weather conditions. The last of these is realised through digital sound processing of the acoustic piano. Each performance of *Climb!* commences at "Basecamp" and concludes at "The Summit," but the route to the top is not fixed. Rather, by choosing outcomes of branching events, a performer can take a multitude of routes along the paths (figure 4.1). For example, at the end of the first movement ("Basecamp") there are three endings the performer can perform. The choice determines whether "Path 1," "Path 2," or "Path 3" is taken. Furthermore, a musical phrase or motif is embedded within the scored material of a majority of these "events." These "challenge codes" function as a musical game: if the phrase is performed correctly, the pianist's journey continues along the same path. Conversely, if the challenge code is not performed correctly, the pianist will branch off from the current path and onto another. This game-like mechanism in *Climb!* builds on a long history of non-linearity and indeterminism in musical composition and performance, from the musical dice games of the late eighteenth and early nineteenth centuries through to the chance-based works of John Cage and Henry Cowell.

Consequently, a performance of *Climb!* does not weave through all twenty-six sections, but rather forges a trajectory through a particular sequence on the basis of choice and challenge. These interactions are controlled by the *Climb!* system software.

Stage set-up

Climb! is written for self-playing Disklavier with a pianist performing on the same instrument. In addition, onstage microphones that capture the acoustic sound of the Disklavier piano are channelled through a MAX/MSP patch running on a laptop computer that applies digital effect processing that is mixed with the acoustic piano sound. Each performance is also accompanied by two visual interfaces: the first consists of onstage projections showing synchronised illustrative graphics providing a visual corollary of the weather conditions; the second is a bespoke web "app" that runs on the audience's mobile phones and that presents a range of supplementary information about the work in addition to the performer's current progress through the indeterminate, branching structure in real-time.

Climb! digital interactions

A performance of *Climb!* encompasses a complex set of digital interactions requiring the application of two bespoke pieces of software in addition to some established products typically used in electroacoustic works. The bespoke software was designed and developed in collaboration with Kallionpää by the Mixed Reality Lab (MRL) at the University of Nottingham and the e-Research Centre at the University of Oxford. The first piece of software is termed *Muzicodes*. It enables a composer/performer to identify musical motifs embedded within a musical work that, when performed, function as triggers for a range of digital interactions (Greenhalgh, Benford, and Hazzard 2016; Greenhalgh et al.

2017).[1] In the case of *Climb!* a number of different types of "codes" are embedded into Kallionpää's scored material—primarily the challenge codes that determine the route that a performer will take through the sections of *Climb!* (shown highlighted in figure 4.2). These codes are typically formed around short sequences of pitches (between one and four notes) to ensure that they are easily performed and consequently serve as triggers. These codes can also trigger and control other performance elements, including the changing weather effects, synchronised projected visuals, and updates to the audience "app" (see figure 4.3).

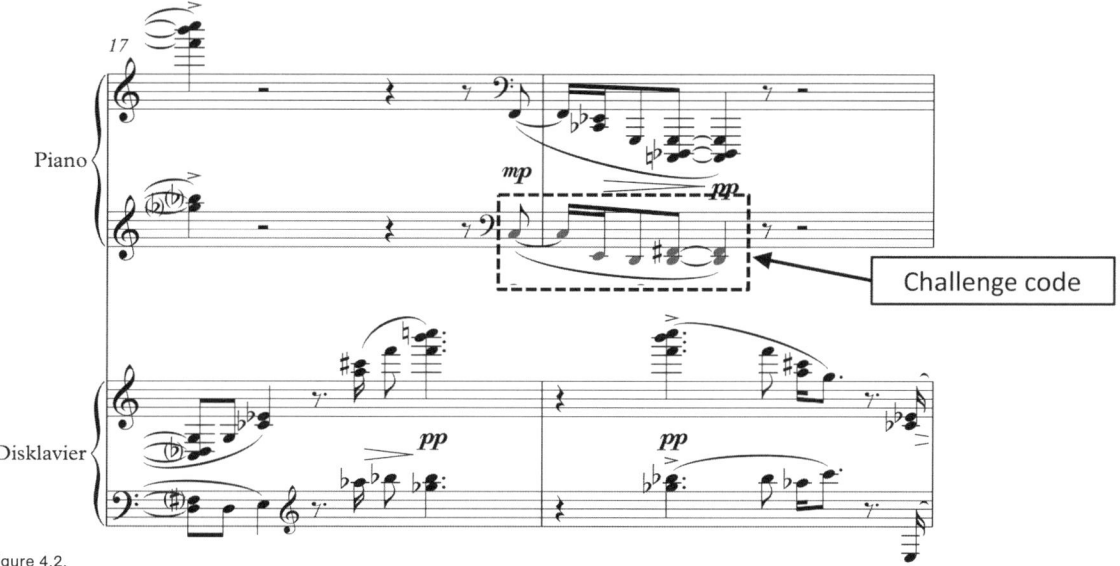

Figure 4.2.

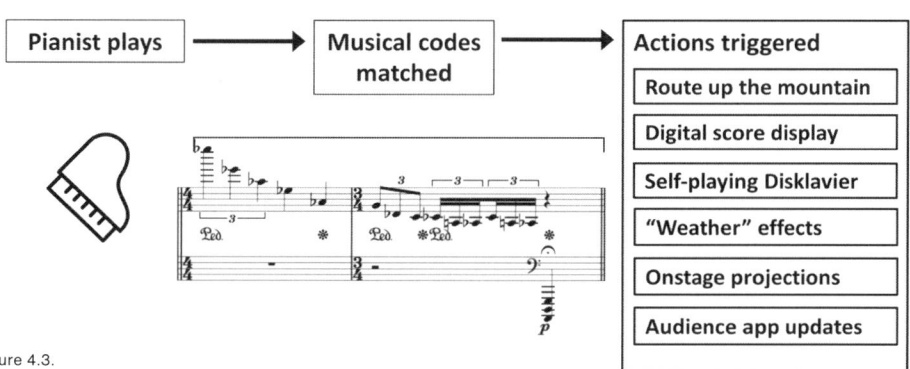

Figure 4.3.

<hr />

1 The Muzicodes approach is distinct from score-following systems that are regularly used in electroacoustic works. These systems typically provide for continuous synchronisation between performer and system, where this synchronisation facilitates a system accompaniment of some description (e.g. Puckette and Lippe 1992; Orio, Lemouton, and Schwarz 2003). Muzicodes listens for discrete musical gestures (i.e., "codes"), creating much flexibility for the composer/performer. Because the presentation of codes can be performed at will, it is not necessary to keep to a fixed sequence of events or time code.

Figure 4.2. Example of a challenge code.
Figure 4.3. Muzicodes system flow.

In addition, the team at Oxford developed MELD (Music Encoding and Linked Data), a bespoke system for real-time rendering of the score displayed on a digital screen for the performer (Weigl et al. 2018). The MELD system also enables real-time highlighting or adaptation of the rendered score materials. The different types of code are colour-coded, so a performer can anticipate their arrival and their function. A successful performance of a code results in those measures being highlighted in red on the digital score display (see figure 4.4). An unsuccessful performance would result in no highlighting. This approach presents immediate feedback as the performer interacts with the system.

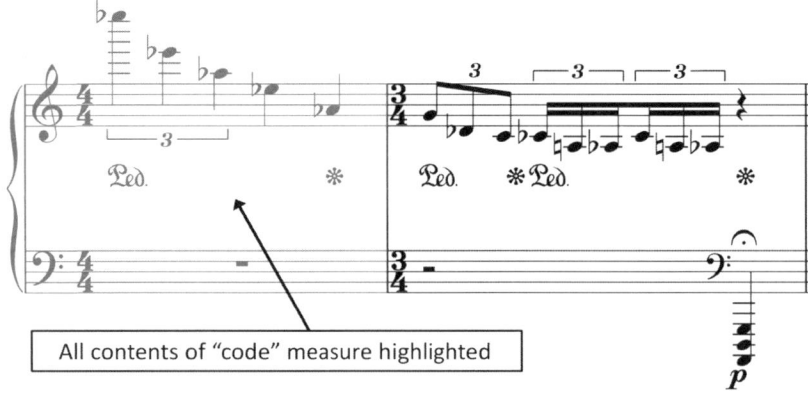

All contents of "code" measure highlighted

Figure 4.4.

2. Perspectives of the composer-performer (Maria Kallionpää)

My approach to composing *Climb!* differed from the usual process, in which compositional and performance phases are separate, because, as the first performer of the work, I was continuously mindful of my own performer's perspective. This enabled me to evaluate the dramatic structure of the piece and also to understand what kind of technical solutions would be optimal. I performed *Climb!* several times in various stages of its development, which enabled the technical team and me to test the interactive system as well as the musical composition in concert situations. The initial prototype of the system and the very first excerpts of the piece were presented in December 2016.[2] The necessity of additional branching options became evident when I performed the premiere of the fully realised, completed version, in which I unintentionally played two very similar performances.[3] Changes were subsequently made to add these new options and also to ensure that a performer would not get stuck in an endless loop.

---

2   The workshops and performances took place between 5 and 8 December 2016 at the annual meeting of the FAST research team in the Cotswolds, UK. The FAST network engages researchers from the Universities of Nottingham and Oxford and also from Queen Mary University, London.

3   The official premiere took place on 9 June 2017 at the Djanogly Recital Hall, University of Nottingham. Kallionpää, the composer of *Climb!*, performed the work twice. The members of the audience filled in the questionnaires between the performances.

Figure 4.4. Score highlighting on a successful "code" performance.

Developing new software according to the needs of a specific composition project may form an integral part of the creative process that cannot be distinguished from the development of the musical material and the structure of the piece (Kallionpää 2014, 39). This was indeed the case with *Climb!*, as my composition work also involved the development of new technological solutions. In the beginning the team had to define what kind of tools and software would best fit the purposes of the project, which were then designed and iteratively customised (i.e., Muzicodes and MELD). There was a constant dialogue between me and the technical team throughout: not only did the music influence the technology but also the development of the software inspired the composition (Kallionpää et al. 2016, 468).

3. Handing over Climb! (Maria Kallionpää, Adrian Hazzard, and Christopher Greenhalgh)

Engaging with Climb!—different perspectives

Following two public performances of *Climb!* given by Kallionpää, a third concert opportunity arose, whereupon we decided to hand over *Climb!* to other performers. The first two *Climb!* performances saw the work played twice within the same concert, an unusual but deliberate approach to expose the work's non-linearity to the audience. Engaging two pianists back-to-back offered the audience two distinct routes through the work alongside two distinct interpretations. Furthermore, we were intrigued to witness the approach and degree of interpretation the two pianists could bring to bear on a performance of *Climb!*, given both the constraints and the freedoms of the work. This approach would also enable us to capture a rich picture of how the two performers would conceptualise, prepare, rehearse, and shape their performances of this work. We presented different materials to each of the two performers.

The two pianists chosen were Anne Veinberg and Zubin Kanga. Both pianists are active in the contemporary music scene and have performance and research interests specifically in working with technology. Veinberg was offered full access to *Climb!* materials whereas Kanga received a restricted set. Specifically, Kanga was not made aware of the location of the challenge codes that determine a pianist's branching route through the movements. Our rationale for this was twofold. First, given the indeterminate, "game-like" approach in this work, Kallionpää was concerned that pianists who know the location of challenge codes may over-rehearse them, thus rendering them less challenging. This would diminish the indeterminacy of the work's form in performance, allowing full control over a piece that is intended to include moments of uncertainty. We wanted to learn whether this indeterminacy would still be realised by Veinberg (who had full access to the codes) and whether she would use the information available to her to shape her rehearsal and performance practice. Furthermore, by withholding this information from Kanga, we could observe how a pianist comes to terms with a highly interactive piece when some of the principal interactions that result from their performance are unknown to them.

Preparations

Our first meeting with Veinberg concerned initial discussions about the concept, score, and practicalities of the performance. Veinberg installed the *Climb!* system software on her laptop computer to enable her to rehearse on both her Yamaha digital piano at home and a Yamaha Disklavier on a few occasions prior to the performance. Thus she was able to prepare and rehearse with what was, for all intents and purposes, a full performance set-up (minus the projected visuals, audience app, and "weather" effects) that included all the resultant system interactions.

Kanga, by contrast, was only told the principal interactions of the computer system; we disclosed that there were musical phrases (i.e., challenge codes) that determined the branching route through the composition but that these were being deliberately withheld because they—in part—determined the "game-like" character of the work. Kanga requested a paper copy of the score and the audio files for his preparation, but we did not offer him the system software to work with at home (as this would expose the location of the challenge codes). Kanga only encountered the full system with Disklavier for a very limited period of rehearsal on the day before and morning of the concert. Kanga requested to use his annotated paper score during the performance itself, as this enabled him to see his markings, discussed further below.[4]

In the following sections, Kanga and Veinberg give their accounts of their experiences with *Climb!*, and their markedly different experiences of preparing and interpreting the work.

4. The performer's experience: Zubin Kanga

First encounter with Climb!

My first thought when I received the score of *Climb!* was astonishment at the size of it—a score of 150 pages for what I was told was a ten-to-fifteen-minute work. But soon I understood that the score contained many possible pathways through the piece and that these would be selected by the system on the basis of my playing certain challenge codes.

As stated above, I was not provided with the challenge codes in the score and I did not have a Disklavier to practise on, which meant that my understanding of how the interaction with the system would work was speculative and abstract. I had extensive experience with live-triggering, live electronics, and unusual methods of control (particularly in *Morphosis* for piano, 3D sensors, and live electronics, which I commissioned in 2014) and had some familiarity with compositions for Disklavier: works with fixed parts, such as *Chunk* (2011) by Cat Hope; autonomously generative/algorithmic works played by Disklaviers, such as Karlheinz Essl's *Lexikon-Sonate* (1992–2018); and Disklaviers used to receive

---

4   Nonetheless, Kanga still needed to use the foot pedal during the performance because the mechanism of pressing the pedal between movements configured and initialised the system for the next section depending on the outcome of the challenge codes (i.e., cueing the required next movement).

MIDI input, process the data, and output a part that duets with the live performer, as in Andrew Brown's *Ripples* (2015). I also had experience as a student using the Disklavier in educational settings (such as recording performances for later reflection). However, I had not yet personally played an interactive work with a Disklavier. It was only on the day before the concert that I had a full understanding of what *Climb!* is, as a piece and as a system.

Resisting the electronic score and experiencing an unknown path in performance

As stated above, I performed the work from a paper score rather than the digital score display. At that point in my career, using an electronic tablet (such as an iPad) was not part of my core practice, so I felt this was not an option I wanted to pursue with *Climb!* More importantly, my markings in the score, which specified pitch names (for pitches with many leger lines), fingerings, and the subdivision of bars and rhythms, could not be transferred into the performance score, which would be generated from the same system as that which drove the Disklavier.

My decision to use the paper score had several major disadvantages. The most important of these was my inability to know where the challenge codes were. These were shown in blue in the electronic version of the score, changing to red as they were played and read by the Disklavier. As stated earlier, the research team deliberately provided me with a paper score for rehearsal on which the challenge codes were left unmarked. If I had chosen to use the digital score display in the performance and pre-performance rehearsals then these codes would have been visible to me, albeit with limited opportunity for me to identify and learn their location and form. With my printed score, I not only did not know the location of these codes but also could not tell whether I had played these passages correctly or "failed."

Because I had no knowledge of the challenge codes, I was "flying blind," simply playing the piece as notated and then waiting until the end of each movement to know whether I would continue up the same path or cross to another one. In most movements, I was wholly unable to guess the location or even size of the challenge codes. This produced a result where, apart from the very first choice at the "Basecamp" (where the three paths were clearly available by choosing from three different endings), I could neither plan a pathway up the mountain nor choose to avoid particular movements. Such lack of control over pathways chosen seemed appropriate to me, however, from my own experience of mountaineering and rock climbing: although a person can plan to take a particular path, environmental conditions, incorrect or out-of-date maps, and other unpredictable features of the landscape often require that choices be made in the middle of a climb to change to another, literal, path.

The question this raises is, do the chance-based decisions encountered in my climbing experiences justify my eschewal of the tablet score? Or would a professional mountain climber prepare a pathway up the mountain more meticulously, as was more the case in Anna Veinberg's performance? For me, it was right to embrace a sense of danger in the lack of control over the pathway while simultaneously feeling in greater control over the score; it allowed me to focus on the musical decisions and the characterisation of each movement rather than to attempt to control the larger game structure.

Perceiving the Disklavier as a duetting partner

The experience of performing as a duetting partner with the Disklavier had similarities both to performing with electronics and to playing with another live pianist, and the combination raised a number of challenges. Like an electronics part, the Disklavier would play through the selected movement without stopping or adjusting to me; since I had no way to control it, I had to fit into its tempi and tempo fluctuations. But in comparison to my previous performances with electronics, I perceived this as a high-risk mode of performance, without the safety that would be provided by a click track. This was especially the case with the longer solos, since these needed to be timed precisely to line up with the re-entry of the Disklavier. One such tricky passage occurred in "Path 1a" (figure 4.5), where the solo pianist has to play continuously at an extremely fast speed to ensure that the part is synchronised with the Disklavier track when it enters.

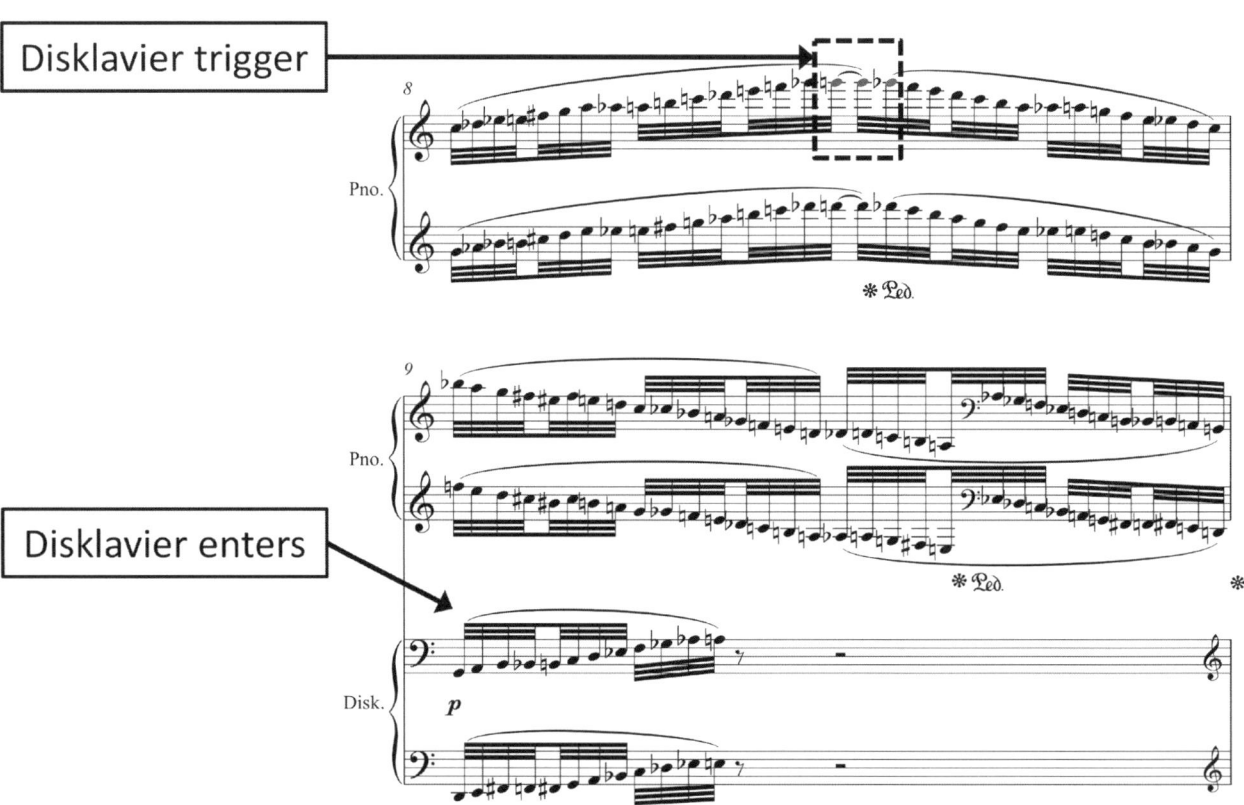

Figure 4.5.

Figure 4.5. Path 1a, bars 8–9.

The accelerandos and ritardandos also required skill to remain synchronised with the Disklavier part. A live performer would most likely aid my performance with visual cues (Williamon and Davidson 2002), but the Disklavier cannot, leaving me only one option: to memorise the pace of each such passage and attempt to match the Disklavier—an option that met with varying degrees of success. For example, the passage in figure 4.6, from "The Summit," was extremely difficult to align with the Disklavier part. The passage in figure 4.7— also from "The Summit"—was tricky for other reasons, requiring that I judge the ritardando to match my predicted timing of the Disklavier's entry: too quick and I would leave a gap between the end of my phase and the Disklavier; too slow and my bar would be interrupted before it was finished. In both cases, the risk of failure was higher than I was comfortable with, despite my strategies for mitigation.[5]

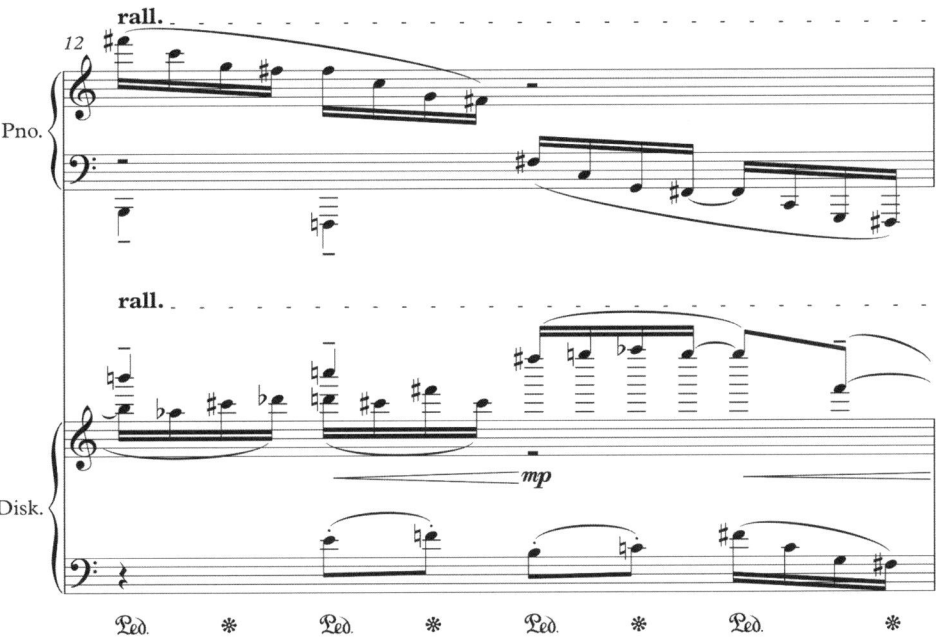

Figure 4.6.

---

5   The balance between mitigating and playing with risk is explored in more detail in Gorton and Kanga (2016).

Figure 4.6. Example of tempo modulations.

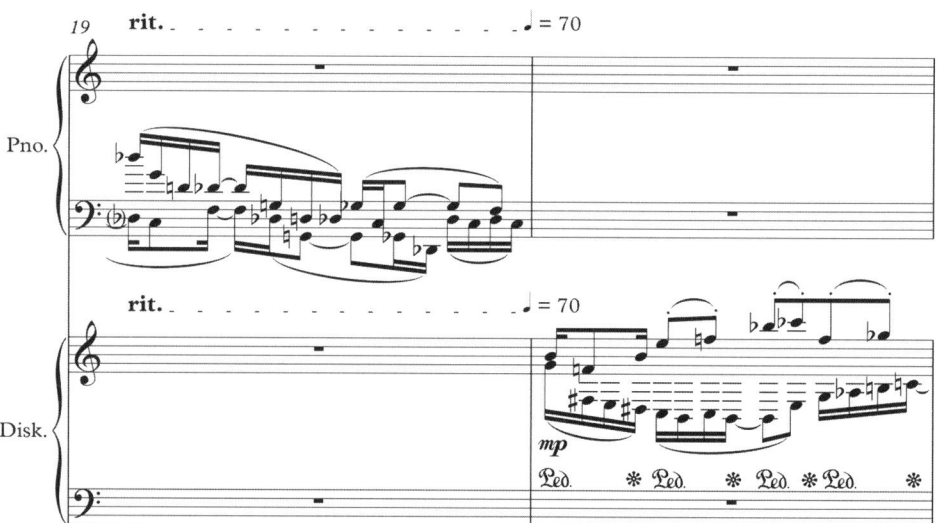

Figure 4.7.

Pauses were similarly problematic to judge, both because I could not count through them in tempo, as in other notated sections, and because the lengths of each of the pauses often differed in ways that were hard to predict. Again, a live performer would visually communicate the length of a pause, and without this visual cue, I continually had to react to the Disklavier, or estimate the lengths of pauses, again with a varying degree of accuracy. Practising my part alongside the audio sound files of the Disklavier parts allowed me to gradually learn how to pace these pauses and the changes in tempo; but, given the number of these instances and the variable pacing, complete and secure accuracy eluded me.

However, there were also aspects of the work that were similar to playing with a live performer, and these mitigated some of the more difficult examples above. When I finally was able to play on the Disklavier the day before the concert, my judgement of pacing and the speed of my reactions improved. Because I could see the keys moving I was afforded a kind of visual reinforcement of what I was hearing, though different from that provided by a real performer who can cue the start of a note or phrase. To some extent, my use of visual stimuli resembled practices found in chamber music (see, for instance, Shaffer [1984], which studies timing in duetting partners who communicate with physical actions, not just disembodied electronic sounds); and this allowed me to perceive the Disklavier even more like a chamber partner, despite its inflexibility (the fugue in "The Summit" being the most obvious example). One negative aspect of this visual reinforcement was that the movement of the Disklavier's keys could sometimes be disconcerting, even though there was little real danger to my

90

Figure 4.7. Synchronising with the Disklavier in "The Summit."

fingers. Thus, in performance (only twenty-six hours after I first experienced the piece on a Disklavier), this sense of disconcertment was still present, and the calibration of my approach to this not-electronics/not-human partner was still in process.

This combination of ways of interacting with and reacting to the Disklavier made *Climb!* a unique performance experience for me in the context of my wider work with interactive systems. There remained an element of risk involved in attempting to anticipate the other part, and I felt that this was appropriate for a piece about mountain climbing. But where there was just unpredictability when rehearsing with the sound files, onstage there was real danger of failure in these interactions with the Disklavier, and this risk of failure was the subject of a number of discussions with the composer.

Preparation and the inevitability of failure

The possibility of failure in *Climb!* was a feature of the performance experience. As already discussed by the composer, the performer cannot "lose" in the choice of pathways—a summit will eventually be reached, even if all challenge codes fail to be activated. But there was still a real possibility, if not inevitability, of failure within each movement—of the two parts coming apart rhythmically or of cues missed completely (as mentioned above).

Writing to me, Kallionpää assured me that failing to play with the Disklavier was part of the piece. It was impossible to play exactly like the machine, and these differences were not to be ironed out—they are what would interest the audience, especially when similar materials appear in both parts in succession. She wrote:

> In my opinion it's not essential that each excerpt sticks to the same metronome marking all the time (I didn't use any click track in my performance and I understood that Anne also would not). Feel free to modify the tempo in the bars where the Disklavier doesn't play alongside you (sometimes the performer also cues the Disklavier in the middle of the piece, in which case it's easier for the performer to distribute the time). Moreover, it's not crucial that everything is highly accurate: one of the ideas of the piece is that a human is playing with (and against) the machine, so it is okay that it is sometimes also audible. (Email, Maria Kallionpää to Zubin Kanga, 3 January 2018)

Although in most sections I still strove to play in time with the Disklavier, Kallionpää's permission to fail allowed me to prepare strategies to recover— for example, finding ways to jump ahead in the "Path 1" sections, in which I would almost inevitably fall behind the very fast Disklavier part. The composer's advice also encouraged me to differentiate my sound and interpretation of the passages from the Disklavier, introducing more varied sounds, articulation, pedalling, and (where possible) rubato, and to embrace the risks of the piece rather than trying to mitigate them completely.

The audience's perception of my human–computer interactions

These differences in the performances of passages shared by my own playing and the Disklavier led me to question how the audience perceived my performance. Would they mistake the Disklavier's notes for mine and believe I was playing many more notes than I was? Or would the flaws and variations in my playing be shown up in stark contrast to the perfection and incredible speed of the machine? At what point do differences stop sounding like interesting differences between human and machine and become more like mistakes? Although some of these questions were addressed in the survey (with a limited audience sample), they remain fundamental issues for any performer tackling this work.

Reflections on the performance

Because I was the second performer in the concert, I had the opportunity to listen to Veinberg's performance. I had already noted the differences in Veinberg's interpretation in comparison to mine during rehearsals (in particular, her more accurate and precise playing with the Disklavier, compared with what seemed like my own wilder approach), so I mainly noted the pathway taken by her and wondered how much my own pathway would vary from this. In performance, I still felt as I had in the rehearsal: I didn't really have control over the pathway through the work. The choice of each subsequent movement could never be predicted; but since I had prepared most possible pathways, I didn't feel surprised or caught unawares by the path the system selected. And more importantly, I enjoyed the unique experience of duetting with the Disklavier, creating hyper-virtuosic moments, as well as strange softer duo interludes, and embracing risk in the unpredictability of the path. The other elements (the video, the electronic processing of sound, the live camera) were all noticeable but secondary aspects; my attention was focused primarily on this duet with the Disklavier.

One of many perspectives

Although I've provided my own perspective on interpreting the piece, this was affected in major ways by my lack of prior knowledge of the work, my use of a paper score, my particular experiences as a chamber musician and soloist working with electronics, and my limited access to the particular system used in the performance. Many of these circumstances and experiences were different, for both Kallionpää and Veinberg. As we will see, Veinberg's experience of the work, despite being in exactly the same venue and concert and on exactly the same instrument, differed from mine in crucial ways.

5. THE PERFORMER'S EXPERIENCE: ANNE VEINBERG

First impressions

I was initially drawn to *Climb!* because its creators described the system as using musical codes (Muzicodes), and I wondered how that might connect to my "CodeKlavier" project, made together with Felipe Ignacio Noriega, which also incorporates the use of musical motifs as computer codes. In receiving the *Climb!* score, my first immediate reaction was—much like Kanga's—shock at the sheer volume of it and nervousness with regards to preparing it in time for our scheduled workshop session just a few weeks later. However, after reading past "Path 1" and receiving some clarifications from the composer, my nerves soon quieted, and I could focus on discovering the work.

I had already participated in several Disklavier projects, including Marcel Wierckx's ongoing series of études, *Duets for Live Coder and Pianist* (Veinberg 2013), and *Zwei Improvisaties* (Veinberg 2014) with Juan A. Romero, so I could anticipate some of the novel human–machine interactions that such works entail: dealing with the machine's tempi and timings, finding my own voice amid the Disklavier's output, and coping with notes being taken away from under my fingers. Hence, at the beginning, these aspects were at the back of my mind, shaping my preparation, interpretation, and performance of the work.

The game of *Climb!* directly influences the piece's structure, but to me the crux of the game lay in human–machine interactions. This is not to dismiss the overarching polyvalent structure of *Climb!* and the decisions entailed to navigate through the system; but since each event was in itself a complete musical micro-composition and since the system was conceived so that it was impossible to "lose" the game, reaching the summit was inevitable and thus not a primary concern in my interpretation.

Submission or assertion

Performing together with a computer-controlled duo partner can lead to a relationship in which the acoustic performer is submissive to their computer counterpart (McNutt 2003). However, when performers view the restrictions placed upon them by the computer as musical motivators for their interpretations, the relationship can be transformed into an assertive one, and this affects the performer's subjective experience of the work.

When first approaching *Climb!*, I was determined to perform the notated score as accurately as possible. I saw the *Climb!* system as an absolute and consistently correct duo partner to whom I should be continuously adjusting. This resulted in an almost obsessive manner of preparation to master the coordination of important entrances between the two parts, but this coordination was never 100 per cent successful. The frustration that emerged from the uncertainty in strictly synchronising entrances made me look for alternative readings that would mask potential rhythmic miscoordinations. I experimented with deliberately breaking chords or placing them before or after the Disklavier entrance, so that such moments would become musical features. I also created contrasts in volume to transform the softer part, whether from the Disklavier or the live piano, into a colouration of the louder one, as a way to mask gaps in timing and create unique sounds. My responses to these timing challenges strongly shaped my interpretation in the associated parts of the work and changed my subjective relation to the Disklavier part from submissive to assertive.

In other parts of the work, in which the Disklavier was not playing, I chose to make my playing overtly rubato so as to claim my own musical space and identity. After all, the full score of *Climb!* could be performed solely by the Disklavier; the result would be similar but more accurate. It can feel intimidating to perform on and with an instrument whose mechanics enable it to reach far greater technical aptitude than one can oneself. For me this was an invitation to exploit the "human" parts of my playing, such as tempo rubato and dynamic fluidity.

The impact of the system set-up on my subjective experience

I had the advantage of knowing where the Muzicodes were embedded in the score, and this enabled me to navigate through the system to construct the narrative of the piece in the manner that I desired. In some ways, I perceived this as a modern-day extension of alternative endings in repeated sections in classical forms, where playing the first option works, like the Muzicode, to repeat the section, while playing the second allows one to move ahead in the structure.

However, was this an advantage? Having access to the system meant that my initial interpretation was clouded by the obsession to play in time and "master" the machine. Listening to the machine playing the duo part from an early stage meant that I spent barely any time considering how the other part *could* sound. I excluded from the interpretative process all considerations about the musical characteristics I would like to hear, could interact with, or might expect from my duo partner; I regarded these as being served to me as objective parts of the music. Consequently, any and all expressivity had to come from my own playing and how it related to the Disklavier part: I could choose to play in a robotic manner to mimic and blend with the Disklavier, or I could play with overt expressivity so as to contrast with the Disklavier. But whatever the stylistic choice, the Disklavier part remained an objective structure in the music that was only ornamented by my expressivity.

In *Climb!*, both pianist and computer share the Disklavier, and this in itself created a game-like interaction between performer and machine. To experience keys that you are about to play literally slipping away from under your fingers is unique to this type of interaction, and such occurrences can play a large role in how one approaches a work. This interaction occurred in a number of places in *Climb!*, but most prominently in "The Stones (part 1b)." The movement is largely built on a series of eighth notes during which the pianist and Disklavier both cycle through the same notes but with different rhythms. Between the parts, overlapping notes are required to render the written score. If played without care, too many notes may end up not sounding, and the phrases will consequently be deformed (see figure 4.8). To combat this, the pianist may opt to play as staccato as possible, thereby increasing the chance that the Disklavier will sound its pitches. This appears to be a technical solution to the problem, but it results in a very appropriate musical interpretation in which the short notes, flooded by the sostenuto pedal, represent the score's suggested imagery of "small stones falling down the path."

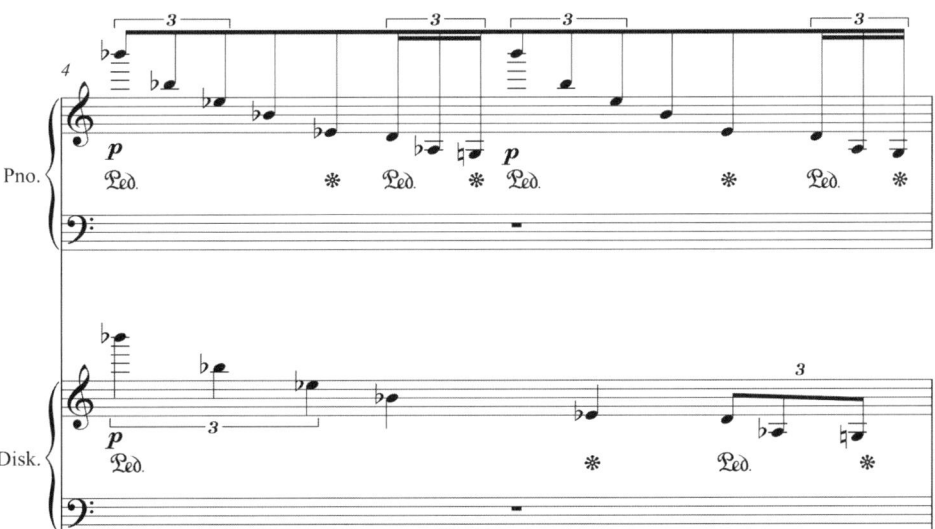

Figure 4.8.

Another aspect of the system design that shaped my interpretation was the rigidity of the Disklavier entrances. A Disklavier file would be triggered after a predetermined time interval following the completion of the associated Disklavier Muzicode. This time interval was set by the creators and did not follow the performer's tempo or the intervening notes. To accommodate timing discrepancies, fermatas were often written on the last note or rest of the pianist's part before the Disklavier entered, but this was not always the case.

As seen in figure 4.9, in "A Sleeping Bear (4a)," a fermata is placed on the first note of the Disklavier part and on the rest at the end of the piano's opening phrase. The Disklavier realised this fermata as a six-second gap between the opening notes and the Disklavier chord, which I felt was a disproportionately long pause given the suggested tempo marking. This created, for me, an undesirable gap or moment of waiting before the Disklavier starts. My artistic solution was to play the phrase rather slowly and with great rubato so that the piano notes would connect to the low cluster that marks the Disklavier entrance. As in "The Stones (1b)," I felt this musical approach helped portray how one might approach a sleeping bear—stepping with caution in speed and volume.

95

Figure 4.8. Bar 4 of "The Stones (1b)."

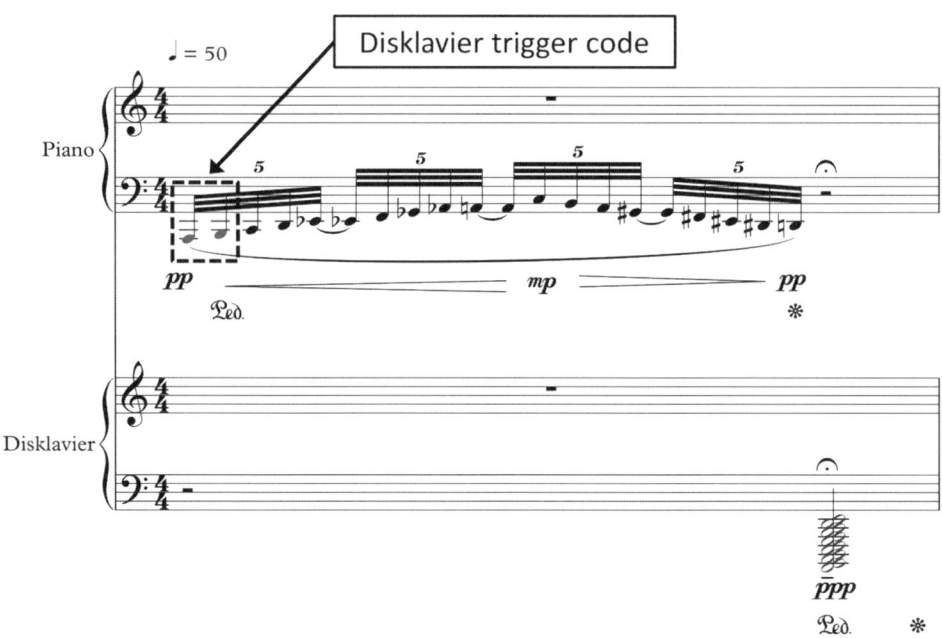

Figure 4.9.

Score indeterminacy: when choosing a path is transformed into interpretation

In contrast to my preparations, which were concerned with covering the full scope of the work and executing every section and Muzicode as accurately as possible, I performed *Climb!* with the intention to change path (i.e., to fail the challenges) as frequently as possible, since this would enable me to perform a wide cross-section of the music. Because the composition was specifically designed so that all paths made musical sense, I was freed from the responsibility to choose a musical path with logical consequences and enabled to simply move between events in any way that the system allowed. This approach came partly from my desire to perform as much of the work as possible and partly from the rare opportunity of receiving an invitation to play wrong notes. However, even when choosing not to execute the Muzicode correctly, I still wanted to keep the intention of the phrase intact; this was most easily done by following the general musical shape of the Muzicode but altering a single note in the sequence.

An unexpected challenge: reflections on the performance

Performances rarely go exactly as planned, and my performance of *Climb!* was not without its surprises. Due to an unexpected technical issue, from as early as the third event in my performance the Disklavier files began to play back at

96

Figure 4.9. Bar 1 of "A Sleeping Bear (4a)."

a slower and more irregular tempo. This created a mild performance "panic" for me: should I should stop the performance and allow the technical team to reboot the system, or should I continue playing and do my best to accommodate the newly varied Disklavier parts? I chose the latter for several reasons:

(1) No one else, including the technical team and composer, seemed to be bothered by the Disklavier issues, and no one initiated a reboot.

(2) I always prefer to "go on with the show" whenever possible.

(3) I would not stop and restart a performance if my human partner unexpectedly played slower or irregularly, so what justification was there for doing that with a computer?

(4) Considering how much of the "game" of *Climb!* had been revealed to me in preparation for the concert, I found it fitting, albeit by chance, that an unrehearsed component would be introduced to me during the performance as if unlocking an extra gaming level.

The irregularities of the Disklavier playbacks presented themselves most evidently in the passages that were most dense, but it took me some time to orient myself and work this out. Only after performing "Path 1b," with its streams of passages in thirty-second notes, in which I finished my part substantially ahead of the Disklavier, was I sure something was wrong. Thereafter, I aimed to climb the path to the summit as directly as possible, which was directly contrary to my initial intention of meandering through *Climb!* for as long as possible. Along the way, I had to adjust to the new, unexpected tempi in the Disklavier part, anticipating them whenever possible.

6. Performers' discussion

The machine as an amalgam of subjectivities

In *Climb!*, the interactivity between human and machine hides a multitude of subjective experiences of the work that enter into play in every performance. The widely varying perspectives, motives, and desired outcomes of the composer and three technologists are integrated into a single voice by performers of the work. Kallionpää is concerned about the many possible pathways through her structures, the range of textures and sounds from the piano, and the combined orchestration of her music created by the real and virtual performers. Meanwhile, the programmers are interested in the application and activation of the challenge codes and the smooth functioning of all the affected systems, from the audience app to the selection of pathways. None of these creators of the work/system are fully aware of the precise function of every component, due as much to the specialised expertise at play as to the distribution of creative roles. But although performers of the work may be aware of these different functions, specialisations, and roles—as well as the many varied intentions that infuse the work—their perceptions are informed only by the output of the Disklavier and the choice of movements in the score.

Do performers experience this amalgam of subjective inputs as a single voice? The case study suggests that, although this is the intention of the creators, the result is more complicated and that the tensions between the competing priorities of the contributors remain present in the final, realised work. Both performers approached the score and the performance as a single work that was coherent in its aims, aesthetic, and technological means. Both also describe performing with the Disklavier part as similar in some ways to performing with another pianist, and both indicate that there is a close relationship between their preparation of *Climb!* and their preparation for two-piano performances. However, both pianists noted tensions inherent in the score and Disklavier part; they also noted tensions between the intentions of the original creators and the decisions the performers took.

The specifics of the MELD notation system, particularly the use of colour and highlighting as codes are played, are clearly programming choices; yet, for Veinberg, they changed her perception of the codes and her preparation for the piece. Veinberg also experienced unpredictability in the machine, uncorrected by the programmers running it, when the Disklavier started to vary in tempo in performance. In this case, the composer's and performer's control and perspective were both thrown off balance by the actions of a machine that was intended to be merely an instrument of their intentions. Kanga experienced different tensions: in the unpredictable audio effects derived from the weather (again the product of the programmers), which seemed to be better regulated in some movements than in others. He also observed that the programmers and the composer had somewhat different aesthetic aims, with the dynamic and dramatic sonic language not necessarily matched with the more static, abstract mountain imagery. Most fundamentally, both pianists realised the sound and playing style of the Disklavier was often more mechanistic and inexpressive than the composer intended, creating substantial differences between their own playing and the Disklavier's performance of the same material, which might have been expected to be indistinguishable. Thus, even though both performers experienced the machine as an amalgam created by multiple authors, these authors' different priorities and the limits of the technology itself meant that the amalgam was far from uniform.

The performers' agency: taming or breaking the machine?

In discussing the subjective experience of the performers, they may seem at times to be passive subjects, responding and reacting to the challenges imposed. But in both cases, they were active interpreters, analysing, challenging, and even subverting these challenges.

Veinberg practised with the system enough to be able to decide when she wanted to activate a code and when she wanted to fail, effectively mapping out her path in a way that resisted the intended mobility of the structure. When the performer chooses when to fail, the system that detects failure becomes the servant of the performer rather than the master. In performance, Veinberg's mastery was confounded by the system's malfunctions (perhaps the computer's own resistance to such insubordination), but Veinberg nevertheless revealed a performer's ability to challenge the system. Kanga tamed the system by constantly varying his approach to the material, changing pedalling, articulation, dynamics, and rubato to accentuate the differences between his own playing and the machine's. This displayed in sharp relief the difference between the machine, which could only continue in a static and fixed performance mode, and a chamber musician, who could respond to these provocations and variations. Moreover, rather than allowing his tempi to be controlled by the machine, Kanga sometimes varied them widely, only linking up again with the machine at the key cue points.

In neither case was the machine broken, and it retained overall control over the sound effects and visuals and over the performance, from choosing movements to playing half the musical materials. But the control structures put in place by the composer and programmers were actively resisted, provoked, and bent by performers unwilling to merely be subjects of their creator's experiments.

7. An audience perspective

The different subjectivities in *Climb!* extend beyond performers' different experiences of playing the work to include how audiences encounter it. To some degree, all musical performances are experienced subjectively according to the performer, occasion, venue, audience, and personal characteristics of listeners, from their prior experiences to their current moods; but the *overtly* subjective structure of *Climb!*, in which performers choose different routes through the piece, opens up new opportunities and challenges for listeners. Crucially, listeners might recognise that each single performance is likely to provide only a partial experience of the piece (though each is complete and coherent in itself), because each takes only one of many possible paths through the work and includes only a subset of its component parts. This naturally invites direct comparisons with other performances that may have taken quite different paths.

These observations led us to design two different visual interfaces to accompany performances of *Climb!*, each intended to fulfil a distinct purpose (Benford et al. 2018). The first, shown in figure 4.10, was a backdrop projected during the performance. We designed this to be broadly impressionistic rather than overtly didactic, intended to enhance the experience of the music and provide some clues about how it was unfolding but not to supply direct explanations. The animated visuals responded to the triggering of Muzicodes and thus followed the structure of the work (the mountain animations changed with each new part, the mountain sides animated when the Disklavier was active, and the image flashed red whenever a Muzicode was triggered), but there was little explicit information about paths chosen, the names of parts, or previous performances.

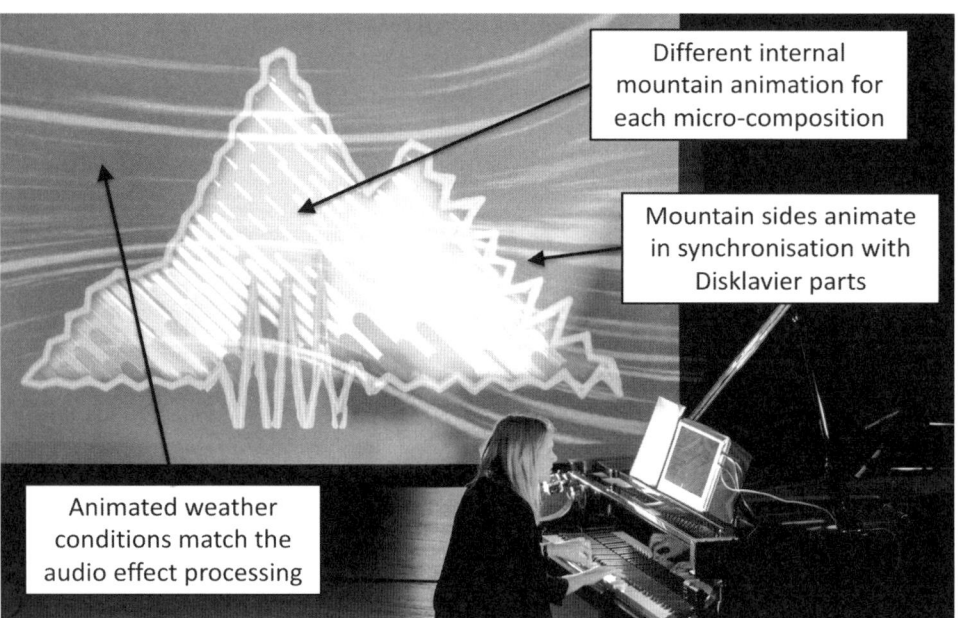

Different internal
mountain animation for
each micro-composition

Mountain sides animate
in synchronisation with
Disklavier parts

Animated weather
conditions match the
audio effect processing

Figure 4.10.

In contrast, a second interface designed for audience members' mobile devices (figure 4.11) was far more didactic in nature, allowing the viewer to follow the path through the current performance, see the names of the various parts, access more detailed programme notes, and directly compare the current path to ones taken in previous performances. Audience members would follow their own interests, voluntarily and subjectively, in choosing whether and how to use this supplementary mobile interface. *Climb!*, then, provided two visual interfaces that directly distinguished between objective and subjective information provided to members of the audience during a live performance.

The audience completed a paper questionnaire immediately after each performance by Veinberg and Kanga.[6] From a total audience of just over fifty people, twenty-four returned completed questionnaires. Overall, the responses were similar to those from the premiere performance by Kallionpää, which are summarised in Benford et al. (2018). For example, in general, the audience enjoyed both performances (the median response was "agree"). Audience members' self-reported knowledge of music and of technology were generally "good," but with individual variations from "very poor" to "excellent." For analysis of the audience's perceptions of duetting with the Disklavier, the differences between Veinberg and Kanga's performances, and *Climb!* as a whole, we drew primarily on the open responses to the questionnaire.

6 Anonymous questionnaire data underlying this paper can be obtained from http://dx.doi.org/10.17639/nott.341. The *Climb!* performance archive is accessible at http://music-mrl.nott.ac.uk/1/archive/explore/Climb (8th Jan. 2018).

100

Figure 4.10. A backdrop projected during *Climb!* provided impressionistic information about the performance.

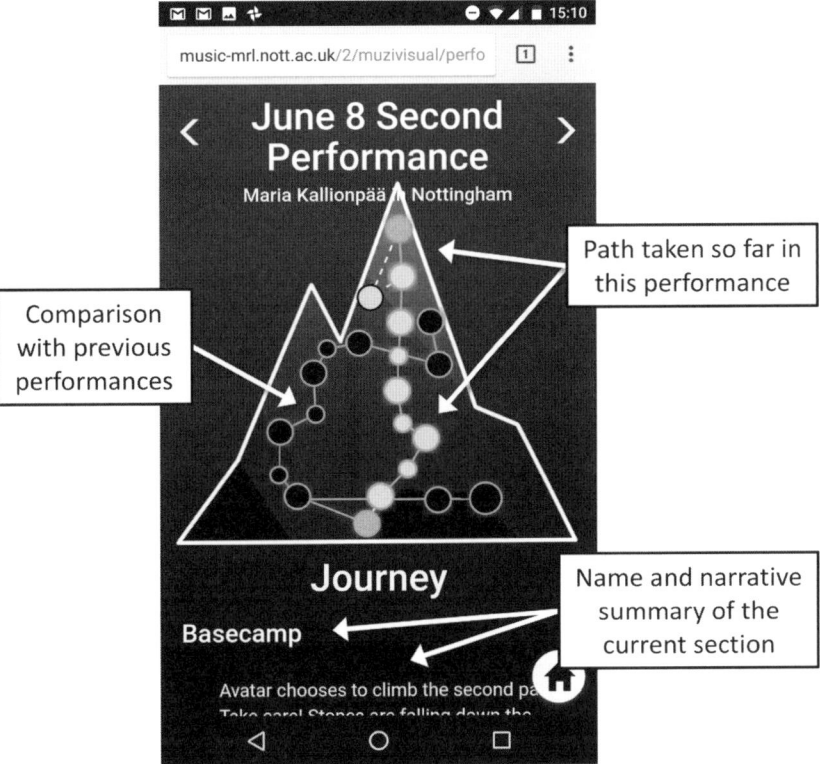

Figure 4.11.

In both performances the audience felt that the performer was exercising at least some control over the system while responding to it. The evidence most commonly cited by the audience was the existence of call-and-response passages between the pianist and the Disklavier. Only one audience member commented on the kind of fine-grained timing and coordination issues of playing with the Disklavier that occupied both performers during rehearsal, noting the "delays in the musical parts" during Kanga's performance. Otherwise, the joint character of the performance seemed essentially unproblematic, either because these issues were satisfactorily resolved in rehearsal or because that level of coordination was hard to perceive without a very detailed knowledge of the piece.

Comparing the two performances, a small number of audience members (who did not normally listen to contemporary music) heard *no* notable differences at all. But in most cases the audience were sensitive to differences in Veinberg and Kanga's performance style and/or to the different routes taken through the piece in each performance. Apart from the different paths taken, the most commonly identified differences were in tempo (of the movements without Disklavier accompaniment, including "Base Camp") and the lengths

101

Figure 4.11. The *Climb!* mobile interface provided more didactic and subjective information.

of pauses between movements, although non-specific differences in "style" were also quite widely noted. One audience member (who reported composing similar music) felt that Veinberg's performance conveyed greater confidence, while Kanga's performance conveyed a greater sense of "danger." Two audience members commented on differences between the paper and digital score, one feeling that the digital score seemed to "work a little better," and another observing that Veinberg seemed to follow the digital score more than Kanga followed the paper score.

The concept of the piece, overall, was apparently appreciated by the audience, and a sense of game and challenge was generally attributed to both performances: "[Veinberg] seemed to be genuinely challenged throughout the game as games should do"; "[Kanga's] gestures really helped me see how hard it was to overcome the challenges." Quite a few audience members reported that learning more about the work and the system in the short talk between the performances or from the mobile app enhanced their enjoyment and appreciation of the piece. The app, in particular, helped many understand the overall progression of the piece; and, from system records of app use, we know that at least twelve phones displayed the app throughout both performances. But fine details of the interaction—such as the precise mechanics of the challenge codes—were not visible to the audience; one remarked, "I tried to figure out how the piano was responding . . . but I couldn't," and several others expressed uncertainty about how the challenges worked.

Finally, even after hearing two performances back-to-back, many audience members reported that they were overwhelmingly inclined to find out more about *Climb!*, go to other performances, or hear recordings of this and other performances.

CONCLUSIONS

By describing *Climb!* from the perspective of the two performers' experiences, with attention to how these related to the expectations of the composer and technical team, we can see how knowledge of an interactive system has a fundamental impact both on a performer's perception of the interactions and on each performer's subsequent preparation and interpretation.

Manipulating the subjective experience of the performer

The double performance of *Climb!* was organised not only to showcase the work and its mobile structure but also to determine whether the composer and system developers could manipulate the performers' subjective experiences of the work and its system. The differing information provided to the performers, particularly regarding the location of challenge codes and their activation, resulted in very different experiences of the work, even though both performers had a good understanding of the system. Veinberg perceived the *Climb!* system to be "reactive," responding to her prepared decisions, whereas for Kanga it was "interactive" but not easily understood: the system sometimes responded as expected and sometimes not, because his expectations were based on guesswork rather than the reliable feedback that Veinberg received from the tablet score. Indeed, before the performance the performers and the composer discussed extensively just what type of "game" *Climb!* is. Veinberg considered it more like role-playing, with choices determining the path one takes; Kanga, in contrast, viewed it more like a game of chance, where control is so minimal as to be irrelevant (Kanga compared the work to the board game Snakes and Ladders). Clearly, even small changes in the information received by performers can affect their entire conceptions and experiences of this work.

Different attitudes to control

The different information and materials provided to the two performers resulted in two contrasting approaches to control: Kanga relinquished control, while Veinberg asserted it. In preparing the performance, Veinberg acquired a detailed understanding of the location and form of the challenge codes as well as access to the interactive computer system. As a result, she became particularly intimate with the scored work and, more importantly, the finer details of her interactions with the system. This explicit knowledge allowed her to infer that she should be able to assert control over all aspects of the work and even to consider herself a "tester" of the system. Her preparations reveal that she believed herself to be in control of the form, the structure, and the forging of trajectories through the set of branching movements, but less in control of duetting with the Disklavier. Kanga, on the other hand, did not know the form or location of the challenge codes and therefore did not believe he had the capacity to control the outcome of the performance's trajectory. Consequently, he chose to embrace the risks inherent in the performance. Overall, in two quite extreme ways, the two approaches confirmed a broader hypothesis: a performer with knowledge of the codes would rehearse them in an attempt to gain control over them, while a performer without that knowledge would simply accept the indeterminate nature of the work.

Forcing interpretation and finding a voice, despite a stubborn partner

Both pianists' approach to forging a personal interpretation of *Climb!* entailed, in part, a desire and the subsequent attempt to distinguish themselves from their mechanical duetting partner, the self-playing Disklavier. In seeking to carve out expressive voices for themselves they differentiated their playing from the strictness and consistency of the Disklavier, albeit in very different ways, using different types of rubato and variation in dynamics and articulation. Both noted the difficulties in timing sections in which the Disklavier was absent, and both addressed these partly through rehearsal but partly also by applying interpretive techniques that blurred or masked timing discrepancies. Veinberg, for instance, used dynamics to create a shadowing effect, while Kanga employed rubato to shift attention to the horizontal rather than vertical aspects of the music.

Although both players noted some similarities to playing chamber music, they stressed the differences: an invisible second performer, the rigidity of the Disklavier's playing, and the absence of cues for phrases or notes, conventionally provided by breathing together or eye contact. As a result, unless they relied on their memories of the timing, with varying success, both performers could only react to the Disklavier cues shortly after hearing them.

Accepting and embracing failure

Both performers' sense of control (although individually different) resulted in an assumption that "failure" would be a primary element of the work—an unusual scenario for a musical performance. Failure in performance took two forms. The first followed from the difficulty, noted above, of duetting with the Disklavier. Playing in synchronism with the Disklavier, while simultaneously playing with a natural flexibility and responding to the Disklavier's sometimes unpredictable fluctuations in tempo, created risks in each movement. Although Kallionpää accepted failures of this kind as "in-built" in the piece, both pianists wanted to minimise the perceivable "mistakes," such as playing noticeably out of time with the Disklavier or, worse yet, losing one's place. The second, more interesting aspect of failure concerned the challenge codes and ways these shaped a performer's trajectory through a given performance. Veinberg, in effect, converted these codes from challenges that might result in failure into conscious choices, so that deliberate failure became a viable option to realise a desired route to the summit. In contrast, Kanga had no way of perceiving success or failure in the codes, which were invisible to him.

Differences in performance as a result of differing subjective experiences of a work

It was notable that, although Veinberg and Kanga felt their two performances were distinctive and different because of their alternative approaches, only broad differences in "style" were perceived by the audience. Quite possibly this indicates a lack of expertise among the listeners: the pianists were both attuned to more subtle differences in approach and performance than was the lay audience. In fact, the two performances are clearly quite distinct in retrospective encounters with the concert recordings. Then, too, it seems doubtful that an audience could recognise differences in approach in those passages in which Veinberg was making conscious decisions while Kanga remained oblivious of the implications. Such lack of expertise is probably not specific to this work: performers are often concerned with factors that, in performance, are not perceptible to the audience (particularly when the work is altogether new), even if these factors are instrumental in shaping the performers' approach or interpretation.

Both performers appreciated and enjoyed the other's performances, while observing differences more subtly than the audience did. Kanga noted the rigour and precision with which Veinberg both played with the Disklavier and determined how to approach each challenge code, while Veinberg noted Kanga's looser approach to playing with the Disklavier, as well as his dramatic shifts in dynamics, tempo, and colour. But, very importantly, both pianists felt that, even after seeing the other perform, their own approach would remain unchanged; each preferred to remain in the position of knowledge or ignorance that had been imposed for this performance.

Final thoughts

This case study has many wider implications for the study of the subjective experience of performers. It is rare to be able to compare two pianists performing the same work back-to-back, and we observed, on the one hand, similarities in the challenges intrinsic in both players' preparation and performance (for instance, in matters of timing) and, on the other, approaches and solutions that were clearly distinct.

One question, in particular, remains open: should future performers be made aware of the challenge codes (as Veinberg was), or should the codes be withheld from them (as was the case with Kanga)? Our observations show that neither approach "broke" the work for either the performers or the audience; rather, both renditions were considered "successful" and the players were admired for their interpretations. It appears, in this case, that intimate knowledge of an interactive system is not necessarily desirable. Indeed, the composer and technology team can censor the details to manipulate a performer's perception of the work. And yet, the performers can—and often do—resist the creators' attempts at control, finding novel ways of exerting their creative authority even when they do not fully understand the inner workings of the system.

This case study has wider implications for all works that explore interactions between live performers and systems that are in some sense responsive. Although interactive systems can model some of the interactions between human partners in chamber music, they inevitably fail to replicate those interactions. In this case, the system both succeeded and failed to conform to the performers' expectations, but the successes and failures were subjectively experienced in entirely different ways by the two performers. It might seem obvious that most computer systems cannot come close to true performing simulacra, but working with these types of systems naturally anthropomorphises them, and perceptions of success and failure are inevitably related to experiences with live chamber musicians. However, perhaps the perception that some aspects of the Disklavier part are comparable to human players is exciting in itself. Indeed, George Lewis, looking back at his landmark *Voyager* system, wrote that the system was not "asking whether machines exhibit personality or identity, but how personalities and identities become articulated through sonic behaviour" (Lewis 2000, 30). Perhaps the model of chamber music should not always be seen as the ideal, and we should also consider person–machine interaction as a new form of collaborative music-making, in which different degrees of technological acceptance or resistance can create entirely new experiences for performers and audiences alike.

ACKNOWLEDGEMENTS

This work was supported by the United Kingdom Engineering and Physical Sciences Research Council (grant numbers EP/L019981/1 and EP/M000877/1), the Kone Foundation, the Leverhulme Trust, and the University of Nottingham's Research Priority Area funding scheme.

REFERENCES

Benford, Steve, Chris Greenhalgh, Adrian Hazzard, Alan Chamberlain, Maria Kallionpää, David M. Weigl, Kevin R. Page, and Mengdie Lin. 2018. "Designing the Audience Journey through Repeated Experiences." In *CHI'18: Proceedings of the 2018 CHI Conference on Human Factors in Computing Systems*. https://doi.org/10.1145/3173574.3174142. Conference held 21–26 April 2018, Montreal.

Chadabe, Joel. 1996. "The History of Electronic Music as a Reflection of Structural Paradigms." *Leonardo Music Journal* 6: 41–44.

Clarke, Eric, Nicholas Cook, Bryn Harrison, and Philip Thomas. "Interpretation and Performance in Bryn Harrison's *être-temps*." *Musicae Scientiae* 9 (1): 31–74.

Gorton, David, and Zubin Kanga. 2016. "Risky Business: Negotiating Virtuosity in the Collaborative Creation of *Orfordness* for Solo Piano." In *Music and/as Process*, edited by Lauren Redhead and Vanessa Hawes, 97–115. Newcastle upon Tyne: Cambridge Scholars Publishing.

Gorton, David, and Stefan Östersjö. 2016. "Choose Your Own Adventure Music: On the Emergence of Voice in Musical Collaboration." *Contemporary Music Review* 35 (6): 579–98.

Greenhalgh, Chris, Steve Benford, and Adrian Hazzard. 2016. "^muzicode$: Composing and Performing Musical Codes." In *AM '16: Proceedings of Audio Mostly 2016*, 47–54. New York: Association for Computing Machinery. Conference held 4–6 Oct 2016, Norrköping, Sweden.

Greenhalgh, Chris, Steve Benford, Adrian Hazzard, and Alan Chamberlain. 2017. "Playing Fast and Loose with Music Recognition." In *CHI'17: Proceedings of the 2017 ACM SIGCHI Conference on Human Factors in Computing Systems*, 4302–13. New York: Association for Computing

Machinery. Conference held 6–11 May 2017, Denver, CO.

Kallionpää, Maria. 2014. "Beyond the Piano: The Super Instrument; Widening the Instrumental Capacities in the Context of the Piano Music of the 21st Century." PhD thesis, University of Oxford.

Kallionpää, Maria, and Hans-Peter Gasselseder. 2016. "The Imaginary Friend: Crossing Over Computer Game Scoring Techniques and Musical Expression." In *EVA London 2016: Electronic Visualisation and the Arts*, edited by Jonathan P. Bowen, Graham Diprose, and Nick Lambert, 42–48. Swindon, UK: BCS Learning and Development.

Kallionpää, Maria, Chris Greenhalgh, Adrian Hazzard, David M. Weigl, Kevin R. Page, and Steve Benford. 2017. "Composing and Realising a Game-Like Performance for Disklavier and Electronics." In *NIME 2017: Proceedings of the International Conference on New Interfaces for Musical Expression*, 464–69. Conference held 15–18 May 2017, Copenhagen, Denmark.

Leman, Marc. 2010. "Music Gesture, and the Formation of Embodied Meaning." In *Musical Gestures: Sound, Movement, and Meaning*, edited by Rolf Inge Godøy and Marc Leman, 126–49. New York: Routledge.

Lewis, George E. 2000. "Two Many Notes: Complexity and Culture in *Voyager*." *Leonardo Music Journal* 10: 33–39.

McNutt, Elizabeth. 2003. "Performing Electroacoustic Music: A Wider View of Interactivity." *Organised Sound* 8 (3): 297–304.

Orio, Nicola, Serge Lemouton, and Diemo Schwarz. 2003. "Score Following: State of the Art and New Developments." In *NIME '03: Proceedings of the 2003 Conference on New Interfaces for Musical Expression*, edited by François Thibault, 36–41.

Montreal: McGill University, Faculty of Music.

Puckette, Miller, and Cort Lippe. 1992. "Score Following in Practice." In *Proceedings of the 1992 International Computer Music Conference*, 182–85. San Francisco, CA: International Computer Music Association.

Shaffer, L. H. 1984. "Timing in Solo and Duet Piano Performances." *Quarterly Journal of Experimental Psychology Section A* 36 (4): 577–95.

Veinberg, Anne. 2013. "Ostinato" from *Duet for Live Coder and Pianist*. live.code.festival 2013, Hochschule fuer Music Karlsruhe. Track 11, MP3 audio podcast, https:// itunes.apple.com/us/itunes-u/live.code.

festival-2013-hd/id821590153?mt=10.

———. 2014. *Zwei Improvisaties für Laptop und Disklavier*. Studiokonzert 2014—III, Hochschule fuer Music Karlsruhe, unreleased live recording.

Weigl, David M., Steve Benford, Chris Greenhalgh, Adrian Hazzard, Maria Kallionpää, and Kevin R. Page. 2018. "Encoding of a Dynamic Composition and Its Performance." Paper presented at 2018 Music Encoding Conference, 23–25 May 2018, University of Maryland.

Williamon, Aaron, and Jane W. Davidson. 2002. "Exploring Co-performer Communication." *Musicae Scientiae* 6 (1): 53–72.

"by way of the BREATH, to the LINE"[1]

Richard Craig

Independent researcher, Glasgow

INTRODUCTION

> Craig brought the concert and this year's festival to an end with Kristian Ireland's *luminous* for amplified alto flute. Over the course of its half-hour duration, I almost wondered whether my heart was going to come to a stop. Articulated with a Feldman-like single-minded patience, it unfolds from extremely quiet pitches emanating via ex- and inhalations, resulting in softly-clashing dyads (out) followed by infinitesimal whispers (in). It was as though Craig were putting down individual aural breadcrumbs to be discovered—or, to switch analogies, like reciting a story or poem one halting word (or even syllable) at a time. Later on, Ireland allows the material to become more extended, which in such a small-scale environment as this (another fitting analogy: as though everything had been shrunken down to microscopic size), such minor extensions felt like major elaborations, almost rudely exuberant despite their unwavering fastidiousness. (Cummings 2017)

The extract above is from the new music blog *5:4* responding to my performance of Kristian Ireland's *luminous* for solo alto flute at the 2017 Alba Music Festival, Edinburgh, Scotland. This work proposes several challenges to an instrumentalist: its duration is circa twenty-eight minutes in length without pause; the piece integrates new breathing techniques to replace standardised approaches to breathing and breath control; and the flute is treated harmonically, rather than as a melodic instrument (figure 5.1 illustrates these points[2]). In this chapter I draw elements of my technical practice with *luminous* into a broader domain, using my engagement with the composition as a performer to outline new methods of approaching performance practices and their annotation.

---

1 An extract from Charles Olsen's poetry pamphlet *Projective Verse* ([1950] 2019).
2 Two extracts of these performances can be accessed at https://soundcloud.com/richard-craig/kristian-ireland-luminous-2012-14 and https://soundcloud.com/richard-craig/kristian-ireland-luminous-extract-2-2012-2014.

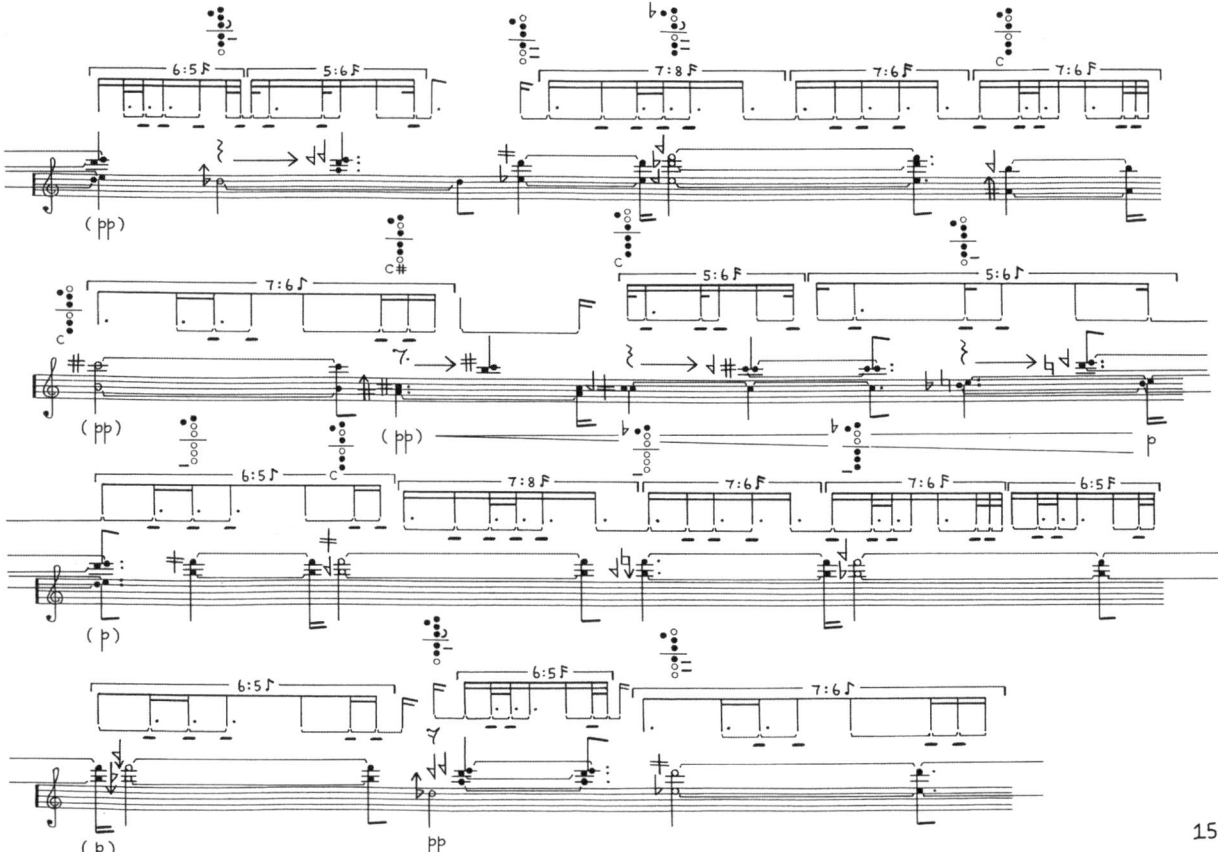

Figure 5.1.

15

This chapter is initially modelled as a set of accompanying notes to *luminous* in lieu of the performance instructions that typically accompany contemporary scores. The writing is in two parts: the first section is conceived principally to address issues of musicianship and the technique I call *ingressive breathing*. I describe the mechanics of this technique, and the way in which it influences the work and the performance practice. Leading from this technical explanation, I then discuss how I conceived the musical structure in my performances and developed an approach to tempo within the work, using this new technique as a parameter. With these technical considerations in place, the second part of the chapter addresses the lack of expressive markings and interpretative approaches in *luminous*, through a musical thematisation of two of the main themes of the piece: the breath and the use of multiphonics. In this second part, I propose a thematisation of *luminous* that incorporates the philosopher Havi Carel's work on the "lived-experience" of illness, prioritising the "pre-reflective, subjective human experience" (2016, 2). This approach is tied to my use of the *ingressive* performance technique, and places the musical material that Ireland uses (namely multiphonics) as a source of physical feedback for my analysis. The latter part of this paper also identifies the technical aspects of the performance as a source of ontological understanding for the performer. In doing so I turn to creating aspects of verisimilitude in my writing (Denzin 2013, 70) and to "resistance" as a mode of performance and practice (Coessens and Östersjö 2014). Ultimately, my work leads to a reconsideration of established concepts of performance and instrumental mastery from an autoethnographical standpoint.

It is important briefly to note why performer notes to *luminous* are required. To date, I am the only musician to perform *luminous*, and the score is not available to other instrumentalists as the performing rights of the composition are limited to myself (as per Ireland's wishes[3]). Furthermore, *luminous* was a performer-led project: I suggested to Kristian that a new piece for solo flute that tackled long-form structures would now be possible. My new technique provided a bridge to challenge the technical limitations of the instrument. In particular, I was interested in developing the flute as a harmonic instrument, in harnessing the potential to sustain more than one pitch (via multiphonics), and in exploring how the breath could be instrumentalised in the harmonic framework of a new piece. Through the integration of my *ingressive* breathing technique, it became possible for these challenges to be engaged with in practice, opening up observations about performance and performance writing.

1. Kristian Ireland's *luminous*

The ingressive playing technique

The composer's programme note to the piece includes the following:

> The modes of playing in the work are distinctly part of Craig's technical approach to the instrument: alternating ingressive and egressive resonance (sound via inhalation/exhalation), and microtonal multiphonics with flexible voicings. In *luminous*, the natural aspects of these materials are allowed to sound and expand as wholly as possible. In sequence, they connect closely and form longer resonant threads. . . . The ingressive/egressive sound and multiphonic voices are extensions of the breathing process.
>
> The form (approximating the Golden Section) and time scale of the work are intentionally expansive. The first 13 minutes, or so, rather than imagined as real time, suggest a moment that is stretched out and prolonged, as an impression or as a loop in the memory. (Ireland 2012–14)

---

3   Until this point, there has not been an explicit need to annotate the score with performance details as the performances since 2014 have been regarded as a process to collect the most relevant information for the work's performance and final score. A finalised version of the work is in preparation.

Many scores encountered by contemporary musicians involve a particular visual intricacy in how the information is codified. This symbolic dimension of the contemporary score, or the *exoteric* representation of music, often draws the musician into a provocative discourse (perhaps even a form of dialectic) when encountering the composition. However, the score of *luminous* is a very different proposal: in the work's first instantiation (as in, through the first encounter with the score) it seems a relatively conventional piece. What becomes clear in my exposition, however, is that *luminous* is an instrumental composition that looks not to the exoteric, or the typical myriad of symbols we often see in scores, but in fact relies upon a more *esoteric* framework. In using "esoteric" as a descriptor here, I am evoking the necessary internalisation, or introspective vigilance, of bodily experiences on the performer's part to give an additional layer of detailing to *luminous*.[4] As such, the information required to perform *luminous* is bound up with the performer's bodily experience and also a particularly body-bound expression that cannot be exemplified in the score or notation.

The technique of *ingressive* breathing sonifies the inhalation of air through the flute, to produce a multiphonic chord. When performed in combination with standard tone production this creates the impression of a continuous sound, similar to that of a violin bow, as opposed to circular breathing.[5] In the score extract given in figure 5.2, the movement of air is shown through the arrows: arrows to the right show exhalation of air, arrows to the left inhalation. Ireland also focuses his attention on the harmonic material through "microtonal multiphonics," and these are also a particular characteristic of the *ingressive* playing technique—the inbreath in this case can be adapted to perform two notes simultaneously. To give an example as to how this new technique compares with the conventional playing method, here is a shorthand explanation from my own notes as to how my *ingressive* technique functions:

> In normal production, the sound of the flute is created by focussing a stream of air across the lip plate, which then strikes the edge of the embouchure hole. When the air meets the edge of the embouchure hole, it is diverted into the flute, thus causing the body of the instrument to resonate according to the fingerings we use. Conversely, my new method draws air back across the flute, into the embouchure, bypassing the body of the instrument as the resonator, and instead using the cavity of the mouth to calibrate the exact pitch. In this case the sound is produced in the mouth, and with the help of a multiphonic fingering. (Personal diary, 2014)

For a wind player, *ingressive* breathing is a counterintuitive approach to making sound: not only does it depart from the standard instrumental tone (where the outbreath and *only* the outbreath engages the instrument), but also the inbreath (typically redundant in musical terms) is heard as a pitched instru-

---

4 My example of exoteric and esoteric was informed by Dixon's "Composition and Adorno's Rhetoric of the New" (2013).
5 The analogy of the violin bow being mapped onto the ingressive technique was a prevalent aspect of my thinking during my experimentation with this technique. As a musical gesture, the analogy of the bow has a much closer link to the origins of the technique than circular (or continuous) breathing.

mental sound and notated as such. In this way, our understanding of the flute as an instrument also undergoes a change. The flute now acts as a filter for the sound: the air passes over the headjoint, into the mouth, and the span of pitches we hear are in fact produced and controlled by the vowel shape in the mouth, not the instrument. In this way the ingressive technique colours the previously transparent action of the inbreath and amplifies aspects of breathing that are typically an intimate aspect of a performance. The technique is used for two-thirds of *luminous* and brings the breath, and its own particular temporal qualities, into a new focus. Instrumentalising the breath in this way places breathing at the forefront of the composition and by association suggests a particular temporal framework for the piece. Furthermore, breathing is often discreetly managed by the performer, but now is placed under particular scrutiny as the rhythmical and harmonic nexus of the piece; I will address this detail of sound production later.

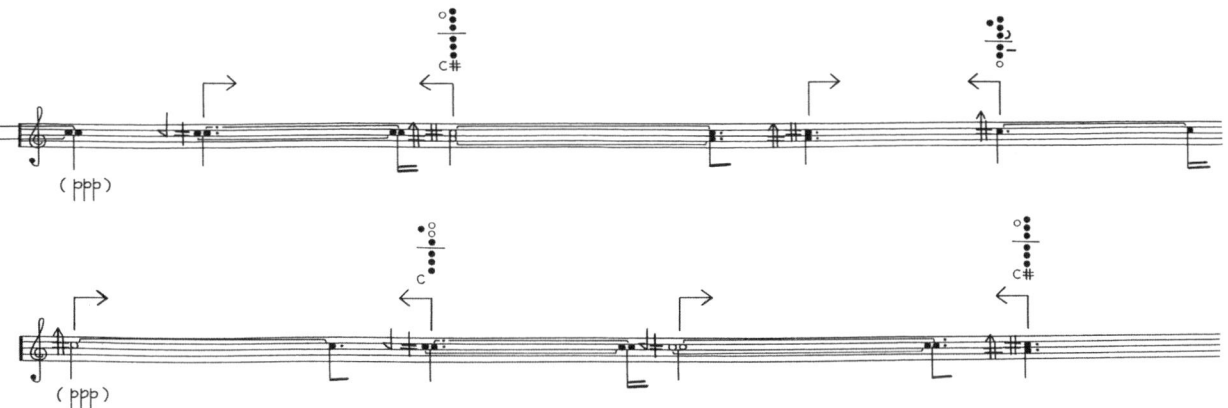

Figure 5.2.

While unusual, *luminous* is not the only work to use breath as a compositional tool or material. Other works in the twentieth century have taken breath as an extra-musical or dramatic device. Heinz Holliger's *Cardiophonie* for solo woodwind performer, for example, uses extreme technical virtuosity, bordering on improvisation, and induces accelerated breathing patterns, thus increasing the heartbeat of the musician. Both the breath and the heartbeat are externalised through a contact microphone attached to the musician's chest, heard by the audience through loudspeakers. Similarly, both Vinko Globokar's *Res/As/Ex/ Ins-pirer* for brass soloist and Mauricio Kagel's *Atem* reach for a more theatrical use of the breath and the voice in their nascent states: here the breath erupts into cries, shrieks, or hiatuses, interspersed with instrumental writing. The breath, to Kagel and Globokar, seems more of a grammatical tool in the overall structure of works conceived as instrumental theatre or music theatre, and a rhetorical device that accompanies other actions. It is, then, a type of breath that plays on pre-emptive or cadential moments that we associate with speech.

113

Figure 5.2. Kristian Ireland, *luminous* (2012–14), 2. ©2014 Kristian Ireland.

More considered attempts at integrating the breath as compositional material into contemporary repertoire can be found in several of Luigi Nono's later compositions too, such as *Das atmende Klarsein* for solo bass flute and choir. Through the media of amplification and live electronics, the breath and its details become magnified, and then captured, sculpted, and layered. Helmut Lachenmann's orchestral and chamber works also use the breath as a colouristic and theatrical aspect, the most relevant example being "*. . . zwei Gefüle . . . ,*" *Musik mit Leonardo* for ensemble and speaker, *temA* (an anagram of *Atem*, meaning "breath" in German) for flute, voice, and cello, and *Dal Niente (Intérieur III)* for solo clarinet. Engaging with the breath in a multifaceted way, Lachenmann and Nono look to the breath or breathing *through* the body of the instrument, with the instrumentalist often covering the mouthpiece with the mouth: the individual musician is more of an actuator of the instrumental sound, and it is the instrument (not the performer's exertions) that create an expressive input. Kaija Saariaho's numerous works for flute similarly pay attention to the breath, but more as a colouristic aspect to her work. In these cases the breath is an acoustic addition to or an actuator of instrumental sound, and this is woven into the compositions as a grammatical tool or a colouristic feature. The focus here is then on the instrument, with little attention to the human presence and the significance of the breath itself. Where *luminous* stands out in this context is in its single-minded focus on the breath as a conjoining of the player and the instrument, using the organic qualities of the performer's breathing and its pacing. In this way, Ireland offers a more detailed examination of the breath and its rhythmical nuances. From a performer-specific point of view, *luminous* facilitates performative introspection and externalises the inflections of the breath and breathing over the approximately twenty-eight minutes of the piece.

Creating a somatic score

Alongside the challenge of using the *ingressive* technique, in *luminous* there are challenges to more fundamental skills of musicianship that we take for granted, in particular with regard to pulse and the understanding of form, over and above aspects of tone production. These questions need to be squared against the overall duration of the piece and the relative lack of information in the score. To approach this, the performer must engage with a recalibration of his or her musicianship and how he or she works with the instrument. The task of the flautist then becomes reorienting a practice that can implement a broader conceptualisation of pulse, and taking experimental approaches to the conception of structure. In turn, *luminous* led me to rethink certain essential categories of instrumental playing, and to question accepted ideas of instrumental mastery as manifested in the classical music tradition.

First, to begin our discussion from a pragmatic stance, two issues present themselves in Ireland's score: (1) The duration of *luminous* is an unusual proposal for the flautist—there are no breaks in the twenty-eight minutes of the piece. (2) There is a need to pace oneself and navigate the large-form structure of the work, while noting that there is little instruction in the score as to how this might be achieved.

Underpinnings and a new musicianship

Moving away from the score, I attempted to notate my considerations in a more direct form, outlining what an alternate approach to Ireland's piece might look like from a more pragmatic perspective. Figure 5.3 conveys, diagrammatically, what I see as the structural underpinnings and technical and performative issues of *luminous*.

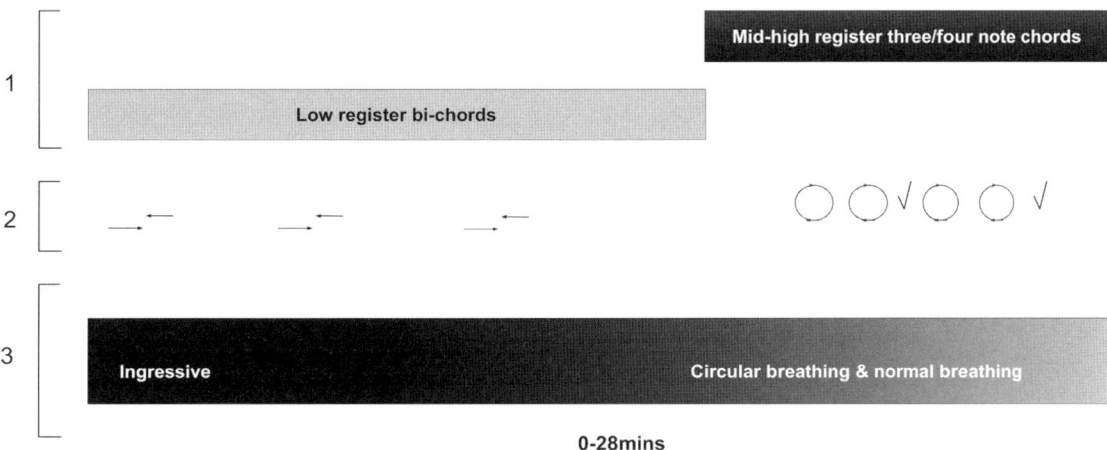

Figure 5.3.

There are three points to note concerning the musical material of the above: the harmonic material, its register, and the technical difficulty it presents, represented by line 1; the breathing patterns and techniques used throughout the piece; and the indications of a physical saturation to the tasks (or a fatigue) that can be gleaned through the combination of lines 2 and 3.

The darker sections are physically demanding, or require a particularly strenuous posture or stance, whereas those in lighter shades indicate a relatively relaxed level of physical engagement. From this basic outline there is an indication as to how the piece can be mapped as a larger event, focussed around a series of quotients and physical processes. As a broader measure of the trajectory of *luminous*, we can see in this diagram how particular techniques define the proportions of the work, and that the breath, or how it is used, is important to its structure. Looking, then, to the phenomenon of the breath in more detail, it is possible to map out smaller units by which to measure the more local detail in the bars.

Rhythm and corporeality

A metricised idea of pulse is a cornerstone of classical music performance practice (though there are, of course, many examples of contemporary art music that subvert this, or dispense with it entirely). However, in this instance we need to consider other points of reference in order to gain some sort of prag-

115

Figure 5.3. The performer's diagrammatic representation of *luminous*.

matic understanding of *luminous*. I propose that the breath, or more specifically the ingressive breathing technique, becomes the temporal focus, and that the performer calibrates a sense of pulse according to a series of breathing cycles, or distinct periods of a particular approach to breathing.

Classical performers are trained to navigate rhythm using a particular unit of a pulse in the score. This ability relies on our ability, to a certain degree, to remain detached from the music we are attempting to play: with this detachment we are able to observe and correct ourselves. However, in *luminous* I found that my approach resembled that articulated by Brian Ferneyhough in his discussion of the importance of *mediating lattices* ([1988] 1995, 43): webs of temporal detailing that mesh the performer's sense of pulse with the objectively mapped pulse of the score. That is to say, in this case the pulse and the notion of the pulse have to be mediated by the body, through the body.

However, it would be incorrect to maintain that a performer's conception of time is here immune to the musical situation and the technical demands of the piece. Furthermore, to rely purely on an internal sense of pulse for orientation is problematic. There is a slippage of the internal clock in circumstances where longer durations and relatively uniform musical material are used. As such, the established understanding of keeping time needs to be reassessed. As noted earlier, many of the answers to these questions in this work entail looking to the esoteric for a solution: to the performer's own clock, as it were, in terms of how the corporeality of the piece, manifested in the skill of a particular technique, lends itself for use as a rhythmical marker. In this situation, I considered the pulse not as a metricised aspect of performance, but as a constituent of two discrete and often unnoticed actions that here form the sonic material of the piece: the outbreath and the inbreath.

Breathing patterns as a temporal marker

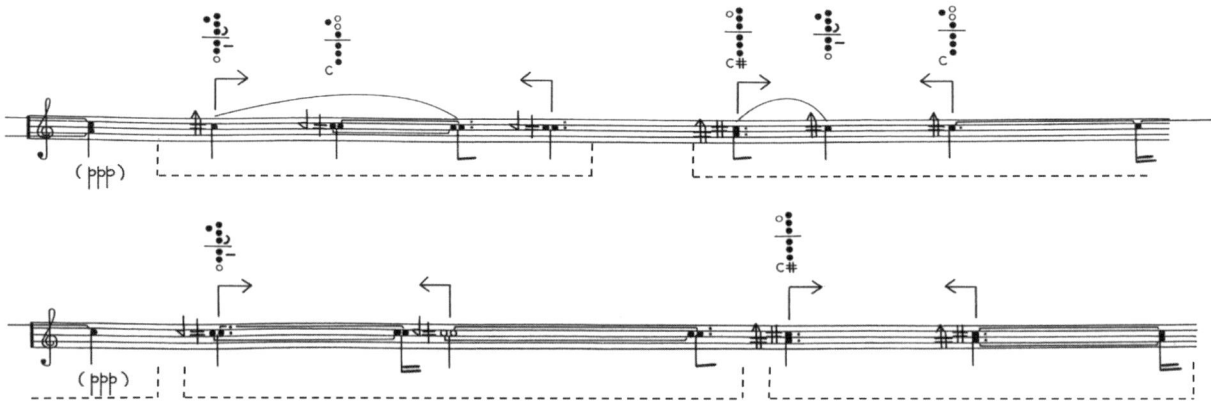

Figure 5.4.

Figure 5.4. Breathing as a temporal marker. Ireland, *luminous* (2012–14), 3. ©2014 Kristian Ireland.

Figure 5.4 is taken from the opening of the work and illustrates how, by using *ingressive* breathing, a complete cycle of a breath (inhalation and exhalation) stands as a temporal unit by which to discern a pulse. Conceptually speaking, this then permits a barring of measures. As such, the figure shows how *ingressive* breathing can be grouped as a temporal indicator. However, within these rhythmic cells, there will naturally be fluctuations in the regularity of the performer's sense of pulse, according to physical limitations or exertions. Emerging from this, I propose a synergy between the score and the control of breath as the guide to navigating *luminous*. Rather than looking to the score for a qualification of the final performance product—and verification of the composer's wishes—this piece can only work by being mediated through an internal compass: a synergy is produced when the demands of the score are aligned through related physical feedback. In this I challenge the conventional need for a succinctly measured performance (as might be taken from the quaver in the score—although this certainly operates as an aide-memoire for me). Instead, a pulse—a sum total of a breathing cycle—takes priority as a unit of time. As an exercise in metric equivalence, this approach forms a major part of my negotiation of tempo and form in *luminous*. It also assists in the negotiation of the local and global aspects of such a demanding work, which are balanced against the temporal structuring of the breath and the *ingressive* technique.

2. EXPRESSIVE TROPES

Multiphonics

If pushed to identify a primary tendency in or characteristic of the musical material of *luminous*, I would point to its inherent instability. In particular, the use of multiphonics and my *ingressive* technique are characteristically unstable musical processes. Both instil a tangible "imprecision" in the work as a whole, and they test particular paradigms of classical music performance. In what follows I discuss the performative difficulty of both techniques as an expressive trope and a form of choreography in *luminous*. Looking to the materials and how their characteristics have formed my interpretation of *luminous*, we find an additional layer of information not explicitly available in the score, yet essential to performing the work.

When composers discuss multiphonics, working collaboratively with performers, their primary concern is their reliability to reproduce exactly what is notated. In *luminous*, forty-three different multiphonics are used. Each chord has its own particular physical posture, airspeed, embouchure adjustment, and fingering pattern. In addition, each chord has a level of instrumental resistance, or a particular technical threshold—the angle of the air, airspeed, and embouchure position—that has to be correct if the chord is to speak. Clearly, there is an intrinsic instability to each chord, and even a lack of certainty as to which pitches will appear, what order they will appear in, and for how long I can manage to sustain them. Rather than considering this a flaw in the performance or instrumental writing, this instability becomes a token of the *physical materiality* of the work, and thus determines how I shape the composition in performance (Callis et al. 2015). The multiphonics have an expressive modality in this situation: there is a distinct instability and a clear sense of precariousness when we hear them in performance. Their vacillation provides a "grain" to the sound, contingent upon the rise and fall of the breath.

This relates to Ireland's compositional process: he treats multiphonics as something to be "stretched out, prolonged and looped" (Ireland 2012–14) during the course of the piece, and there are indications as to what the impact of Ireland's compositional strategy might be upon the physical integrity of the performance (or, the performative "accuracy," in my interpretation of the piece). Through Ireland's processes of repetition and elongation, there is also a gradual compromising of the material and, from a performance viewpoint, a physical depletion (or fatigue) enacted compositionally but effected in performance. I identify this, in particular, as a palpable sense of physical decline and, more generally, in the practice of *luminous* as a type of physical entropy (Iddon 2006, 93). It is the case, then, that the performer instils a fallibility or physical compromise in the piece that stands in the way of the idealised score. In this way, inadvertent additions and erasures become significant aspects of the twenty-eight minutes of the piece.

The breath

Havi Carel writes that the breath is a "complex phenomen[on], with several levels of expression and a multifactorial physiological, psychological, and spiritual/cultural underpinning" (2016, 109). As I have illustrated, the breath and breathing have a much more conspicuous role than usual in *luminous*, inviting a more detailed discussion in phenomenological terms. For most of us, breath and breathing are for the most part unmeasured experiences that accompany our daily existence in an unconscious manner. In a similar process to other body sensations, breath is often "neutral and tacit" (ibid., 56) in our daily lived experience.

It is only when we push ourselves, or experience a physical disturbance or illness, that we move beyond a bodily or psychological threshold and the breath comes to the foreground of our awareness, an outward indicator of a physical disruption (Carel 2016, 108). Taking this concept of a transmutation from the esoteric to the exoteric into musical territories, we can say that *ingressive* breathing poses an intervention in my typical approach to the breath and the quotidian aspect of instrumental performance. Essentially, there is a disruption to the transparency of the breath and breathing.[6] The breath, thematised as it is in *luminous*, crosses a particular instrumental, physical, and psychological threshold that can hold "several layers of expression" (ibid., 109). The breath is then an externalising conduit in *luminous*. In this sense, I would go so far as to say that

---

6   The concept of transparency is taken-up and developed by Carel (2016, 55–56) from Sartre's proposal of the healthy body: "[a] consciousness (of) the body is lateral and retrospective; the body is the *neglected*, the *'passed by in silence'*" (Sartre [1958] 1989, 330). Carel (2016, 56) also quotes Leder (1990, 1): "while in one sense the body is the most abiding and inescapable presence in our lives, it is also essentially characterized by absence. That is, one's own body is rarely the thematic object of experience."

luminous is as much a form of body choreography as it is a composition for flute,[7] and the complicated and nuanced process of bodily perception and musical performance, theoretically and discursively, can co-exist in this case study. As a closing suggestion to this proposal of physical tropes and their outward characteristics, I offer my own shorthand notes that formed an attempt to capture the experience of *ingressive* breathing. There is a clear sense of awkwardness and lack of continuity to the experience, and an awareness that facets of instrumental playing are being forged anew: "my descriptive focus falls to the sound of discreet rasps, crepitations and the sense of apnea from the inward breathing action of the ingressive technique. It is a sound content which is also anatomically oriented, whilst remaining inconclusive as to where exactly it is located. In *luminous* we have the apparatus of the voice and the mechanics of sound production seemingly engaged in a reverse manner" (personal notes, 2016).

Interventions and verisimilitude

From my descriptions of the technical aspects of *luminous*, it is apparent that in the process of performance there has been a degree of sensitisation to the concepts I have outlined and to working with the instrument in a new way. There emerged, as a result, a better understanding of the body-centric proposition of *luminous*, and of a certain physical "resistance" that is in play against an engrained practice or cultural instantiation of practice. However, conveying all this poses a particular challenge. In *Interpretive Autoethnography*, Norman Denzin (2013, 70) suggests that conveying a truth in autoethnographic experience entails a degree of responsibility: the researcher seeks a verisimilitude that "evokes a feeling that the experience described is true, coherent, believable, and connects the reader to the writer's world." Denzin proposes that such a text is one that can evoke as much as inform the reader of praxis. Taking this suggestion into my approach to *luminous*, I have pursued a more existential type of enquiry as to how I might best convey the processes and understanding manifested in performing, aiming to find an approach that would mirror the radical intervention that occurred in my instrumental and personal understanding of performing, the score, and the composer. To this end, I drew on the work of the philosopher Havi Carel, and in particular her writings on physical decline, developing from this a form of body-centric observation that has now become part of my approach to *luminous*. In *Phenomenology of Illness*, Carel recounts (from personal experience as well as case-study materials) how the disturbance of illness manifests itself physically, and ontologically—these two categories combine, becoming a symptomatic reduction of power to act or plan our daily lives.

---

7   The choreographic implications of composed instrumental action are further discussed by Catherine Laws later in this book (136–37). More extensively, in chapter 8, Nguyễn Thanh Thủy and Stefan Östersjö discuss the ways in which their collaborative project *Inside/Outside* took analysis of the gendered nature of instrumental gesture as the basis for developing an installation and performance for choreographed musicians.

Looking more closely at Carel's phenomenological account of illness, it becomes clear that she grasps it as an intervention into our day-to-day experience, and that in this lies an abrupt reassessment of our power or confidence to control tasks. Carel notes the way in which the body can be limited, or depleted, while illness takes hold, and in this our prospective self (our capabilities, or plans, or repertoire of skills) is folded back into the physical realities of the situation (Carel 2016, 95). In the case of *luminous*, while I am engaged in the piece and the long-form procedure that Ireland has set in motion, I simultaneously and continually reflect upon and reconsider the consistent demands upon my breathing and the level of instrumental control. As such, this type of focus consumes previously hierarchical and established aspects of my technique (sound control and intonation, for example). When these physical limitations are met with the requirements of the score, I am forced to collapse "back onto my actual physical being" and be grounded by the body and its overriding requirements in my performances (ibid.). Here, the score merely reminds me of the duration and chords, and provides little detail as to how to wrestle with the phenomena of performance. Interestingly, such grindingly problematic and uncharted experiences also highlight an entirely new level of attention in my technique: a sensitisation, even a relearning, which, in working against a standardised technique "requires serious effort and continuous work" (ibid., 3) to maintain.

Interventions

Taking this theme of decline into the more general sphere of performance studies, such notions are in fact vital interventions into our conceptions of "mastery," and "a breathtakingly intense experience" (Carel 2016, 3): they cut through and correct a particular world view of practice and self-management. What was previously simple and unconscious becomes complex, confused, and doubtful. The technical or conceptual disturbances I encountered shifted my focus and forced me to question my own capabilities. In *luminous*, the disruption of core aspects of my instrumental skill—producing a stable sound, the control of breathing, and the elongation of the breath—exposed a "blind confidence" in my technique. A particular "bodily-certainty" or the "subtle feeling of 'I can' that pervades our actions" (or, in my case, pervades an accomplished sense of praxis) is problematised (Carel 2016, 90).

Musical decline, as I recount it here, is then a constant engagement of—a monitoring, self-diagnosing, even a halting sense of—our limitations. My thematisation of *luminous* also conveys a particular understanding of the changes to my practice, and an attempt to render the immediacy of this through the language: "a sense of urgency and a demand to do something about the pain, discomfort, or nausea through which the body comes to the fore. There is a heightening of bodily focus at times of illness and disruption" (Carel 2016, 60).

At the outset of *Phenomenology of Illness*, Carel (2016, 41–43), draws upon S. Kay Toombs's analysis of bodily decline and illness, and how it acts upon our perception of everyday experience. From Carel's overview, the following three points reflect my experience with *luminous*:

1. Loss of continuity

   The breath, and its blending into everyday experience and performance practice, was disturbed in my work with *luminous*. Breathing is now a much more conscious musical gesture that requires careful thought in the context of this piece. By using my new technique of breathing in *luminous* I have created a self-observational process from a previously involuntary action, in which "normal flow" is conspicuous and alludes to a heightened sense of self-awareness and interiority.

2. Loss of transparency

   Carel notes that a loss of transparency is a "dramatic resistance in the exchange between body and environment" (2016, 58) and, more specifically in my case, a jolting removal of a sense of mastery with the instrument and my bodily-management of this. The discombobulation of my everyday instrumental practice results in a coarseness of experience, which can be heard in the technical tropes of the piece. In this case aspects of "mastery," in the musical sense, are channelled into a moment-by-moment account and an inability to plan too far ahead, due to the length of the piece and the precarious nature of the multiphonics. Carel points out that with this loss of transparency (of mastery, or fluency of skill in everyday life), there is also a loss of spontaneity (ibid., 41–43). In this instance, a singularity of expression and focus takes hold in *luminous* through the numerous technical and physical restrictions.

3. Inconsistency, from a lack of "faith"

   This constitutes a retrospective note in my practice, from an inductive perspective in relation to my previous experiences before *luminous*. I now have a deeper understanding of practice (or *habitus*) before this intervention took place. My plans or ability to foresee and adjust to oncoming challenges in *luminous* fold back into what is physically possible. My practice was fractured or displaced when first engaging with *luminous*; "the ability to project oneself," a self-certainty, or selfhood, is questioned in these circumstances, when confronted with a composition of this duration and somatic complexity. Carel (2016, 95) writes: "The limitless sense of myself, of my open horizons, as extending beyond myself and into the world collapses back onto my actual physical being; it becomes an act of conscious planning to see how far I can, or dare, project myself onto the world."

Pathophilia

Carel argues that "illness is potentially edifying and instructive not only in a personal sense but also in a general philosophical sense" (2016, 12). There is an instinctive concern surrounding any metaphor of illness (Sontag [1978–89] 1991), and so I am keen to temper the discussion in terms of the redemptive qualities that can be associated with decline. More pointedly, Carel suggests that we can wear "illness as [a] potentially edifying, positive, purifying, and instructive" process (2016, 12). Reflecting upon this aspect of my approach, the metaphorical clothing of decline around this composition *has* been an instructive, sensitising, and regenerative process for my understanding of performance and practice. To that end, there is an outward trace to my thinking, or a regenerative aspect, and not surprisingly one that characterises *luminous* as a cathartic process.

As a token of this pathophilic approach or recovery, by adapting and incorporating Carel's writings into my musical practice, my focus on decline has magnified the interconnectedness between the instrument and the instrumentalist in a way that goes beyond what we would, in conventional musical practice, deem a form of resistance, mastery, or virtuosity. Reflecting upon Carel's thematisation of illness as a metaphorical and philosophical tool has initiated a fluidity between experience, instrument, score, and the reporting, revealing, and understanding of practice. By extension, attempting to notate this interconnectivity of instrument and instrumentalist has demanded an ongoing internal reciprocity in trying to record the immediacy of a practice and develop an exacting textual validity.

CONCLUSION

The "transparency" of my everyday artistic practice has been tested to an unusual degree in *luminous*. My technical innovations, and Ireland's organisation of these in the composition, have contributed to a radical shift in how I embody and describe the experience of performing and understanding a work. In a broader way, *luminous* has also opened up a new approach to considering how the instrumentalist can be more central to the conception of composition, and in what sense—where, when, and how—an "instrumentation" takes form.

Placing all this within the context of current research concerning the "habitus," or more precisely the "hexis," of performance and practice offers a useful perspective. Coessens and Östersjö note (2014, 336): "For the musician then, *hexis* is constitutive of artistic choice, reflection, and action. The artistic virtue that is embodied in the musician's hexis is reflective of a broader aesthetic context and one's (artistic) goals in life and as such is an expression of a critical relation between the two." Coessens and Östersjö also set in place the "complex interplay between processes of 'resonance' and 'critique' or 'resistance'—a 'critique' that constitutes this denial of habit [my established, engrained practice] in musical performance" (ibid., 341). The resistance here is perhaps more accurately situated in this paper as an exposition of my aversion to established and inherited practices: rather than cultivating a pristine notion of instrumental practice or virtuosity as enshrined by the classical tradition, in Ireland's piece I have restricted *myself* to a limited instrumental vocabulary. Furthermore, my work was not focussed around the epiphenomenon of the score, the composer, or continual collaborative practice, as for example in David Gorton and Stefan Östersjö's "*Austerity Measures I*: Performing the Discursive Voice" (2019), or a critical point for the theory of resistance as a creative tool in musical performance, as Coessens and Östersjö (2014) present it. Instead,

I have shown that an intersubjective resonance is involved here,[8] aimed at a particular strain of technical and interpretational knowledge (one that lay outside the purview of the composer and the score). Moreover, this tension has spawned series of contingencies in *luminous* as to how I view and mediate standardised approaches to score reading and performance hierarchies.

Luminous has allowed me interpretative space to consider a method and its implementation, and it is this bespoke approach that suggests an additional point of action for future collaborations. In addition, not only has the composer–performer dynamic been parried here, but also the relationship of performer and instrument has come into a new focus. As a result, my understanding of the categories of instrument and the instrumentalist have been altered, with the normal distinctions rethought as a merging of two species of technologies: the human and skill-based with the machinery of the flute.[9] Such a moulding is eloquently captured by Walter J. Ong ([1982] 2002, 82): "The fact is that by using a mechanical contrivance, a violinist or an organist can express something poignantly human that cannot be expressed without the mechanical contrivance. To achieve such expression of course the violinist or organist has to have interiorized the technology, made the tool or machine a second nature, a psychological part of himself or herself."

Capturing performance or performance as text is of course an abstraction, and performance writing is reliant on the powers of metaphor for its enlivening. In my description of *luminous*, the pursuit of conveying an existential dimension to performance has entailed looking toward an *obeisance* of the body, not the score, bringing what I consider an emboldening of a vulnerability and imperfection to the musical sphere. It is then not mastery per se that I am bringing out here, but bodily conditions that are seldom considered to impinge upon the realms of musical practice: "Vulnerability, limitation, and finitude are fundamental features of human life not only in its physiological objective mode, or as abstract knowledge, but also in its experienced, subjective mode, as informing our ways of being in the world" (Carel 2016, 63).

---

8 The phrase "intersubjective resonance" echoes the terms used by Juliana Hodkinson in her chapter earlier in this book. However, rather than the solo performance of a piece composed by another, Hodkinson's context is rather different: her focus is her practice as a composer-performer, the concern being the manifestation of this "resonance" between those participating in an event of sound-making, whether as performers, listeners, or both. In this respect, my use of this term extends the notion she introduces.

9 The relationship between performer and instrument is further discussed in *Voices, Bodies, Practices*, the partner volume to this book, especially in chapter 1 by Gorton and Östersjö (2019, 40–42) and subsequently in chapter 2, in which the "merging" of performer and instrument is problematised (Laws 2019, 107–11).

References

Callis, Sarah, Neil Heyde, Zubin Kanga, and Olivia Sham. 2015. "Creative Resistance as a Performance Tool." *Music & Practice* 2. Accessed 14 October 2019. https://www.musicandpractice.org/volume-2/creative-resistance-as-a-performance-tool/.

Carel, Havi. 2016. *Phenomenology of Illness*. Oxford: Oxford University Press.

Coessens, Kathleen, and Stefan Östersjö. 2014. "Habitus and the Resistance of Culture." In *Artistic Experimentation in Music: An Anthology*, edited by Darla Crispin and Bob Gilmore, 333–48. Orpheus Institute Series. Leuven: Leuven University Press.

Cummings, Simon. 2017. "Recognition, Raw Ambition and Raw Power: Alba New Music 2017." *5:4* (blog), 13 October. Accessed 10 February 2020. http://5against4.com/2017/10/13/recognition-raw-ambition-and-raw-power-alba-new-music-2017/.

Denzin, Norman K. 2013. *Interpretive Autoethnography*. 2nd ed. Qualitative Research Methods 17. Los Angeles: Sage.

Dixon, Martin. 2013. "Composition and Adorno's Rhetoric of the New." *Scottish Music Review* 3: 1–27.

Ferneyhough, Brian. (1988) 1995. "The Tactility of Time." In *Collected Writings*, edited by James Boros and Richard Toop, 42–50. Abingdon, UK: Routledge. First given as a lecture (Darmstadt, 1988).

Gorton, David, and Stefan Östersjö. 2019. "*Austerity Measures I*: Performing the Discursive Voice." In *Voices, Bodies, Practices: Performing Musical Subjectivities*, by Catherine Laws, William Brooks, David Gorton, Nguyễn Thanh Thủy, Stefan Östersjö, and Jeremy J. Wells, 29–79. Orpheus Institute Series. Leuven: Leuven University Press.

Iddon, Martin. 2006. "On the Entropy Circuit: Brian Ferneyhough's *Time and Motion Study II*." *Contemporary Music Review* 25 (1–2): 93–105.

Ireland, Kristian. 2012–14. *luminous*. Unpublished score.

Laws, Catherine. 2019. "Being a Player: Agency and Subjectivity in *Player Piano*." In *Voices, Bodies, Practices: Performing Musical Subjectivities*, by Catherine Laws, William Brooks, David Gorton, Nguyễn Thanh Thủy, Stefan Östersjö, and Jeremy J. Wells, 83–167. Orpheus Institute Series. Leuven: Leuven University Press.

Leder, Drew. 1990. *The Absent Body*. Chicago: University of Chicago Press.

Olsen, Charles. (1950) 2019. *Projective Verse*. Accessed 14 October 2019. http://writing.upenn.edu/~taransky/Projective_Verse.pdf. First published 1950 (*Poetry New York* 3).

Ong, Walter J. (1982) 2002. *Orality and Literature: The Technologizing of the World*. New York: Routledge. First published 1982 (London: Methuen).

Sartre, Jean-Paul. (1958) 1989. *Being and Nothingness: An Essay on Phenomenological Ontology*. Translated by Hazel E. Barnes. London: Routledge. First published 1943 as *L'être et le néant* (Paris: Gallimard). This translation first published 1958 (London: Methuen).

Sontag, Susan. (1978–89) 1991. *Illness as Metaphor and AIDS and Its Metaphors*. London: Penguin. *Illness as Metaphor* first published 1978 (New York: Farrar, Straus & Giroux); *Aids and Its Metaphors* first published 1989 (New York: Farrar, Straus & Giroux).

Performing Being a Pianist

Gender and Embodied Subjectivity in Performing Annea Lockwood's *Ceci n'est pas un piano*

Catherine Laws

University of York; Orpheus Institute, Ghent

Introduction

This chapter explores the dynamic interaction of composer, performer, and instrumental agencies in a particular case study: my development of a new version of *Ceci n'est pas un piano* (2002), for piano, recorded text, electronics, and video, by the New Zealand–born composer and sound artist Annea Lockwood (available as an audio recording).[1] I am interested in how these agencies entwine within an apparently singular performative identity and how, in particular, the piece thematises the body at the piano in particular ways.[2] In what follows, I unpick the status of this body-subject and its gendered qualities, examining the space opened up between the physically present performer—who forms a version of herself through a particular embodied engagement with the piano as physical object, sound source, and cultural agent—and the absent performer evoked by a recorded text.

In many ways *Ceci n'est pas un piano* follows traditional Western classical modes of practice. There is a score, manifesting a work-concept by a composer; unlike some of the case studies in this volume, this piece was not produced by the composer in collaboration with this performer. While my own work as a performer is very often collaborative or co-creative, in this case the piece was initially written for another pianist, Jennifer Hymer. Indeed, it was through Hymer's 2010 recording of the piece that I became aware of it. Likewise, realising the piece for performance involved a process of practice almost entirely independent of the composer, with just occasional moments of consultation

---

1 Audio recording of *Ceci n'est pas un piano* by Annea Lockwood, with text by Catherine Laws, performed by Catherine Laws and produced by Jon Hughes, available at https://soundcloud.com/user-120758327/ceci-mix-27th-july-2015.

2 I have written about this piece more briefly elsewhere, but somewhat differently, in order to examine (a) the nature of the collaboration with Lockwood (Laws 2018); and (b) its role in the context of a larger production, *Player Piano*, in which it is performed alongside other pieces (Laws 2019). Inevitably, the current chapter reiterates some of the earlier description of the piece in order to provide the basis for the subsequent discussion. However, the analysis here is more detailed, and the focus is upon the interaction of autobiographical text and music in the context of gendered, embodied subjectivity.

along the way. However, in certain respects both the materials of this piece and the process by which it was developed for performance reveal much about the complexities that underlie apparently conventional and straightforward divisions of labour. Moreover, and importantly in this context, the pianist's agency and embodied subjectivity are explicitly invoked in this piece. This arises partly from the ways in which the performer engages with the instrument—and the ways in which Lockwood's choices, here, point up this embodied engagement—but also from the incorporation of a narrative: a recorded text, played back as part of the piece, which draws attention to the performer, her role, and her relationship to her instrument.

THE TREACHERY OF SOUNDS

The title of the piece invokes René Magritte's *The Treachery of Images* (1929): a beautifully painted picture of a pipe, rendered as realistically as possible but incorporating the painted caption "Ceci n'est pas un pipe." This is perhaps the most famous of a series of such paintings produced by Magritte starting in the late 1920s, concerned with the problematics of representation: they all combine apparently realist paintings of objects with words that point out the representational status of the images. Magritte himself reportedly commented: "could you stuff my pipe? No, it's just a representation, is it not? So if I had written on my picture 'This is a pipe,' I'd have been lying!" (Torczyner 1977, 71). Magritte's essay "Les mots et les images," which also appeared in 1920, in a volume of the journal *La révolution surréaliste* (The surrealist revolution), provided a parallel critique, focusing on the gap between representation and experience that subsequently became the reflexive basis of so much Western art-making of the twentieth century.

Ceci n'est pas un piano works somewhat analogously, showing us a piano and inviting us to listen to it while simultaneously telling us that this is not a piano: it implicitly suggests that we might consider the relationship between the signifier "piano" and what we experience in performance. Musically, the piece sometimes uses the piano conventionally, with standard playing on the keys. However, many of the sounds are produced from inside the instrument by playing the strings, the struts, the wooden body, and so on. Indeed, for almost the first six minutes—approximately half the piece—all the musical sounds are produced this way, using not only the fingers but also a range of objects: stones, ribbons, rubber and metal balls, mallets, and, at the end of the piece, an e-bow (figure 6.1 shows the basic performance situation).

Particularly in an audio recording, when the listener cannot see the physical actions that produce the sounds, some of these sounds might well not be thought to originate solely from the piano, even by someone used to hearing extended techniques; one might think that many had been electronically enhanced or manipulated, when in fact only very low-level amplification is used. Given the title, we might understand this as a critique of Schaefferian sonorous objectness. For Pierre Schaeffer (2004), the focus on sonorous objects in acousmatic music facilitated concentration on "the perceptive reality of sound as such, as distinguished from the modes of its production and transmission" (77). In contrast, Lockwood seems to invite us to question this mode of listening, foregrounding what Schaeffer describes as "the curiosity put into play" with acoustic sound (77), in which the interpretative relationship between the objective sound source and the subjectively perceived sound is of prime importance in determining the significance of what is heard. In this way, by simultaneously using this soundworld while also presenting us with a grand piano (visually, but also when we hear its more conventional use later in the piece), and telling us "this is not a piano," Lockwood seems to invite us to question the sonic associations that the idea of "piano" brings into play and to consider the treachery of *sounds*.

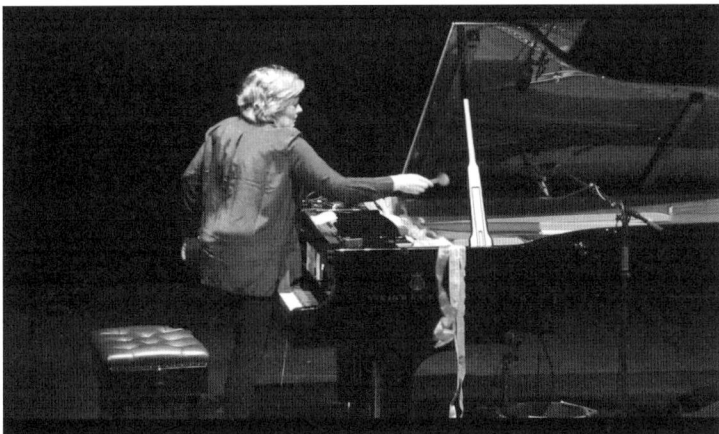

Figure 6.1.

However, all this is only one aspect of a performance of this multi-layered piece. The description thus far concentrates primarily on what we hear, musically—that is, on the use of piano *sound*. In performance, though, the production of sound is, of course, perceived in part through the physical activity of the pianist; this is the case in any piano performance, but more so here due to the extended gestures in and around the instrument. I will examine this more fully later, when I consider the significance of the physicality of performance in relation to the production of embodied subjectivity. For now it suffices to say that, importantly, the music in this piece operates in dialogue with words, and the nature of the text is such that it, too, directs attention significantly beyond pure sonic objectness and towards the embodied, situated act of a performer playing an instrument.

THE TREACHERY OF WORDS

Ceci n'est pas un piano explicitly invokes the pianist's relationship to her instrument as part of its thematics. Throughout the first two-thirds of the piece, the musical materials weave around a recording of a pianist who speaks in personal

Figure 6.1. Still from Annea Lockwood, *Ceci n'est pas un piano* performed by Catherine Laws, Scenic Stage Theatre, York, 5 May 2016.

terms about this relationship. There is, in this way, a reflexive engagement with the relationship between the pianist's live playing and the recorded comments on aspects of her life and work—that is, with her creative identity and embodied subjectivity. Sometimes the voice is played through a speaker positioned under the piano, as close as possible to the soundboard, in the exact position that will, with the particular piano in the specific space, provoke the most sympathetic resonances from the instrument when the pedal is down. In other sections of the piece, the recording is relayed through a transducer inside the piano, which likewise sets the instrument in motion, producing additional frequencies: again, the pedal is held down throughout. Finally, there are times when the text is relayed through both channels at once. Thus, whenever the recorded speaking voice is heard, its production through the instrument provokes related overtonal resonances: it becomes a kind of piano voice. Moreover, the recorded text is mastered by Lockwood to enhance, subtly, certain vocal frequencies ready for playback through the body of the piano. As discussed below, each process mediates the voice a little differently: the voice is recognisably the same, but its timbre changes according to its allocation to the different speakers, in turn provoking different overtonal resonances from the instrument, the nature and extent of which of course vary with the size and model of the piano and the acoustics of the space.

A microphone is used to pick up some of the tinier sounds inside the piano, such as those produced by stones or fingernails on the strings, and these sounds are also fed through the speaker under the piano. There is no external PA system: all sound runs through the piano. Importantly, then, the voice always emanates from the piano, not from speakers separately located in the performance space. The voice that speaks in the first person about performance—about playing the piano, the relationship to the instrument, and its physical experience—does not emanate directly from the performer, but neither is it spatially separated: the performer's body and the speaking voice are close, both within the space of the piano, and the sound-producing actions of the pianist become integrated sonically and spatially with the speaking voice, all sounds emerging through the body of the piano.

The text used when I perform this piece, and in my recording, is written and spoken by me. However, as noted above, *Ceci n'est pas un piano* was composed for another pianist, Jennifer Hymer. The original recorded text was of Hymer talking about *her* pianistic experience, her life, her pianos, her sense of her body at the instrument; her text begins "I have the hands of my grandmother. My mother has them as well, and my cousin Maja."[3] In consultation with Lockwood and Hymer, I made my own vocal recording, which Lockwood then mastered (as she had Hymer's). As a result, the text of the new version is about me: about my relationship to the piano, my performing body, and aspects of my life in relation to piano playing. However, I had to fit my words into the timings of the piece, since the score often specifies precisely the interaction of text and

---

3 This recording is available on a CD of Hymer's performances also entitled *Ceci n'est pas un piano* (Hymer 2007).

piano sounds. My verbal narrative was therefore constrained structurally by the composer's and the first performer's formal decisions. More significant is the thematic relationship: inevitably, my approach to writing was influenced by Hymer's recollections as presented in her recorded text.

Hymer talks not only about her relationship to piano playing but also specifically about her own piano and her connection to it. Moreover, she refers to the domestic context in which it is housed, to the ways it is used by herself and by her children as an object of play, rather than an expensive, refined machine for the production of high art. I have long been interested in the performer's embodied relationship to the instrument and also the nature and status of the piano; in particular, these things have become the focus of some of my recent collaborative projects (see Laws 2019). Had I been the first performer of this piece, my ongoing interests might well have led me to speak, in my recording, about the physical experience of playing: about my hands and about the moments of deeply felt embodiment and disembodiment one can experience, almost simultaneously, in performance. These things are in my final text, and probably would have been there without Hymer's original as a prompt. The same could be said of our parallel interests in the cultural status of the piano and our ambivalent relationship to virtuoso solo performance.

Nevertheless, Hymer's influence is apparent to me, especially retrospectively. My commentary speaks of the relationship between piano performing and everyday life: there are references to the piano as a domestic object in the home ("dropped and bashed when we've moved house"), used for serious work, but also for amusement, for play with (and "thumped by") children, and there are also suggestions of the interplay between everyday physical activity, piano practice, and the ways in which these manifest in physical changes over time: "Arthritis runs in my family, and I do worry what that might mean for me. So far I've been lucky, but with every little twinge I imagine the worst. Paranoid pianist." Many of these consciously echo Hymer's original text, but the experiences described are mine. This is, then, my voice, an autobiographical monologue, but Hymer is very much in it.

Ceci therefore provides the audience with a textual body, in the literal sense of its mediation via spoken language; a body that connects to but does not coincide with the live, performing body. The text speaks of the body at the piano, and it speaks through the piano, with piano resonances, but even if the speaker of the text is understood to be the pianist seen and heard by the audience, and even if the content of the speech refers to the embodied experience of live performance, a disjunction between the discursive mediation of the body through composed and recorded text—produced in another time and place—and the "now" of the body active in the moment of performance is apparent. Bodies are never simple or singular, as Mark Evans notes: "the actor [or performer, more widely] is constructed through not one body, but many" (2009, 170). The hands seen to play the piano in *Ceci* are simultaneously the instigators of sound, expressive objects of visual attention, and subject to verbal contemplation—contemplation that explicitly invokes their complex agency: "These hands of mine: I sometimes wonder where they come from, how they got this way. . . . Whose hands are these, anyway? They're so much mine, they know so much of what I know, maybe more than I do. They can find notes, feel distance, decide on musical emphasis. But other people, teachers and composers, have moulded them too, pushed them into peculiar shapes over and over, until I can no longer say what's truly natural to them."

As Anna Fenemore notes, the body is always both "an aesthetic and performative entity," "both a site for representation (something that can be 'read') . . . and . . . a 'lived' entity" (2011, 21). It is always mediated by words—in the explicit sense of being described, accounted for, circumscribed in language—but is also always textual, always open to "reading" in its broader inscription within semiotic systems. However, it is also resistant to that textualisation, always "there," acting and feeling in ways that are not always possible to capture, always changing: "Although it can transmit signs and meanings, the body resists signification and meaning" (Ramirez Ladrón de Guevara 2011, 25).[4] *Ceci*, with its layering of bodily presence and absence, its simultaneous presentation of different manifestations of the body, seems to work precisely with what Peggy Phelan describes as "the anxiety raised by the gap between the discursive construct 'the body' and the affective experience of embodiment" (1993, 171).

This is not . . . me?

The textual component of *Ceci n'est pas un piano* warrants further discussion. Beyond its discursive mediation of the body, its autobiographical content contributes to the complexities of subjectivity produced in performance. Autobiographical modes of performance, such as verbatim theatre, have often been adopted by those who feel their voices, their stories, have not been heard. In recent decades, a good example is provided by the recourse to personal experience in feminist writing, theatre, and performance art. As Maggie Gale and Viv Gardner note (2004, 4), much autobiographical work by theatre women can be read, in part, "as an attempt to re-insert themselves, not as individuals, but as part of a constructed 'group identity' or community, into a theatre history, a cultural moment or a performance space, from which they—as women—have been rendered 'absent' or 'disappeared.'" Linda Park-Fuller notes (2009, 25), similarly, that theatre affords opportunities not only to "to write oneself 'into' the picture from which one has been absent" but also to "make discoveries about one's own experience" and to "'re-create' oneself, through oneself."

In the context of Western classical music, the performer as creative entity is a relatively absent figure; while the history of music is replete with accounts of composers' lives, ideas, intentions, and working practices, we have learned relatively little about such things with respect to performers. It is true that a number of historical treatises on performance practices have remained in circulation, alongside more recent books on instrumental technique and certain matters of style and interpretation. However, barring a few exceptions, mostly

---

4   Helena De Preester articulates this very clearly: "in performance, the body abruptly and explicitly comes into visibility and resists forms of objectification that may put it to rest, to clarity and obviousness" (2007, 352).

from the last two decades,[5] these are mostly restricted to a subset of practical matters, very different from the "life and work" accounts of composers or parallel discussions of the conceptual or philosophical underpinnings of composers' work. In *Ceci n'est pas un piano*, by setting the musical content—expressive of a combined composerly and performative voice—in dialogue with the performer's usually unheard voice, speaking of things that ordinarily reside only in her private world, Lockwood foregrounds the customarily hidden performing subject, producing her as an embodied subject with a life of her own.

This piece can, of course, be performed by anyone. To date, though, the only performers (as far as Lockwood and I am aware) have been two women: Hymer and myself. That the speaking voices are those of women pianists is additionally significant. The development of the modern grand piano facilitated the composition of ever more complex and difficult music; as I have discussed elsewhere (Laws 2019, 98–99), the figure of the virtuoso pianist, able to project intricate musical structures and complex harmonic soundworlds by means of the sophisticated manipulation of this extraordinary machine, personifies the notion of absolute music as the highest art form in the nineteenth century and beyond. Notwithstanding important historical exceptions such as Clara Schumann and Myra Hess, and even though there are, today, many more women prominent in the field, the virtuoso tradition is predominantly male, characterised by extreme prowess, power, mastery, and musical transcendence. This is one of the reasons for my own ambivalence with respect to solo piano performance: there is, simultaneously, a sense of the piano being part of "myself"—inextricably part of who I am, how I take effect in the world—together with an alienation from the world of mainstream pianism and what it might mean to be considered a pianist (a sentiment that is projected onto my body in the text of *Ceci*: "I'm not sure they're pianist's hands, really"). Likewise, the conventional world of piano virtuosity is not Lockwood's either: as I discuss below, her relationship to the instrument and its cultural status is rather different. With respect to this history, it is significant that the performers of *Ceci* choose to speak not just of matters underlying the act of performance but also of their lives as women.

At the same time, autobiographical performance is never simple or transparent. As Suzette Henke observes, it offers agency to a marginal self but also produces a "newly revised subject," a "semifictive protagonist" (2000, xv).[6]

---

5   I am thinking, here, of studies that move beyond the question of the artistry of performance—whether technical or interpretative—into wider questions, such as a performer's ideas, aesthetic stance, the relationship between life and work, or the formation of performing voice and/or identity. Perhaps most striking are the small number of books written as first-person critical accounts of the production and mediation of the embodied sense of self through musical performance, such as Naomi Cumming's *The Sonic Self* (2000), or Elisabeth Le Guin's *Boccherini's Body* (2005).

6   Claire MacDonald (1995, 189) notes that "when a performance artist stands up in front of an audience she is assumed to be performing as herself. By putting her own body and her own experience forward within a live space the artist becomes both object and subject within the work and is able to use the live space to articulate that relationship." This is perhaps exaggerated in *Ceci n'est pas un piano*: recording and playback turn the voice of the speaking subject into a material object, while the live performing subject is objectified in those words and must confirm, temporally, to the timings of the recorded phrases; nevertheless, the live performing subject has the power to work *with* that material, making sounds that can either support or drown out the recording.

Autobiography is always already performative in the broader sense derived from Judith Butler (1988): we put out a circumscribed version of the self, producing a partial, edited "me," instantiating, stabilising, and fixing in time something that is complex, dynamic, in process, and resistant to representation. As Nicola Shaughnessy says (2004, 39), "the autobiographical mode is usually identified with prose and, less frequently, with poetry: it is often a confessional discourse which, in the former medium especially, reveals the unity and 'truth' of the writing self through a linear, semi-novelistic narrative of self-becoming. But as post-structuralist and feminist work on autobiography has demonstrated, the apparent coherence and facticity of the autobiographical text's mediation of the space between the 'self' and the 'life' is misleading."

The act of recording aspects of a life in words, in any kind of fixed medium—whether words on a page or as recorded speech—and then presenting it in live performance, through reading or playback, exposes that gap: we are confronted by the "pastness" of something that purports to be true of the presented self. Trịnh T. Minh-ha makes a distinction between women's autobiographical writing that aims to disclose some essence, to consolidate truths about women's experience, and writing that opens up questions about the status of the self. The latter offers possibilities but not answers; it is aware of its own constructed status, is "scriptive" (Trịnh 1989, 28). Moreover, we might say that autobiography in a performance context is doubly performative, in that it draws the broader performativity of selfhood that is always in operation into a context marked explicitly *for* performance. This is expressed in my text for *Ceci*, which at certain points implies a question about what it is to be a pianist, suggesting an uncertainty about whether I am one while at the same time acknowledging that in certain respects I present myself as one by enacting expected modes of pianistic behaviour: "Sometimes in performance it's as if I become detached from my hands: they're outside me, dancing for me. Watching films of my playing has the same effect: there's an agility, an assuredness I don't recognise. I'm performing being a pianist."

With *Ceci n'est pas un piano*, this "scriptive" self, produced by a text that is on one hand confessional and on the other, in its very documentation, revealing of its own provisionality, gains additional complexity when brought into relation with the individuated, embodied action of sound-making: that is, with a different kind of performance of "voice"—a *piano* voice. The audience hears two voices, two narratives, even: the metaphorical "voice" expected in musical performance—that is, the performer's "voice" manifested in the particularities of her approach to instrumental sound (i.e., "my instrument is my voice")—is coupled with an actual voice, that of a pianist, talking about herself, about things central to performers' lives (and in this case particularly women's and mothers' lives) but usually peripheral to musical performance. This opens up a space between the physically present performer, who forms a version of herself through a particular embodied engagement with the piano as physical object, sound source, and cultural agent, and the absent performer, whose speaking voice we hear and who focuses on the backdrop, expressing things about the relationship to the piano and performance that would normally remain hidden, while forming this version of herself very consciously in words, knowing that these will be fixed, played back time and time again.

Moreover, as Linda Alcoff writes, "In speaking for myself, I . . . create a public, discursive self, which will in most cases have an effect on the self experienced as interiority" (1991–92, 10). With repetition and the passing of time, the effect of the recorded voice is at once one of increasing familiarity and one of increasing strangeness. I wrote the words, which are about myself, and spoke them into a microphone. And they *were* me, they *felt* truthful; but, in writing thus, I signed off a version of myself, turned that version into an object. Further, in then speaking the words aloud for recording I *performed* this: I knew the kind of vocal tone I wanted and the effect of intimacy I wanted to convey, and the recording technician produced a suitable product. I performed a version of subjective authenticity, manipulating a representation of inwardness, self-disclosure. I thereby produced a not-quite-I, at a distance to myself. As Deirdre Heddon writes, "There is the self who was and the self who is. There is the self who is performed, and the performing self. . . . Every autobiographical act requires taking some distance from the self" (2008, 27). This estrangement increases as time goes on: I perform with myself speaking in the present tense about a baby who is now six years old, a granddad who is now dead. Recalling Park-Fuller's words (2009, 25), quoted above: each time I perform the piece, I create myself through myself.

Of course, the listener does not have access to this inside information; but hearing apparent self-disclosure in performance always opens up the question of authenticity. The question is redoubled by the fact that the voice is recorded and the live performer does not speak (except through the piano). The voice thus emphasises non-presence, produces a temporal non-identity between embodied subject and textual subject, where identity would otherwise be implied: is it necessarily the case that the speaking self and the physically present self coincide? Interestingly, in post-performance discussions with audience members, I have often been surprised how many people assume that it is someone else, not I, who has composed and is speaking the text.

It seems that the composer certainly did not assume that the performer would always necessarily be the author (and speaker) of the text, even though both Hymer and I wrote and recorded our own lines. When I first contacted Lockwood about the piece, she sent the score but also a copy of the backing track recorded by Hymer. I had always taken it for granted that performing this piece would involve writing and recording my own text, but clearly Lockwood had thought otherwise. When I asked about this, she responded positively, generously agreeing that I could write and record a new spoken text. I did so, and Lockwood then mastered this for use in performances (with some back and forth between the two of us about the creative decisions in the production process, particularly with respect to equalisation of the vocal frequencies, which Lockwood worked with carefully, due to their role in provoking additional resonances from the piano). It seems significant, though, in the light of the above discussion, that Lockwood had not assumed any identity between performer and speaker.

Writing about the role of text in his composed theatre works, Heiner Goebbels (1997) comments: "on stage I try to blur or even break the identity between speech and speaker in order to make the 'speaker' disappear. There are two reasons for this: first, to rescue the language, to develop the hearing of language independently, and second, to acquire an actor who can not only physically elaborate what he or she has already said but who can present himself or herself as an independent body—to arrive finally at having two bodies: the text as a body and the body of the actor." Something similar is at work in *Ceci*. To suggest that the speaker "disappears" is, to my mind, an exaggeration, but the split between the performing and textual bodies is comparable.

Jen Harvie (2004, 194) notes that autobiographical performance "might be particularly at risk of being understood as essentialist because the performer is present and embodied in it. This presence may appear to invest the autobiographical narrative—as well as the essentialist link between body and gender—with especially resonant authority." On one level, the disjunction employed by Lockwood (and Goebbels) strategically sidesteps this risk. Moreover, as *Ceci* progresses, that fissure expands, particularly as we hear the vocal quality change when the mediation shifts from the speaker under the piano to the transducer. Heard through the transducer (which contains a much smaller speaker), the frequencies are more restricted and the vocal sound has to be further (and differently) boosted to provoke additional frequencies from the piano. The effect is less natural, more obviously recorded. While the voice is audibly that of the same person, the change seems to carry the sonic suggestion that it might emanate from a different time and place, beyond those implied by the voice heard through the speaker under the piano: it seems more distant, suggesting that it recollects a past self rather than manifests a present self.

The effect of this is to call into question the singularity or individuality of the performing subject, to offer intimations of its composite multiplicity. In this way, like many contemporary theatre or live art performances involving women's autobiography, *Ceci* draws on the power of intimate testimony while exposing the impossibilities of pure or essentialist self-representation.[7] As Lynn C. Miller and Jacqueline Taylor argue, "the story of women's autobiography is the story of resistance to the disembodied, traditionally masculine 'universal subject'" (2003, 4).[8] Accordingly, *Ceci n'est pas un piano* seems to offer a "view from a body," as demanded by Donna Haraway: "always a complex, contradictory, structuring, and structured body, versus the view from above, from nowhere, from simplicity" (1988, 589).

---

7   Kwame Anthony Appiah notes this paradox of authenticity and constructedness in the politics of identity: the need for experience to be voiced—the demand for and power of testimony—is set against the dangers that the one narrative comes to be essentialised. He writes: "Invented histories, invented biologies, invented cultural affinities come with every identity; each is a kind of role that has to be scripted, structured by conventions of narrative to which the world never quite managed to conform" (Appiah 1992, 174).

8   Shirley Neuman makes a similar point (1992, 225): the female performing subject in this context is "neither the unified subject of traditional theory of autobiography nor the discursively produced and dispersed subject of poststructuralist theory. . . . It is a complex, multiple, layered subject with agency in the discourses and the worlds that constitute the referential space of his or her autobiography."

Embodied voice(s)

I have argued above that the textual component of *Ceci n'est pas un piano* in itself opens up questions of subjectivity: it is positioned as a first-person narrative but mediated by recording and playback through the piano to produce a complex, discursive, performative (or "scriptive") self. How, then, does this relate to the musical content? As noted above, for roughly the first half of the piece, what we hear are non-standard piano sounds, produced inside the instrument, combined with the recorded text. Some of the piano music is precisely composed and notated; some of it is improvised within certain constraints. The sounds produced are not the usual tones produced by piano hammers on strings; and that sets the sounds, to an extent, in relation both to the title, which apparently questions what a piano "is," and also to the text, which speaks of the physical relationship to the instrument. To be sure, the extended piano techniques used here are by no means new. It is now nearly one hundred years since Henry Cowell composed *Aeolian Harp* (1923), which uses only the insides of the piano—plucked and strummed piano strings. Likewise, in recent decades the idea of exploring the "whole" instrument has become relatively commonplace in new music: performers often work with preparations of different kinds, on the strings or otherwise, to alter the sound; or they produce sounds from various parts of the instrument, striking, knocking, bowing, tapping, and so on, with a variety of objects.[9]

Nevertheless, certain of Lockwood's choices are striking in terms of the specific qualities of sound produced. Chime balls rolling on the strings or tiny stones wobbling on them, the particular ways in which strings are bowed or swiped with a fingernail—all these are subtle variants on extended piano techniques that are regularly used by improvisers and found elsewhere in the contemporary piano repertoire. The particularities here draw the performer into experimenting with the details of these modes of sound production as part of the process of practising—into a fresh and explicit awareness of the affordances of the instrument, experienced through embodied interaction with it. Such moments are built into the performance, notably in the more improvisatory sections in which the pianist is clearly directly engaged in her own playful exploration of the sound-world thus made available—something that is quite apparent in live performance, though perhaps not so evident in an audio recording. In particular, in one section (from 4:18 on the recording) Lockwood invites the pianist to improvise for several minutes, making particular use of a rolled rubber ball, mid-register stokes of a superball mallet, and flicked bass strings that will bring out harmonics.

However, Lockwood's choices of instrumental tools are also striking with respect to the particular forms of physical interaction with the instrument that they demand. Four brightly coloured metallic ribbons are used to bow the strings; the gesture required to make the strings ring properly is expansive,

---

9   Luk Vaes (2009) provides the most thorough account of the history of extended keyboard techniques and piano preparations.

even flamboyant—more so even than when pianists bow the instrument with what are, now, the quite conventional tools of fishing wire or horsehair, and particularly so for someone who is not very tall: in order to pull the ribbons far and hard enough to produce the required sound, I have to stretch onto my tiptoes and extend the pulling gesture as high as possible and some way sidewards (see figure 6.2).

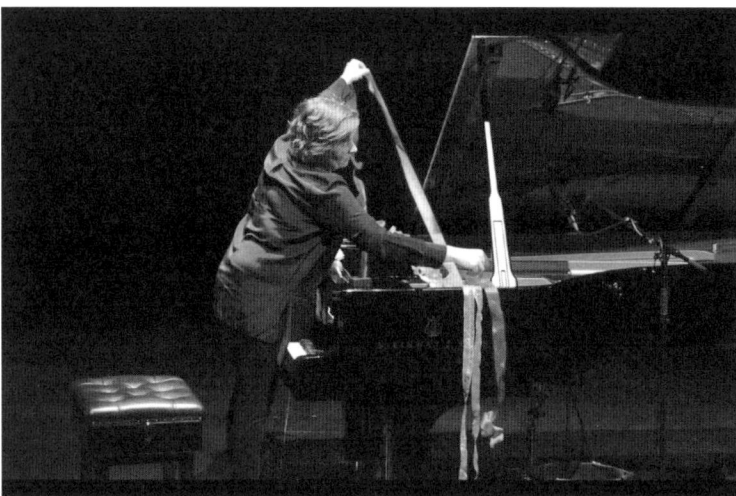

Figure 6.2.

Other sounds require me to lean as far into the instrument as I can, to reach sections of the strings or struts that are a long way from the keys, thereby producing the kind of performing experience that I refer to in my text, in which I speak of "burrowing into the instrument's own space" and comment that "what I do love is getting right inside the instrument, head under the lid of a big resonant grand, with the overtones bouncing around, the blooming buzzing confusion, where you can't tell what's in your head and what's outside it." These, then, are examples of how the piece affords the performer a certain gestural expressivity. Attention is drawn to the specifics of the individual physical engagement: the significance of bodily action in the formation of musical meaning cannot be ignored.

At the same time, the composer's "voice" is certainly "in" the performer's engagement with the instrument. In addition to playing notes on the piano, the performer, as described above, enacts a kind of choreography in and around the piano, a necessary consequence of some of Lockwood's instructions. As well as bowing with ribbons and rolling and bouncing balls, Lockwood requires the performer to use fingers and objects to pluck, flick, strike, and stroke various parts of the instrument, thereby characterising the performer's intimate engagement with the instrumental body. The care with which Lockwood specifies the modes of sound production extends to the precise choice of tools: on sending me the score she included a kit with some of the necessary objects—

Figure 6.2. Still from Annea Lockwood, *Ceci n'est pas un piano* performed by Catherine Laws, Scenic Stage Theatre, York, 5 May 2016.

the right kind of ribbon, for example—to ensure I could produce the correct range of sounds. As a result, there is an element of Lockwood composing not just the notated music but also the performer's body.[10]

On the one hand it is certainly true that all notated music for instrumentalists configures the body that produces the sound; composers usually have at least some awareness of the physical consequences of writing music for performance on a particular instrument (even if they then choose to stretch or even ignore the implicit physical limitations). Beyond this, in recent years a number of composers have become interested in taking the physicality of musical performance as their starting points, composing (and often notating) bodily actions or details of instrumental gesture from which sound then results, rather than vice versa.[11] *Ceci n'est pas un piano* sits some way between these two approaches, composing the situation in a way that focuses attention on the performer's embodiment but also allows the particularities and the agency of the individual body to emerge. Lockwood composes the nature of the sonic and physical engagement with the instrument, at the same time giving the performer a materially significant creative role to play through creation of the text and in the improvisational sections.

In this sense, Lockwood's composerly "voice" retains its presence even in the aspects of performance that would seem to be more attributable to a specific player. However, she plays with this dynamic, creating structures and sound possibilities that not only afford the performer considerable agency but also draw attention to the operation and potential significance of that agency. Her decision to work with the instrument in an unconventional manner, focusing attention on the wider situation of piano performance, and with a text that is explicitly concerned with a performer's relationship to the instrument, marks the situation as determinedly expressive of particular musical identities, arguably foregrounding the specificity of the performer's creative activity relative to that of the composer.

Here, the performer's embodied "voice" is perhaps more radically present than in most performances of composed music. What certainly happens is that the piece draws attention to the piano as something *played*, foregrounding the performer as an embodied subject who encompasses a life beyond this piece. However, *Ceci* also repudiates the simplistic view that the discursive voice—constituted in the performing subject—can be equated with the performer "herself": the complexities of textual mediation, of the relationship between the embodied self and the self that is spoken into being, and of the manifest and entangled dynamics of composer and performer agencies all work to

---

10   In the previous chapter, Richard Craig (119) notes, similarly, the ways in which the physical demands of producing the sounds of *luminous* effect a form of choreography. Chapter 8, "Inside the Choreography of Gender," by Nguyễn Thanh Thủy and Stefan Östersjö, further discusses the gendered aspects of instrumental gesture.

11   For example, in some recent composition the conventional priorities of sound and movement are fully reversed. Examples include Simon Steen-Andersen's first *Study for String Instrument* (2007), where it is the players' movements in time (not the resultant sounds) that are notated, or a number of Aaron Cassidy's pieces, where he employs "physicality and gestural choreography as a primary determinant for material" (Cassidy 2004, 47). For further discussion see Laws (2019, 103–6).

undermine conventional and naive understandings.[12] "This is not a piano," in this sense, might not simply be a statement about the materiality of piano sound, or the cultural status of the instrument (though these are certainly implicated); rather, it might perhaps constitute a larger question about what, or perhaps who, is experienced in a performance. The performance self-consciously stages musical subjectivity in process. We hear and see the interaction of composer and performer agencies with the materiality of piano sound but also with the materiality of the textualised self, and all feed into the emergence of an embodied performing subject: an entity we can call "the performer" but that is manifestly multiple and always changing, self and others in one.

THIS IS A PIANO?

So far I have mapped the performing subject that emerges in *Ceci n'est pas un piano* as discursive and multiply constituted in three ways. First, the performative narrativity of the autobiographical text, juxtaposed with the live performing body, produces the performing self as simultaneously significant and in process, multiple in its instantiation. Second, a particular form of performer intersubjectivity is made evident here, due to the ways in which my own performance of selfhood is constituted through Hymer's. This is a more extreme version of something common to all solo performance (though not often acknowledged), in that the apparently singular performing "voice" is always formed socially, through processes of identification with and differentiation from other, similar practitioners (peers, teachers, famous performers both revered and disliked, and so on). Third, although the embodied performing subject is foregrounded, it is nevertheless produced in part through composerly choices in the particular uses of text and music, the performance tools, and the more precisely scored moments: a dynamics of co-creation, rather than a hierarchy of creator and interpreter, is made apparent.

Beyond this, as I have discussed in more detail elsewhere (Laws 2018), in first encountering this piece, my strong attraction to it derived partly from my immediate sense of a common ground of understanding with the composer, even though we had never met or otherwise communicated. I felt myself to be somehow already "in" this piece, due to its particular exploration of the relationship between performer and piano—physical, musical, and cultural. These were all things with which I was already concerned, as both a performer and musicologist. That the nature of the piano and reflections on being a pianist form both the subject and the content of this piece meant that playing it represented more than a performance opportunity; it created a context for exploring the ways in which the piece itself, and the processes of (re)making it for performance, might open up questions about the construction of musical subjectivity through performance and the distribution of creative agency between composer, performers, and instruments.

---

12 This relates to the notion of the discursive voice developed by David Gorton and Stefan Östersjö in *Voices, Bodies, Practices* (2019, 29–79).

I have outlined above how some of this is manifested. However, the piano, as an entity in itself, plays a particular role in the piece; that is, the performance is in certain ways predicated upon the wider significance of the piano. In addition to the live playing and the recorded text, the piece includes a video: a sequence of stills taken from Lockwood's series *Piano Transplants*, from the 1960s, 70s, and 80s, which involved leaving pianos outside in a range of contexts, such as gardens, beaches, and ponds, and then returning to observe what happened over a period of time (see figures 6.3 and 6.4).[13]

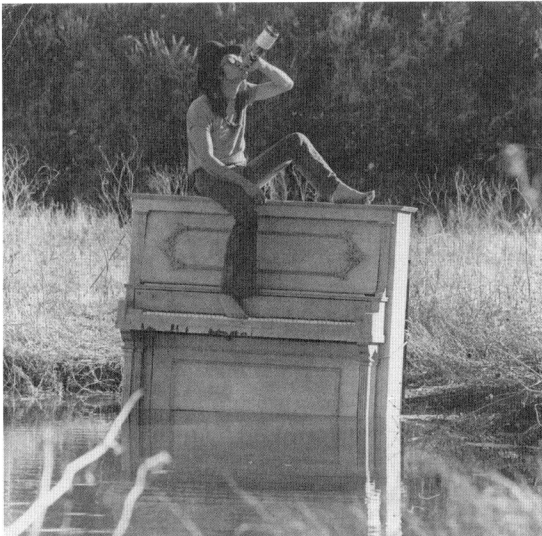

Figure 6.3.

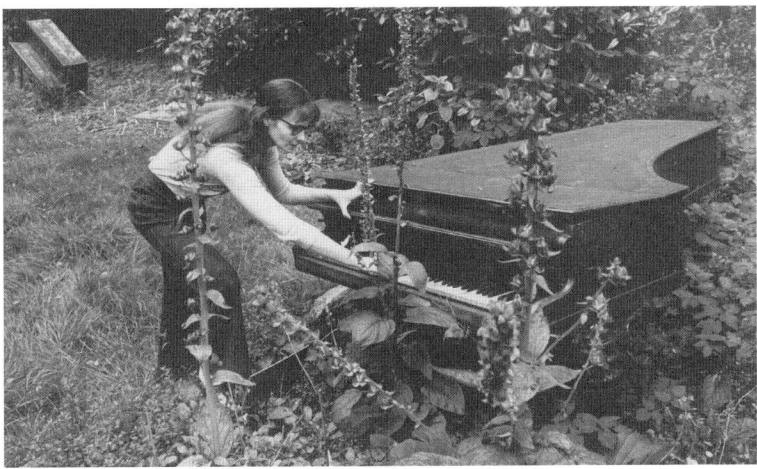

Figure 6.4.

---

13   For the scores of Lockwood's *Piano Transplants*, and images from her realisations, see Lockwood ([1968–72] 2020).

Figure 6.3. Annea Lockwood, "Piano Drowning (1972, Amarillo, Texas)" from *Piano Transplants* series. Photo by Richard Curtin.

Figure 6.4. Annea Lockwood, "Piano Garden (1969–70, Ingatestone, Essex)" from *Piano Transplants* series. Photo by Chris Ware.

Placing these complex, expensive art-making machines outside, at the mercy of wind and rain, water and mud, is on one level an act of violence. But it also relieves these pianos of the grandness and cultural weight that they often carry. These documented actions seem to question the piano's cultural status, perhaps even its place in the world.[14] This adds an additional perspective to the treatment of the piano in *Ceci n'est pas un piano*, furthering the ways in which the title and use of instrumental sound invite reflection upon quite what a piano is.

The piano itself has several voices in this piece, and the compositional structure marks them out as distinct, at least superficially. As noted above, the piano keys are not used in the first half of the piece. For the first few minutes, the instrumental sounds from inside the piano and the lines of text remain relatively discrete: performer and recording politely take turns, as if in conversation (see figure 6.5).

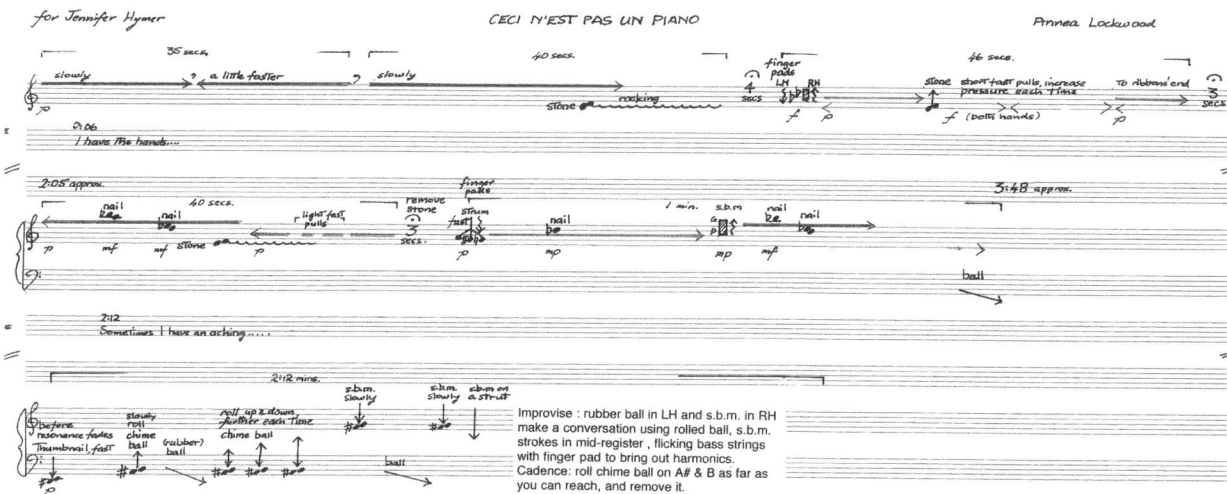

Figure 6.5.

However, running through all this are the soft reverberations emanating from the body of the piano: with the pedal wedged down, each of the instrumental interjections rings on, even if quietly. Similarly, since the voice is played back through the body of the piano, the speaking voice is always a piano voice; and this, too, rings on, quietly, in the background. Beyond the performer and recording, a third agent is, therefore, subtly intimated: a piano voice that is provoked into action, differently, by both the live performer's actions and the absent performer's voice but that is not fully under the control of either. The duration and character of the resonating overtones is dependent on the size, design, and tuning of the individual piano, the details and configuration of the technology, and the acoustic of the space. From the very beginning, then, the

---

14 Lockwood is by no means alone in exploring, artistically, the piano as a cultural object. See Laws (2019, 140).

Figure 6.5. Score extract (opening and improvisation section), Annea Lockwood, *Ceci n'est pas un piano* (2002).

question of voice and agency is complex: although the three components of performer, instrument, and text can be heard as separate, they are also, simultaneously, interdependent. Likewise, the piano "voice" manifests doubly in this opening, speaking first through the articulated sounds of its strings and struts being bowed, plucked, and struck, and second through the ongoing reverberations that are only partly dependent upon those articulations: again, the two voices can be perceived separately, despite a degree of co-dependence.

After a few minutes, the conversational exchange dissipates, first with a slightly longer passage in which there is no text, only the sounds of the chime ball, rubber balls, and superball mallets on the strings (from 3:20 on the recording). Then the voice switches channels into the transducer, with a noticeable shift in vocal timbre and a consequent foregrounding of its recorded quality. On one level, these two changes have the effect of making us listen to the piano sounds and the voice differently, perhaps more as sonic entities in themselves than as part of a dialogue that (in the text) refers to and (in the performer's gestures) enacts the embodied performer–instrument relationship. However, this quickly develops into the improvisation section mentioned above: for several minutes the performer freely explores the soundworld in relation to the continuing text, playing with the sounds and the interactions of their resonances. In my recording, the sounds build up here considerably: the voice, through the transducer, sounds more strident, but as I play, the words gradually become overwhelmed by the piano resonances. The textual clarity of the first few minutes of the piece, with its well-mannered dialogue, is undermined, the words sometimes audible but often submerged in swirls of piano sound. The performer here seems to have a particular kind of power: either to let the voice speak or to produce enough piano noise to engulf it, subsuming verbal signification into musical.

However, the distribution of power here is not quite that simple. The unpredictability of the system undermines the performer's control, enforcing a dynamic, reactive, more truly improvisational state. The resonant backdrop, produced by the piano in response to the two different sound sources, comes and goes according to the interactions between what and how I play at a given moment and how those sounds activate additional frequencies that are then held in the pedal resonance. In the opening, the extent of piano resonance differs subtly from one performance to another according to the size, model, and tuning of the piano and in relation to the spatial acoustics; here, with the louder and timbrally different vocal input and a wider range of sounds and dynamics in the piano playing, the variations suddenly become not only more obvious but much more volatile. The recorded sounds and those I make intermingle to produce additional frequencies, and this internal dynamic system of resonance is quite unstable. Piano sounds that I might expect to have a certain resonant quality take on additional overtones that in turn interact with the unpredictable textual resonance. Things can take off in unexpected ways: there are times when the piano-resonance system seems to have an agency of its own, the situation feeling more fluid than one would normally expect when fixed media are played back. Even though I cannot perceive the origin of some resonances and certainly can only partially control them, they manifest as mine in the context of performance: I am produced in and through these interactions of voice as much as I produce them. As Naomi Cumming asks, in *The Sonic Self*, "does the self form the sound or the sound the self?" (2000, 7).

This section ends about halfway through the piece, when chords start to be played on the piano keys (from 5:49). From this point onwards, the piano music interweaves conventional playing with sounds from the insides of the instrument. However, there are two further moments that are particularly striking with respect to piano sound and identity. Around two thirds of the way through the piece, the wedge is removed from the pedal and the spoken text ends. The pedal continues to be used throughout the rest of the piece, but in conventional fashion, operated by the foot in relation to phrasing and harmonic reverberation. Resonance continues to be important, especially for some of the louder playing in this final section, which includes clusters played by the fists on the keys, the clubbing of fingers on strings, and the scraping of thumbnails along strings to produce a sharp, ringing effect. Nevertheless, the piano is no longer a permanently activated resonator. Moreover, when the wedge is removed, the sound dissipates, with only the very soft reverberations of rubber balls on strings ringing on. The next thing we hear (from 7:53) is standard piano playing: pure, conventional piano sound, in the form of an expressive arpeggiated phrase with the notes held down and without an added layer of text or prolonged reverberations from previous phrases (see figure 6.6).

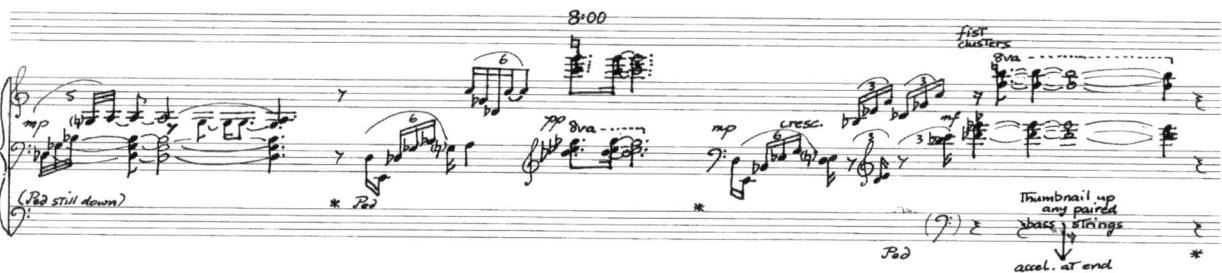

Figure 6.6.

The resulting chord has been briefly held while the pedal is lifted; then, for a fleeting but conspicuous moment before the next, similar phrase, there is a hiatus in the sound for the first time in the whole piece: no piano resonance at all. This short passage, starting with the removal of the pedal wedge, is particularly arresting because it constitutes a shift away from the speaking voice, which never returns, and from the ongoing reverberations. For a moment, the sound of the piano, in a more recognisable form, is exposed, together with the silence that surrounds it.

As these phrases continue, we seem to experience a return to the conventions of piano performance: a silent performer plays the instrument, controlling the sounds notated by a composer. This is perhaps emphasised in my performance

Figure 6.6. Score extract, Annea Lockwood, *Ceci n'est pas un piano* (2002).

by the fact that at this point I sit down on the piano stool for the first time in the performance, assuming the usual position of the pianist. I am not tall enough to play inside the piano while seated, so to avoid constantly getting up and down I prefer to play even the keyed music of the earlier sections from a standing position. This moment, then, feels significant: a reversion to the classic mode of piano performance, with somewhat conventional expressive piano materials in the form of a sequence of rolling arpeggios. This, surely, *is* a piano, a piano as we know it. And this is a pianist, being a pianist. But a question follows: what was that thing that we heard so much of until now, subtly at first and then more persistently and invasively—was it the voice of the resonant beast?

Unsurprisingly, this moment does not last very long. The arpeggios extend and crescendo, gradually reincorporating the punctuating sounds from inside the piano (starting with a fingernail swiping a string), until finally they transform into a sequence of rising clusters played by the fists. This continues into a climactic passage in which loud chords and clusters on the keys alternate with powerful booms and ringing tones from inside the piano that are produced by beating and scraping the fingers on strings and with the superball mallet. The "simple" moment is all but obliterated; and while the tumult of sound quickly disperses, what we are left with, at the end, is a different kind of piano voice: a single tone produced by an e-bow on a string, forming a second striking moment in which piano sound is exposed starkly and clearly. The pianist moves the e-bow into position to set it in action, then leaves it, sits back down, and moderates the harmonics of the tone by varying the pedal pressure, before finally letting the sound die out (see figure 6.7). Look: no hands. A piano tone, but not pure and simple: varying in its harmonic content, and not a tone we are used to. The pianist is not needed for its operation: the pedal could simply be wedged and the tone would sound. But it is her action—the subtle adjustments to the pedal pressure—that in fact gives the tone nuance, exposes its complexity.

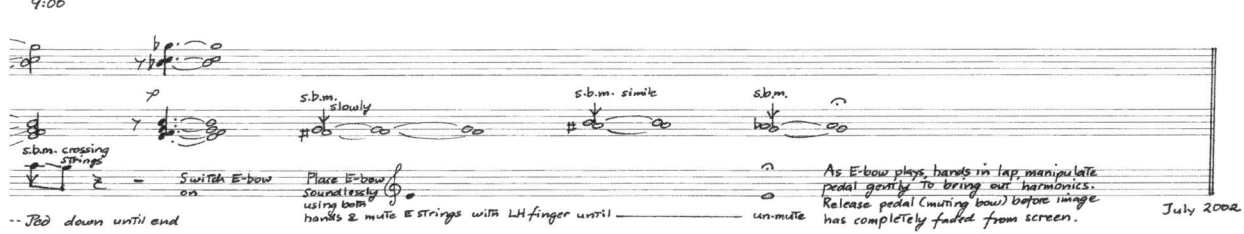

Figure 6.7.

In these various ways, through the inclusion of the video of her *Piano Transplants* but also through this complex exploration of piano sound, the sense emerges that in composing for the piano Lockwood sought to explore the possibilities afforded by the instrument as a mechanical and cultural object with a kind of agency of its own: with the piano's "thing power," as Jane Bennett puts it (2010, 2), in her arguments for greater acknowledgement of the active power of nonhuman agents.[15] Lockwood explicitly engages with the piano's characteristics, challenges, and limitations, but she also invites the performer to take this further: by composing the text and subsequently in weaving her piano playing around it, the performer significantly modulates the experience of the pianistic world and our interactions with it. All this fed into my sense of identification with the piece, building on my own ambivalence with regard to solo piano performance, my love of its rich soundworld, and my wider concerns with the significance of embodiment in performance.

Whose voice is it, anyway?

Ceci n'est pas un piano is reflexively concerned with identities—explicitly with the identities of both piano and pianist. Developing the piece for performance exposed, materially and significantly, the co-constitutive roles of composer, performers, instrument, and context, their contingencies and co-dependencies. Writing about the experience of this piece from the perspective of performance, it is all too easy to present the situation as if there is a clear, split selfhood at work: a physically present, performing self and an absent, verbally reflecting self. However, as I have noted, each of these voices only masquerades as singular: the recorded voice conceals its formation, which depends on those of Hymer, Lockwood, and, at a deeper level, many others; and the embodied performing self has been formed mimetically and antagonistically through interactions both with the context defined by the composer and with significant pianistic others. But even this still neglects the ways in which each identity is *material* for the other. The performing self plays the recorded self, weaves sound around and through it; the performing self—the embodied piano voice—has the power to drown out the reflective, textual voice. However, the bodily "I" is a referent both in the sound—constituted by gesture and effort—and in the words, which speak *of* the body: the body is mediated, and hence to an extent controlled, by the sound. Finally, the piano at times seems to be exposed as an entity in itself, determining the qualities of sounds and their interactions, surpassing the power of either the fixed recording or the performer's in-the-moment decisions; yet its selfhood itself relies on the input of both performer and the recording. Every entity, then, has a kind of singularity; but every singularity is produced in and through the other(s).

One of the reasons I wanted to perform Lockwood's *Ceci n'est pas un piano*—and the reason to write about the processes involved—is that it exposes some of the complexities of the piano in order to reflexively reimagine the embodied self as manifested in performance. Deirdre Heddon argues that autobio-

---

15 Bennett's objective, building from Latour's actor–network theory, is to enable us to acknowledge the shared materiality of people and things—to consider the ways in which we are affected by the things around us—so as better to understand the interactions and distributions of agencies. Juliana Hodkinson, in her chapter in this book, makes a similar plea (drawing directly on Bennett) for better acknowledgement of the affective power of the interactions of not just subjects but also objects.

graphical performances, by simultaneously making recourse to lived experience and self-consciously restaging the becoming-self, are oriented to the future, to transformations of selves, relations, and understanding: "they are performances of aspiration and possibility . . . Looking at the past through the present we are urged to consider the future and what we choose to make there" (Heddon 2010, 172). Likewise, because musical practices do not just express identities but actively construct them, working through identity and difference in the musical imaginary has powerful transformative potential. As Simon Frith suggests, how we "place ourselves in imaginary cultural narratives" (1996, 124) becomes key to relationships between musical and socio-political matters.

Ceci n'est pas un piano seems, in a beautifully playful and creative way, to explore the instrumentalist's body not merely as a vehicle for realising musical intentions, whether of composer or performer, but rather as significant in its apparent presence and its simultaneous, persistent mediations: significant precisely because it is modified by years of practice, subjected to the disciplines of instrumental training and by the demands of repertoire, but also by other, non-musical, social and cultural experiences. To be sure, compositional authority defines the specific context, thematically, musically, and, to an extent, choreographically, as discussed; but by considering the wider context of the piano and piano performance, *Ceci* invites reflection on the ways in which a performing subject is caught in, even produced by, a system of regulation. At the same time, it opens up a space of creativity and resistance for the performer.

The particularities of enaction within that system are brought to the fore: the images invite us to question the nature of the instrument; one hears the voice of the usually silent performer; and the piece directs attention to nuances of particular sounds made by a particular body. Yet all this operates in and through a regulatory context of piano performance and composerly intention—whatever the images and the thematic context, this is a piano piece for a performance space written by a composer. The system can only be reproduced and perpetuated, however, by the subject that it produces, and in that dynamic lies the potential to do something differentiated and meaningful: to grow something from the very reflexive frictions intrinsic to the composer-performer-instrument dynamic.

This is not, then, simply a dialogue, whether between text and music, voice and body, corporeal self and reflecting self, performer and instrument, or, less explicitly, composer and performer(s); rather, it is a composite, interwoven monologue of embodiment. Ultimately, this dynamic, unstable system—merging agencies of body, sound and discourse, composer and different performers, instruments and space—facilitates a restaging of the situation fundamental to any performance: the networks of intersubjectivity, affordance, and resistance at play. What we see and hear both is and is not a piano, is and is not a pianist, is and is not a "work" by a composer. *Ceci n'est pas un piano* asks us what those things are and how they come to be; it playfully and performatively exposes the different entities embodied by an apparently singular performing subject.

CODA

This chapter is primarily concerned with critically examining the process of developing a new text for *Ceci n'est pas un piano* and the subsequent experience of performing the piece: it has since been performed multiple times, in different contexts. The audio recording linked to in the chapter was produced early in that same period, in 2015. However, more recently, and in parallel to the process of writing this chapter, I decided to develop a film version of my performance as part of my series of "piano films": filmic versions of theatrical pieces for piano developed in collaboration with film maker Minyung Im and a number of composers (available at bit.ly/pianofilms). For *Ceci*, the film context offered the opportunity further to explore matters discussed in this chapter, especially the embodied relationship to the piano and the wider status of the instrument: its weight, both physically and metaphorically, and its materiality. As such, the film combines footage from performance (using the audio recording referenced in the chapter) with location filming inspired by Lockwood's *Piano Transplants*. The film is available at https://vimeo.com/421565655: *Ceci n'est pas un piano* by Annea Lockwood; text, performance, and film concept by Catherine Laws; film by Minyung Im; sound recording produced by Jon Hughes; sound mastered for film by Lynette Quek.

REFERENCES

Alcoff, Linda. 1991–92. "The Problem of Speaking for Others." *Cultural Critique* 20: 5–32.

Appiah, Kwame Anthony. 1992. *In My Father's House: Africa in the Philosophy of Culture*. New York: Oxford University Press.

Bennett, Jane. 2010. *Vibrant Matter: A Political Ecology of Things*. Durham, NC: Duke University Press.

Butler, Judith. 1988. "Performative Acts and Gender Constitution: An Essay in Phenomenology and Feminist Theory." *Theatre Journal* 40 (4): 519–31.

Cassidy, Aaron. 2004. "Performative Physicality and Choreography as Morphological Determinants." In *Musical Morphology: New Music and Aesthetics in the 21st Century, Volume 2*, edited by Claus-Steffen Mahnkopf, Frank Cox, and Wolfram Schurig, 34–51. Hofheim: Wolke Verlag.

Cumming, Naomi. 2000. *The Sonic Self: Musical Subjectivity and Signification*. Bloomington: Indiana University Press.

De Preester, Helena. 2007. "To Perform the Layered Body: A Short Exploration of the Body in Performance." *Janus Head* 9 (2): 349–83.

Evans, Mark. 2009. *Movement Training for the Modern Actor*. New York: Routledge.

Fenemore, Anna. 2011. "Body: Introduction." In *Performance Perspectives: A Critical Introduction*, edited by Jonathan Pitches and Sita Popat, 21–22. Basingstoke, UK: Palgrave Macmillan.

Frith, Simon. 1996. "Music and Identity." In *Questions of Cultural Identity*, edited by Stuart Hall and Paul du Gay, 108–27. London: Sage.

Gale, Maggie and Viv Gardner. 2004. "Introduction; Women, Theatre and

Performance: Auto/Biography and Performance." In *Auto/Biography and Identity: Women, Theatre and Performance*, edited by Maggie B. Gale and Viv Gardner, 1–8. Manchester: Manchester University Press.

Goebbels, Heiner. 1997. "Text as Landscape." Translated by Heike Roms. https://www.heinergoebbels.com/en/archive/texts/texts_by_heiner_goebbels/read/240.

Gorton, David, and Stefan Östersjö. 2019. "Austerity Measures I: Performing the Discursive Voice." In *Voices, Bodies, Practices: Performing Musical Subjectivities*, by Catherine Laws, William Brooks, David Gorton, Nguyễn Thanh Thủy, Stefan Östersjö, and Jeremy J. Wells, 29–79. Orpheus Institute Series. Leuven: Leuven University Press.

Haraway, Donna. 1988. "Situated Knowledges: The Science Question in Feminism and the Privilege of Partial Perspective." *Feminist Studies* 14 (3): 575–99.

Harvie, Jen. 2004. "Being Her: Presence, Absence and Performance in the Art of Janet Cardiff and Tracey Emin." In *Auto/Biography and Identity: Women, Theatre and Performance*, edited by Maggie B. Gale and Viv Gardner, 194–216. Manchester: Manchester University Press.

Heddon, Deirdre. 2008. *Autobiography and Performance*. Basingstoke, UK: Palgrave Macmillan.

Henke, Suzette A. 2000. *Shattered Subjects: Trauma and Testimony in Women's Life Writing*. Basingstoke, UK: Palgrave Macmillan.

Hymer, Jennifer (piano). 2007. "Annea Lockwood: *Ceci n'est pas un piano*." On *Ceci n'est pas un piano: Works by Godfield, Hajdu, Lemke, Lockwood, Milliken, Stahnke, Tan Dun*. Ambitus Musikproduktion, none96925, compact disc.

Laws, Catherine. 2018. "This Is Not A . . . ." In *Collaborative and Distributed Processes in Contemporary Music-Making*, edited by Lauren Redhead and Richard Glover, 167–84. Newcastle upon Tyne: Cambridge Scholars Publishing.

———. 2019. "Being a Player: Agency and Subjectivity in *Player Piano*." In *Voices, Bodies, Practices: Performing Musical Subjectivities*, by Catherine Laws, William

Brooks, David Gorton, Nguyễn Thanh Thủy, Stefan Östersjö, and Jeremy J. Wells, 83–167. Orpheus Institute Series. Leuven: Leuven University Press.

Le Guin, Elisabeth. 2005. *Boccherini's Body: An Essay in Carnal Musicology*. Berkeley: University of California Press.

Lockwood, Annea. 2002. *Ceci n'est pas un piano*, for piano, video, and electronics. http://www.annealockwood.com/compositions/.

———. (1968–72) 2020. *Piano Transplants*. Accessed 6 February 2019. http://www.annealockwood.com/compositions/piano-transplants/.

MacDonald, Claire. 1995. "Assumed Identities: Feminism, Autobiography and Performance Art." In *The Uses of Autobiography*, edited by Julia Swindells, 187–95. London: Taylor and Francis.

Magritte, René. 1929. "Les mots et les images." *La révolution surréaliste* 5 (12): 32–33.

Miller, Lynn C., and Jacqueline Taylor. 2003. "Editor's Introduction." In *Voices Made Flesh: Performing Women's Autobiography*, edited by Lynn C. Miller, Jacqueline Taylor, and M. Heather Carver, 3–14. Madison: University of Wisconsin Press.

Neuman, Shirley. 1992. "Autobiography: From Different Poetics to a Poetics of Differences." In *Essays on Life Writing: From Genre to Critical Practice*, edited by Marlene Kadar, 213–30. Toronto: University of Toronto Press.

Park-Fuller, Linda M. 2000. "Performing Absence: The Staged Personal Narrative as Testimony." *Text and Performance Quarterly* 20 (1): 20–42.

Phelan, Peggy. 1993. *Unmarked: The Politics of Performance*. Abingdon, UK: Routledge.

Ramirez Ladrón de Guevara, Victor. 2011. "Any Body? The Multiple Bodies of the Performer." In *Performance Perspectives: A Critical Introduction*, edited by Jonathan Pitches and Sita Popat, 21–32. Basingstoke, UK: Palgrave Macmillan.

Schaeffer, Pierre. 2004. "Acousmatics." Translated by Daniel W. Smith. In *Audio Culture: Readings in Modern Music*, edited by Christoph Cox and Daniel Warner, 76–81. New York: Continuum. Essay first published 1966 in *Traité des objets musicaux* (Paris: Seuil).

147

Shaughnessy, Nicola. 2004. "The Disappearing Subject in Susan Glaspell's Auto/Biographical Theatre." In *Auto/Biography and Identity: Women, Theatre and Performance*, edited by Maggie B. Gale and Viv Gardner, 39–57. Manchester: Manchester University Press.

Steen-Andersen, Simon. 2007. *Study for String Instrument #1*. Copenhagen: Edition S.

Torczyner, Harry. 1977. *Magritte: Ideas and Images*. New York: H. N. Abrams.

Trịnh T. Minh-ha. 1989. *Woman, Native, Other: Writing Postcoloniality and Feminism*. Bloomington: Indiana University Press.

Vaes, Luk. 2009. "Extended Piano Techniques: In Theory, History and Performance Practice." PhD thesis, Leiden University. https://openaccess. leidenuniv.nl/handle/1887/15093.

Charlotte Moorman and "Avant-Garde Music"

A Feminist History of Performance Experimentation

Eleanor Roberts

University of Roehampton

Performance practices of women artists had a pivotal impact in propelling the paradigmatic shift from modernist avant-gardism to other, pluralistic modes of experimentation and innovation across artistic disciplines in the late 1960s and 1970s. Anticipating and paving the way for the development of new forms (such as live art) that would emerge decades later, interdisciplinary artists, including Carolee Schneemann, Charlotte Moorman, Yoko Ono, VALIE EXPORT, and many others, forcefully exposed gendered conceptions (and misconceptions of "authenticity" and authorship), challenged formal borders and boundaries, and transformed understandings of subject and object and their dialogic inter-relationships. Importantly, they also redefined how the artist is understood in relation to society.

However, these significant contributions remain under-historicised. While much has been achieved by feminist artists, historians, and others in identifying those who have previously been neglected or who have an uneasy relationship with conventional means of historicisation, there remains a tendency for many contemporary scholars and institutions to reproduce received narratives of singularly great men. Subsequent theorisations have similarly reinforced questionable historical models based on patrilinear, hierarchical succession (and this remains the case in many studies of music history); for example, Peter Bürger's well-known study situates avant-gardism and experimentation since 1960 as a "neo-avant-garde" unduly indebted to modernist forebears (1984, 58). In contrast, the present chapter suggests a re-evaluation: How might avant-garde (or neo-avant-garde) experimentation across disciplines (in this instance, across visual art, music, and performance) in the late 1960s be theorised and historicised? In a feminist historiographical mode, I complicate and expand on often fragmentary information from institutional archives with anecdotal, experiential, and potentially messy forms of performance documentation that are less typically acknowledged as valid sources. My discussion builds to and from a reading of an event that took place at London's Institute of Contemporary Arts (ICA) in 1968. Titled "Avant-Garde Music," this consisted of a collection of performances by Charlotte Moorman—an influential US-based artist, curator, and trained cellist—in collaboration with the Korean-born artist Nam June Paik. Ultimately, I argue that Moorman's work, in particular, both demands and enables different ways of understanding how new forms of art, music, and performance emerged in the mid-to-late twentieth century (particularly in relation to notions of authorship), also challenging some of the gendered assumptions of previous received histories.

As I have implied, innovative practices in performance art and new music that emerged in the 1960s were defined by institutions in relation to, or as derived from, mythic forefathers of preceding modernisms from the first half of the twentieth century. For example, at the opening of its grand new premises on The Mall in 1968, London's ICA gallery was characterised—both by its director and by commentators—in relation to a designated "patron saint," in this case the French Futurist Guillaume Apollinaire (Lynton 1968, 6). A "hero-poet" (Shattuck [1950] 1971, 5) whose works included erotic fiction, poetry, visual art, and cultural criticism, Apollinaire was influential in the development of several movements, including cubism, Dada, and surrealism, and his works were known for their qualities of "modernism, spontaneity, and surprise" (Bohn 1976, 49).[1] While these might seem fitting constitutive characteristics for a key venue for experimental art, music, performance, poetry, and film-making, Apollinaire's posthumous appointment as patron saint amplifies some of the gendered assumptions of the male-centred art historical canon. Shortly after the gallery's opening, Carolee Schneemann offered an eloquent response to this situation with a performance titled *Naked Action Lecture* (ICA, 1968), which was programmed as part of a double bill along with a screening of her "love-fuck" film *Fuses* (1965).[2] Documentation of the event is scant in the ICA archive; however, Schneemann took steps to document her own "istory," as she calls it, a gender-neutral term designed to shed light on the gendered characteristics of history as a discourse (Schneemann [1974] 2003, 138). From the artist's own account and a number of reviews (Schneemann [1968] 1997, 180–81), we know that the performance-lecture centred on Schneemann comparing her own practice (with slides of her painting, light boxes, and photographs from her kinetic theatre projects) to works by European and American modernist greats like Paul Cézanne, Claude Monet, John Marin, and Willem de Kooning.[3] As part of "split second stops for questions and answers" with the audience among the cascade of images (Schneemann [1968] 2010, 138), Schneemann posed questions: "Can an artist be an art istorian? Can an art istorian be a naked woman? Does a woman have intellectual authority? Can she have public

---

1 Apollinaire was also an artilleryman and infantry officer for the French army during World War One. During the conflict he was hospitalised by shrapnel wounds to the head and reportedly wrote a number of works while recovering in hospital. He died in 1918 in the influenza pandemic. See Shattuck ([1950] 1971).

2 A publicity poster, advertising *Fuses* as Schneemann's "love-fuck," can be found at "Publicity: Posters and Flyers, 1969–1980," TGA 815/2/3/10/5, David Mayor Collection, Tate Archive, London. However, ICA staff edited out Schneemann's confrontational "fuck" and advertised it instead as her "Love Film"; see Michael Kustow, press release 13 June 1968, TGA 955/13/1/4, ICA Collection, Tate Archive, London; ICA Bulletin, May–June 1968, TGA 955/14, ICA Collection, Tate Archive, London.

3 It is important to note that Schneemann's *Action Lecture* also argued for the importance of women artists such as Berthe Morisot and Joan Mitchell.

authority while naked and speaking?" (Schneemann [1968] 1997, 180). In a further act of montage, Schneemann undertook the entire lecture while undressing and dressing in and out of overalls, before asking for two volunteers from the audience to join her in nudity. Schneemann and two "brave fellows" concluded the performance part of the evening by brushing wallpaper glue onto each other's bodies before leaping into a pile of shredded paper below the stage (Schneemann [1968] 2010, 138).

After the artist departed from the space, tarred and feathered with paper, *Fuses* was screened—a twenty-two minute silent film that depicts Schneemann's long-term, three-year action of having sex with her partner (the composer James Tenney) on camera, after which the celluloid was burned, baked, cut, and painted to achieve a partially abstracted, textured aesthetic similar to auto-destructive forms.[4] Various screenings had produced mixed audience reactions, but, according to Schneemann, the work was met with a remarkably stony (if not hostile) reception at the ICA ([1974] 2003, 138). In a letter to Jan Van der Marck on 29 July 1968, Schneemann reported that "the discomfort of the audience was palpable!" and that at the end of the evening an "irate red jowled General with a cane rose from his seat and proclaimed: 'Only a demented frigid nymphomaniac could make such a thing!'" ([1968] 2010, 138). Schneemann's work and its reception in this context speaks to the reality that representations of women (if they are represented at all) in history are frequently plagued by gendered assumptions of artistic and intellectual deficiency and tied to familiar caricatures of raging, perverse, naive, and narcissistic women artists.

Schneemann's life and work has been the subject of a number of important studies and publications, but Charlotte Moorman, another notable visitor to the ICA from the United States in 1968, has until recently received less critical and scholarly attention in histories of art. Moorman was born in a small southern city, Little Rock, Arkansas. She studied at the Juilliard School of Music for a year before going on to play with the American Symphony Orchestra from 1964 to 1966. Concurrently with these classical activities, Moorman established herself as a key figure in intermedia art experiments and activities and founded her enormously influential Annual New York Avant-Garde Festival in 1963. The scope of collaborators and associates grew year by year to include, among others, Schneemann and Tenney, fellow artists Shigeko Kubota, Yoko Ono, Joseph Beuys, Allan Kaprow, Alison Knowles, and Hans Richter, artist-poet Emmett Williams, and new-music composers John Cage and David Tudor. Schneemann and Moorman were friends and worked with each other on a number of projects in New York, from the first Festival of the Avant-Garde (1964), which Moorman organised. It was then that Schneemann played a significant role by encouraging Moorman, for the first time, to realise the potential of her naked body as a visual element in her work (Rothfuss 2014, 102). Moorman continued

---

4   Auto-destructive art is a type of work, pioneered by the artist Gustav Metzger from the late 1950s, that involves processes of destruction, transformation, and material disintegration. It includes works that "automatically" self-destruct because of chemical or other physical components, as well as instances in which the artist or participants manually "destroy" or break up work to create something else. Yoko Ono was the only woman to present art work at Metzger's pivotal Destruction in Art Symposium (London, 1966), but Schneemann did participate in subsequent related events. See Stiles (1987; 1992, 98).

to support Schneemann, and she included her work as part of the Festival of the Avant-Garde from 1965 through the 1970s. Moorman, who died of breast cancer in 1991, aged 57, is among the artists and friends memorialised in Schneemann's installation *Mortal Coils* (1994)—sadly, Schneemann herself died in 2019, also due to breast cancer.[5] There are a number of articles, chapters, and shorter studies of Moorman's work, but it was only relatively recently (during the course of this research) that Joan Rothfuss published her excellent, comprehensive account of Moorman's remarkable life and work, *Topless Cellist: The Improbable Life of Charlotte Moorman* (2014). Subsequently, Lisa Graziose Corrin and Corrine Granof published the edited collection *A Feast of Astonishments: Charlotte Moorman and the Avant-Garde, 1960s–1980s* (2016), another valuable resource, which emerged from a touring exhibition of Moorman's work and archival materials.[6]

Moorman's work—not unlike Schneemann's—has been unhelpfully characterised as excessively theatrical, amateurish, inauthentic, and variously limited by, or confined to, sex and sexuality. This chapter, however, seeks to reclaim the anecdotal, messy, or fragmentary archival material and oral accounts—such as the story of the "red jowled General"—which might appear to bolster the marginal status of women but can instead be used to re-centre or reclaim the supposed inauthenticity of the woman artist as a critical gesture. My focus on the London performance of "Avant-Garde Music," which took place three months after Schneemann's aforementioned intervention at the ICA, reveals generative ways through which one can re-evaluate how Moorman and women artists intervened into a cultural climate in which key male figures of modernism had been secure in their integration into institutions of art as patron saints. In her use of the naked and explicit body in performance, Moorman—alongside peers such as Schneemann—is exemplary in her pursuit of new acts of artistic infidelity, which laid the groundwork for later developments in feminist art and interpretation. In performance studies and related fields, for example, Rebecca Schneider's totemic study *The Explicit Body in Performance* (1997) marked renewed attention to ways in which women's use of their own explicit bodies and sexual agency holds potential not only to shift the "terms of transgression" (4) but also to disrupt misdirecting binaries such as those organised around women's supposed victimhood at the hands of men. I am interested, then, in building upon existing feminist research (such as Schneider's) that has theorised the (woman) artist's explicit body in performance as not merely a defiling presence in the context of the museum (as Schneemann's "red jowled General" saw her) or in music performance, but as productively disruptive. In particular, Moorman's example shows ways in which conventions and assumptions of authorship and authenticity in contemporary art after 1960 might be radically destabilised. This is something that is taken up in work such as Annea Lockwood's *Ceci n'est pas un piano*, as discussed by Catherine

---

5 Documentation of *Mortal Coils* can be found at http://www.caroleeschneemann.com/mortalcoils.html.
6 That attention to Moorman continues to grow many years after her death is simultaneously a happy and, in some ways, a bitter situation. Moorman's legacies should rightly be acknowledged, and yet their posthumous re-evaluation highlights the well-known problem of women artists of this period being overlooked during their actual lifetimes.

Laws in the previous chapter, and in the collaborative performance installation *Inside/Outside*, by the ensemble The Six Tones, choreographer Marie Fahlin, and sound artist Matt Wright, the focus of the next chapter, by Nguyễn Thanh Thủy and Stefan Östersjö: both of these works playfully disrupt conventional notions of the musical performing body. Unlike more typical theorisations of feminist practice, Moorman's performance foregrounds the possibilities of an intervention that is both deeply loving *and* profoundly critical of received (male-centred) histories.

Unlike Schneemann's work, Moorman's can be located more specifically and securely in relation to intermedia art and Fluxus-related practices that were often self-styled as neo-avant-garde.[7] While Moorman herself was not part of the international network of Fluxus artists—particularly because Fluxus founder George Maciunas (also based in New York) did not approve of her work (Rothfuss 2014, 88, 124)—she was nonetheless a part of its wider artistic and social context. In 1964, Moorman met Nam June Paik—then a Fluxus member who was also classically trained as a pianist—after seeking him out (on the composer's instruction) to take part in her production of Karlheinz Stockhausen's music theatre work *Originale* (1961) for the second Annual Festival in 1964.[8] Against the wishes of Henry Flynt and other members of Maciunas's Fluxus group, who had boycotted the production,[9] Paik happily agreed to take part (he announced his resignation from Fluxus), and their long-term collaboration was forged (Rothfuss 2014, 124). Her naked and sexually provocative performances with Paik would earn Moorman the moniker "topless cellist," especially after she was found guilty of indecent exposure and given a suspended sentence by Judge Milton Shalleck in New York in 1967 (ibid., 175–205).[10] The charge was brought after plainclothes police shut down her performance of *Opera Sextronique* (1967), a work originally written for Moorman by Paik and presented at the Film-Makers' Cinematheque (figure 7.1).

The work called for Moorman to perform "topless, then bottomless, and finally completely nude," but she was arrested before the third aria (Rothfuss 2014, 175). Topless, but before she had a chance to remove her skirt, she was dragged from the stage by the police amid chaotic scenes created by a protesting audience and a scrum of journalists. Though Rothfuss argues that Moorman herself was "probably responsible for the leak" that prompted police to arrive at the venue, Moorman did not anticipate that she would be arrested or that she would be refused permission to dress before being taken into custody, taken

---

7   Intermedia art is a term that emerged in the 1960s. It was used by artist Dick Higgins to describe new art practices that challenged disciplinary distinctions, such as those between music, poetry, and visual art, by incorporating a variety of media in a single work. Fluxus, a related term, refers to a specific network of artists operating within the broader category of intermedia art. Fluxus was started by artist George Maciunas; while the group was ostensibly open, membership appears to have been based on Maciunas's and others' approval or acceptance. See Dick Higgins and Hannah Higgins ([1965] 2001).

8   According to Rothfuss (2010, 146), Paik was also pleased with the encounter, having finally found a woman who would consider performing naked.

9   Maciunas and others boycotted the production on the grounds that Stockhausen was considered a "Cultural Imperialist" and "Ruling-Class Artist" (see Piekut 2011, 66–69).

10 See also David Bourdon (2000).

away to spend the night in a cell.[11] In court, the prosecution characterised *Opera Sextronique* as "a sick publicity stunt" (ibid, 192–93); but, according to Rothfuss, the conviction rested on the assertion that "topless cellists could not be artful because [the judge] had never seen one described in classical painting, poetry, or prose" and hence concluded that "perhaps, then, the breast in those milieux is not artful" (ibid., 201). Since Moorman's performance of *Opera Sextronique* was not considered to be art, it was presumed to be merely an act of indecency.

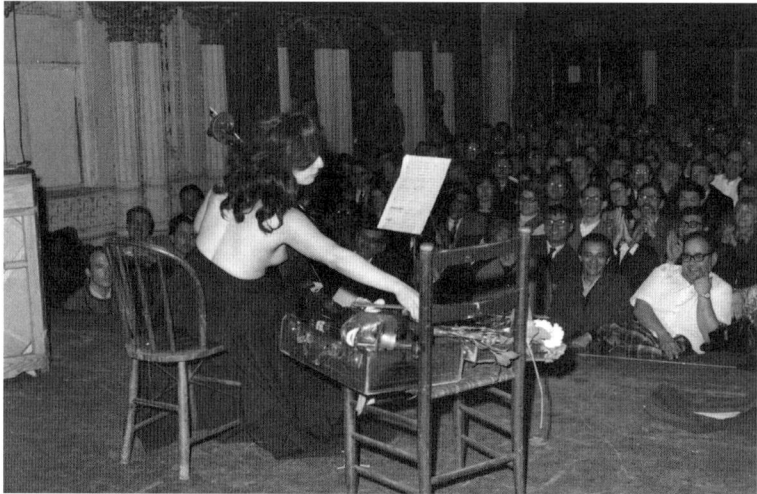

Figure 7.1.

Rendering Moorman's performance as an "indecent" act places it within a set of art and non-art binaries constructed on assumptions of artistic legitimacy that are frequently bound up with representations of sex. These binaries have been understood by feminist critics as both misleadingly constructed and insidiously gendered, as Jennifer Doyle (2006, xvii) has argued persuasively in relation to art and pornography. Interestingly, Paik actively and outspokenly pursued ways in which art and sex might overlap for a number of years prior to *Opera Sextronique*. In the early 1960s, for example, he had written a score for Alison Knowles—who was at the time the only woman in the Fluxus group—that was sexually explicit (Rothfuss 2014, 88). *Serenade for Alison* (1962) involved Knowles stripping off "panties" of different colours and discarding them in various ways, leading to a final display of nakedness.[12] However, Paik was unable to convince Knowles to perform the piece as he had written it; she felt it isolated and foregrounded the "femaleness" of her body and what she termed the "objectness of woman" in a limiting way (Rothfuss 2014, 89). Indeed, as we

---

11 Moorman was wearing a skirt and a coat that *Life* magazine editor David Bourdon had draped over her shoulders as she left (Rothfuss 2014, 186).

12 The score for *Serenade for Alison* can be found at TGA 815/2/2/4/163, David Mayor Collection, Tate Archive, London.

Figure 7.1. Charlotte Moorman, performing at the Film-Makers' Cinematheque, 125 West 41st Street, New York. Credit: New York Daily News Archive / Hy Rothman, 1967. Courtesy of Getty Images.

have seen in the case of Schneemann, women's occupation of sexually explicit roles or poses has frequently been used to deny their claims to seriousness. Whereas men's representations of nude women are frequently accepted into institutions housing artistic activity, women's presentations of their own live bodies have been considered to be outside the purview of valid or accepted (high) culture. For instance, although Moorman was charged, Paik was released from custody in the early morning following his arrest. Assumptions about the artistic agencies of Paik and Moorman come into question here: whereas Paik is comparatively sheltered as the legitimated author of *Opera Sextronique*, Moorman is assumed to be one of many interchangeable performers and hence guilty of indecent exposure (Rothfuss 2010, 145). These assumptions are made despite the facts that Moorman was well known as an artist and that she had also toured, in Europe in 1965 and 1966, performing intermedia art, Fluxus scores, and related works from around the world. Bitterly and ironically—especially so, when one considers that in the conventional Western classical tradition it is the (male) composer to whom artistic authorship, and hence responsibility, is usually uncritically ascribed—Moorman is only assumed to be responsible when the work is pulled into charges of indecency.

To return to the ICA, and taking modernist avant-gardism as a framing device employed by that institution in the late 1960s, a struggle seems to have taken place between competing forces of historical succession (what becomes "new"), citation (against or alongside which the "new" is defined), and slippage between different moments and practices. Frequently, what brings those forces together—as Mignon Nixon has suggested of surrealism—are cultures of brotherhood (or fatherhood) and discipleship, which may involve seemingly contradictory modes not only of fraternity (or paternity) and reverence but also of profanity (Nixon 2005, 4). These cultural lineages, however, become troubled by the figure of the "woman artist," as has been demonstrated by a number of feminist art historians that include Nixon (2005), Schneider (1997), Amelia Jones (2004), and others. For example, in her book *Fantastic Reality: Louise Bourgeois and a Story of Modern Art*, Nixon (2005) identifies ways in which Louise Bourgeois's employment of "the comic gesture and the hysterical pose" (4) in her work recasts discipleship, as she "burlesques her many frustrated attempts to court a master" (25) in a milieu from which she was professionally rejected in the earliest stages of her career in the 1930s and 1940s. Questions of identity and authorship, which—as Nixon says—have more typically secured coherence and unity between an artist's works in art historical interpretation (2), are then thrown into states of conflict. In the case of a surrogate son, for example, "rebellion [against the father figure] is the proof and fulfillment of the patriarchal bond"; but this bond is unavailable to a surrogate daughter of the modernist avant-garde, whose admirations are conversely (Nixon argues in Freudian terms) channelled away towards her (hetero)sexual relations with other men (27). Indeed, as Nixon has explained, for Bourgeois and surrealism, major themes or representational modes are dramatically changed in meaning by the agitated—or, rather, agitating—authorship of the woman artist. Consider, for example, the aesthetics or representations of hysteria: "[For

Bourgeois,] hysteria's potential to resist patriarchal authority is double-edged. For the hysterical position surrealism celebrates—marked by passivity, fragmentation, and helplessness—holds the danger for a 'woman artist' of being confused with femininity itself. It is one thing to identify, as an artist, with the hysteria of the other, as the male surrealists did: to turn hysterical might feel exciting or terrifying, liberating or rebellious. It is something else to lay claim, as a 'woman artist,' to the hysteria that is culturally synonymous with being a woman" (32). The double-dealing authorship of a woman artist who disturbs the patriarchal bonds of the modernist avant-garde is thus consistently shadowed by myths of her unified and unifying femininity. This is particularly evident in Moorman's reception as a "surrogate daughter" of male artists.

Indeed, throughout histories of avant-garde art, women who use their own bodies to express aesthetics or modes of sex or sexuality in their work have been regarded with suspicion. For instance, in *Irrational Modernism: A Neurasthenic History of New York Dada*, Amelia Jones establishes that Elsa von Freytag-Loringhoven ("the Baroness") was a pioneering and influential figure in New York Dada circles in the 1910s and that she may even have been responsible for (or at least had a strong influence on) the creation of some of its most famous ready-made works, such as the sculpture titled *Fountain* (c.1917) that is typically credited to Marcel Duchamp (Jones 2004, 10). However, in her outlandish style and openness about sexuality she became the subject of male peers' "lingering sexual conservatism" and misogynistic characterisations of her as an excessive or tasteless figure (ibid.). Rothfuss has pointed out similar biases against Moorman that include failures to recognise her artistic agency: "Her body was the vehicle for two of [Paik's] aesthetic experiments: the fusion of classical music with sex, and the humanisation of technology . . . She was [perceived as] a naïf who blindly carried out his instructions, even after doing so got her arrested and convicted of lewd behaviour" (Rothfuss 2010, 145).

In autumn 1968, Paik was exhibiting a number of TV sets and his humanoid *Robot K-456* (created with Japanese artist-engineer Shuya Abe in 1964) as part of the *Cybernetic Serendipity* show (2 August–20 October) at the ICA.[13] This hugely popular exhibition, which showcased various syntheses of art and technology, remains relatively well known today and has been commended for marking a "change in thinking" of major arts institutions towards video art (Rogers 2013, 138). On the evening of Monday 23 September 1968 Moorman joined Paik at the gallery to perform their evening of avant-garde music in the Nash House auditorium.[14] The press release sensationally (though accurately) announced that Moorman was to "play dustbins, whistles, balloons, guns, door buzzers, etc." The credits for the intermedia programme (billed here as "mixed media") were listed as follows:

---

13 Papers relating to the exhibition *Cybernetic Serendipity*, TGA 955/7/2/7, Tate Archive, London. Paik's *K-456* is a radio-controlled construct that walked, "talked," defecated dried beans, and for a time boasted a penis as well as breasts; see also Wulf Herzogenrath (1988, 21).

14 Due to demand, a second late-night concert took place the following Saturday; see "Avant-Garde Music at the ICA: First Concert by Charlotte Moorman and Nam June Paik," press release, 18 September 1968, TGA 955/13/6/16, ICA Collection, Tate Archive, London.

ENTRANCE MUSIC . . .	[George] BRECHT- [James] TENNEY
PER ARCO . . .	GIUSEPPI CHIARI
26.1'1499" . . .	JOHN CAGE
VARIATIONS ON A THEME BY SAINT-SAENS . . .	NAM JUNE PAIK
SPRINGEN . . .	HENNING CHRISTIANSEN
A NEW FILM . . .	STAN BRAKHAGE
INSTRUMENTAL MUSIC . . .	TAKEHISA KOSUGI
VARIATION No. 3 . . .	JOHN CAGE
EXIT MUSIC . . .	BRECHT-TENNEY[15]

Archival evidence suggests that perhaps unsurprisingly, given the history of Paik and Moorman's previous collaborations, the evening did not play out in this orderly fashion. An article by Edward Greenfield in the *Guardian* tells us that the event ran late and that in fact the Brecht-Tenney (George Brecht and James Tenney) piece was not played at all because, as Paik told an increasingly restless audience, the tape, which contained a "sort of feeling of music, rather than actual sound," had been "left at the BBC" (Greenfield 1968, 6). On the basis of Greenfield's account, the first presentation was actually *Instrumental Music*, a score by Japanese artist Takehisa Kosugi, with whom Moorman had previously worked on her Annual Festivals[16] and who had also assisted Paik and Moorman at the raided performance of *Opera Sextronique* (Rothfuss 2014, 113).

For *Instrumental Music*, Moorman would begin playing her cello, and a collaborator (in this case, Paik) would trace and cut out the outline of her shadow from fabric or paper hung on a back wall. In some performances, fabric was placed directly over Moorman's body and cut out around her as she lay on the floor (Rothfuss 2014, 151). Interestingly, the cutting of fabric or paper over, around, or against the body is a recognisable trope in intermedia art, as represented in extant scores.[17] While there is virtually no documentation of *Instrumental Music* at the ICA, critics did describe Moorman's performance of a related score by Kosugi called *Chamber Music* (at least part of which exists in the form of a score titled *Anima 2*).[18] For this piece, Moorman would crawl into a large nylon bag with various zippers sewn across its surface, drag her cello in alongside her, and then roll around inside. Video documentation of Moorman performing *Chamber Music* at Caracas Contemporary Art Museum in

---

15 A second document advertises the second appearance, including works by "JOSEPH BEUYS, GEORGE BRECHT, ROBERT BREER, EARLE BROWN, JOHN CAGE, GIUSEPPI CHIARI, HENNING CHRISTIANSEN, KEN JACOBS, TAKEHISA KOSUGI, YOKO ONO, JAMES TENNEY AND NAM JUNE PAIK." TGA 955/13/6/16, ICA Collection, Tate Archive, London.

16 Moorman's fourth Annual Festival (1966), in which Kosugi performed, was a free event held in Central Park, reportedly seen by 15,000 spectators and passers-by. Hans Richter, Richard Huelsenbeck, Joseph Beuys, Shigeko Kubota, Allan Kaprow, Alison Knowles, Bob Watts, and Emmett Williams were among the artists involved. See David Bourdon (2000, 80–82).

17 Many Fluxus and intermedia scores have been published since the 1960s, including artists' own auto-historicisations and edited collections such as *The Fluxus Performance Workbook* (Friedman, Smith, and Sawchyn 2002).

18 *Anima 2* is among the Takehisa Kosugi scores published in *The Fluxus Performance Workbook*. It requires a "chamber which has windows," out of which one should "put out" different parts of the body (Kosugi 2002, 75).

1969 (Performancelogia Performance Art Archive 1969), together with another later performance for camera (Stern 1980), gives us a clearer sense of her performance style.[19] Moorman pushes and pulls at the zips from within the bag to reveal mischievous peering eyes, the naked flesh of her leg, her buttocks, the cello's neck, her hair—before zipping up and retreating again into the bag. Moorman's use of the bag here seems to partake of her subversive approach to conventions of concert wardrobe: she usually performed in formal gowns, technological underwear designed for her by Paik, such as *TV Bra for Living Sculpture* (1969), or nothing at all. This insight into Moorman's playful sensibility in performance enables a fuller understanding of the character of the ICA programme: following *Chamber Music*, Moorman continued with her interpretation of the next score, John Cage's *Variation No. 3*, including replacing her bow with a bunch of flowers, frying eggs, gurgling Coca-Cola, and playing a doorbell.[20] Moorman also inserted new elements into the scores; for instance, as part of John Cage's *26'1.1499"*, she performed an act conceived by Paik and titled *Human Cello* (1965), in which she discarded her cello to play Paik's naked back instead. Stripped to the waist, Paik would kneel and press his face into Moorman's breasts as she "slapped, plucked, and bowed" a string stretched across the length of his spine (Rothfuss 2014, 113). A projected backdrop of video clips from previous performances ran throughout. For Greenfield (1968, 6), the evening was "fun," but ultimately characterised by an enduring feeling of "waiting," never amounting to more than a collection of "disjointed squibs."

In her *Naked Action Lecture*, Schneemann critically intervened into patriarchal conceptions of authorship by putting herself in conversation with Cézanne and other modernist "greats." Moorman's performances of scores written by others, in which she presents her own body as both subject and object (here, as a musical instrument), prompt a related but distinct set of questions about histories of avant-gardism and more specific notions of artistic *agency*. The conditions of art production within and around the collective milieu of intermedia artists in the 1960s, of which Paik and Moorman were a part, bring into sharp focus increasingly destabilised distinctions not only between authorship and agency but also between the "authentic" and "inauthentic." The neo-avant-garde practices of these artists *did* consciously echo those of the Dadaists that converged particularly in Europe and New York in the 1910s and 1920s. As John Cage famously wrote, "One way to write music: study Duchamp" (Cage [1963] 1967, 72). Similarly, Ina Blom writes of what she calls a "tele-touch" that cuts through time, between early Dada and "Neo-Dada" of the 1960s, and

---

19 My use of footage of a different performance in the absence of archival material is justified on the grounds that my methodology here also reflects the "infidelity" or "infidel" feminist strategies that I begin to explore in this chapter.

20 Cage's score is correctly titled *Variations III*; see https://johncage.org/pp/John-Cage-Work-Detail.cfm?work_ID=235. Typographical variation in the programme for "Avant-Garde Music" is minor, but at the same time draws further attention to issues of Moorman's infidelity to those whose status as authors is more secure. This seeming discrepancy between versions might be considered in terms of generation loss between copies and the authentic original. However, in this chapter I unsettle the notion of the singular authentic original in the context of intermedia art. Therefore the variation may *seem* to bolster notions that Moorman was a sloppy copyist, but it also points to the process of transformation that differentiates Moorman's work from Cage's.

prevents positioning Dada in any single spatial-temporal location (2001, 210, 212). Moorman's appearing and disappearing body in works such as *Chamber Music* (a score originally written in Japan and performed around the world) is co-mingled with the cello, as interchangeable limbs (a foot, a wooden neck) emerge from within the bag. As the body of the cello and the body of the artist are muddled together, the performance seems to exemplify what Peter Bürger theorised to be the project of the historical avant-garde: to sublate art into the "praxis of life" (1984, 53–54). However, Bürger also argues that by the time of the "neo-avant-gardes" of the 1960s this project had failed: "Since now the protest of the historical avant-garde against art as institution is accepted as *art*, the gesture of protest of the neo-avant-garde becomes inauthentic" (53).

Bürger's suggestion of a dichotomy between the "authentic" (if ultimately failed) protests of the historical avant-garde and their later, "inauthentic" counterparts mirrors patterns of criticism that diminish Moorman's artistic agency in comparison to the "authentic" authors whose works she performs. That Moorman's body has been deemed to be a "vehicle" for works by others, as Rothfuss (2010, 145) has shown, is illustrative of wider assumptions that women artists (particularly as "performers") are always indebted to a great male author. Indeed, the trope of the (woman) artist as "copyist" has many historical antecedents. This "copyist" status has held changing meanings and implications at different points in history; for example, as the craze for embroidered "copies" of "old master" paintings played out in the eighteenth century, women artists such as Mary Linwood were initially celebrated in high art circles and academies for their artistry and craftsmanship but were subsequently challenged in their "legitimacy" as artists and struggled to escape "amateur" status (Lindberg 1998, 507–9). For Moorman, suspicion among her peers arose when it was felt that she overshadowed the work at the expense of fidelity to the score or when she failed to demonstrate the modesty required to foreground the work of the composer (the "true" artist). As Rothfuss details, Moorman's performances were despised by George Maciunas and Fluxus members, Jasper Johns said that Moorman should be "kept off the stage," and John Cage (also sometimes considered a Fluxus artist) "came to abhor the way she performed" his works (Rothfuss 2014, 77). Indeed, Cage's publisher had written to him to say that "the best thing that could happen for [Cage], would be that Charlotte Moorman would die" (235).

To return to *Chamber Music* and Moorman's body-becoming-cello or body-as-instrument, a comparison with now-canonical antecedents illuminates how agency and authenticity have been historically conceived. The image of a woman's body *as* musical instrument, for instance, recalls New York Dadaist Man Ray's well known photograph of Alice Prin (also known as Kiki de Montparnasse) titled *Le Violon d'Ingres* (1926). In this work, as Kirsten Hoving Powell writes (2000, 772), Man Ray invokes Jean-Auguste-Dominique Ingres's neoclassical rendering of a seated female nude in *La Baigneuse Valpinçon* (1808). Like Ingres's bather, Man Ray's image is of an anonymous woman, naked save for a turban covering her hair; her head is turned as she gazes off into the unseen distance, and the smooth cleft of her full buttocks emerges from sumptuous folds of fabric. In both images there is a smoothing, flattening, and distortion of the woman's figure as represented by the artists. Man Ray irreverently foregrounds his manipulations, rounding out and smoothing off the woman's body in the photograph with a pencil and adding in the sound holes of a violin with Indian ink on her back (Hoving Powell 2000, 780). There is fantasy at play in these images by Ingres and Man Ray, and it is important to observe that the women are represented as objects of male desire or pleasure ("violon d'Ingres" is a colloquialism meaning hobby). Their bodies are depicted as instruments and vessels of the artists' creativity, emblematised in the "hollowing out" of Kiki's body-as-violin.

Hoving Powell points out that the title of Man Ray's work suggests several readings of the central ambiguity between the woman's body as a homage to Ingres and the French use of the phrase "violon d'Ingres" to refer to a secondary pastime (often that one is bad at).[21] This has been variously interpreted as an expression of Man Ray's heterosexual desire (or, perhaps more specifically, his desire for Kiki) or of his wilfully playful, "not serious," approach to art—or both (Mundy 2008, 47). Hoving Powell also points out the troubling linguistic resemblance to the French word for rape (*violons*), before—perhaps questionably—edging around this to conclude that, primarily, the title is indicative of sets of oppositions, of both "respect and ridicule" in this "appropriated" nude (Hoving Powell 2000, 772). As a canonical figure in French art, Ingres held a complicated position amongst Dadaists: he was regarded as influential, in his retrospective aesthetic and concern with imagery from the past (thus supporting the various "primitivisms" of the historical avant-gardes), but he was also treated ironically by highly experimental artists.[22] Hoving Powell suggests that Man Ray's imitation of Ingres's bather in *Le Violon d'Ingres* "pays homage to the master, while also deriding the tradition he represents" (781). She also argues that Ray's "deformation" of the woman's body, which appears distorted and limbless, is primarily an attack on classicism and the "classical unity" of the body, rather than an attack on women's actual bodies (as the apparent wordplay on "rape" might suggest) (789).

Although Hoving Powell's study suggests a number of ways in which Man Ray's work might be put to feminist use or made subject to feminist criticism, it falls short of explicitly addressing the ways in which the image operates in its patriarchal functionality, whereby the construction of women's bodies fails to reach beyond their gendered objectification. Usefully, Nixon has suggested ways in which modernist avant-garde histories might be understood through their frequent deployment of obscene or dirty jokes, in which women's bodies become anchors for patriarchal bonds between men: "The purpose of obscene jokes, Freud contends, is sexual exposure. An obscene joke is also, according to him, an intimacy shared between men (specifically, upper-class men) with reference to an absent woman—a woman whose absence is an essential condition of the joke. . . . As with obscene jokes in general, the woman's absence from the

---

21 This phrase reportedly stems from Ingres's hobby of playing the violin with varying degrees of success (Hoving Powell 2000, 772).
22 Notably Francis Picabia; see also Hoving Powell (2000, 775).

scene in which pleasure is taken ensures that the men's enjoyment will not be spoiled, that the object of the joke will not object, will not become a resistant subject" (Nixon 2005, 63).

Of course, *Le Violon d'Ingres* cannot be adequately theorised merely as a dirty joke. As a work of art it does a number of other things—making visible the process of artistic production and wryly playing with tradition, cultural seriousness, and hierarchical orderings of (male) artists. However, while the work might constitute a valid expression of Man Ray's sexuality on one hand, on the other hand the dismemberment, warping, and anonymity of the woman's vehicular body is inextricably bound up with other patterns of patriarchal representation and reinforces the male author's control over the woman-as-object. Historically, women's bodies have been appropriated and objectified as vehicles in the service of myriad agendas—including, as Nguyễn Thanh Thủy and Stefan Östersjö point out in their chapter in this book, the re/constitution of national(istic) identity. In Moorman's case, as her body becomes interchangeable and merged with the body of a cello in *Chamber Music*, questions emerge about how her performance, as a kind of "mouthpiece" for an external (male) artistic authority, relates to the circuitous interconnection of tribute and disparagement illustrated in Man Ray's avant-gardism. Agency—so startlingly obliterated in the women's bodies depicted by Man Ray and Ingres—is brought into particularly sharp focus by the popular assumptions, explained and critiqued by Rothfuss, that Moorman was merely a vehicle or instrument for realising the visions of "true" artists (Paik) or, worse, that she was a cultural "Harlot" and thief (Rothfuss 2010, 145). From such perspectives, although Man Ray is seen to actively appropriate another artist's imagery, Moorman merely re-enacts or plagiarises a kind of authentic original. As a woman, she is assumed to be unable to intervene into masculinist traditions of art and the consequent attacks on women's bodies in the historical canon.

As the patriarchal bonds described by Nixon, around which avant-garde histories and practices are typically constructed, are out of Moorman's reach, her embodiment of sexuality takes on different connotations. In his *Guardian* account of *Chamber Music* at the ICA, Greenfield writes: "An occasional clonk of pleasure came from the cello at what Miss Moorman was evidently doing to it, but these were the spontaneous murmurs of love, not recognisable music. The ostentatious unzipping of a zip and the sudden emergence of sensuous lips, of a mass of hair, of a naked foot—these were the 'events' of the piece, superbly surrealistic, but tickling the nerves less and less as one waited" (1968, 6). Greenfield characterises Moorman's performance by describing unseen acts of "love" and the erotic implications of her joyful (yet serious) writhing around in the bag. The erotic aspects of the performance are also evident in footage of the 1969 performance at Caracas Contemporary Art Museum (Performancelogia Performance Art Archive 1969), in which Moorman's thigh emerges from a zip to straddle the cello-body, "clonks of pleasure" sounding from within. Indeed, in this footage, the contrast between Moorman's white stockings and suspenders and her naked flesh as the fabric of the bag slips further down causes a young teenage boy in the audience to turn away, looking at his friends, shrugging off his embarrassment with a nervous laugh. But a corollary implication in Greenfield's account is that Moorman's performance lies outside recognisable (one might as well say "legitimate") spaces of art and musical performance. Interestingly, where Greenfield saw "love," Michael Nyman (1999, 88), who reviewed the performance for the *Spectator*, saw war—a cello being "fought" with. On Moorman's work more generally, he writes: "Moorman's cello has surpassed any other instrument, in any era, in the number of uses it has been put to. It is attacked when a recording of aerial bombardment is played; it is fought within a large bag with zippered orifices; it is frozen in a block of ice, and then the ice bowed until it melts and Moorman can get at the cello; Paik's back is bowed as if it were a cello, and the instrument itself it used as a sexual organ" (ibid.). Here, Nyman is more generous in crediting Moorman's work for its multiplicity, particularly by allowing that it might represent both love *and* aggression simultaneously; however, he nonetheless conflates Moorman's cello with her own body, defined by its implicitly feminine and essential "sexual organ."[23] Indeed, the conflation between the curved body of the cello and the body of a woman had at this point become a recognisable cliché.[24]

As noted above, Hoving Powell (2000) argues that in Man Ray's work the woman's body is tactically appropriated by the artist from a forefather, drawing on an authentic original to create a new (but nonetheless authentic) work that partakes of both homage and derision. However, the context for intermedia art, of which Moorman is part, puts questions of authorship, appropriation, and the authentic in a different light. Five years before the ICA show, *Chamber Music*, or at least its semblance, was performed by Takehisa Kosugi in Tokyo at the open entry 15th Yomiuri Independent Exhibition in 1963.[25] Kosugi was a Tokyo-based composer, artist, and violinist who pioneered intermedia and

23 A worthwhile comparison can be made with the use of the piano by Annea Lockwood, discussed in the previous chapter by Catherine Laws. Subsequently, Laws commented to me that Lockwood's treatment of the piano in her "transplants" might seem similar to the ways in which Nyman characterises Moorman's treatment of her cello: both are placed in unusual contexts and engaged in actions designed to provoke reactions, especially from those used to seeing expensive musical instruments treated as precious objects deployed in the service of high art. In an email exchange, Laws commented to me that "Nyman's account repeats the conflation of cello and woman's body that is, as described above, so pervasive, the pianos in Lockwood's transplants can be visited or perhaps even played but stand proudly alone, as if having found a new environment, independent of conventional performance." Moreover, rather than a merging with the instrument, Lockwood's composition *Ceci n'est pas un piano*, and Laws's text for the piece, explore both our assumptions about the nature of the piano and, in particular, the tensions and constraints of the embodied performer–instrument relationship. As further examined in Laws's extended discussion of body–instrument relationships in the partner volume, *Voices, Bodies, Practices* (Laws 2019, 107–11), the notion of instrumental "incorporation" is simultaneously attractive and problematic, not least for pianists.

24 On the cliché of conflations between the body of the cello and the body of the woman, I thank Catherine Laws for her response to my paper, "Anecdotal Interventions: Performance Art in 1970s London and Feminist Historiographies," at the seminar Performance, Subjectivity, and Experimentation in Artistic Research, Orpheus Research Centre in Music, Ghent, 25 February 2016.

25 The Yomiuri Independent Exhibition was an annual open entry fine art show with no selection process (although exhibitors were required to pay a fee). It was sponsored by the Yomiuri Shimbun Company, a newspaper publishing house, and existed between 1949 and 1963. Faced with increasingly out-of-control submissions year after year, exhibition organisers at the hosting Tokyo Metropolitan Art Museum enacted "Standards for Showing Exhibits" in 1962, which stipulated various rules against unpleasant and dangerous works. The show was suddenly discontinued in 1964, shortly before the sixteenth exhibition was due to take place. See Nakazawa (2014).

Fluxus-related forms both individually and as part of the improvisation ensemble Group Ongaku [Music Group] in the 1960s and 1970s. In an act titled *Chamber Music/Anima 2*, Kosugi climbed inside a white bag, which he titled *Chieronomy/Instrument*.[26] Interestingly, Kosugi foregrounded the bag itself (as an instrument) as the art object, though this may have been because the show didn't recognise performances as admissible fine-art entries (Nakazawa 2014). However, to place *Chamber Music* as an authentic score created solely by Kosugi is more difficult than it may first appear. *Chamber Music* was performed simultaneously alongside a piece by Sho Kazakura, *Stuff Comes from Somewhere and Goes Somewhere* (1963), which, according to film and media scholar Julian Ross, consisted of "a piece of rope draped from the ceiling and onto the floor (submitted in the category for sculpture)," with which Kazakura danced, naked from the waist down (email, Julian Ross to the author, 16 May 2014).[27] Kazakura and Kosugi were frequent collaborators in various groups that often overlapped or metamorphosed into one another, for instance in the Neo-Dada Organizers and the collective Group Ongaku.[28] These collectives of changeable members created frameless works and political demonstrations that ran and blurred between and away from one another in the field of what William Marotti calls "art activism" in late 1950s and 1960s Japan (2013a, 8). Crucially, both artists had previously been involved in presenting a piece titled *Ritual for Closed Vagina* at a Kyoto screening a year earlier, in which Kazakura, not Kosugi, first performed inside a bag.[29] The collaborations between Tokyo groups are also visible in Yoko Ono's experimentation with similar ideas during and after 1964, first with *Bag Piece* (which involved two people undressing and dressing) and later with John Lennon and their "bagism" at the end of the decade (Yoshimoto 2005, 98). Thus, the quest for singular authorship and, indeed, the very notion of an original or authentic textual source are destabilised further by conditions of collectivity and re-enactment in the protean fields of intermedia art. In Moorman's work, even the law attests to this when it sees her, not Paik, as responsible for the "indecent exposure" in *Opera Sextronique*. My aim here is not to refute Kosugi's claim to authorship of *Chamber Music* in order to secure authorship for Moorman. Rather, I chart the work's history to illuminate the need for historical research to recognise that any iteration at any time confers agency and to acknowledge the problematics of authenticity, which is now a highly unstable basis for interpretation.

---

26 There were two bags submitted to the show, one blue and one white, alongside a third "sonic installation." See also William Marotti (2013a, 173).

27 William Marotti also offers an account of the event but marginalises the importance of the rope. Marotti claims instead that Kazakura "completely dispensed with the artwork itself. His submission was himself" (2013a, 172). This seems to sit slightly uncomfortably with other references to submission requirements for the "sculpture" category (to which both Kosugi and Kazakura applied) and with Marotti's own report that the performance was shut down by museum staff on a daily basis. An image of the event can be found in Marotti (2013b).

28 An account of the Neo-Dada group and other overlapping collectives of 1960s Japan can be found in Marotti (2013, 173, 187).

29 According to Julian Ross (email to the author, 16 May 2014), *Ritual for Closed Vagina* first took place at a screening of *Closed Vagina* (1962), a film made under the collective name Nichidai Eiken (Nihon University Film Studies Club) but led by Masao Adachi, in Kyoto at the Gion Kaikan, May 1962.

Such frustrated attempts to locate the work's "origin" reveal that it is pointless to view Moorman's event as a recital of a piece that actually "belongs" to Kosugi (or, even, to Kazakura). Rather, since Moorman takes an active role in shaping the works through her performance, we are confronted with the indeterminacy and negation of source that characterises the global network of intermedia artists in the 1960s. By naming Kosugi the composer, Moorman points to the expanded sociality of the field and highlights the conventions of concert practice as objects of play; the formalities constitute an important component of the work, and yet toying with them exposes their rigidity as absurd. Moorman's use of the term "concert" had already been denounced by an angry public and created legal difficulties when it was used to advertise her first Annual Festival in 1963, since the festival's new music challenged patrons' expectations of what a "concert" would contain.[30] This example reinforces the idea that her long-term objective remained to sabotage and renegotiate distinctions between cultural forms. In an interview, Moorman said Kosugi wrote *Chamber Music* for her in 1965; quoting Kosugi, she said, "Music does not aim at sound itself, but is in a complex conception. First, forget about sounds. Sounds must be free." She added, "I think that really says it for the whole movement that I'm involved in, the way we feel about all art forms and definitions . . . You've got to forget the definition" (Stern 1980). Moorman seems to call here for freeing and "expanding" art, which might be imagined as a linear "progression" of experimentation, "moving on" from the old in favour of something new. Her actions, however, can be more accurately theorised along the lines of Schneemann's "love-fuck," which gestures to a relation that is loving but nonetheless critical—to "fuck" but also to "fuck with." The avant-garde histories that have been developed and reworked over time as modernist tradition are represented but also seem to fall apart, retrospectively reaching for a time "before" the definition, while necessarily sharing its present existence. In one of Paik's papers (found in the David Mayor Collection at Tate Archive) he asks, "Why repeat? Repetition is the character of biological existence. More or less."[31] The impossibility of birthing new ideas in a world where sounds are forgotten or redundant seems to leave only the artistic possibilities of eternal repetition or self-destruction.

While acknowledging Paik's gesture to the biological, however, this suggestion of repetition is rendered acutely *inorganic* by the disruptive force of Moorman's theatricality. Rather than a quality that detracts from her seriousness as a highly skilled and faithful interpreter of textual originals, this theatricality actually becomes the very condition around which her avant-garde potential might be defined. Bürger writes (1984, 72): "The organic work of art seeks to make unrecognizable the fact that it has been made. The opposite holds true for the avant-gardiste work: it proclaims itself an artificial construct, an arti-

---

30 Ticket holders of Six Concerts '63, particularly one woman described by Moorman as a "little tourist lady," complained to Moorman that to describe such an event as a "concert" was false advertising, as some of the works did not take the form they were expected by patrons to take (classical-style music). Afterwards, Moorman used the term *avant-garde*, despite not particularly liking the phrase because, she argued, it pointed to a "future time" rather than an urgent "present time" (Varble [1973] 2003, 173).

31 Nam June Paik, untitled document, folder entitled *Nam June Paik*, TGA 815/2/2/4/163, David Mayor Collection, Tate Archive, London.

fact. To this extent, montage may be considered the fundamental principle of avant-gardiste art. . . . Paradoxically, the avant-gardiste intention to destroy art as an institution is thus realized in the work of art itself."

While it is accurate to point out that Moorman credits work as "belonging" to other composers, she also occupies a far more complicated, perhaps irreconcilable position—something other than ones deriving from historicisations that assert that modernist or Dadaist impulses overturn the "traditional" in favour of the "experimental." The latter are complex but ultimately subjugating, and arguably macho, as they play into notions of succession, enlightenment, and chronological "progress." I suggest that Moorman's performance might indeed be an exemplary instance of ways in which the naked woman, the absent object of the joke (to recall Nixon's point again), becomes a live and resistant subject—one that makes its attacks in other ways.

A memorable section of the archive footage of a performance of *Chamber Music* shows the bag, its surfaces pulsating, before Moorman emerges from within, awkwardly mooning her audience, as she exposes only her naked buttocks, which peek out from the bottom of the bag (Performancelogia Performance Art Archive 2012). Considering this comic gesture, her act can be interpreted as a clear rebuttal of social conventions in the art-museum-as-temple. Yet, just as her body leaks out from the zippers of the bag, her acts blurring into and away from one another, she also defies this reading in other respects, as well as "fixing" effects of interpretation and categorisation more broadly. Greenfield's *Guardian* review of an evening at the ICA of wandering "fun" and an odd assortment of "disjointed squibs" is primarily shaped by a perception of Moorman's excessive and frivolous theatricality, which renders the textual authority of the composer increasingly impalpable. Yet, while toying with their authority, Moorman also held a profound respect and admiration for her composers, and there remains a deep, seemingly paradoxical seriousness in Moorman's homage to Kosugi and her cultural "forefathers." One article in the *Observer* claimed she "worships" Paik, adding "perhaps if she could laugh a little . . . But no, it is a highly serious event" (*Observer* 1968, 36). Many similar accounts are also grounded in Moorman's own deference. The poster for the 1967 *Opera Sextronique* event, which carried a manifesto written by Paik, sheds further light on the tension between the "serious" and the "not serious" in their work:

> After three emancipations in twentieth century music (serial, indeterminate, actional) I have found that there is still one more chain to lose. That is PRE-FREUDIAN HYPOCRISY. Why is sex a predominant theme in art and literature prohibited ONLY in music? How long can New Music afford to be sixty years behind the times and still claim to be a serious art? The purge of sex under the excuse of being "serious" exactly undermines the so-called "seriousness" of music as a classical art, ranking with literature and painting. Music history needs its D. H. Lawrence, its Sigmund Freud. (Quoted in Nyman 1999, 88)[32]

---

32 Paik considered the lack of sex in music to be a signifier of its being "behind" other arts and strangulated by convention. This was a view shared in different manifestations in the global experimental music scene from the late 1950s. See also Marotti (2013a, 181).

Moorman completely embraced the idea that sex was key to "emancipating" music (as a "classical art"), which Paik had been working towards for some time before their collaborations began (as in his score for Alison Knowles). We don't know whether Moorman was considering similar ideas prior to meeting Paik, partly because, unlike Paik, archival materials (particularly relating to her early practice) have only recently become publicly available. However, it is clear that among the reasons for Moorman's willingness and keenness to perform Paik's sexually suggestive scores, apart from her strong faith in him as an artist, is that, as Schneemann related, following her first naked performances, Moorman had said quite simply, it "felt wonderful!" (Rothfuss 2014, 58). The role of pleasure then, ties Moorman's performance to Schneemann's in its blasphemous and dissident comic value, the assumed frivolousness of which is in itself harnessed as a major component of the serious critical achievement of the work.

Like earlier women artists who were needlework "copyists," Moorman challenged distinctions between high and low art spaces. In an interview Moorman said, "I'm very bored with the concept that art is for a few people—the chosen few. I participate in the activities organized by big museums and big establishment performances, but I have a secret love for reaching people who don't get to museums or concerts normally. . . . I'm very interested in fun and not making art such a snobbish, mysterious thing" (Varble [1973] 2003, 175).

Perhaps Greenfield's perplexity can be explained by an understandable but ultimately pointless impulse to see the work as a mystery to be solved, to be productive, to give an "answer"; whereas for Moorman, the key to the work is in the critical and aesthetic possibility of a play with and through desire. As we have seen, responses to Schneemann's *Naked Action Lecture* and Moorman's performance "Avant-Garde Music" illuminate common tropes: women are "not artists"; they are sexual objects, "demented frigid nymphomaniacs," naïfs, victims, mere instruments, or copyists of "great" men. In their innovations in performance with their unruly and explicit bodies, Schneemann and Moorman subverted these conventional interpretations and established a foundation for later practices. Such acts by women artists harness the political potential of their own bodies (from which traditional conceptions of "seriousness" would require them to flee) to carry out acts that could be described as infidelities or blasphemies in the art-museum-as-temple. I do not interpret such acts, however, simply as destruction per se, but as strategic and critical reconfigurations; their creators take profound pleasure in the works of those "patron saints" with which they engage, even while trashing the temple. They resist confinement in a separate space marked "woman artist"; rather, they expose most forcefully new, generative ways in which tenets of modernism more broadly might be historicised—for instance, in relation to persisting misconceptions of authenticity and the hierarchical orderings of the patrilinear canon. Here, I have looked to move beyond the familiar caricatures of women artists in performance as raging, perverse, naive, or narcissistic in order to address the relevance of the artists and their works beyond gender-specificity, to recognise their criticality and their sophisticated, complex, and considerable achievements.

REFERENCES

Blom, Ina. 2001. "The Touch through Time: Raoul Hausmann, Nam June Paik and the Transmission Technologies of the Avant-Garde." *Leonardo* 34 (3): 209–15.

Bohn, Willard. 1976. "Guillaume Apollinaire and the New York Avant-Garde." *Comparative Literature Studies* 13 (1): 40–51.

Bourdon, David. 2000. "A Letter to Charlotte Moorman." *Art in America* 88 (6): 80–85, 135–37.

Bürger, Peter. 1984. *Theory of the Avant-Garde*. Translated by Michael Shaw. Minneapolis: University of Minnesota Press. Translation based on *Theorie der Avantgarde*, 2nd ed. (Frankfurt am Main: Suhrkamp, 1980) and selections from *Vermittlung—Rezeption—Funktion* (Frankfurt am Main: Suhrkamp, 1979).

Cage, John. (1963) 1967. "26 Statements re Duchamp." In *A Year from Monday: Lectures and Writings*, 70–72. Middletown, CT: Wesleyan University Press. First published 1963 (*Mizue* [September], Tokyo).

Corrin, Lisa Graziose, and Corrine Granof, eds. 2016. *A Feast of Astonishments: Charlotte Moorman and the Avant-Garde, 1960s–1980s*. Evanston, IL: Northwestern University Press.

Doyle, Jennifer. 2006. *Sex Objects: Art and the Dialectics of Desire*. Minneapolis: University of Minnesota Press.

Friedman, Ken, Owen Smith, and Lauren Sawchyn, eds. 2002. *The Fluxus Performance Workbook*. Rev. ed. Digital supplement to "On Fluxus," special issue, *Performance Research* 7 (3). http://performance-research.net (site discontinued).

Greenfield, Edward. 1968. "Charlotte Moorman at the Institute of Contemporary Arts." *Guardian*, 24 September: 6.

Herzogenrath, Wulf. 1988. "The Anti-Technological Technology of Nam June Paik's Robots." In *Nam June Paik: Video Works 1963–88*, edited by Gerlinde Gabriel, 6–31. London: Hayward Gallery.

Higgins, Dick, and Hannah Higgins. (1965) 2001. "Intermedia." *Leonardo* 34 (1): 49–54. Written 1965; first published 1966 in *Something Else Newsletter* 1 (1).

Hoving Powell, Kirsten. 2000. "*Le Violon d'Ingres*: Man Ray's Variations on Ingres, Deformation, Desire and de Sade." *Art History* 23 (5): 772–99.

Jones, Amelia. 2004. *Irrational Modernism: A Neurasthenic History of New York Dada*. Cambridge, MA: MIT Press.

Kosugi, Takehisa. 2002. "Anima 2." In Friedman, Smith, and Sawchyn 2002, 75. Date of score unknown.

Laws, Catherine. 2019. "Being a Player: Agency and Subjectivity in *Player Piano*." In *Voices, Bodies, Practices: Performing Musical Subjectivities*, by Catherine Laws, William Brooks, David Gorton, Nguyễn Thanh Thủy, Stefan Östersjö, and Jeremy J. Wells, 83–167. Orpheus Institute Series. Leuven: Leuven University Press.

Lindberg, Anna Lena. 1998. "Through the Needle's Eye: Embroidered Pictures on the Threshold of Modernity." *Eighteenth-Century Studies* 31 (4): 503–10.

Lynton, Norbert. 1968. "Apollinaire, Drunk on a Universe." *Guardian*, 5 November: 6.

Marotti, William. 2013a. *Money, Trains, and Guillotines: Art and Revolution in 1960s Japan*. Durham, NC: Duke University Press.

———. 2013b. "Timely and Untimely Politics: Art and Protest in Early 1960s Japan." SOAS University of London. Accessed 22 January 2020. http://www.soas.ac.uk/wg-beasley/file89425.pdf.

Mundy, Jennifer. 2008. "The Art of Friendship." In *Duchamp, Man Ray, Picabia*, edited by Jennifer Mundy, 8–57. London: Tate.

Nakazawa, Hideki. 2014. "The Discontinuation of the Yomiuri Independent Exhibition." Accessed 22 January 2020. http://aloalo.co.jp/arthistoryjapan/3b.html.

Nixon, Mignon. 2005. *Fantastic Reality: Louise Bourgeois and a Story of Modern Art*. Cambridge, MA: MIT Press.

Nyman, Michael. 1999. *Experimental Music: Cage and Beyond*. 2nd ed. Cambridge: Cambridge University Press.

Observer. 1968. "Naked Art Form." September 29: 36.

Performancelogia Performance Art Archive. 1969. "Charlotte Moorman: 'TV-Bra for Living Sculpture' (1969) y 'Chamber Music' (1969)." YouTube video, 06:59, posted by "Performancelogia

Performance Art Archive," 3 June 2012. Accessed 21 January 2020. https://www.youtube.com/watch?v=_5WSoK5_Qao.

Piekut, Benjamin. 2011. *Experimentalism Otherwise: The New York Avant-Garde and Its Limits*. Berkeley: University of California Press.

Rogers, Holly. 2013. *Sounding the Gallery: Video and the Rise of Art-Music*. New York: Oxford University Press.

Rothfuss, Joan. 2010. "The Ballad of Nam June and Charlotte: A Revisionist History." In *Nam June Paik*, edited by Sook-Kyung Lee and Susanne Rennert, 145–68. London: Tate.

———. 2014. *Topless Cellist: The Improbable Life of Charlotte Moorman*. Cambridge, MA: MIT Press.

Schneemann, Carolee. (1968) 1997. "Naked Action Lecture June 27 1968 Institute of Contemporary Art [sic] London." In *More than Meat Joy: Performance Works and Selected Writings*, edited by Bruce R. McPherson, 180–181. Kingston, NY: Documentext / McPherson.

———. (1968) 2010. Letter from Carolee Schneemann to Jan Van der Marck, 29 July 1968. In *Correspondence Course: An Epistolary History of Carolee Schneemann and Her Circle*, edited by Kristine Stiles, 137–38. Durham, NC: Duke University Press.

———. (1974) 2003. "Istory of a Girl Pornographer." In *Imaging Her Erotics: Essays, Interviews, Projects*, 137–38. London: MIT Press. Essay written 1974.

Schneider, Rebecca. 1997. *The Explicit Body in Performance*. Abingdon, UK: Routledge.

Shattuck, Roger. (1950) 1971. "Introduction: Apollinaire, Hero-Poet." In *Selected Writings of Guillaume Apollinaire*, translated and edited by Roger Shattuck, 3–54. New York: New Directions. First published 1950 (London: Harvill Press).

Stern, Fred, dir. 1980. "Charlotte Moorman—Interview 3." YouTube video, 11:53, posted by "Alex Mirutziu," 4 December 2012. Accessed 21 January 2020. https://www.youtube.com/watch?v=ruSPHwioVIo.

Stiles, Kristine. 1987. "Synopsis of the Destruction in Art Symposium (DIAS) and Its Theoretical Significance." *The Act* 1 (2): 22–31.

———. 1992. "Survival Ethos and Destruction Art." *Discourse* 14 (2): 74–102.

Varble, Stephen. (1973) 2003. "Interview with Charlotte Moorman on the Avant-Garde Festivals." In *Critical Mass: Happenings, Fluxus, Performance, Intermedia and Rutgers University 1958–1972*, edited by Geoffrey Hendricks, 173–180. New Brunswick, NJ: Rutgers University Press. Interview conducted summer 1973.

Yoshimoto, Midori. 2005. *Into Performance: Japanese Women Artists in New York*. Piscataway, NJ: Rutgers University Press.

Inside the Choreography
of Gender

Nguyễn Thanh Thủy

Malmö Academy of Music, Lund University

Stefan Östersjö

Piteå School of Music, Luleå University of Technology

*Inside/Outside is an
installation and performance
for three choreographed
musicians. On the basis
of a gender analysis of
traditional Vietnamese music
in Vietnamese TV shows, the
piece presents three
musicians as wax dolls in
glass boxes in a dark room.*

INTRODUCTION

This chapter is a set of reflections on the process of making *Inside/Outside*, an installation built on a concept by Nguyễn Thanh Thủy (Vietnam) and developed in collaboration between The Six Tones (Vietnam/Sweden),[1] the choreographer Marie Fahlin (Sweden), and sound artist Matt Wright (UK). The piece was filmed by Maria Norrman and is available online (https://www.youtube.com/watch?v=hZ8iP1Swumg). We discuss the choreography of gender (Foster 1998) in the performance of traditional Vietnamese music and the role of the body in the play with gendered identity that is launched in performing the piece.

*   *   *

*But who are these musicians?
They play Asian instruments
and wear traditional
Vietnamese queen costume but
one of them appears to be a
Western man. What is Inside
and what is Outside in this
self-reflective imagery?*

---

1 Since 2006, The Six Tones has been bringing art music from Vietnam and Europe together, touring as an instrumental music group or in music theatre projects, and working with choreographers. We play traditional Vietnamese music in hybrid settings for Western stringed instruments and traditional Vietnamese instruments. We improvise in traditional and experimental Western idioms and commission new music by composers in Asia as well as in Western countries. The Six Tones are Nguyễn Thanh Thủy (who plays *đàn tranh*), Ngô Trà My (who plays *đàn bầu*), and Stefan Östersjö (who plays guitar and also many other stringed instruments). See www.thesixtones.net.

The role of women performers in traditional Vietnamese music

The history of Vietnam is largely also the history of colonialism and occupation from neighbouring countries; its cultural history is deeply connected to the transcultural and intercultural[2] exchanges created through this violent past.[3] At the same time, Vietnam is itself a country with many minority cultures, but with a majority population that has dominated economic and cultural development, the Kinh people. What is commonly referred to as "traditional Vietnamese music" is the ancient traditions of the majority population; largely a music deeply intertwined with traditional theatre, it was developed at royal courts in the Nguyễn dynasty and before.[4] Even though Chinese notation was used in much of this music, it was essentially orally transmitted. Vietnamese cultural norms, up to the creation of the socialist republic, were built largely on Confucianism, a patriarchal society in which women were regarded as inferior and excluded from many cultural activities and other domains of public life. Hence, musical performance and acting in theatre was largely a male occupation. Lauren Littlejohn (2017, 4) observes how Confucius, in his writings, "insisted that music must be proper and musicians must be virtuous; thus, men concluded they were more capable and assumed superiority in the realm of music." However, over the past sixty years, women have done more than merely enter the traditional music and theatre scene in Vietnam: today, most concert performances are entirely dominated by women.

*   *   *

---

2 Wolfgang Welsch (1999) defines *interculturality* as based on an essentialist understanding of cultures as "spheres or islands" while aiming to overcome the unavoidable clashes that are the result of such cultural difference. *Multiculturality* he understands as a representation of a similar approach, specifically addressing the conflicts between cultures when they co-exist in the same society. Finally, he sees *transculturality* as "a consequence of the inner differentiation and complexity of modern cultures" that is characterised by entanglement and networking which has led to increasing hybridisation (197, emphasis removed).

3 Contacts between different cultures are the source for many processes of musical change. They lead to "creative transformation, which may be termed syncretism, synthesis or transculturation," and which "may result in a greater level of individual or corporate creativity than before," and which, further, in the process of making sense of the other culture's music, give rise to new understandings and ways of teaching music (Kartomi 1994, ix). Eventually, "whole styles, repertoires, genres . . . may change as a result of convergences in contact situations" (ibid.). But the history of music also gives numerous examples of collisions between cultures, in which the dominant class instead suppresses indigenous musicians (Kartomi and Blum 1994), issues that are also evident in Ortiz's writings on Cuban music (1947), in which the term *transculturation* was coined.

4 There are several examples of purely instrumental music, such as funeral music, the *nhã nhạc cung Đình Huế* (court music of *Huế*,) and *nhạc tài tử* (a form of chamber music with its roots in the very south of the country). While most instrumental music in Vietnam has been drawn from theatre music, *nhạc tài tử* is an example of the opposite. This music, which was initially played in groups in private settings in villages, became the basis for a new form of theatre when in the 1920s theatrical elements were added to the music in performance; the outcome was a new form of theatre, with colonial influences, called *cải lương* (reformed theatre.)

My mother was a Tuồng actress.
In traditional theatre, there are stereotypes for
male and female behaviour, just as for good/evil;
virtuous/immoral; hero/mean person, etc.
Since I was a child, I have seen my mother
embodying different characters onstage.
But in Vietnamese society, there was no possibility
for a girl to choose to perform differently.
I was taught to always be a good girl according
to the norms I learnt from my mother.

*   *   *

The histories of this music and the role of women performers are essential for an understanding of the artistic work discussed in this chapter. A significant step in this development came in 1927 when the colonial powers at the time opened the French Conservatory of the Far East (Conservatoire Français d'Extrême-Orient) in Hà Nội. A typical expression of the "mission to civilise" (*mission civilatrice*) that guided French colonial politics, the short-lived institution was in essence a failure. Nevertheless, it permitted a select few upper-class Vietnamese to study Western instruments, Western music theory, and composition. Even though the school was only open for three years (because France was bankrupt and could not afford to support the school), together with music training in many churches in the country, it led to the emergence of a first generation of Vietnamese composers, musicians who studied the performance and composition of classical Western music, and songwriters[5] who built on Western music theory and used Western notation to create a (modern) Vietnamese new music called *tân nhạc/nhạc cải cách* (renovated music). In 1930, the colonial government's shrinking budget forced the conservatory to close, and for many years, music teaching again became a private matter.

*   *   *

In the installation you will
find headphones with
which you can enter a sonic
world "inside" the main
performance in the video.
As well as musical
fragments, there are stories
told by the individual musicians
that place their performances
against a tension between
traditional Vietnamese culture
and a globalised society.

---

5 For a further discussion of the fate of the conservatory, its colonialist background, and its impact on Vietnamese musical society, see McClellan (2009), who summarises the response among Vietnamese musicians as follows: "There is no doubt that the Conservatory held an attraction for musically talented Vietnamese. The result of the performance examinations from 1929 and 1930 show Vietnamese students receiving many of the highest honors, and one year later at the recitals organized by the Conservatory, Vietnamese students outnumbered the French students chosen to perform as string soloists. By 1930 over twice as many native students as French students were enrolled in the Conservatory (137 to 60)" (ibid., 322).

Traditional music remained largely unaffected by Western music until the 1950s. Paradoxically, the strong impact that Western music has had on traditional Vietnamese music in modern times has its origin in the politics of the communist government, a transformation of traditional culture in the name of nationalism.

In 1954, when the war with the French was won, North Vietnam started on a dual mission: to build a new socialist country from the ashes of war and to simultaneously continue the civil war with help from the world's largest communist power, the Soviet Union, since Moscow hoped to consolidate and expand communism in the Asian hemisphere through Vietnam. The Soviet Union gave moral, logistical, and military support to North Vietnam by sending aid and specialists, but they also accepted many Vietnamese students in higher education. When Trường Âm Nhạc Việt Nam (the Vietnam School of Music, which later became the Hà Nội Conservatory of Music) was established in 1956, very few teachers in the classical music department conformed to international standards:[6] many were self-taught or had studied privately or only for a short time in the conservatory. However, the level of Western classical music performance rose quickly in the 1960s with the possibility of studying in the Soviet Union. In the traditional music department, there was only one teacher when the school opened, the old master Vũ Tuấn Đức.

In 2016–17, Nguyễn Thanh Thủy made a documentary film, *The Culture Soldiers*, based on interviews with musicians in Hà Nội, most of them belonging to the first generation of students and teachers in the department for traditional music at the Hà Nội Conservatory of Music. The *đàn nhị*[7] player Thao Giang describes the paradoxical situation for traditional music performance at this time. The government wished to reintroduce traditional music to the cities, from which, in the colonial days, it had been largely absent. However, this was attempted by bringing the traditions into academia, where the pedagogy was based on the use of Western notation, and by reintroducing traditional music to city audiences in concert halls, a site where this music had not been presented before:

> People immediately laughed when they saw me bringing the *đàn nhị* onstage. People had no idea that the *đàn nhị* could be played solo onstage, be played as the violin or the piano, or other Western instruments. It was so unusual. I was so serious, took my seat and therefore people laughed again. They laughed at everything I did. They found it so strange. Throughout the long period of the anti-French resistance and the Indochina war, people didn't get to see traditional instruments like that. Only then, when we had built the conservatory of music. When I played the first note, people applauded cheerfully. It happened the same with the *đàn bầu*[8] or the *đàn*

---

6 Two pianists, Thái Thị Liên, who had studied at the Prague Conservatory, and Vũ Thị Hiền, who had studied in Paris with Alfred Cortot, were the exception.

7 Also called the *đàn cò*, the *đàn nhị* is a Vietnamese bowed string instrument with two strings. The word *nhị* means "two" in Vietnamese. Its sound box is generally covered on one end with snakeskin.

8 The *đàn bầu* is a Vietnamese monochord. Its playing technique is harmonics, the pitch of which is modulated by shifting the basic pitch of the string. It is an instrument that perfectly embodies the fundamental building blocks of traditional Vietnamese music and allows the performer a wide range of ornamental figurations and vibrati.

tranh.[9] People had no idea that the traditional instruments could be presented that way. (Nguyễn 2017)

In 1962 the Central Traditional Music and Song Ensemble (Đoàn Ca Nhạc Dân Tộc Trung Ương) was created, which became the spark for the development of a new type of staged musical performance (Đào 1977). In 1964, the Ministry of Culture decided to establish an orchestra of about sixty players, in collaboration with the Hà Nội Conservatory of Music (Bộ Văn Hoá 1964). The leading composer in the development of a repertory of "renovated music" was Nguyễn Xuân Khoát, educated at the Conservatory of the Far East and the first president of the Vietnam Composers Association. Here we can see how colonial heritage becomes entangled with the strife involved in creating a new, postcolonial nationalist identity. The aim was not to preserve musical culture but to create a socialist folk culture. Tô Ngọc Thanh, the General Secretary of the Vietnam Folklore Association, captures this governmental approach to traditional music in the following statement: "*Nhã nhạc* is considered by many to be an academic art and as such is not popular among people nowadays. Very few people understand enough about it to enjoy it fully. It is for this reason that it has almost disappeared" (Salemink 2007, 565–66). In the *Vietnam Courier*, Đào Trọng Từ further claims that "The repertory also needs to be improved in the direction of a deeper national character and to include the musical treasures to be found in the different traditional sung theatre genres—cheo, tuong, and cai luong—and the instruments of mountain minorities such as the Meo tongued flute, the Tay Nung guitar, while being open to influence by great classical forms in western music—sonate, symphony, concerto" (Đào 1977, 30). As Ingrid Bertleff concludes (2006, 72), "these attempts have resulted in what is now known as neo-traditional music: the fusion of regionally and ethnically diverse musical practices into a homogenous music of national representation." But, of course, nationalism was not the only driving force behind the development of this music. As noted by Miranda Arana (1999, 30), composers who had been trained in the Western tradition now "hungered for a sense of connection to their roots, and began to look for musical inspiration from their own less familiar traditions."

Another form of impact from the Soviet Union was the general approach to traditional and folk music, through the systematic implementation of educational methods based on the use of staff notation, a mode of transmission that is fundamentally different to the oral basis on which a master and an apprentice would normally engage in the teaching and learning of traditional Vietnamese music.

Since the 1950s, music has been used in the north of Vietnam as a vehicle for political propaganda. During the war and especially afterward, numerous competitions and festivals were organised by the government with the aim of establishing a new type of socialist musical culture. Lê (1988, 94) notes how "in

---

9   The *dàn tranh*, also called the *dàn thập lục*, is a Vietnamese plucked zither, similar to the Chinese *guzheng*, the Japanese *koto*, the Korean *kayagum*, and the Mongolian *yatga*. It has a long soundbox with steel strings, movable bridges, and tuning pegs positioned on its top.

the arts, many concepts and practices were borrowed from the Soviet Union and China. The Leninist and Maoist concept of arts as politically functional tools was adopted as the fundamental guideline for Vietnamese revolution-ary arts." Just as in the Soviet Union, partyism and nationalism were deemed central qualities to be projected through artistic production. The creation of orchestras for neo-traditional music was one driving factor in the implemen-tation of a new culture of public performances in concert halls. Ingrid Bertleff, looking at how the *đàn bầu* was constructed as a symbol of nationalism by the regime, observes how this politically driven development resulted in a music culture in which "the visual aspects of performances and verbal expressions of Vietnamese music have become more important than the music itself. Music has become a show for sightseers. The listening experience has become sec-ondary" (Bertleff 2006, 72).

*   *   *

When the audience moves through the space, the reflections in the boxes create a primary level of being inside and outside. You see yourself inside the box, and you see the performers reflected in each other's boxes.

*   *   *

This movement from private settings—in which male performers would per-form to an aristocratic audience—to public concerts, has been accompan-ied by a shift from male to female musicians. A very similar process has been observed in South Korea (Mueller 2013). In Korea, the practices of traditional music have their origins in Confucian ideals, which created a music culture in which the presence of women was seen as improper other than in women-only circles.[10] Hence, traditional music, at court and in rituals, was for men only. The shift to the situation today, where the majority of performers are female, has been simultaneous in the two countries. While the shift from male to female performers has been equally striking, and occurred at around the same time, in Korea, the forms of representation are sometimes different. Mueller (2013) gives several accounts of women cross-dressing in order to perform certain forms of music that are particularly related to male costume. In Vietnam, the same style for traditional music performance has been introduced as is dis-cussed by Mueller in crossover ensembles in Korea, where the (all-female) performers are presented in revealing clothing and are normally posing with instruments rather than playing them.

---

10 Joseph Lam (2003) discusses in more detail this history and its situatedness in Confucian norms in China in two distinct periods, the Han dynasty (140 BCE–220 CE) and the late Ming period (roughly 1368–1644).

To access documentation of musicians working in the Tuồng[11] and Chèo[12] theatres in Hà Nội, Nguyễn Thanh Thủy contacted the management and retrieved complete lists of the musicians employed. Here we can see that the dominance of male musicians was complete in the first generation. Over the years, both theatres employed only a few female *đàn tranh* players. Nevertheless, theatre ensembles are the exception that confirms the rule: since public concerts and TV shows began presenting traditional Vietnamese music, women have taken centre stage. The musicians in a theatre orchestra are not onstage but in a pit, just like in a Western opera house. Further, it should be noted that these musicians are educated in the theatres, and not at the Vietnam National Academy of Music, where women have become dominant in recent decades.

In 1986, as a response to the declining economy, the Sixth Party Congress decided to launch a series of reforms with the aim, like China, to "introduce market forces without altering the foundations of its political system" (Spitäller and Lipworth [1993], 4). This economic renovation, *Đổi Mới*, transformed the stagnant peasant economy of Vietnam into a vibrant, market-driven capitalist system (Freeman 1996). However, the economic liberation brought Vietnam straight into a new phase of rapid industrialisation and globalisation that had both positive and negative effects on Vietnamese society. Among many other things, tourism played an important role in bringing about these changes, as it did also in the reformation of the music of minority people in the country (O Briain 2016). Eventually, this affected the growth of the traditional music revival movement, where, for instance in Huế, "the preservation of court music has also been enhanced by tourist performances" (Norton 2009, 53).

Nation-branding is a term we find useful to refer to phenomena observed globally since the 1990s. In developing countries, and in post-socialist economies, these tendencies have been very strong. Nadia Kaneva (2012, 4) argues that "in its most expansive articulations, nation branding refers to much more than slogans, logos, and colourful advertisements. Rather, it seeks to reconstitute nationhood at the levels of both *ideology* and *praxis*, whereby the meaning and experiential reality of national belonging and national governance are transformed in unprecedented ways." In a recent study concerned with the role of media in such political undertakings, Göran Bolin and Per Ståhlberg (2015, 3076) observe how "television and television channels and streamed video services such as YouTube also are used as platforms for the distribution of mediated information—that is, they are the cultural technologies used by various agents in the nation-branding process." Vietnam is no exception, and the role of women in the representation of traditional music has been deeply intertwined with the emergence of TV shows and other commercialised forms of propaganda. This development started slowly in the 1970s, with the first television broadcast by VOV (Voice of Vietnam) taking place on 7 September 1970, but has exploded in later years. In 1990, the Samsung company negotiated the establishment of a local TV assembly plant with Vietnamese officials; the mar-

---

11 Also called *hát tuồng* or *hát bội*, it is a form of Vietnamese theatre. *Tuồng* is often referred to as classical "Vietnamese opera" influenced by Chinese opera.

12 A form of musical theatre, traditionally performed by Vietnamese peasants in northern Vietnam.

keting of the new sets shifted from state stores to numerous small private shops in every city and town within range of a TV transmitter (Marr 1998). As of 2004, it was estimated that VOV programmes reached more than 90 per cent of all households in Vietnam. The impact of national branding, the rising economy, and the sudden effects of globalisation through the internet and tourism radically altered the premises for traditional Vietnamese music, and for the musicians who are part of maintaining its cultural heritage. As put by the Vietnamese media artist Nguyễn Trinh Thi: "I think that women—not only in Vietnamese cinema—are usually there to be looked at. During the war and the socialist times, the image of women was used for propaganda purposes, to garner support from everyone, regardless of their gender, for war and socialism building efforts. And it's not like things got any better in our present times" (Magiera 2016). In an interview for *The Culture Soldiers*, Thanh Tâm—the first woman to play the *đàn bầu* professionally—comments on how the concert culture of traditional music reflects a shift in how music is experienced in Vietnam: "Before, we only listened to music. Today we listen and watch music at the same time" (Nguyễn 2017). This is why women took over the stage: because they "are more beautiful." She further claims that this is particularly true when they wear traditional dress. Again, as observed by Bertleff (2006), the emergence of women on the concert stage is immediately related to a concert culture dominated by visual experience, and objectification of women.

THE CHOREOGRAPHY OF GENDER

In 1998 Nguyễn Thanh Thủy received the first prize in the national *đàn tranh* competition in Hồ Chí Minh City. By winning the competition, she became a public representative of traditional Vietnamese music, often appearing on TV shows—still a novelty at the time in Vietnam—and in public concerts.[13] In these TV shows, she would always be recorded in scenic outdoor settings with waterfalls, romantic parks, and so on, never on a concert stage. Even the department for traditional music in the Vietnam National Academy of Music adopted the same aesthetics, as described here by Nguyễn Thanh Thủy:

> In 2001 the head of department at the Vietnam National Academy of Music decided to make a promotional DVD with traditional music. In it, they made me pose for a performance of a three minute piece, and the recording of it brought me to two different provinces with scenic landscapes and put me into a lot of suffering, for instance when performing in a stream balancing dangerously on a float. It should be noted that I did not know how to swim at this time. Also, on the float I was bitten by insects that, together with my fear of falling into the water, made this video recording session a truly horrific experience despite the pastoral appearance it may have in the photo. (Östersjö and Nguyễn 2013a, 90, as quoted in Nguyễn 2019a, 12)

---

13 A typical production that can be found on YouTube was recorded by HTV (Ho Chi Minh Television) in 2000, shot by a waterfall and a bonsai garden in Ho Chi Minh City. Two excerpts can be found at https://www.youtube.com/watch?v=oNhgCUkoLEA and https://www.youtube.com/watch?v=X-y8NV3KA9w.

Musical training of female performers in Vietnam involves learning gendered gesture, further amplified or underlined in contemporary TV productions. The concept for *Inside/Outside* is drawn directly from the experience of such objectification of women and the making of the piece demanded an in-depth engagement with the choreography of this institutionalised phenomenon.

The complexity of how nation branding has affected traditional music performance, and brought this cultural heritage onto TV shows, often combined with the "improvement" of the musical material through Western-style arrangement in neotraditional style, is thoroughly discussed above. But the emergence of a particular choreography for the performance of traditional instruments, such as taught today in the Vietnam National Academy of Music, demands further reflection.

Building largely on the writings of Judith Butler, "doing gender" has often been discussed in terms of performance. This performance of gender is constituted largely of the repetition, most often of verbal acts, that are "naturalised" in the body (Butler 1999, xv). In an attempt to move from the verbal domain to embodied ways of "doing" gender, Susan Leigh Foster (1998) suggests that a better way of thinking of these socially defined behaviours, distinct from our biological nature, is through the "social and historical analytic framework for the study of gender" that is offered by the "tradition of codes and conventions through which meaning is constructed in dance" (ibid., 5). While a theory of performativity focuses on the discussion of the individual execution of such codes, an analysis of the choreography of gender permits a more overarching perspective:

> Choreography resonates with cultural values concerning bodily, individual, and social identities, whereas performance focuses on the skill necessary to represent those identities. . . . Like performativity, choreography consists in sets of norms and conventions; yet unlike performativity, or at least its general usage thus far, choreography encompasses corporeal as well as verbal articulateness. Choreography therefore serves as a useful intervention into discussions of materiality and body by focusing on the unspoken, on the bodily gestures and movements that, along with speech, construct gendered identity. (Foster 1998, 5)

On TV shows with traditional music, it has become most common to present women performers as collectives, rather than in the small groups with differentiated voices and instruments that historically was the norm in this music. Take for instance a group of musicians playing the Vietnamese four-stringed lute, the *đàn tỳ bà*. Here, universal behaviours such as rocking movements—normally a way to synchronise the music between performers—have been turned into decorative elements and are exaggerated with a particular choreographic effect.

Nguyễn Thanh Thủy and Stefan Östersjö

Multiple perspectives on musical gesture

A musician's movements in performance are on the one hand a public display of highly subjective and individual experiences of interactions with fellow players, instruments, and other cultural materials; but they must be understood too as culturally situated, as the result of being socialised into behaviours that can also be understood from a gender perspective. Differences in physical gesture between men and women are part of a sign system by which gender is defined. Jill Halstead (2005, 222) finds gender to be essential for "understanding any performance practice that involves human bodies; nowhere is gender more directly created, perceived, enacted or challenged than through the display of the body and the dynamic of its gestures." The role that gender plays in the way musical practice is organised has been observed by music ethnologists and anthropologists looking at many different societies (George 1993; Koskoff [1987] 1989; Williams 1998). Music-making is a social practice, on the one hand flowing out of human relations—both between musicians and between performer and audience—and, on the other, reflective of power structures in the society in which it is situated: "The questions raised have to do with the role music-making plays in producing or subverting gender-based hierarchies of prestige and authority: Does music support or threaten predominant ideas about gender? How does it shape the way in which women and men experience sexual hierarchy? Can music-making itself be a form of sexual politics?" (George 1993, 1–2). Hence, in order to arrive at a comprehensive understanding of the function of musical gesture in a specific cultural setting, multiple analytical perspectives are called for. How can we best approach the cultural and subjective layers of a musician's actions in performance? We have already seen how gender analysis may provide an essential perspective. But again, if the performance of gender is also to be found in a choreography of movement, in these "unspoken" processes of signification parallel to language, how can this knowledge be approached and communicated?

As noted in the introduction to this book (14), the human body is multi-layered, and our experience of the body can be understood from the perspectives of the body image and body schema, where the former is related to our perception of the body and the latter to action (Pitron and de Vignemont 2017, 115). While the body schema can be understood as "a system of preconscious, subpersonal processes" (Gallagher and Cole 1995, 370), the body image on the other hand is "conscious and . . . personal" (De Preester 2007, 355, emphasis removed). Gorton and Östersjö (2019) draw some conclusions regarding the methodological implications of this distinction and find that "on the level of the body image, performative knowledge may be accessible through introspection and reflexive research methods, such as is common in autobiographical forms of artistic research. . . . An inquiry into the formation of embodied knowledge on the level of the body schema could also be approached through reflexive methods, but such an inquiry is more thoroughly conducted through combining these with observation and measurement. Hence, a discursive understanding of performative knowledge can only fully be accessed through interaction with other paradigms, employing both qualitative and quantitative research methods" (Gorton and Östersjö 2019, 38).

Marc Leman (2010) proposes a three-layered analytical perspective on musical gesture, where the third-person perspective permits measurements to be made to establish repeatable data about a certain gesture type. He further discusses the social interactions typical of a second-person perspective and ways of approaching different layers of subjective understandings from a first-person perspective.

In a series of artistic research projects, The Six Tones have analysed the artistic process using methods such as the stimulated recall[14] of video documentation. In our analysis of working on *Inside/Outside* we have attempted to embrace these multiple perspectives to capture some of the complexity of gesture and its cultural meanings. In this process, we used open coding (Benaquisto 2008); but of particular importance for the analysis were the annotations added to each selected portion of the video. In the analysis, we looked at first- and third-person perspectives in analysing both the choreography of gender (Foster 1998) in traditional music performance and when looking at the choreography in *Inside/Outside*.

Both these perspectives are important in order to unpack the process of creating *Inside/Outside*. Nguyễn Thanh Thủy describes her experience in the following way:

> When creating the solo choreography in collaboration with Marie Fahlin, I was challenged to negate some of my habits as a *dàn tranh* player, especially related to the hand and arm movements. The control and grace which would constitute the norm in traditional music performance were here replaced by wider and more aggressive movement sets, directed all around my position in the glassbox, and not always towards the instrument. At the same time, while performing in the glassbox in queen costume, make-up and hairdo, I was also aware of embodying the role of a female traditional music performer, and the public persona that this assumes. (Nguyễn, pers. comm., 2017)

This account reflects an experience of a multi-layered body.[15] While the habitus of a performer must largely be referred to the level of the body schema, the "public persona" that Nguyễn refers to is experienced on the level of the body image. On the other hand, when consciously disrupting the entrained behaviour of *dàn tranh* playing, the choreography of hand and arm gestures brings these subconscious layers to awareness.

---

14 The term was coined by Benjamin Bloom in 1953, in a paper that discussed a study using audio recordings of classroom teaching as stimuli, aiming to allow the student to relive the original experience and give an account of their original thought processes (see further Bloom 1953; Nguyễn and Östersjö 2013b; Brooks, Östersjö, and Wells 2019). See also chapter 3 of this volume.

15 The multilayered nature of the body in performance is also discussed by Catherine Laws in her chapter in this volume (129–30): she considers the live performing body in juxtaposition with its textual mediation, as well as its simultaneously discursive and affective qualities.

Georgina Born (2011) discusses the processes of identity formation in musical practice as situated in four social planes,[16] ranging from the more intimate relations between musicians in an ensemble, to the "imagined communities" that music creates, to a third plane, in which "music is traversed by wider social identity formations, from the most concrete and intimate to the most abstract of collectivities—music's refraction of the hierarchical and stratified relations of class and age, race and ethnicity, gender and sexuality" (ibid., 378); finally in the fourth plane, the arena of public and private institutions can be analysed.

Subjectivity in musical performance, then, emerges from internal and external processes, situated in a multi-layered body but also in society; thereby, it can only be understood through a comprehensive analysis through the personal to the political. The "public persona" of a female Vietnamese performer is drawn very much from a collective identity as a Vietnamese woman, which has strong foundations in the blend between communism and nationalism that constitutes the ideology of the country. In the documents of the Third Party Congress in 1960, the government of the young Democratic Republic of Vietnam clearly stated the aim to build a culture on the basis of socialism and nationalism (Văn Kiện Đảng 1960). Wendy Duong, in a comprehensive analysis of the current state of gender equality in Vietnam notes how nationalist perspectives tend to blur questions of women's rights: "In colonial or post-colonial societies, nationalist-strategists (who were mostly men) commonly advocated women's liberation to instill unity and conscript the female labor in the fight for national independence and reconstruction. Third World gender equality, therefore, easily becomes intertwined with the rhetoric of anti-colonialism and patriotism" (Duong 2001, 283).

In Vietnamese society today, collective identity is given much more emphasis than individual identity, and thereby "swallows gender issues and stifles the attempts of women to achieve personal freedoms" (Duong 2001, 289). But this "fallacy of the trio" (ibid.), as Duong refers to this blurring of nationalism, socialism, and women's rights, is only part of the complexity of contemporary Vietnamese society. The norms of Confucian ideologies are still highly present in society,[17] and kept alive through traditionally inspired poetry. Thus, traditional poetry can at times be more influential than the rule of law. On the other hand, this has also meant that governmental campaigns can instruct women to embrace both socialist and Confucian ideals, such as famously expressed in the

---

16 For a detailed discussion of identity formation in relation to the musical performance of cultural identity—identity as difference, as personal and social, as a process, and as narrative—see the next chapter, "Identity Performance and Performing Identity: Performing Isang Yun's *Fünf Stücke für Klavier* (1958)" by Jin Hyung Lim.

17 In Vietnam, the co-existence of Confucianism and nationalism has deeply influenced the way communist ideology was implemented in the country. Alexander Woodside ([1971] 1998, 210) concludes that Confucianism puts family considerations before global ones and men before women. Benedict Anderson (2006, 113–19) identifies colonialism and the bureaucratic systems, or the infrastructure modelled on Western societies, to be a strong factor in the rise of nationalism in Vietnam. However, the sense of a nation goes much further back in history and Brantly Womack (2006) argues that the "patriotic resistance to foreign invaders" (63) is to be understood as a stronger force than the communication system. Surely, nationalism played a significant role in Vietnam on the country's path toward communism. Ho Chi Minh himself admitted that "it was patriotism and not communism that originally inspired me" (quoted in Karnow 1997, 134).

so-called Three Criteria Campaign: "study actively, work creatively, raise children well, and build happy families."

> Post-1946 Socialist Vietnam brought about a kind of social emancipation for women; "women's liberation" and participation in social and political life were important elements in the anti-colonial movement, even though the traditional Confucian role of women as caregivers was still very much emphasized. After liberation, women's equal rights with men in both the public and private domains were legally recognized. In this new Socialist Vietnam, women became responsible for both family and nation or, in the words of one national slogan used in the 1960s and 1970s, "good at national tasks, good at household tasks." (Schuler et al. 2006, 386)

The focus on such a collective identity has had a direct impact on the development of a concert culture for traditional Vietnamese music, in which women play a central role, as symbols of the nation and as symbolic representations of a society that maintains a paradoxical objectification of women in parallel with a politics of emancipation and "equal rights." The complexity of this social, cultural, and political entanglement is discussed in Spivak's essay[18] on the voice of the subaltern: "Between patriarchy and imperialism, subject-constitution and object-formation, the figure of the woman disappears, not into a pristine nothingness, but into a violent shuttling which is the displaced figuration of the 'third-world woman' caught between tradition and modernization, culturalism and development" (Spivak 1999, 304). Although women performers in traditional Vietnamese music of today are indeed seen—and very much so, given the increasing focus on visual appearance in musical performance discussed above by Bertleff—they are only present as "women-manipulated-as-sign" (Spivak 1999, 149). The issue here, which Spivak reminds us of, is that these women are not given a voice, and, as seems to be a typical trait of patriarchal societies, are not allowed control over their bodies, nor over body movement.

Dress, gender, and identity

Gendered identity has always been performed, often subconsciously, through choice of clothing. In modern society, fashion permits a more dynamic relation to the expression of individual identity (Arvanitidou and Gasouka 2011). In Vietnam, the relation between traditional and modern society can be understood for instance from the Party Central Committee's statement in Resolution no. 5 of 1998, expressing the intention to "build a progressive culture imbued with national identity" (Salemink 2007, 563). This aim can be seen as one of the fundamental grounds on which the development of a modern concert culture for traditional music, displayed on TV shows rather than in its traditional settings, has been created. Salemink (2007) discusses a number of similar manifestations of the same politics, perhaps most clearly expressed in the creation of a fashion show at the Huế festival in 2002. By far the most

---

18   Cited here from the reworked version in her book *A Critique of Postcolonial Reason: Toward a History of the Vanishing Present* (1999).

important cultural event in Vietnam, this festival receives substantial attention from the government. While traditional forms of expression constitute the point of departure for most events, the creation of a "national identity" ultimately serves to present the "present political regime as the natural successor to the Nguyễn, thus representing the government as 'authentic' and hence legitimate" (Salemink 2007, 564–65). The biggest audiences at the 2000 and 2002 festivals were attracted by the fashion shows by the couturier Minh Hạnh. Both of these shows built on her practice of creating fashion from the traditional female dress, the *áo dài*, which has a particularly iconic function in the identity of the city of Huế. This identity was expressed differently in the two shows: the first drew strongly on the traditional violet silk famously worn by women in Huế, while the second was developed specifically on models from the ancient Royal Court.

The initial ideas for the design of the costume in *Inside/Outside* aimed to create a critique of traditional music performance on TV shows. Here, the *áo dài* has always been a means to represent women within the frame of traditional culture, but in the TV shows, the traditional origin of the dress, as well as of the music, is contrasted with other visual, choreographic, and musical components. A similar observation is made by Salemink, in a further discussion of the fashion shows at the Huế festival, in which it is argued that the models

> represent an aesthetic image of modernity, albeit in Vietnamese style, and constitute a reason for pride in the physical shape of the female half of the country's population. This gendered and embodied vision of the nation is considered attractive because it is simultaneously modern and uniquely Vietnamese. The quintessential female embodiment symbolising the nation is clothed in the *áo dài*, the tight long tunic worn over a pair of long pants that became fashionable in the 1920s and became an icon for newly traditional national dress since the 1960s. In the various editions of Festival Huế since 2002, a *lễ hội áo dài* (*áo dài* festival) consisting of a parade of hundreds of women and girls wearing *áo dài* was part of the public "Off" programme. Clearly, the "Eyes of the Moon" fashion show was contextualised by an aesthetic politics that featured women's bodies in quasi-traditional national dress, and this partly explains the popularity of the fashion show in comparison with other artistic performances at the Huế Festival. (Salemink 2007, 568)

In *Inside/Outside*, we wished to address exactly this kind of cultural politics and we wanted the costume to be reminiscent of the *áo dài*. However, we also wanted to create a reference to the costume used in traditional Tuồng theatre. Our costume maker, Nguyễn Xuân Sơn, made the further suggestion also to draw on models from the ancient royal court in Huế; all this eventually led us to the decision to use the costume of Nam Phương Hoàng Hậu, the last queen of Vietnam, as the primary reference. This meant that the colour would be golden, and this in turn motivated the golden frames we used for the set of glass boxes in the first production of the piece in Hà Nội. Golden coloured dress was only worn by the royal family, and the punishment was severe for anyone who challenged this rule. Further, for Vietnamese viewers, this "queen costume" suggested that, just as the queens resided in one of the castles within the "forbidden city,"[19] these individuals in the glass-boxes are permanently kept as objects in the "museum" for traditional music performance that the installation evokes. But what was the function of the costume from the performer's perspective? Ngô Trà My reflects on the role of the costume as follows:

> Because of the specifics of the outfit, initially, as it was too large for me, I had to find a way to move in it so that it would work in the narrow space inside the glass box, with the *dàn bâu* inside which [it] is not easy to shift around. Then, when performing the choreography, I noticed how the dress would fold and unfold as I moved in ways that would add new qualities to the gesture. The costume became almost like an instrument with which I could perform the choreography, aiming to move smoothly in the box, but also to always create beautiful imagery with the dress. (Ngô, personal communication, 2018)

Just like a musical instrument, the costume has particular affordances and resistances (see further, Clarke 1995; Coessens and Östersjö 2014), and therefore it has agency in the artistic process, and in the moment of performance. Elizabeth McMahon (2000, 112) finds how, in Shakespeare, "cross-dressing functions to destabilise categories of sex, gender and sexuality and their conventional alliances." She further observes how this practice is manifest in many different forms in contemporary society, and continues to provide a "temporary freedom from the constraints of gendered identity" (ibid). Ngô Trà My describes the experience of "being 'someone else,' of playing a role" (pers. comm., 2018)[20] and it can be concluded that the costume was an important factor in the creation of such a performative situation. While the only performer who was actually cross-dressing in the piece was Stefan Östersjö, Ngô Trà My also describes the experience of performing in the installation as a play with identity: "Actually, I have the feeling of being 'someone else,' of playing a role, when I get the dress on and perform in this *áo dài*. It makes me feel like a princess in the king's palace, but the dress itself, with its qualities, also 'creates' choreography which matches the character" (Ngô, pers. comm., 2018). We return below to the role of "play" in the ways in which the artistic methods employed in the creation of *Inside/Outside* may also have allowed the individual performers to address their personal experiences of performing gender in musical socio-cultural settings. But first, we will take a closer look at the role of analysis in the creation of the piece.

---

19 Although the situation for women in the royal court at Huế was, relatively speaking, less severe than in China, there was little or no freedom for a queen or a concubine. Wendy Duong claims that "oppression of women was portrayed by early French colonists as they came into contact with life of the *Hue* imperial court: forty-three women serviced the emperor's quarters, thirty women functioned as his guards, thirteen others took care of his hygiene, clothes, nails, hair, cigarettes, and ink. At night, the women slept around his bed, prepared to serve as shields in case of an assassination attempt. Description of the twenty-five-year-old Emperor Dong Khanh, who reportedly had 100 royal concubines, was as follows. Every day a group of women took turns servicing him. At least five women were around all the time, taking care of his hygiene, preparing his turban, manicure, perfumed oil, with the goal that every detail be perfect" (Duong 2001, 215n88).

20 Further discussed in the final section.

FROM GESTURE ANALYSIS TO THE CREATION OF THE CHOREOGRAPHY

Inside/Outside was premiered in Hà Nội at the Chèo Theatre in November 2012. In the performance, the spectators first find three glass boxes, illuminated from different sides by spotlights in the darkened room. In each box there appears to be a statue of a musician in traditional Vietnamese queen costume. On 6 March 2015, a new video installation version of *Inside/Outside* was presented for the first time in a new exhibition at the Museum of World Culture, Gothenburg. The film was shot by Maria Norrman at the Inter Arts Center, Malmö, in December 2014. Throughout the entire working process, all sessions were documented on video. A substantial portion of clips from this documentation is available online (Nguyễn 2019b).[21]

In the making of *Inside/Outside*, qualitative analysis constituted an important factor in the artistic process. Already in the first coding sessions, we experienced the opacity of the other, as we had many times before when engaging in the inter-subjective process of stimulated recall. We have observed elsewhere, with reference to Édouard Glissant's call for the "right to opacity," that in intercultural collaboration, "We must not understand the unknowable. The individual character of each performer must be highlighted to create a discursive heterogeneous voice" (Nguyễn and Östersjö 2019, 252–53). This entails a certain fragility in the collaborative process, through which artistic outcomes may be unpredictable but also tend to be situated in a liminal space between traditions and aesthetic paradigms.

In our initial coding sessions, we attempted to analyse gendered gesture in traditional music performance on TV shows. In several of the selected clips, the two Vietnamese members of the group were themselves performing. The two Western artists experienced how a sense of being "outside" became increasingly stronger. The process of making the piece emphasised how different cultural understandings of gender issues are. Throughout the working period, Fahlin and Östersjö curiously tried to figure out what the core issues and concerns were and what the proper way to address them in artistic form in the Vietnamese context would be. Just as we have encountered in many forms in musical collaboration, perhaps the identity of the final piece was indeed drawn also from this field of tension between different cultural perspectives on choreographies of gender?

With a catalogue of performance-related movements—identified in the video analysis—as a point of departure, the three performers and the choreographer continued the development of the piece in working sessions at the Inter Arts Center, Malmö. Here, Marie Fahlin engaged in a dialogue with each performer on their individual response to these gestures from TV shows.[22] Hence, the choreographies were not taught to the performers but rather drawn from their bodily response to these materials. Among the extended sound-produ-

---

21 Video clips and a further discussion of the collaborative process of making the piece can be found at https://researchcatalogue.net/view/55919/386485.

22 See Nguyễn (2019b, videos V2.7b and V2.9).

cing gestures were for instance elbow movements particular to the plucking action on the *đàn tranh*. The musicians of The Six Tones and Fahlin had studied a video in which a group of *đàn tranh* players, led by their teacher at the academy, performed the same gesture—an extensive suffix following the plucking action—in precise synchronisation. These elbow movements became a fundamental material in sections two and four of the piece. In the third section, the choreography followed more closely the actual behaviours one finds in traditional music performance on TV shows. Here, the performance of a traditional song, *Dạ Cổ Hoài Lang*, was synchronised through extensive rocking movements.

For the two Vietnamese musicians, this process also became a vehicle to intentionally address how they had been socialised into these gendered behaviours and to explore ways in which their bodies could also "perform differently," as it was later phrased by Nguyễn Thanh Thủy (pers. comm., 2015). This critical dimension of the work was expressed in the coding of the video from the premiere. For instance, Nguyễn commented as follows on a transitional section in the piece, where she expresses an intentional critique of the performance conventions of the TV shows, also referring directly to the cameras: "I felt here like I turned my back to the camera (even if the room doesn't really have a back and front . . .) and when I performed these gestures I explicitly tried to expose my back to the camera through exaggerated sound-producing gestures and rocking" (Nguyễn, annotation to video, 2012). Through several statements like this, one can conclude that, in many instances, Nguyễn would perform the choreography with the direct intentions of "subverting gender-based hierarchies of prestige and authority" (George 1993, 2). As will be further discussed below, other examples of a similar kind are found in accounts from Ngô Trà My. In the next section we will look at how the close relation between sound and movement in the compositional process had a direct impact not only on the articulation of a politically informed critique through the piece, but also on the embodied experience of creating the performance.

A SPACE BETWEEN SOUND AND MOVEMENT

The music, by The Six Tones and Matt Wright, builds layers of acoustic and electronic sound from two traditional Vietnamese pieces. The music was made in parallel with the choreography, sometimes defining the structure of the bodily movements but more often being drawn directly from the choreography. A large-scale musical form was developed before the first workshop. It consisted of improvisations on two traditional Vietnamese songs, *Dạ Cổ Hoài Lang* and *Vọng Cổ*,[23] first on *đàn tranh* and then with electronic materials created by Matt Wright. This draft form was further developed in the workshop and became the

---

23   This music is deeply interlinked: the later piece is in fact a development of the former. *Dạ Cổ Hoài Lang* was composed in 1918 by Cao Văn Lầu (1892–1976), also known as Sáu Lầu. In this process, Nguyễn Khải Thư (2012, 259) notes how *Dạ Cổ Hoài Lang* "transformed from a two-beat version, to four-, eight-, sixteen-, thirty-two-, and sixty-four-beat versions, with the thirty-two-beat version being most commonly used today."

basic framework within which the finer details of the composition emerged. But, while the initial structure was defined by its musical materials and had a rather simple form in four sections, a more complex form emerged from the interaction between movement and sound. Parts one and three are most closely linked to *Vọng Cổ* and *Dạ Cổ Hoài Lang*, and to some of the methods employed by The Six Tones when improvising or composing music with materials from traditional music. In the first section, short and often very fast fragments of *Vọng Cổ* create a dense web. The choreography is created by expanding the sound-producing movements by playing "in the air." In the third section, the music is created by simple looping of phrases from *Dạ Cổ Hoài Lang*, and the choreography mimics and exaggerates the typical "rocking" movements that you might see on TV shows. These two sections have remained the same since the first draft version of the music. The two solo choreographies, discussed in more detail below, may serve as an example of the further interactions between music and movement. Already at the outset, the aim was for the electronics to be generated live, in order for the electronic sounds to be responsive to the choreography, and for the form to be malleable.

The solo choreography with Nguyễn was drawn quite directly from the movements found in the dialogue between her and Fahlin. The interaction with the electronics, performed by Matt Wright, would tend towards a call-and-response-like structure, where the choreography would at times excite sound on the instrument, followed by movement "in the air" where the electronics would respond to and sonically enhance the ongoing choreography. Here, Matt Wright's performative skills were an essential factor; and as the piece has toured, the extent to which the sections can be expanded and contracted, in response to the evolving choreography, but also to the response from the audience, has been striking:[24]

> Crucially the structural elements of the electronics (by this I mean the clear sonic cues built into the ongoing compositional progress of the music) were performed/triggered in response to the musical "tempi" of the musicians. Conversely, the live processing followed the choreography, based on the notion of "turning movements": little cycles/loops of delay and spatialisation that overlap in asymmetric patterns to create a dense web of sound from simple, often single notes on the instruments. Those simple sounds from the instruments were themselves often the result of a choreographic gesture, rather than the sole reason for it.
>
> Therefore, I tend to think *chronologically* when following the structural narrative of the music, but *spatially* when responding to the choreography and any resultant sounds this might suggest. This dialectical tension between chronological/spatial is analogous for me to the tension inherent in notions of "inside" and "outside," as if our agreed musical structure is an agreed inside, whilst the live processing is something deliberately outside our compositional agreement, something potentially risky. (Wright, pers. comm., 2018)

---

24 Put simply, we have experienced many times how, in performances in which the space has been packed, each section needs to progress much more slowly, for the audience to be allowed to gradually move around and capture the choreographies in each of the boxes. In other situations, such as a show when we had many schoolchildren in the gallery, we made our way through the entire piece in twenty minutes (instead of the average 30) without losing any of the compositional structure.

Another layer of sonic material in the performance was the audio through headphones presented by each of the glass boxes. For the premiere in 2012 we created audio tracks with music played on the instrument inside the box. After the premiere of the piece we decided to make a further analysis of the work, looking at the choreographies and working mainly from a first-person perspective. We had no intention that this analysis would inform further artistic work since we felt that the process was finished with the premiere in November 2012. However, the analysis carried out in 2013 and 2014 created a more articulated understanding of the working process and the individual experiences of all three performers, of both the cultural context for traditional music in Vietnam and the individual identity of each performer. This analysis gave us the idea of creating headphone tracks that would be based on the individual coding of video carried out by the three performers. The three performers made recordings in which they gave personal accounts of how they had been socialised into male Swedish or female Vietnamese performers respectively and further, of their experiences of performing the piece. These recordings were eventually edited and processed into individual tape parts, still containing some elements of instrumental playing from "inside" the box. The headphone tracks were presented for the first time in the video installation version of *Inside/Outside*, which was commissioned by the Museum of World Culture, Gothenburg, in 2015. The headphone tracks can be accessed on Research Catalogue (Nguyễn 2019b).[25]

The solo choreographies performed by Östersjö and Nguyễn display a close link between bodily movement and resulting sound. In the former, Östersjö was standing, holding the *tỳ bà*. This is visually significant, since holding the lute in this way alludes to traditional paintings of women playing the lute, but it is difficult to play the instrument in this position, since the instrument has a constant tendency to fall out of one's hands when held upright. But above all, the solo involved a constant turning movement, like a ballerina in a music box; the musical material was shaped according to the speed and direction of these turns. Here, the footwork came to shape the musical form of the entire solo, underlining the interdependence of movement and music. Coessens and Östersjö note how "'winding up' and 'releasing' the ballerina shaped the music in accordance with these movements and vice versa. Imperfections in the turning movement and the timing of when to start 'unwinding' the mechanism immediately affected the ongoing music" (Coessens and Östersjö 2014, 340).

A specific musical idea was for the electronics to follow the turning movements around the room through the four-channel speaker set-up. Matt Wright designed a software patch with Ableton Live,[26] built on the idea that the most effective physical gestures would be those resulting in clear, short attacks on the instrument(s), such as a plucked string. These short sounds were then processed through asymmetrical delay patterns and spatialised so that each of

---

25   The headphone tracks and a filmed performance of the piece can be found at
      https://www.researchcatalogue.net/view/55919/55933.
26   Ableton Live is a software music sequencer and digital audio workstation. In contrast to many other
      software sequencers, Ableton Live is designed to be an instrument for live performances as well as a
      tool for composing, recording, arranging, mixing, and mastering.

the four speakers had its own rhythmic identity. This entailed that one short sound from the instrument—recorded *inside* the glass box—could cascade out of the box and fill the performance space with constant "turning movements" as mentioned above.[27]

GENDERED IDENTITIES AT PLAY

This solo is a good example of the gendered movement differences that Östersjö experienced in the creation of the piece; Coessens and Östersjö further discuss how "in the first days of rehearsal, this physical movement totally outside the habitus of a classical performer turned Östersjö's body into a space of resistance" (Coessens and Östersjö 2014, 340). Here, the body into which Östersjö has been socialised, through education and professional practice, becomes an obstacle to performing a choreography drawing on female movement types. In the audio track for the headphones, Östersjö reflects on this choreography: "Trying to move like a woman in the choreographies made me very strongly aware of muscles I had never used. Already to rise and get seated like a woman hurts, you realise how our bodies are disciplined from early childhood towards this bodily behaviour. My attempts to make my body move like a woman became for me an attempt to express sympathy with the many women performers I've come to know throughout the years I've been in Hanoi."

The making of this solo choreography brought out the sense that while the Vietnamese performers were "inside" the project, the Western artists remained, in a sense, "outside" it. This experience of looking at a cultural phenomenon from the outside was particularly great at the start, when Marie Fahlin and The Six Tones worked on the video analysis at EMS in Stockholm. Since the Western artists did not share the experience of performing traditional music in TV shows, and since the perspectives on gendered behaviour were different too, it was challenging to create a shared understanding of the aims and means of the project. But, just as argued above by Östersjö and Nguyễn (2013b, 2019), an acceptance of the opacity of the other can result in a particular dynamic in the creative process. In the case of this choreography, such a dynamic can be seen in the interaction between the two. Fahlin expressed a particular interest in Nguyễn's hands, as a representation of the embodied and encultured knowing of a Vietnamese female musician; this also related directly to the finger plectrums used on the *đàn tranh*, which can be made of either plastic or metal. She referred to these as "the deformed *đàn tranh* fingers" and would talk about how the hands of a musician are marked by experience (Fahlin, pers. comm., 2015).[28] A Vietnamese choreographer may have looked differently at the plectrums on

---

27 See The Six Tones (2014, 19:30).
28 The performer's hands, as carriers of embodied knowledge, experienced from both within and without, provide a similar point of focus in the text Catherine Laws wrote for her realisation of Annea Lockwood's *Ceci n'est pas un piano*, and in her subsequent discussion of performing that piece in this volume (128–130, 132): "Whose hands are these, anyway? They're so much mine, they know so much of what I know, maybe more than I do. They can find notes, feel distance, decide on musical emphasis. But other people, teachers and composers, have moulded them too, pushed them into peculiar shapes over and over, until I can no longer say what's truly natural to them."

her fingers but, to Fahlin, the hands of the *dàn tranh* player afforded the possibility of a transformation from gracious control towards a more threatening and aggressive expression. For the two collaborators, the making of this choreography became one of the clearest expressions in the piece of an actual critique of the current state of affairs in the business of nation branding through traditional music. As expressed by Nguyễn in the headphone track by her box:

> In this solo, choreography gestures from *dàn tranh* playing are even more disconnected from normal playing. In my mind I imagined this to be like going crazy over the situation in the glass box. . . . I first thought of this as just pretending to play, like in the opening. But then I felt that the critical stance was so much stronger here. I am not just "pretending to play" like in the playback recording for a TV show but here I am mocking the whole situation with the disconnected hands and only one of them actually playing. The viewer's attention is drawn (I believe) to the hand that is not playing and, just as with TV shows with traditional music, they are watching the wrong thing.

The making of the headphone tracks summarised much of the individual experiences from the entire working process, as the above quotation illustrates. As Östersjö concluded in a recent book chapter (2017, 100), "not only could the headphone tracks constitute a window for the audience onto the inside of the piece's choreography but also the making of these recordings constituted an end point in an inwards journey for the participating artists." This inward journey started with the analysis of videos of television shows and an emerging understanding of the body image of a female Vietnamese musician. The headphone tracks constitute an artistic translation of the embodied knowledge of the three performers, a knowledge that has taken shape through the play instigated by making *Inside/Outside*. In the headphone tracks, embodied knowledge is translated into an artistic format but simultaneously also into the discursive domain. But the multilayered and bilingual design of the tape compositions in the headphone tracks does not provide the "expression of a single subjectivity of the performer" but rather gives a display of the "many fictive subjectivities that have been activated in the making of *Inside/Outside*" (Östersjö 2017, 101).

Although gendered identity is performative, it is still not really possible to alter one's body image at will during the short duration of an artistic production. In what way does the making of a piece like *Inside/Outside* allow the participating artists to address the choreography of gender in their respective cultures?

Here, Gadamer's discussion of the ontological nature of the artwork is helpful, in particular, how it is drawn from the human activity of "play." Gadamer ([1989] 2004) builds an understanding of the relation between art and truth starting from an analogy between the player and the play and artistic creation. Play creates a space where the participant must embrace the rules of the game with a particular seriousness: "Play fulfils its purpose only if the player loses himself in play" (103). It is essential that in play, as well as in artistic creation, the subjectivity of the individual artist is in a sense bracketed by the rules of the emerging artwork itself. Gadamer continues, "in cases where human subjectivity is what is playing, the primacy of the game over the players engaged in it is experienced by the players themselves in a special way" (106). "All playing is a being-played. The attraction of a game, the fascination it exerts, consists precisely in the fact that the game masters the players" (107).

Such an experience is certainly present in Ngô Trà My's reflection on the performances, and how the costume not only permitted the experience of "playing a role" but also even "creates the choreography" (and thereby, perhaps also the music), as cited above. The agency of the costume is part of the game, and Ngô has a sense of being played when performing in the piece. But this experience is also what creates the possibility of bypassing the cultural codes guiding the performance of traditional music, and performing differently. After the premiere and the first performances, all the artists gathered for a joint conversation that was recorded on video. Fahlin asked Ngô how she would describe the change that Fahlin observed in her performance from the early workshop stages to the premiere. Ngô's response is again expressive of the complexity of her experience, and of how the process of making the piece laid the ground for a different approach to her body image as a performer. In the qualitative analysis of the video from the premiere, Ngô Trà My described how she, at times would think of the situation in the glass box as a metaphor for the traditional performer's context in contemporary society. This could then result in more aggressive movement types, such as attempts at what she calls "breaking out": "Actually, I feel very upset about the situation of traditional music today in Vietnam, where all aesthetic values are turned upside down, and there's no way to escape or change it. I want to find a different path, by breaking with it, to get out of the box, but I can't. That's why I make these aggressive movements in the choreography, like breaking out through the glass" (Ngô, pers. comm., 2018).

By engaging with the body images at play in the choreography of gender in Vietnamese traditional music, moving in-between different layers of collective and individual identity becomes possible through the rules of the game at play. In making *Inside/Outside*, the artistic methods that we agreed on were central. Taking body movements identified in TV shows as the basic material from which we improvised new movements in dialogue with the choreographer created a different experience, in which a particular distance to these body images could allow a more critical understanding to be articulated and a movement between the inside and the outside of a particular choreography of gender.

But what could the political significance of this manifestation of individual choreographies of gender in the performance of traditional Vietnamese music be? We find useful the definition of political space proposed by Rebecca Adami, articulated through her reading of Adriana Cavarero's philosophical reflections on voice. Adami (2014, 169) develops a critique of ontologies that define human rights and political space through the "political imaginary of human rights as nation-states"; she argues that the failure of such perspectives is found in their inability to articulate a political space for the stateless, immigrants, and cultural minorities. Here, she turns to Cavarero, and her notion of a relational understanding of a political space, constructed through the individuality of "voice" through which the political is articulated as "the reciprocal communication of voices who raise their uniqueness in relations that can take place anywhere" (ibid., 176). Cavarero argues for an ontology of political space articulated beyond *logos*, through the unique sonic engagement through which any human can interact: "In the voice both uniqueness and relation—indeed, uniqueness as relation—manifest themselves acoustically without even taking account of what is Said. The voice, which is embodied in the plurality of voices, always puts forward first of all the *who* of saying" (Cavarero 2005, 30). Cavarero suggests an understanding of political space in which the relation between speech and politics is replaced by uniqueness, plurality, and relation. Adami (2014, 177) concludes that "Relatedness in this sense does not occur between a social utopia of equals who are seen as equal in rights and dignity, or through a kind of sameness, where people belong to the same nationality or are citizens in the same polis. Rather, relatedness comes in this sense through voicing what is urgent for 'you' and 'me' that we can act upon politically." Given the emphasis on collective identity discussed above, we argue that the voices of female performers of traditional Vietnamese music are disregarded and indeed suppressed by the institutional/governmental "other."

Nevertheless, a parallel to the movement beyond logos proposed by Cavarero is found in Foster's proposal for an analytical perspective on the choreography of gender (1998). Perhaps "voice" in the political perspective discussed here can be even more clearly represented by a multimodal understanding of choreography and gesture. *Inside/Outside*, then, seeks to create a space in which individual voices can be articulated through body movement, initially for the two Vietnamese performers of the group. But, also, the piece wishes to draw the viewer into a situation that dissolves the binary of public and private, through the play with inside and outside in the multiple reflections in the space, and by allowing the viewer to enter into the private space articulated by each performer in the headphone tracks. Ann Cooper Albright (1997) observes how such a shift of relation between performer and audience—"when the act of watching transforms into the act of witnessing" (xxii)—can make the spectator uncomfortable, often by "shifting the dynamics of the traditional gaze" (ibid). Yet the "traditional gaze" of a spectator well versed in the performance tradition from which the choreography is drawn is inherently different to that of a Western viewer, who may not grasp the very detail of the critique expressed in the choreography.[29] Instead, it may be that it is a Westerner's "traditional gaze" when viewing an Asian woman that is questioned as the viewer is drawn into this personal sphere. At the same time, it is essential to bear in mind, as pointed out by Trịnh Minh-ha, how voice is not only inherently authentic but also constructed, through a performative act that again accentuates the in-betweenness of today's multicultural society: "Voice: in the confines of this relationship with the body, from the inside out, between absence and presence, desire. The voice of the name appearing on the image is a fiction. The speaker, the news reporter,

---

29 Jin Hyung Lim makes a similar point, in the next chapter (223), with regard to the ways in which the perception of "Western" and "Eastern" elements in Isang Yun's music, and their mediation via her own understanding, manifested in performance, varies according to the listener's culturally situated experience.

or the narrator has a fictive identity, for I is a fiction of identity. Not all of what is seen, heard, smelled, tasted and felt is representable, for I represent not I" (Trịnh 2011, 77). Further, these observations resonate with the discussion by Catherine Laws, earlier in this book, of the manipulated subjective authenticity—the not-quite-I—reproduced in autobiographical performance.

The process of creating *Inside/Outside* constituted a situation in which the subjectivity of the individual artist is in a sense bracketed by the rules of the emerging artwork (Gadamer [1989] 2004). Hence, when the artists engage with the body images at play in the choreography of gender in Vietnamese traditional music, moving between different layers of collective and individual identity becomes possible through the rules of the game at play: a play with fictive and real layers of identity, negotiated through performance.

References

Adami, Rebecca. 2014. "Human Rights for More than One Voice: Rethinking Political Space Beyond the Global/Local Divide." *Ethics and Global Politics* 7 (4): 163–80.

Albright, Ann Cooper. 1997. *Choreographing Difference: The Body and Identity in Contemporary Dance*. Hannover, NH: Wesleyan University Press / University Press of New England.

Anderson, Benedict. 2006. *Imagined Communities: Reflections on the Origin and Spread of Nationalism*. New ed. London: Verso.

Arana, Miranda. 1999. *Neotraditional Music in Vietnam*. Kent, OH: International Association for Research in Vietnamese Music.

Arvanitidou, Zoe, and Maria Gasouka. 2011. "Dress, Identity and Cultural Practices." *International Journal of the Humanities* 9 (1): 17–25.

Benaquisto, Lucia. 2008. "Codes and Coding." In *The Sage Encyclopedia of Qualitative Research Methods*, edited by Lisa M. Given, 2 vols., 1:86–89. Thousand Oaks, CA: Sage.

Bertleff, Ingrid. 2006. "Can Musical Instruments Be National? The Symbolic Use of Musical Instruments in Vietnamese National Representation." *ICTM Study Group on Folk Musical Instruments: Proceedings from the 16th International Meeting*, 66–76. Meeting held 5–8 April 2006, Vilnius, Lithuania.

Bloom, Benjamin S. 1953. "Thought-Processes in Lectures and Discussions." *Journal of General Education* 7 (3): 160–69.

Bolin, Göran, and Per Ståhlberg. 2015. "Mediating the Nation-State: Agency and the Media in Nation-Branding Campaigns." *International Journal of Communication* (9): 3065–83.

Born, Georgina. 2011. "Music and the Materialization of Identities." *Journal of Material Culture* 16 (4): 376–88.

Bộ Văn Hoá. 1964. "Quyết Định về việc thành lập Nhà Hát Ca Múa Nhạc Việt Nam." 534-VH-QĐ. Accessed 2 Oct 2019. http://hethongphapluatvietnam.com/quyet-dinh-534-vh-qd-nam-1964-ve-viec-thanh-lap-nha-hat-ca-mua-nhac-viet-nam-truc-thuoc-bo-truong-bo-van-hoa-do-bo-van-hoa-ban-hanh.html.

Brooks, William, Stefan Östersjö, and Jeremy J. Wells. 2019. "Footnotes." In *Voices, Bodies, Practices: Performing Musical Subjectivities*, by Catherine Laws, William Brooks, David Gorton, Nguyễn Thanh Thủy, Stefan Östersjö, and Jeremy J. Wells, 171–232. Orpheus Institute Series. Leuven: Leuven University Press.

Butler, Judith. 1999. "Preface (1999)." In *Gender Trouble: Feminism and the Subversion of Identity*, 10th anniversary ed., vii–xxvi. New York: Routledge.

Cavarero, Adriana. 2005. *For More than One Voice: Toward a Philosophy of Vocal Expression*. Translated by Paul A. Kottman. Stanford, CA: Stanford University Press. First published 2003 as *A più voci:*

Per una filosofia dell'espressione vocale (Milan: Feltrinelli).

Clarke, Eric. 1995. "Expression in Performance: Generativity, Perception and Semiosis." In *The Practice of Performance: Studies in Musical Interpretation*, edited by John Rink, 21–54. Cambridge: Cambridge University Press.

Coessens, Kathleen, and Stefan Östersjö. 2014. "Habitus and the Resistance of Culture." In *Artistic Experimentation in Music: An Anthology*, edited by Darla Crispin and Bob Gilmore, 333–47. Orpheus Institute Series. Leuven: University Press.

Đào Trọng Từ. 1977. "Vietnamese Traditional Dance." *Vietnam Courier* 67: 25–30.

De Preester, Helena. 2007. "To Perform the Layered Body: A Short Exploration of the Body in Performance." *Janus Head* 9 (2): 349–83.

Duong, Wendy N. 2001. "Gender Equality and Women's Issues in Vietnam: The Vietnamese Woman—Warrior and Poet." *Pacific Rim Law and Policy Journal* 10 (2): 191–326.

Foster, Susan Leigh. 1998. "Choreographies of Gender." *Signs* 24 (1): 1–33.

Freeman, Donald. 1996. "Doi Moi Policy and the Small-Enterprise Boom in Ho Chi Minh City, Vietnam." *Geographical Review* 86 (2): 178–97.

Gadamer, Hans-Georg. (1989) 2004. *Truth and Method*. 2nd ed. Translated by W. Glen-Doepel, translation revised by Joel Weinsheimer and Donald G. Marshall. London: Continuum. First published 1960 as *Wahrheit und Methode: Grundzüge einer philosophischen Hermeneutik* (Tübingen: Mohr). 2nd ed. of translation first published 1989 (London: Sheed and Ward).

Gallagher, Shaun, and Jonathan Cole. 1995. "Body Schema and Body Image in a Deafferented Subject." *Journal of Mind and Behavior* 16 (4): 369–90.

George, Kenneth M. 1993. "Music-Making, Ritual, and Gender in a Southeast Asian Hill Society." *Ethnomusicology* 37 (1): 1–27.

Gorton, David and Stefan Östersjö. 2019. "Austerity Measures I: Performing the Discursive Voice." In *Voices, Bodies, Practices: Performing Musical Subjectivities*, by Catherine Laws, William Brooks, David Gorton, Nguyễn Thanh Thủy,

Stefan Östersjö, and Jeremy J. Wells, 29–79. Orpheus Institute Series. Leuven: Leuven University Press.

Halstead, Jill. 2005. "'The Night Mrs Baker Made History': Conducting, Display and the Interruption of Masculinity." *Women: A Cultural Review* 16 (2): 222–35.

Kaneva, Nadia. 2012. "Nation Branding in Post-Communist Europe: Identities, Markets, and Democracies." In *Branding Post-Communist Nations: Marketizing National Identities in the "New" Europe*, edited by Nadia Kaneva, 3–22. New York: Routledge.

Karnow, Stanley. 1997. *Vietnam: A History*. 2nd rev. ed. London: Penguin Books.

Kartomi, Margaret J. 1994. Preface to Kartomi and Blum 1994b, ix–xiii.

Kartomi, Margaret J., and Stephen Blum, eds. 1994. *Music-Cultures in Contact: Convergences and Collisions*. Basel: Gordon & Breach.

Koskoff, Ellen. (1987) 1989. *Women and Music in Cross-Cultural Perspective*. Urbana: University of Illinois Press. First published 1987 (New York: Greenwood Press).

Lam, Joseph S. C. 2003. "The Presence and Absence of Female Musicians and Music in China." In *Women and Confucian Cultures in Premodern China, Korea, and Japan*, edited by Dorothy Ko, JaHyun Kim Haboush, and Joan R. Piggott, 97–120. Berkeley: University of California Press.

Leman, Marc. 2010. "Music, Gesture, and the Formation of Embodied Meaning." *Musical Gestures: Sound, Movement, and Meaning*, edited by Rolf Inge Godøy and Marc Leman, 126–53. New York: Routledge.

Lê Tuấn Hùng. 1998. *Đàn Tranh Music of Vietnam: Traditions and Innovations*. Melbourne: Australia Asia Foundation.

Littlejohn, Lauren J. 2017. "Confucianism: How *Analects* Promoted Patriarchy and Influenced the Subordination of Women in East Asia." Young Historians Conference. Accessed 2 Oct 2019. http://pdxscholar.library.pdx.edu/younghistorians/2017/oralpres/9.

Magiera, Magdalena. 2016. "Nguyễn Trinh Thi 'Eleven Men.'" *Vdrome*. Accessed 2 October 2019. http://www.vdrome.org/nguyen-trinh-thi.

Marr, David G., ed. 1998. *The Mass Media in Vietnam*. Canberra: Department of Political and Social Change, Research School of Pacific and Asian Studies, Australian National University.

McClellan, Michael E. 2009. "Music, Education and *Français de couleur*: Music Instruction in Colonial Hanoi." *Fontes Artis Musicae* 56 (3): 314–25.

McMahon, Elizabeth. 2000. "Crossdressing." In *Encyclopedia of Feminist Theories*, edited by Lorraine Code, 112. Abingdon, UK: Routledge.

Mueller, Ruth H. 2013. "Female Participation in South Korean Traditional Music: Late Chosŏn to the Present Day." PhD thesis, University of Sheffield.

Nguyễn Khải Thư. 2012. "A Personal Sorrow: *Cải Lương* and the Politics of North and South Vietnam." *Asian Theatre Journal* 29 (1): 255–75.

Nguyễn Thanh Thủy, dir. 2017. "The Culture Soldiers." Research Catalogue video, 21:05. Accessed 2 Oct 2019. https://www.researchcatalogue.net/view/55919/462606.

———. 2019a. "The Choreography of Gender in Traditional Vietnamese Music." PhD thesis, Lund University.

———. 2019b. "The Choreography of Gender in Traditional Vietnamese Music." Research Catalogue. Accessed 28 January 2020. https://www.researchcatalogue.net/view/55919/386485.

Nguyễn Thanh Thủy and Stefan Östersjö. 2019. "Arrival Cities: Hanoi." In *Voices, Bodies, Practices: Performing Musical Subjectivities*, by Catherine Laws, William Brooks, David Gorton, Nguyễn Thanh Thủy, Stefan Östersjö, and Jeremy J. Wells, 235–94. Orpheus Institute Series. Leuven: Leuven University Press.

Norton, Barley. 2009. *Songs for the Spirits: Music and Mediums in Modern Vietnam*. Urbana: University of Illinois Press.

O Briain, Lonan. 2016. "Domesticated Noise: The Musical Reformation of Identity in Urban Vietnam." *Journal of Sonic Studies* 12. Accessed 2 Oct 2019. https://www.researchcatalogue.net/view/282456/282457/4338/0.

Ortiz, Fernando. 1947. *Cuban Counterpoint: Tobacco and Sugar*. New York: A. A. Knopf.

Östersjö, Stefan. 2017. "Thinking-through-Music: On Knowledge Production, Materiality, Embodiment, and Subjectivity in Artistic Research." In *Artistic Research in Music: Discipline and Resistance; Artists and Researchers at the Orpheus Institute*, edited by Jonathan Impett, 88–107. Orpheus Institute Series. Leuven: Leuven University Press.

Östersjö, Stefan, and Nguyễn Thanh Thủy. 2013a. "Inside/Outside: Towards an Expanded Notion of Musical Gesture." In *Sound, Music and the Moving-Thinking Body*, edited by Marilyn Wyers and Osvaldo Glieca, 85–93. Newcastle upon Tyne: Cambridge Scholars Publishing.

———. 2013b. "Traditions in Transformation: The Function of Openness in the Interaction between Musicians." In *(Re)thinking Improvisation: Artistic Explorations and Conceptual Writing*, edited by Henrik Frisk and Stefan Östersjö, 184–201. Malmö: Malmö Academy of Music.

Pitron, Victor, and Frédérique de Vignemont. 2017. "Beyond Differences between the Body Schema and the Body Image: Insights from Body Hallucinations." *Consciousness and Cognition* 53: 115–21.

Salemink, Oscar. 2007. "The Emperor's New Clothes: Re-fashioning Ritual in the Huế Festival." *Journal of Southeast Asian Studies* 38 (3): 559–81. Accessed 2 Oct 2019.

Schuler, Sidney Ruth, Tú Anh Hoàng, Song Hà Vũ, Hùng Minh Trần, Thanh Mai Bùi, and Vũ Thiên Phạm. 2006. "Constructions of Gender in Vietnam: In Pursuit of the 'Three Criteria.'" *Culture, Health & Sexuality* 8 (5): 383–94.

Spitäller, Erich, and Gabrielle Lipworth. [1993]. *Viet Nam: Reform and Stabilization, 1986–92*. Washington, DC: International Monetary Fund.

Spivak, Gayatri Chakravorty. 1999. *A Critique of Postcolonial Reason: Toward a History of the Vanishing Present*. Cambridge, MA: Harvard University Press.

Trịnh T. Minh-ha. 2011. *Elsewhere, Within Here: Immigration, Refugeeism and the Boundary Event*. New York: Routledge.

Văn Kiện Đảng. 1960. *Diễn Văn Khai Mạc Đại Hội*, 5 September. Accessed 2 October 2019. http://tulieuvankien.dangcongsan.vn/ban-chap-hanh-trung-uong-dang/

194

dai-hoi-dang/lan-thu-iii/dien-van-khai-mac-dai-hoi-dai-bieu-toan-quoc-lan-thu-iii-cua-dang-1456.

Welsch, Wolfgang. 1999. "Transculturality: The Puzzling Form of Cultures Today." In *Spaces of Culture: City, Nation, World*, edited by Mike Featherstone and Scott Lash, 194–213. London: Sage.

Williams, Sean. 1998. "Constructing Gender in Sundanese Music." *Yearbook for Traditional Music* 30: 74–84.

Womack, Brantly. 2006. *China and Vietnam: The Politics of Asymmetry*. New York: Cambridge University Press.

Woodside, Alexander Barton. (1971) 1988. *Vietnam and the Chinese Model: A Comparative Study of Vietnamese and Chinese Government in the First Half of the Nineteenth Century*. Cambridge, MA: Harvard University Press. First published 1971 (Cambridge, MA: Harvard University Press).

Identity Performance and Performing Identity

Performing Isang Yun's
Fünf Stücke für Klavier (1958)

Jin Hyung Lim

Keimyung University

The purpose of every musical activity—composing, performing, and listening—is that it is experienced.[1] As Tia DeNora says (2003, 4), reality—the perception and understanding of lived experience—"cannot be fully addressed by words, measurements, concepts, and categories, all of which must be understood at best as approximations of reality, as socially constituted ideas or images of phenomena." Peter L. Berger and Thomas Luckmann ([1966] 1991) define *reality* ("a quality appertaining to phenomena that we recognise as having a being independent of our own volition" [13]) and *knowledge* ("the certainty that phenomena are real and that they possess specific characteristics" [13]) as being always in a state of flux, however objective and fixed they may, at times, appear. In short, reality is socially constructed and knowledge is perceived through certain prismatic reflections within a society.

Performance, as an ephemeral art, is explicitly in flux, but what is less obvious is that in this very state it expresses the flux of the reality and knowledge that feed into and underpin it. A performer's reality and knowledge not only determine performative decisions derived at least in part from one's cultural experiences and social circumstances; emotional understanding also has a significant role to play, whether it is the recognition of emotions "in" or expressed "by" the music, the performer's emotional response to the music (or generated by playing it), or both. However provoked or manifested, emotion is always influenced by personal experience and knowledge: emotion is social (Oxford English Dictionary 2020). As Michael Boiger and Batja Mesquita (2012) observe, emotions arise in relation to social interactions and relationships (221). Therefore, subsequent emotional experiences are determined by but are also constitutive of the social, political, and cultural contexts in which they emerge (227): "In sum, we take social construction of emotion to be an iterative and ongoing process that unfolds within interactions and relationships, which derive their shape and meaning from the prevailing ideas and practices of the larger socio-

---

1 Unless otherwise stated, all translations are my own.

cultural context. At different times, and in different contexts, the resulting emotions will be different" (222).

As a performer, what is my response to any knowledge of a musical work that I might have, especially an understanding of the composer's cultural, historical, political, and musical identities? Is imparting this information to the audience—conveying some form of this understanding—part of my role? Or is it sufficient to "deliver the piece," believing that matters of identity and cultural expression manifest themselves in the music "itself"? Furthermore, if I do wish to communicate implied cultural or political meaning in my performance, what does this mean in practice?

Madan Sarup (1996, 28) suggests that identity is a good "tool" for understanding a person's way of life in social, political, and philosophical terms. As a performer as well as a musicologist, my work here combines performance-led investigation with other forms of research, in order to examine how Korean-German composer Isang Yun's diasporic, cultural, and political identities are manifested in his first piano work, *Fünf Stücke für Klavier* (1958). I seek to understand the ways in which Yun's music reflects—or perhaps more accurately performs—his multiple identities in various cultural-historical contexts, and subsequently what this means when I play this music.

Isang Yun (1917–95) was a Korean-German composer whose work combined Eastern and Western musical elements. He experienced an enormously dramatic life in both the East and the West (Byeon 2003). This included surviving two wars, as well as being kidnapped by South Korean agents and being sentenced to death under the South Korean Anti-Communist Laws due to his contact with North Korea. After international pressure brought about his release, Yun left South Korea to live in exile in Germany. Yun's experiences and the social and political phenomena he encountered inevitably influenced his music, and many of his works carry political overtones. Yun's encounters with the new ideas and experimental sounds of the European avant-garde at the Darmstadt Festival in 1958 and 1959 led him to develop a complex musical identity that combined these influences with other cultural aesthetics, including Korea's musical heritage and Eastern philosophy.

In this essay, I define aspects of identity briefly according to four categories—identity as difference, as personal and social, as a process, and as narrative—and explore the significance of identity, how it is constructed, and its social role. This feeds the discussion not just of Yun's diasporic identity but also my personal experiences of being displaced in different countries for the past twenty years: it becomes relevant to the question of composer and performer identities. The focus, then, is an exploration of Yun's social and diasporic identities in relation to his first piano piece, *Fünf Stücke für Klavier*, a work that in many respects presents as a Western, post-serial piano composition, but which in fact reveals a complex range of cultural and political references. Furthermore, I contend that a musical performance is a personal, social, political, and cultural act—the embodiment of a performer's multiple identities. I am interested in how performative agency can invoke questions of identity.

IDENTITY PERFORMANCE AND PERFORMING IDENTITY

Recent decades have seen something of a "performance turn" in musicology (Cook 2014), moving beyond the idea that performers are transparently the voices of composers towards a fuller understanding of quite how and why "music is a performing art" (Cook 2001, par. 19). As Richard Taruskin argues (1982), we can only realise "the composer's intentions as far as our knowledge of them permits" (340): musical performance is substantially an expression of the performer's cultural and social identity, thereby more fully "let[ting] the culture speak" (342). In recent years, scholars including Max Paddison (2004), Stan Godlovitch (1998), Nicholas Cook (2001, 2014), and Philip Auslander (2004, 2006) have emphasised the performative domain of music. As Godlovitch (1998) notes, only performance makes musical works accessible to the ear (2), and the emergence of musical meaning depends upon the combination of the score (where one is in operation), conventional practices, and the performer's contributed subjectivity (85). Considering that one performs *something*, but in and through a social context (interacting with listeners, and often other performers), Nicholas Cook (2001) argues, "To understand music as performance means to see it as an irreducibly social phenomenon, even when only a single individual is involved" (par. 14). In this sense, Cook contends, we should understand a score as something like a musically notated script that choreographs socio-musical interactions, and from those interactions we "understand music as both reflection and generator of social meaning" (par. 31).

Philip Auslander, in response to Cook, emphasises the concept of persona in musical performance: music is not just the act of performing *something*, but requires an agent or a collective agent who makes the performing action. Drawing on the work of Simon Frith in *Performing Rites* (1996b), Auslander (2004, 6) identifies three key aspects of a performer: the real person (the performer's personal identity), the performance persona (the performer's stage personality), and the character he or she plays in. Auslander describes the term *persona* as a performed presence, in-between the performer's "real" identity and the character of the music he or she is playing (ibid., 6n14). Seen in this context, my three key players in performance would be Jin with her personal identity as a human being, Jin as a pianist who has had training in music and musical practice throughout her life, and Jin as the performer portraying a character of the music. For example, I would possess individual, different, and characteristic conceptions when I play Chopin's nocturnes compared with Bach's toccatas. In addition, the performing gestures (looking up or down, flat or curved fingers, light or heavy touches) I make to search for the most convincing tones on the piano, which I imagine in my inner ear, will be different as specified by what, when, where, and how I play.

Overall, then, performance is at once a personal, social, and political act: performative power engages critically and imaginatively with questions of identity through a process of communication. As Auslander says (2006, 101), this means "thinking of musicians as social beings—not just in the sense that musical performances are interactions among musicians (as Cook suggests), but also in the

larger sense, that to be a musician is to perform an identity in a social realm."
We don't just see the real person playing in a concert hall: we follow the entity
"that mediates between musicians and the act of performance. When we hear
a musician play, the source of the sound is a version of that person constructed
for the specific purpose of playing music under particular circumstances" (ibid.
102). Ultimately, as Marissa Silverman says (2007, 109), "interpretation is the act
of bringing one's whole being—intellectual, social, cultural, artistic, physical,
emotional and personal—into the performing event." Consequently, the listener does not experience some pure exemplification of organised sound, but
a revelation of the performer's expression of self-in-relation at a particular time
and place.

Why identity?

As Kathryn Woodward notes (1997, 2), identity is marked by "polarisation." As
social beings, we tend to differentiate between "us" and "them," depending on
how and where we are positioned in relation to others and especially whether
we operate within or outside groups constructed around the status, views, or
practices of societies, religions, ethnicities, cultures, economics, and politics.
That is to say, identity depends on whether we share a sameness or confront an
otherness, on conjunction and disjunction, internal and external, personal and
social: identity presents as double-sided.

My research addresses four aspects of identity. The first concerns difference:
identity as formed via interactions with others. As Pullen, Beech, and Sims
comment (2007, 2), identity "respects the sameness and difference [in] that it
implies and works within the tension between the two." In their view, work and
organisations are prior parts of identity in contemporary times, and different
activities in organisations have a significant impact on people's identities—as
significant as people's identities impact on organisations (ibid.). As Hall states
(1987, 45), in accordance with the previous discussions, "all identity is constructed across difference and begins to live with the politics of difference."
Hence, identity is shaped by how we perceive ourselves, as well as how others
recognise us through what we are not: difference.

With regard to the second aspect, my research explores how identity is both
personal and social, and how these two facets relate to one another. Woodward
(2002, xi–xii) scrutinises the social constitution of identity: "Identity has to be
socially located because it is through the concept of identity that the personal
and the social are connected. Identity occupies that interstitial space between
the personal and the social." Thus, identity is relational and social, constituted,
and negotiated via numerous kinds of relationships. Identity can be read differently, by different people, according to social context (ibid.). Richard Stevens
(1996) argues that a person's identity is the combination of personal identity
and social identity (19–20), and that personhood is inherently a social phenomenon (2, 22). By recognising Yun's social relationships in different social contexts, therefore, we can better understand this aspect of Yun's music and how
it expresses his relationship to the cultures in which he operated. Moreover, by

exploring Yun's background in this way, as well as examining and practising his music, the question of *my* identity as a performer arises: it becomes significant in relation to the cultural context, Yun's compositional choices, and the performance process. From such an enquiry, we gain a deeper understanding that reaches towards a more complex sense of the relationship between culture, identity, music, and expression.

The third aspect examines the notion that identity is always contingent on and changes constantly via experience and negotiations with others in particular circumstances. In opposition to the essentialist perspective of identity as fixed and static, Stanley Aronowitz states ([1992] 1995, 115): "there can be no 'essential' identity." He elaborates: "while in some contexts it appears that oppression is firmly situated in skin colour, sexual practices or national origins (in which cases identity appears anchored in the human condition), in other contexts the sources for oppression may appear entirely different." Aronowitz (ibid., 114) draws on the work of George Herbert Mead (1938, 53) to emphasise that society and its institutions determine the ongoing process of individual formation. Therefore, experience is the practice of assimilation of the surrounding environment (Aronowitz [1992] 1995, 114); ultimately, as Aronowitz says: "We may now regard the individual as a process constituted by its multiple and *specific* relations, not only to the institutions of socialization such as family, school and law, but also to significant others, all of whom are in motion and constantly changing. . . . New identities arise; old ones pass away (at least temporarily)" (ibid., 115).

Martin Parker and Stuart Hall also note the provisional nature of identity. Hall (1996, 4) states that identities are fragmented and fractured, "constantly in the process of change and transformation." Forced and free migration, and the processes of globalisation in the so-called postcolonial world (ibid.), encourage the increase of migration, and migration creates multiple identities in response. The meaning of identity in the postcolonial world has drifted from a defined phenomenon to something more akin to a "way of living." As Parker concludes, "[identity] is becoming more fluid and complex" (2007, 61).

Finally, I explore identity as narrative. Jonathan Rutherford (1990, 24) comments that "Identity then is never a static location, it contains traces of its past and what it is to become. It is contingent, a provisional full stop in the play of differences and the narrative of our own lives." Identities are constructed not only by external factors: we also shape our own identities by making choices and negotiating the consequences at every moment. Stevens (1996, 23) suggests that our experiences, actions, and events in every corner of our lives create some kind of narrative. In this account, understanding identity seems to unfold a narrative. Hall (1987, 44) summarises the argument as follows: "Who I am—the 'real' me—was formed in relation to a whole set of other narratives. I was aware of the fact that identity is an invention from the very beginning, long before I understood any of this theoretically. Identity is formed at the unstable point where the 'unspeakable' stories of subjectivity meet the narratives of history, of a culture."

These aspects of identity—as difference, as personal and social, as a process, and as narrative—underpin the ways in which I examine the work of Isang Yun and performances of his piano music. Yun's different personal identities—as Korean, German, a young man in a colonial country, a music teacher, the head of a household, and a kidnapped and exiled composer—shaped his social, international, diasporic, political, and cultural identities. As Paul Gilroy argues (1997, 311), identity's "capacity to be changed, reshaped and redefined, its malleability, is cultivated and protected as a source of pleasure, power, danger and wealth." Such capacity for gendered identity to be changed and redefined, and indeed the power and pleasure that follows from the play with gendered identity provided by the making of *Inside/Outside*, is discussed by Nguyễn and Östersjö above, in chapter 8. In this regard, Yun's multiple identities display a considerable degree of plasticity, simultaneously static and fluid, with the different components connecting with outside influences—contexts, cultures, and ideas—across time and space. Similarly, these various identities pervade his works: the question, then, is how this is manifested in his composition and what this might mean for a performer. As Catherine Laws notes (2005, 146), performance decisions, whether conscious or not, are on one level ontological, "in their performance of ways of being in the world—ways of telling stories, of expressing something of meaning, of constructing a different sense of self in relation to the world." When performing Yun's works, my identity mediates but is also constituted in part by my own way of engaging and negotiating Yun's identities, through my various interpretative decisions and ways of presenting the music to the audience.

Diasporic identity

Lawrence Grossberg (1996, 89) argues that the central concept of identity in both theoretical and political discourses is a "modern" development, in response, particularly in the last one hundred years, to global culture, travel, exchange, and exploitation, leading to increased awareness of cultural differences. When people are displaced, they experience more conflicts and greater confusion about who they are. For me, this is useful for connecting the questions that arise in considering Yun's music to his displacement: the observations of Grossberg and others prompt me to ask what it means to be in a certain place at a certain time—what is different and what is the same in two cultures—and therefore how Yun's identity is produced amid all this.

According to Paul Gilroy (1997, 341), the term *diaspora*, arose specifically as a result of the exile and scattering of Jewish populations. In the first issue of *Diaspora* journal, the editor, Khachig Tölölian (1991, 4), defined the term succinctly: "The term that once described Jewish, Greek, and Armenian dispersion now shares meanings with a larger semantic domain that includes words like immigrant, expatriate, refugee, guest-worker, exile community, overseas community, ethnic community." Su Zheng adds (2010, 11): "During the last decade of the twentieth century, it also became an alluring key concept in organizing contemporary intellectual ideas, exploring the politics of identity, and characterizing experiences of hybridity, difference, displacement, and transgression." In other words, the concept of diaspora is complex and conflicted, involving consciousness of geography and genealogy that is always relational to both spatial distinction and historical displacement. Hence, as Grossberg (1996, 92) notes with reference to James Clifford, "diaspora emphasizes the historically spatial fluidity and intentionality of identity."

In his essay "Diasporas in Modern Societies: Myths of Homeland and Return," William Safran (1991) clarifies the integral conditions of diaspora, and James Clifford (1994, 305) summarises this in one sentence: "A history of dispersal, myths/memories of the homeland, alienation in the host . . . country, desire for eventual return, ongoing support of the homeland, and a collective identity importantly defined by this relationship." Yun's multiple identities are shaped by a range of factors: his exile, longing for his homeland, and lifelong desire to return to South Korea; his exploration of his musical identity through participation in the Darmstadt Summer Courses, encountering the two extremes of hyper-determined and experimental approaches; his organising of a concert for the reunification of the two Koreas as a form of reconciliation through music.

As discussed, identity can change depending on where one is, as well as what one does, how one behaves, what one wishes to express, and how one expresses it in a given context. However, these things change over time. Diaspora is not only about one's history; it is also about being open to newness. As Hall (1990, 235) states: "diaspora identities are those which are constantly producing and reproducing themselves anew, through transformation and difference." In artworks, including music, diasporic identities motivate complex intercultural and multicultural structures: Edward Said (1993, 7) stresses that the struggle over geography sparked ideas, images, and imaginings. Mark Slobin (1994) argues that music can be a primary mode of expression of the diasporic experience, connecting homeland and here-land via a complex system of sound: "it is an extraordinarily multilayered channel of communication, nesting language itself, that primary agent of identity, within a series of strata of cultural meaning" (244). Furthermore, Slobin stated, "music offers a richness of methodological possibilities and points of view, opening new windows on diasporic neighborhoods" (243). Indeed, music seems to be one of the primary means of identification for the collective diasporas (245). When living in Korea, Yun immersed himself in Western music techniques: there are only brief hints of traditional Korean music. After moving to Europe, however, he employed more Korean musical ideas and techniques, adjusting musical sounds and techniques from his homeland to fit the grammar of Western contemporary music (Shin-hyang Yun 2005, 37–38).

My diasporic identity

In my personal experience of living in Canada, France, Belgium, and the United Kingdom, over the past twenty years, I have found that community has a strong impact on one's diasporic identity. In his essay "Home and Identity,"

203

Madan Sarup (1994) affirms this: "identity can be displaced; it can be hybrid or multiple. It can be constituted through community: family, region, the nation state. One crosses frontiers and boundaries" (89). Sarup was born in India and lived in the United Kingdom for over fifty years, yet did not feel British: he saw himself as an exile, or as displaced (89). He asks: "where is home [for migrants in particular]?" (90). I find myself hesitating when I try to answer this. During the more than ten years I spent in Canada, I lived in different places, with the various duties and benefits associated with life in that country: I paid taxes, was able to access the healthcare system, attempted to fit into a dynamic, multi-cultural country with an open-minded attitude, gained support for my musical career within and outside institutions, and developed personal and social relationships. However, almost every year (sometimes twice a year) I returned to my hometown in South Korea, to my parents and old friends. This trip became like a ritual event, which I called *recharging myself at home*. Although there were many benefits to experiencing new cultures and activities in new places, I found that living away from my homeland was quite exhausting and lonely. After reading Sarup, I realised that one's home is not just a geographical place in which one is situated at the time, but is a signifier of personal memories and imagined situations: "A home truth is something private. Many of the connotations of home are condensed in the expression: *Home is where the heart is*. Home is (often) associated with pleasant memories, intimate situations, a place of warmth and protective security amongst parents, brothers and sisters, loved people" (Sarup 1994, 90).

Regardless how many years I lived in Canada or how much I enjoyed such a multi-ethnic country, I was always an outsider and felt displaced. For many subsequent years my place of residence was the United Kingdom, but I still travelled to South Korea regularly to meet my family and old friends, to speak my mother tongue, and to eat Korean food, including homemade kimchi. Most of all, I grounded myself in my origin during these trips and revisited my roots, thus recharging myself at home. According to Sarup (1994), when people explore or learn about their "roots," they gain a renewed pride in their identity (92). Moreover, "the concept of home seems to be tied in some way with the notion of identity—*the story we tell of ourselves and which is also the story others tell of us*. But identities are not free-floating, they are limited by borders and boundaries" (91). This is because we are born into established relationships, which are linked to a place (93).

Displaced individuals often need to seek the familiar scents and tastes of their homeland cultures to reinforce and reaffirm this aspect of their identities. Moreover, certain ethnic and cultural diasporic communities seem to have a stronger sense of collective identity than others: "Any minority group when faced with hostile acts does several things. One of its first reactions is that it draws in on itself, it tightens its cultural bonds to present a united front against its oppressor. The group gains strength by emphasizing its collective identity. This inevitably means a conscious explicit decision on the part of some not to integrate with 'the dominant group' but to validate its own culture (religion, language, values, ways of life)" (Sarup 1994, 91). As Hall notes (1987, 46), "[identity] insists on difference—on the fact that every identity is placed, positioned, in a culture, a language, a history. Every statement comes from somewhere, from somebody in particular. It insists on specificity, on conjuncture." The members of a diasporic community not only participate in the sense of physical and social displacement, but also share the sense of distinctiveness due to the certain cultural homogeneity produced by participation in traditions, customs, and particularly language. I only fully understood and appreciated my own "Koreanness" after I moved to Canada. As Hall writes: "It may be true that the self is always, in a sense, a fiction, just as the kinds of 'closures' which are required to create communities of identification—nation, ethnic group, families, sexualities, etc.—are arbitrary closures; and the forms of political action, whether movements, or parties, or classes, those too, are temporary, partial, arbitrary" (Hall 1987, 44). As I searched for ways to express my Korean cultural identity in a foreign country, I found fellowship in the diasporic communities by becoming an active member of the Korean-Canadian Association of Ottawa, organising several performances, and inviting traditional Korean musicians and dancers from South Korea, as well as being an organist at a Korean Catholic church.

From my own diasporic experiences, diasporic identity gives rise to another phenomenon: feeling peripherally situated and unsettled. Hall (1987) notes that "migration is a one way trip. There is no 'home' to go back to" (44): people who are displaced, whether through free will or necessity, take on a new identity, are given a new identity, a "marginal identity" (44), and are never centred. This phenomenon encourages societies to create arenas or events for each minority group to express and share differences by interacting with other groups. As an example, Ottawa, an ethnically diverse city, hosts the annual Canadian Tulip Festival. Each year, over thirty different ethnic communities perform their traditional music and celebrate their cultures, as well as introducing their traditional foods to the other communities. As the artistic director of the Korean board of the festival in 2008 and 2009, I conducted performances of popular and traditional Korean music and dance along with over fifty performers. In this context, the festival creates a multicentric setting for marginal identity, as well as acting as a cultural mediator in a multicultural society.

In "Music and Identity" (1996a), Simon Frith describes musical experience as reflecting and producing one's identity. As a pianist, performing music is a means of understanding different aspects of my identity. I am Korean, but was brought up playing Western classical music and then studied music in different Western countries, expanding my connection to the various kinds of music around me. My experience of music as a pianist articulates my identity in flux, in relation to given times and places: this is examined more specifically later in this essay, in relation to performing Yun's *Fünf Stücke für Klavier* (1958). First, I map the important aspects of Yun's biography, focusing on his diasporic identity, in order to explore how music is expressive of aspects of individual and collective identity.

Yun's diasporic identity

Isang Yun was born on 17 September 1917 near Tongyeong, a small harbour town in what is now South Korea, during the Japanese occupation of Korea (1910–45). According to Seon Wook Park (2017, 37–48), Yun's musical material was shaped by Tongyeong, as he was exposed to shamanic rituals, the Lotus Lantern Festival, Buddhist chanting of the sutras, *pansori*, the sounds of fishermen working, and the quiet sea at night. Yun explained this influence as follows: "To me, my homeland and my music are deeply interrelated. My music was born through my country, while my country embraces my music as its offspring, which supports fruitful music in return" (Yun 1991c, 73). Influenced by his father, Ki Hyun Yun, a scholar of poetry, Yun entered a Chinese literary institute at age five before attending a standard elementary school. At the literary institute, he read Lao-tzu and Confucius, whose ideas later permeated his compositions.

In his youth, Yun began to study the violin, and was fond of listening to Ravel, Fauré, and Debussy, particularly Ravel's String Quartet in F major (1903). He made his first self-taught attempts at composition aged 13 (Seon Wook Park 2017, 69–70). Yun's advanced music education began in Japan in 1933, when he entered the Osaka Conservatory to study cello and music theory, before going on to study counterpoint and composition in Tokyo. With his mother's death, Yun returned to Tongyeong. About fifty years later, he composed the second movement of his Symphony No. 4 "Im Dunkeln singen" (1986) in memory of his mother. In 1939, Yun made his second trip to Japan to study under Ikenouch Domojiro in Tokyo (ibid., 108). However, after two years, Yun (with all other Korean students) was forced to return to Korea in the immediate aftermath of the Japanese attack on Pearl Harbor in 1941.

In 1942, Yun decided to join his town's underground resistance against the Japanese occupation. This was his first political activity. Three years later, he was tortured and then imprisoned for two months—jailed not because of his resistance activities, but because of his compositions in Korean. By this time, Japan had forbidden all Koreans from writing, talking, and singing in Korean; to do so was regarded as an anti-Japanese crime (Seon Wook Park 2017, 115–22). After Korea's liberation from Japanese colonial rule in 1945, Yun's professional musical career began with the founding of the Tongyeong Cultural Society (ibid., 87), which organised concerts, plays, and lectures for the public.

With the outbreak of the Korean War in 1950, Yun founded the Wartime Composers Association, later renamed the Korean Composers Association. At this time, he was teaching music at Busan High School as well as holding a lectureship in composition at Busan National University. Soon afterwards, he moved to Seoul with his wife and taught music theory at several universities there, while also being active as a lecturer and writer. In Yun's writings of this time we can glimpse something of his philosophy regarding art and society: "An artist as a member of a society has a responsibility to support citizens to grow. Art is the product of its time, citizens have their own sensibilities and reasons, yet society should be open to all different kinds of arts to prevent deadlock and decomposition" (Yun quoted in Noh 1994, 333). Clearly, Yun believed that artists cannot be separate from, but are part of, society: an artist should pay attention to what is happening and respond to the particular circumstances. In 1956 Yun won the Seoul City Culture Prize for two early works, a piano trio and a string quartet. This achievement motivated him to continue his studies in Europe: first at the Paris Conservatory with Toni Aubin and Pierre Revel, who had both been pupils of Paul Dukas, then at the West Berlin Hochschule with Boris Blancher, Reinhard Schwarz-Schilling, and Josef Rufer, a student of Schoenberg's. Under the influence of these musicians, Yun explored the atonal techniques of the Second Viennese School.

Yun first participated in the Darmstadt Summer Courses for New Music in 1958 and 1959. At Darmstadt he encountered leading post-war avant-garde composers, including Karlheinz Stockhausen, John Cage, Pierre Boulez, Luigi Nono, and Bruno Maderna, which simultaneously distracted and confused him (Byeon 2003, 108). Yun's experiences at Darmstadt acted as a mirror: he sought a musical stance by reflecting the music of the avant-garde composers (74). Two of Yun's works of this time incorporated avant-garde techniques and had successful debut performances: *Fünf Stücke für Klavier* (1958) was performed at Gaudeamus-Musikfest in Bilthoven, and *Musik für sieben Instrumente* (1959) at Darmstadt (287).

In 1963, Yun visited North Korea: an illegal act under South Korean law. Viewing North Korea positively, he did not consider this trip particularly controversial; after all, East and West Germans crossed the Berlin Wall freely at that time (Cho 2018, 163). Furthermore, North Korea's economic growth in the 1960s exceeded that of South Korea, and several South Korean students from Berlin considered the idea of visiting North Korea to be an enticing prospect (ibid.). In an interview with Rinser, Yun said: "My trip [ended] with a double result: with great admiration for the achievements in construction and with deep consternation about the change in landscape, and even more so the people. Thus, my trip to North Korea actually went in such a manner, and [I was] not as a communist sympathizer and spy chief as I was accused" (Byeon 2003, 224).

In 1964, the Ford Foundation granted a permit that allowed Yun's family to join him in Berlin. In the same period, he began to gain international recognition as a composer. Two years later, Yun was invited to the United States to deliver lectures in Aspen, Chicago, Los Angeles, New York, San Francisco, and Tanglewood (Hauser 2009, 7). In 1967, Yun's growing musical career and more settled personal life were snatched from him when the South Korean Central Intelligence Agency (KCIA) kidnapped him during an event dubbed the "East Berlin Spy Incident" (explained more fully below). After his release in 1969, Yun started life anew in Germany, becoming a German citizen in 1971, and never returned to South Korea.

Yun was awarded the Kiel Cultural Prize in 1969; from that year on, he received regular commissions from international organisations, including for an opera at the 1972 Summer Olympics in Munich, which employed the slogan "the unity of all cultures" (Hauser 2009, 10). He was appointed as a lecturer at the Musikhochschule in Hanover (1970–71), and then as a professor at the Hochschule für Musik in Berlin (1970–85). Concurrently, Yun continued his social and political activities: he affiliated himself with Korean Exile Organisations, as well as participating in an international conference of Korean refugee organisations in Tokyo in 1976 (ibid.). As Laura Hauser writes, "Yun was continually concerned with peace on the Korean peninsula. His hope was for the reunification of North and South Korea, and the existence of a democratic government" (ibid.). Unsurprisingly, Yun became the leader of the European branch of the National Alliance for the Country's Reunification in 1977 (Howard 2006, 132).

Yun never visited South Korea after his exile in 1969, yet he visited North Korea several times after his release from imprisonment by the KCIA: from 1979 on, Yun made several visits to Pyongyang (since his first trip in 1963) (Cho 2018, 165; see also Jee-hyun Kim 2008, 18). In 1984, the Isang Yun Music Research Centre was founded in Pyongyang, and the Isang Yun Music Festival has been held annually ever since: as part of this, Yun gave lectures and organised concerts including international musicians (Seon Wook Park 2017, 530). Throughout the 1980s, until his death in 1995, Yun was extremely active compositionally and received numerous prizes and other accolades. He died of pneumonia on 3 November 1995 in Berlin and was buried in the city's Gatow cemetery.

Yun's biography is suggestive of complex identity. He was always located between South and North Korea, as well as between East Asia and Western Europe. In conversation with Luise Rinser, Yun stated: "I am not a typical East Asian, nor am I Europeanized. I bear the characteristics of the two cultures" (Byeon 2003, 286). Because of his cross-cultural experiences in the East and the West, Yun's works reveal the influence not only of Western modernist and experimental composers but also of Korean musical heritage and Eastern philosophy: these led to the development of Yun's own unique compositional technique, *Hauptton*. Moreover, the experience of exile changed him, having a profound influence not just on his socio-political outlook but also on his approach to composition.

I lived in Korea until 2000, but never encountered Yun's music in classes or concerts. The South Korean government lifted the prohibition on Yun's music in 1993 (Ko Eun Lee 2012, 14); nevertheless, some South Koreans still consider Yun to be somehow attached to North Korea and for that reason reject his music. However, in recent years certain incidents suggest a shift in opinions: when celebrating the centenary of his birth in 2017, the first lady of South Korea, former classical singer Jung-sook Kim, paid tribute to Yun and visited his grave in Berlin. In 2018, the South Korean government transferred Yun's body to the garden of the Tongyeong International Music Foundation: he finally returned home twenty-three years after his death.

Yun's political identity, *Musik Im Exil*

According to Christian Martin Schmidt (1992, 12), Yun's works were born as *Musik im Exil* due to his treatment by his home country. Schmidt further adds that Yun's work can be fully understood by treating his music as a product of his unique situation and life circumstances. As Bhuchung Sonam, himself a Tibetan exile, explains, exile refers not just to place but also to the person: it is "a state of physical displacement and longing for the native land . . . place of birth, or of origin or sometimes just the idea of home. On a more subtle level an exile is some sort of a social outcaste, an outsider—one who intentionally remains outside the mainstream social intercourse" (Sonam 2005, quoted in Oha 2008, 82). Similarly, Obododimma Oha (2008, 87) describes exile as "a removal from home [that] orchestrates an *in-betweenness*: the exiled person is neither here nor there, even in the choice of language to express self. Exile is *somewhere*, but psychologically, the exiled person is *nowhere*." Tetsunori Koizumi (1993, 117–18) identifies two kinds of exiled peoples: those who are "pushed out" by political oppression or power struggles, often as a result of political actions or the expression of offending views, and others who are "pulled into" leaving to receive benefits with which they expect to be rewarded. Yun's case certainly fits the first category.

After General Chung-hee Park seized control of South Korea following the 1961 military coup, Yun established the Korean Society with his friends in Germany (Byeon 2003, 163). The goal of this group was to promote the establishment of democracy in South Korea; the Society harshly criticised the authoritarian Park and his repressive military government. In 1963, together with his wife, Yun visited Pyongyang. This trip to North Korea was not overtly political but reflected Yun's desire to see in person the other half of his home country, especially the famous Sashindo tomb fresco (220), one of Yun's greatest sources of artistic inspiration (8).

However, this trip to North Korea had dire consequences a few years later. In 1967, the KCIA kidnapped Yun from Berlin and smuggled him to South Korea, along with over 150 Korean intellectuals from many other countries (Byeon 2003, 180). After kidnapping Yun, the KCIA drugged and severely tortured him, extracting a false confession of spying for North Korea that resulted in a death sentence under the draconian Anti-Communist Law (204).

Yun's imprisonment resulted in international uproar. The West German Government threatened to reduce its economic support to South Korea as a political counteraction against illegal acts undertaken on West German soil (Yulee Choi 1992, 141). Yun's professional and social circle in Berlin set up a committee to press for his release. Many internationally prominent musicians gave fundraising concerts to support the committee: In 1967, the president of the Hamburg Academy of Arts, Wilhelm Maler, wrote a letter to the South Korean government calling for Yun's release from prison: 161 distinguished musicians signed a petition supporting Maler's letter demanding Yun's release: these included Earle Brown, Edward Staempfli, Karlheinz Stockhausen,

Elliott Carter, Ernst Krenek, Herbert von Karajan, Wolfgang Fortner, Mauricio Kagel, György Ligeti, Hans Werner Henze, and Rolf Liebermann; Claudio Arrau supported the campaign by cancelling his recital in Seoul (Yulee Choi 1992, 207–9). After two years, this pressure brought about Yun's release and he returned to Berlin—this time as an exile. However, tarred as a North Korean sympathiser, Yun's music was officially banned in South Korea, a ban that was only rescinded in 1993 (Suja Lee 1998, 2:99).

After this experience, social and political ideas began to seep into Yun's music: his works began to display stronger political overtones. Furthermore, Yun led the European branch of the overseas National Alliance for the Country's Reunification (Howard 2006, 132), which resulted in the first—and also last—united concert with musicians from the two Koreas. Speaking at a ceremony at which the University of Tübingen bestowed an honorary doctorate upon him, Yun emphasised that "through my humanistic and political experience of 'kidnapping' [to Korea] and the social-political development in the West, I aim to express my social stance with more distinct musical language" (Yun 1991b, 49). He further stated: "Basically to me art and politics are segregated. I am only a musician, nothing else, I have nothing to do directly with politics. As a musician I have only one goal: to follow my artistic knowledge and its high demand for purity and great dimensions of consciousness. . . . Always in a catastrophe, an artist is also a human like all others, and must do something for all, hence, to get involved in politics" (Byeon 2003, 298). Yun seems to be saying that he is only an artist. However, at the same time, he notes that political events had a deep effect on his musical language. Certainly, Yun's music is not overtly political, but politics can manifest itself in music in complex ways.

Before Yun was kidnapped and exiled in 1967–69, he had already experienced a period of social and political change, including three different wars: the Second World War, the Korean War, and the Cold War. Although the music he wrote during this time was not explicitly political, it inevitably reflected his identity. However, after moving to Europe Yun withdrew all the music he composed during his time in Korea and Japan (Schmidt 1992, 12): thus, his first published work is *Fünf Stücke für Klavier*, written in Europe in 1958. Yun stated that he was unsatisfied with the works he had written in Korea, but this decision was also a statement about identity, and hence, given the context, a political act.

Moreover, on his release the Korean government forced Yun to sign a contract with three rules (Seon Wook Park 2017, 454). First, he must never mention anything of what happened in the period of his imprisonment between his kidnapping and his exile. Second, he must never mention details of his trials. Finally, he must never talk about South Korea negatively (ibid.). It was not until seven years after his release that Yun first mentioned his kidnapping and time in prison, and in observance of the contract, his pieces from this period have no programmatic titles that could in any way relate to these circumstances. Yun confessed that he had suffered mental trauma with serious depression for ten years after his release. Can we really claim that all Yun's music written during these seven years is wholly abstract and apolitical? Ron Eyerman (2002, 46) discusses the ways in which music, as a cultural artefact, can carry memory, "linking past, present and future" for individuals and collectives, in relation to their communities and histories. Adorno (1976, 197) refined this thought: "The social distribution and reception of music is mere epiphenomenon; the essence is the objective social constitution of music in itself." In short, music is engaged with social relations, which change in flux. Whether or not Yun wanted his music to reflect his political experiences, something of it carries through: all art reflects the artist's identity, mediated socially.

Performing *Fünf Stücke für Klavier* (1958)

As noted in the introduction to this book, Simon Frith (1996a) argues that "identity is not a thing but a process—an experiential process which is most vividly grasped *as music*" (110). Music is not a fixed work but rather a storytelling process; like identity, it requires an openness to imaginative experience in relation to social, political, and cultural contexts. As Frith postulates, "music seems to be a key to identity because it offers, so intensely, a sense of both self and others, of the subjective in the collective" (110). Moreover, Frith notes that music does not just reflect identity, but also produces it: "the issue is not how a particular piece of music or a performance reflects the people, but how it produces them, how it creates and constructs an experience—a musical experience, an aesthetic experience—that we can only make sense of by *taking on* both a subjective and a collective identity" (109). Philip Auslander (2006, 101), likewise, argues for music as performative of social identity: "to be a musician is to perform an identity in a social realm." Performing music involves presenting a version of self—an identity—mediated by what is written in the score (ibid.).

In recent years, study of diasporas has greatly increased, and this has been followed in musicology (Solomon 2015, 202): as Georgina Born and David Hesmondhalgh (2000, 25) argue, "In contrast with ethnomusicology's former object of study—'traditional musics'—it is diasporic music that has moved to the center of attention." Beyond this, though, Thomas Solomon (2015, 214) suggests that diasporic music is particularly rich as a carrier of identity: "because of its portability and the way it affords deeply felt, embodied experiences, music is an especially powerful tool for articulating diasporic consciousness."

My own performance-led research examines Isang Yun's *Fünf Stücke für Klavier* (1958), as a case study for the understanding of diasporic music.[2] This includes score-based work that traces Yun's typical use of musical symbols and signs, identifying aspects of his diasporic identity in his use of both Eastern and Western musical traditions. The composer employs these elements throughout the composition, and understanding this affects my realisation of the work in performance, determining how I communicate with the audience using my performative agency in relation to my own social, cultural, and embodied understanding: by means of my own identity.

---

2 A recording of a performance of *Fünf Stücke für Klavier*, given as part of a lecture-recital in 2015, is available at https://www.youtube.com/watch?v=CU7O9ucnnDo&t=116s.

Yun completed *Fünf Stücke für Klavier* in 1958 while he was studying at the Berlin Hochschule; it was premiered by Herman Keuyt at Gaudeamus-Musikfest in Bilthoven in the Netherlands in 1959. In this early work, Yun's encounter with avant-garde composers encouraged him to use the twelve-tone technique. However, his early adaptation of Eastern cultural and musical trad-itions is also evident, when we dig a little deeper. On a simple level, this piece sounds like a Western serial piano piece, with Yun adapting the twelve-tone technique according to his personal taste: as Edward Park (2014, 27) states, the piece "expresses the academic aspect of a composer who has mastered the twelve-tone technique" and thus "it is hard to find unique Korean musical color in this suite." Nevertheless, aspects of Korean musical tradition and Eastern philosophy, which were to become more prominent in Yun's later work, are subtly embedded. Ko Eun Lee (2012, 90) argues that Yun's particular use of the tone row is linked to an Eastern philosophical conception of the single tone, so as "to highlight their functions as both a whole and a part." Indeed, Yun once said that "the single tone is the musical phenomenon. Each tone has its own life" (Byeon 2003, 138).

Beyond this, I argue that we can identify the stark contrasts of the piece in relation to the philosophical ideas of yin and yang: a particular approach to the balance and harmony between opposing forces. This understanding then informs my own performance. In what follows, I do not attempt to interpret or to produce a comprehensive analysis of the piece. Rather, I identify three key aspects of the ways in which the musical language of the piece manifests different facets of Yun's complex identity, particularly those that interest me as a performer: first, Yun's use of both the twelve-tone technique and Eastern scales; second, other kinds of instrumental references to traditional Korean music; third, the relevance of certain symbolic points in Yun's life, drawn from my knowledge of the composer and the ways in which he himself sometimes referenced political or spiritual ideas in his music (quite explicitly, in his later music).

References to the Western and Korean musical systems

The first movement of *Fünf Stücke für Klavier* is divided into two sections: adagio and andante (see figure 9.1 for the adagio). One might argue that this move-ment is strongly situated in Western modernism, given its post-tonal sound-world and its selective deployment of twelve-tone techniques: for example, the very first melodic phrase, rising from the first notes in the left hand across into the right, comprises all twelve tones (though at the entry of the right hand, the accompaniment repeats pitches just heard).

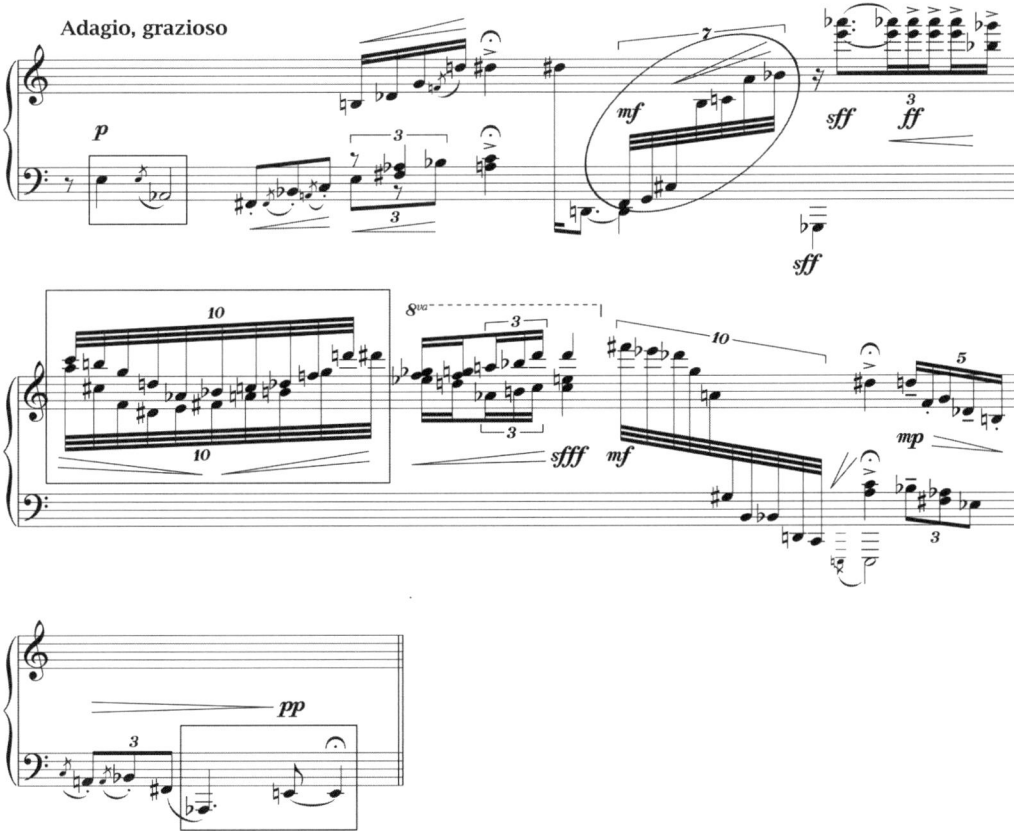

Figure 9.1.

However, Yun employs both Eastern and Western musical traditions in the very opening of *Fünf Stücke für Klavier*. Mi-ock Kim (2010, 64) found that the adagio section includes the Eastern *Saeya* motif as well as the Western tone row. The *Saeya* motif refers to the traditional Korean folk song *Saeya, Saeya, Pahrang Saeya* (Bird, bird, blue bird) (Taehyun Kim 2013, 38).

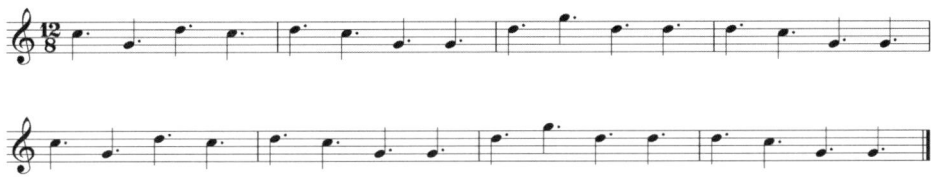

Figure 9.2.

As is shown in figure 9.2, the *Saeya* motif represents the "upward [or downward] progression of the two intervals, the perfect 4th and the major 2nd" (Mi-ock Kim 2010, 90); Yun added this motif to the adagio section, as can be seen in the upper part of the left hand at the end of the second system in figure 9.1

213

(the descending B♭–A♭–E♭, which reiterates in slightly modified form the left-hand accompaniment in the very first phrase). Importantly, this moment is set against a reverse iteration of the opening tone row, and this is how the adagio ends. Consequently, the first tone row and the *Saeya* motif both appear simultaneously at the beginning (in a modified version) and end of the adagio section: as Mi-ock Kim says, the *Saeya* motif remains as an embedded figure under the tone row (ibid., 64). In this regard, the motif acts as a manifestation of Yun's East Asian identity, but juxtaposed with the Western tone row.

In the first movement, Yun wrote two brief but obviously symmetrical passages—which is one characteristic of twelve-tone technique compositions—manifesting Western identity. Not only are the pitch classes reversed in the retrograde row forms, but the rhythmic patterns and registral placements also appear in retrograde: an ascending motion (F, G, C♯, B, C, A, B♭) in the adagio (given in the circle in figure 9.1) appears as a reverse descending motion (B♭, A, C, B, C♯, G, F) in the andante (the circle in figure 9.3); in certain respects the beginning and end of this movement form a palindrome.

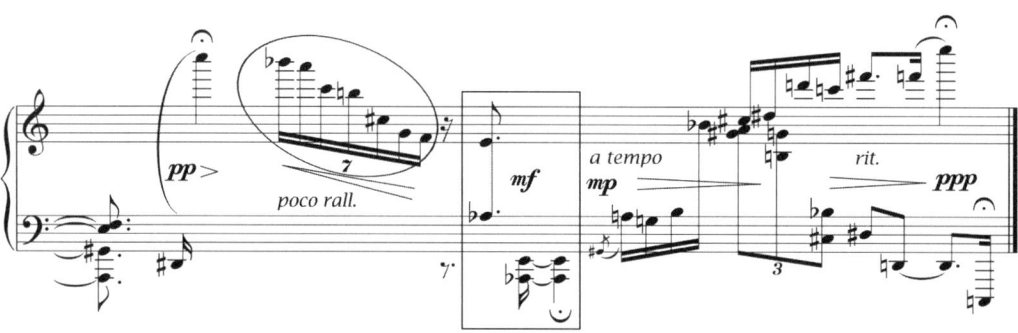

Figure 9.3.

Somewhat similarly, but more locally, at the beginning and end of the final section of the movement (shown in figure 9.3), two large intervals appear as rhetorical expressions: the very soft, wide leaps, with pauses on the highest notes, first swooping upwards, and then (for the last two notes) down again, over an even wider space and even quieter. What does this mean to me as a performer? In order to play these intervals, in which two separate notes are very far from one another across vertical pitch space, my arms need to stretch sufficiently to cover the entire keyboard horizontally; thus, I enjoy the feeling of spaciousness in both directions. This reminds me of Yun's long-lasting hope for the reunification of the two Koreas without a border. In this case, I cannot think of any concrete reason for identifying things in this manner. However, exploring Yun's life and music seems to have shaped my cognitive processes in certain ways. In addition, the descending septuplet with *poco rall.* in figure 9.3 proposes not only an engagement with the gradually slower motion, but also that more weight is put on the right hand as the music develops, similar to an emotional gesture.

214

Similar approaches are found later in the piece, but with other scales. The "romance-like" second movement opens with an elegant linear melody (Yun quoted in Sparrer 2008, 11), another example of the coexistence of Eastern and Western musical traditions (see figure 9.4). The opening *piano dolce* melody for the right hand introduces a G–E–D♯ motif that appears several times in the movement (Sae Hee Kim 2004, 42), followed by a full pentatonic scale (D♯, F, A♭, B♭, C) (ibid., 26) and concluding with a diminished triad (C, A, F♯). The pentatonic scale is equivalent to the Korean mode *pyeongjo* on D♯. Many people will recognise the broader Eastern reference, and perhaps some will spot the more specific Korean focus; again this acts as a symbolic mediation of cultural identity as manifested in Eastern music traditions.

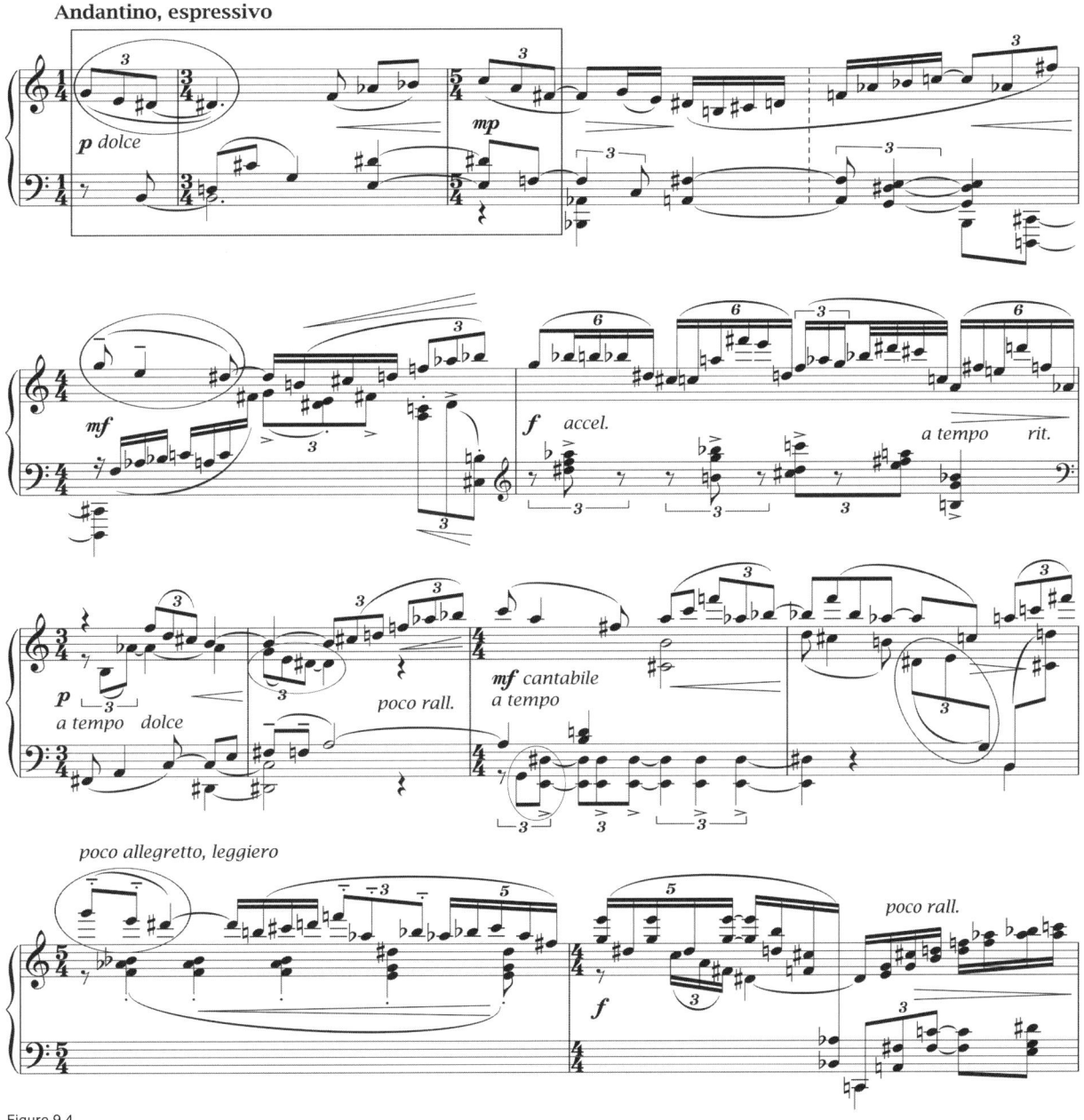

Figure 9.4.

Figure 9.4. *Fünf Stücke für Klavier*, movement 2, bars 1–11. © Copyright 1958 by Bote & Bock Musik- und Bühnenverlag Gmbh & Co. Reproduced by permission of Boosey & Hawkes Music Publishers Ltd.

The chromatic accompaniment for the left hand completes the aggregate, forming a twelve-tone row (G, E, D♯, B, D♮, C♯, F, A♭, B♭, C, A, F♯) in the box in figure 9.4. This row then appears more clearly in sixteenth notes for the right hand in the following bar (bar 3), at the stronger dynamic level of *mezzo-piano*. The version of the row in bar 3 does not state the pentatonic scale as clearly: only four notes (F, A♭, B♭, C) are adjacent. In this way, Yun introduced two different melodic elements simultaneously: a Western European-style twelve-tone row and a more Eastern-sounding pentatonic scale.

Moreover, the G–E–D♯ motif (circled in figure 9.4) itself has an interesting possible heritage: according to Sparrer (2008, 11), "the thematic core of the second piece—a falling minor third and a semitone—pays homage to Schoenberg's *Klavierstück* op.11 no.1." This thematic core depicts Yun's social and situational identities, because he was studying with Schoenberg's pupil, Josef Rufer, at the West Berlin Hochschule while composing *Fünf Stücke für Klavier* (Seon Wook Park 2017, 279).

References to Korean music

The opening improvisatory adagio section of the first movement (see figure 9.1) aroused my interest in a particular style that reminds me of Korean court music, such as *Sujecheon* (meaning "Long life everlasting as the sky" [Kwon 2012, 48])—perhaps this was because I had been exposed to court music while I was living in Korea, and also because while I was studying Yun's life and works I had noted that some of his compositions have cultural overtones of traditional Korean music. *Sujecheon* is considered the oldest of all Korean court orchestral works and is performed in an elegant manner (ibid.). In addition, *Sujecheon* usually consists of prolonged notes in a slow and meditative tempo (Soo-yon Choi 2006, 33). The adagio section of the first movement employs a free, recitative-like style: there is no metre, nor are there bar lines (Sae Hee Kim 2004, 35). J. W. Turner (2013, 218) notes that the unmetred rhythm in a slow tempo of Yun's *Glissées pour violoncello seul* (1970) suggests Korean court music and Buddhist chants. Moreover, the influence of *Sujecheon* can be found in Yun's other works: for example, Keith Howard (2006, 130) notes that Yun seems to associate his piece *Loyang* (1962) with *Sujecheon*. Consequently, my performance of the movement connects different identities, imbued with my personal memory of Korean music in conjunction with Yun's cultural identity, manifested in the score. My knowledge of different musical traditions and experience of their different sounds influences how I perform this piece.

The thirty-second-note (demisemiquaver) passage in the box at the start of the second system in figure 9.1 is the centre of the adagio, in which there are brief diatonic passages: the right hand plays A♭, B♭, C♮, D♭, and F♮, which are all part of the A♭ major scale, and the left hand plays D♯, E, F♯, A♮, B♮, and G♮ from the E-minor scale. The emphasis on the central point of the figure—using a sudden reduction in dynamic to the lack of sounds and a focus upon tones—is similar to the lack of an object in this style of negative space in Eastern paintings, reflecting its characteristics of dialogue, infinity, freedom, openness, and receptiveness (Lim 2019, 184–92). This focus on empty space originates in the Taoist view, wherein *negative* means something that is "negated" or "denied," implying a sense of void. By decreasing the dynamic level in this way, the composer can force the audience to pay closer attention. This negative accent simultaneously opens up a dialogue between the diatonic passages and the dissonant chords, opening a space for the listener's imagination. This has implications for performance: I often attempt to slow down the passage to express the diatonic colours amid the more atonal moments.[3]

In the second movement, the opening G–E–D♯ motif in the first measure in figure 9.4 is repeated throughout the movement using different rhythmic patterns to produce a syncopated effect. In contrast to the unmetred first movement, the second movement has time signatures that change frequently ($\frac{1}{4}$–$\frac{3}{4}$–$\frac{5}{4}$–$\frac{4}{4}$–$\frac{3}{4}$–$\frac{4}{4}$–$\frac{5}{4}$–$\frac{4}{4}$–$\frac{4}{4}$–$\frac{3}{4}$). The choices here create a sense of ebb and flow, or expanding and contrasting motions, which mediate the momentum of the piece. The opening motif (marked with a circle in figure 9.4) in the first system often appears on the downbeats. To me, the motif's journey embodies Yun's wandering identity between home and elsewhere. Amid the shifting metres, Yun maintains a quarter-note (crotchet) pulse. Therefore, the regular appearance of the motif on the downbeats, alongside the maintenance of an underlying beat throughout the movement, produces a sense of solidity and continuity; an identity that I can't help linking to Yun's persistent sense of his Korean identity when he encountered sameness and difference during his life journey.

Likewise, knowing Yun's interest in Taoism (discussed below), the irregular time signatures and the regular appearances of the motif seem to co-exist as the two cosmic forces of yin and yang. As a performer, I am aware of some salient patterns in the score, such as the opening motif in this movement (and its possible reference back to Schoenberg's *Klavierstück* op.11, no.1); I emphasise these patterns in performance in order to communicate them in different voices, in which the motif is manipulated and changed, yet retains the core of its identity. Perhaps similarly, MyeongSuk Park (1990, 29) states that Yun's use of this motif suggests a sense of free repetition, recalling a particular characteristic of Korean court music.

It is also important to note the different roles assigned to the right and left hands in this movement. As shown in figure 9.4, the right hand plays a straightforward linear melody, creating the sense of one line and implying active motion, whereas the left hand plays sustained notes and chords (bars 3–4, 8–9, 10, 12, 13, 16, 20–21), implying passive motion. Thus, the opening andantino of the second movement features a melody and accompanying texture. Moreover, the right hand controls the metric pulse rhythmically, with notes on many downbeats, while the left hand avoids conspicuous downbeats. This arrangement is very similar to the traditional Korean musical genre *pansori*.

---

3   Although I believe that negative space appears in Yun's other works, including *Interludium A* and *Duo für Viola und Klavier*, I do not address these in this study, but leave them as the subject of further research.

Pansori originated during the Joseon dynasty (1674–1720) and became fashionable from the eighteenth century onward (Cultural Properties Administration 2000, 19). It is a form of musical storytelling, often referred to as Korean solo opera, which requires one *sorikkun* (a voice) and one *gosu* (a drummer) (Ko Eun Lee 2012, 11). The meaning of the term *pansori* is derived from two separate words: *pan*, meaning "a place where people gather," and *sori*, meaning "sound" (ibid.). A vocalist alternates the spoken narrative with a sung section. The *changgo*, the most common type of drum in Korea, is used to accompany the singer. In 2013, *pansori* was declared a UNESCO Masterpiece in the Oral and Intangible Heritage of Mankind (Howard 2006, 80). The most popular *pansori* is *Simcheongga* (The song of Simcheong); Yun composed an opera entitled *Sim Tjong* for the 1972 Summer Olympics in Munich in his later years.

In this movement, Yun adapted *pansori*, with its operatic combination of speaking and singing, somewhat similar to the genre of melodrama that inspired Schoenberg's use of *Sprechgesang* (spoken singing). Of course, *Pierrot Lunaire*, op. 21 (1912), is not a twelve-tone work. However, Schoenberg's use of *Sprechgesang*, adapted from European traditional melodrama, is well known and influential.

In the last movement ("Allegretto"), Yun produces a more spacious and playful effect. In the first six bars (shown in figure 9.5), the alternation of a single line and three voices may refer to *nodongyo*, a genre of traditional Korean folksong. In *nodongyo*, a leading voice alternates with that of a group, forming "a narration of call and response in [an] agricultural scene" (Dong-hoon Lee 2000, 65). The genre encompasses work songs sung by farmers or fisherman to reduce the hardship of hours of labour. Thus, it is a communicative form containing diverse stories in terms of different kinds of works and processes (ibid., 5–6). This influences my playing, in that my performing attitude changes according to the alternation of solo and collective voices.

The piece ends with *sf* on the last chord, creating a similar effect to the percussive clap of the *pak*, a traditional Korean instrument, illustrated in figure 9.6 (MyeongSuk Park 1990, 57–58; see also Chae 2003, 34). Korean instruments are divided into eight families on the basis of the material of which they are made—metal, stone, silk, bamboo, gourd, earth, skin, and wood—with *pak* belonging to the wood category. It is made of five or six wood sticks thirteen inches long connected by a strap; this instrument appears at the beginning and end of traditional Korean court music performances, producing a crisp percussive clap (Feliciano 1983, 38).

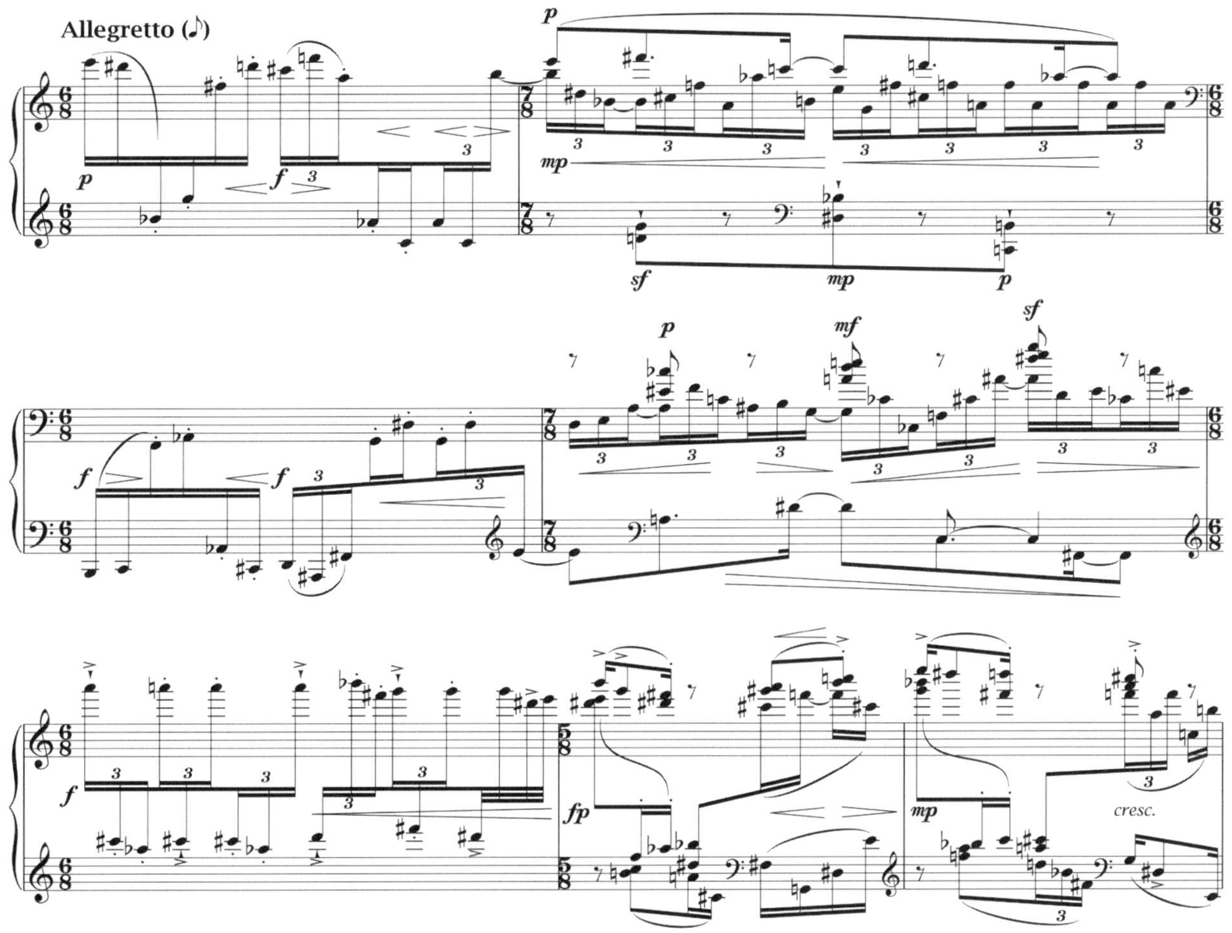

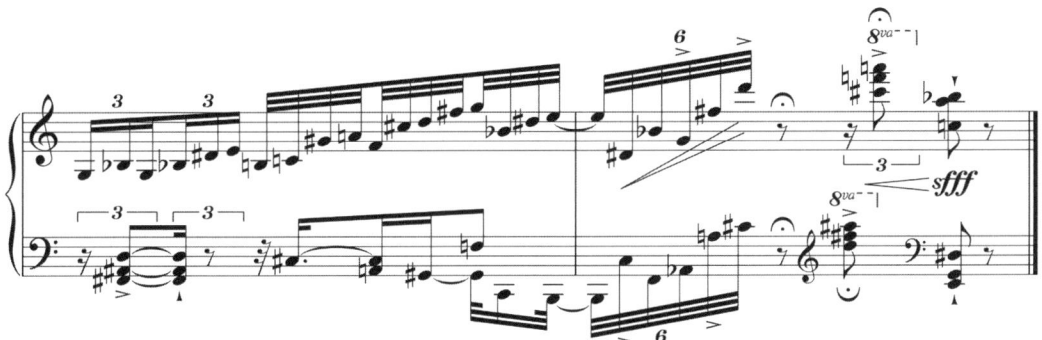

Figure 9.5.

Figure 9.6 .

Figure 9.5. *Fünf Stücke für Klavier*, movement 5, bars 1–7. © Copyright 1958 by Bote & Bock Musik- und Bühnenverlag Gmbh & Co. Reproduced by permission of Boosey & Hawkes Music Publishers Ltd.

Figure 9.6. *Fünf Stücke für Klavier*, movement 5, bars 18–19. © Copyright 1958 by Bote & Bock Musik- und Bühnenverlag Gmbh & Co. Reproduced by permission of Boosey & Hawkes Music Publishers Ltd.

Korean people have long believed that the *pak* invites a clean state of mind and pushes listeners towards "right thinking" (Young Woon Kim 2015, 113): as Hye-jin Song (2008, 162) writes, "Because it has no after-tone, the sound of struck wood gives an impression of straightness, and has traditionally been regarded as the musical expression of a righteous image." The *pak* player is generally the director of the Korean court music ensemble. Da-mi Oh (1999, 44) calls attention to the crescendo immediately before the last chord of *Fünf Stücke für Klavier*: due to the nature of the piano—with tones fading away as soon as they sound—it is impossible to produce this crescendo in practice. According to Da-mi Oh, when using this dynamic indication Yun suggested that a pianist should focus on expanding the spacious density within the crescendo, which reaches its limit and bursts forth in the last chords, and the *pak*-like full stop at the end (ibid., 44–45). This theoretical and practical understanding of the piece, invoking the *pak* and thus Korean court music, affects and changes my way of playing the piece, leading me to perform it in a majestic manner.

Political and spiritual references

From his childhood onwards, Yun was exposed to Eastern philosophies and ideas. Many of Yun's works explicitly represent Taoist concepts, such as *Loyang* (1962), *Der Traum des Liu-Tung* (*The Dream of Liu-Tung*, 1965), *Die Witwe des Schmetterlings* (*The Widow of the Butterfly*, 1968), *Ein Schmetterlingstraum* (*A Butterfly Dream*, 1968), *Sim Tjong* (1972), *Der weise Mann* (*The Wise Man*, 1977), and *Silla* for orchestra (1992). Yun presented his thoughts on Taoism in his lecture "Philosophy" at the Salzburg Mozarteum in 1993:

> Taoism is not a religious medium, but is a philosophical and spiritual attitude.... *Tao* in Chinese is interpreted as "Path" (*Weg*), yet *Weg* in German is not enough to express the extraordinary meaning [of *Tao*]. In Taoism, men and the universe exist in the huge absolute being [referred to as "the one" in the *Tao Te Ching*]. In addition, there is a huge being in Taoism, and it makes movements without discontinuation. This movement goes far away and makes its return [to its original state]. Although "movement" (*Bewegung*) exists ceaselessly, it is also "stillness" (*Nichtbewegung*) because of its [recurrent] returns.... The movement happens inherently. [*Tao*] is the spirit and anima of a man, which represents a small unit of the microcosmos.... The principle of Taoism represents four main components in the universal space, and one of them is the human being. (Yun and Sparrer 1994, 28–29)[4]

Yun himself explained how his compositions embodied Taoist principles; these are ubiquitous in his compositions, but sometimes manifest in loose or subtle ways (Henseler 1992, 75). For example, in the first movement, three fermatas appear in the adagio and three more in the andante (see figures 9.1 and 9.3). The contrast between pause and movement is similar to the yin and yang forces of activity and passivity, to which Yun often referred and which derive from the Taoist idea of unity: "Yin and yang are (together) one absolute, the absolute is basically infinite" (Liu 2005, 39).

---

4   This quotation is also cited by Young Ju Lee, who gives her own translation (2009, 18).

E♮ and A♭, the tonic notes of the two scales discussed above with reference to the idea of negative space (shown in the box at the start of the second system of figure 9.1), are the first two notes of the piece (the box at the first system of figure 9.1), and they also appear at the end of the adagio (the box at the third system of figure 9.1) and immediately before the epilogue in the andante (the box in figure 9.3). These two notes not only form the pillars of the first movement but in certain respects seem also to express Yun's East Asian cultural identity. The appearance of the E–A♭ dyad at the very beginning and at the end of the adagio forms the contour of an arch, as if it begins in nothingness and returns to its origin, in reference to Taoism. This musical gesture summarises one of my arguments for the contrasts and combinations of languages embedded in the music.

Rising gestures are important to Yun's music: in later compositions they become more explicitly symbolic (as in the Cello Concerto, where Yun referred to the cello's rising and leaping gestures as "desire and demand for freedom, purity, and absoluteness" [Byeon 2003, 309]). In *Fünf Stücke für Klavier* the third movement is the most passionate, with extreme dynamic levels (*pp–fff*), an urgent sense of activity from quickening rhythms, expressive markings such as *con forza* and *con anima*, and repetitive, crescendo rising gestures. Figures 9.7, 9.8, and 9.9 illustrate that the three rising gestures (in bars 1–3, 12–13, and 20–21) act as pillars in the movement. The opening allegro (see figure 9.7) begins and ends with this rising gesture, which returns once more to conclude the entire movement. The gesture uses highly dissonant chords and always features a crescendo to *fff*. In his lecture "Debussy and I" in July 1986, Yun (1991a, 72) described the meaning of these rising gestures as follows: "My music is more purpose-oriented, the rising gesture of the melody implies certain characteristics. The constant rising gestures in my compositions signify emancipation."

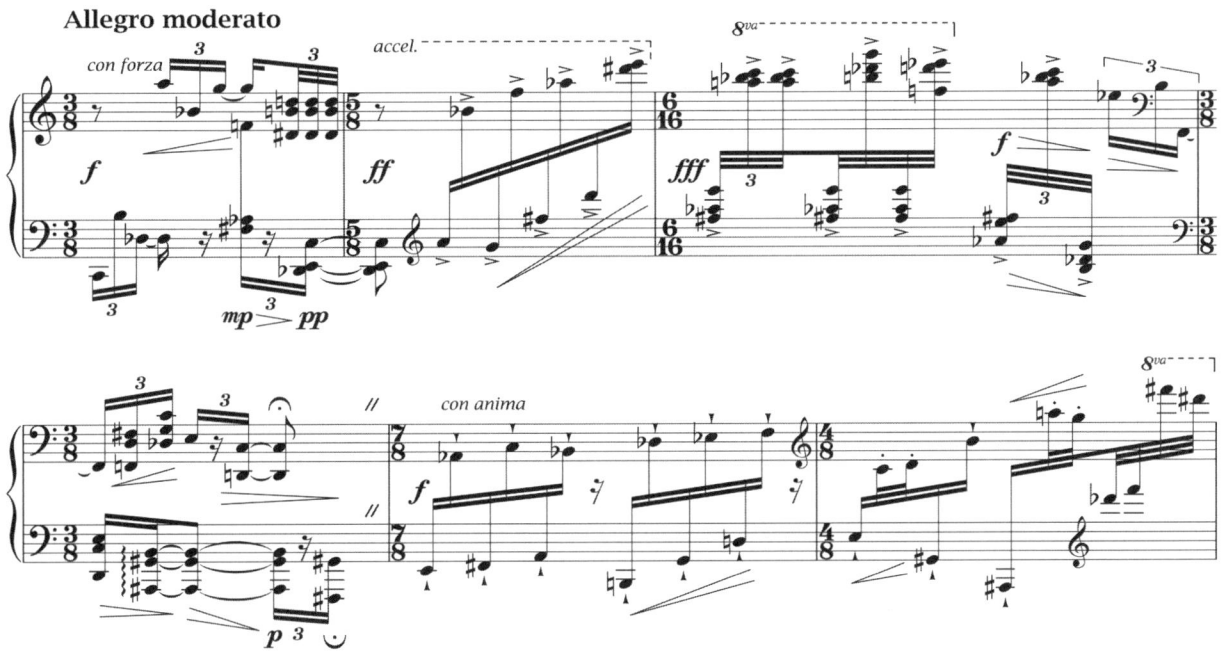

Figure 9.7.

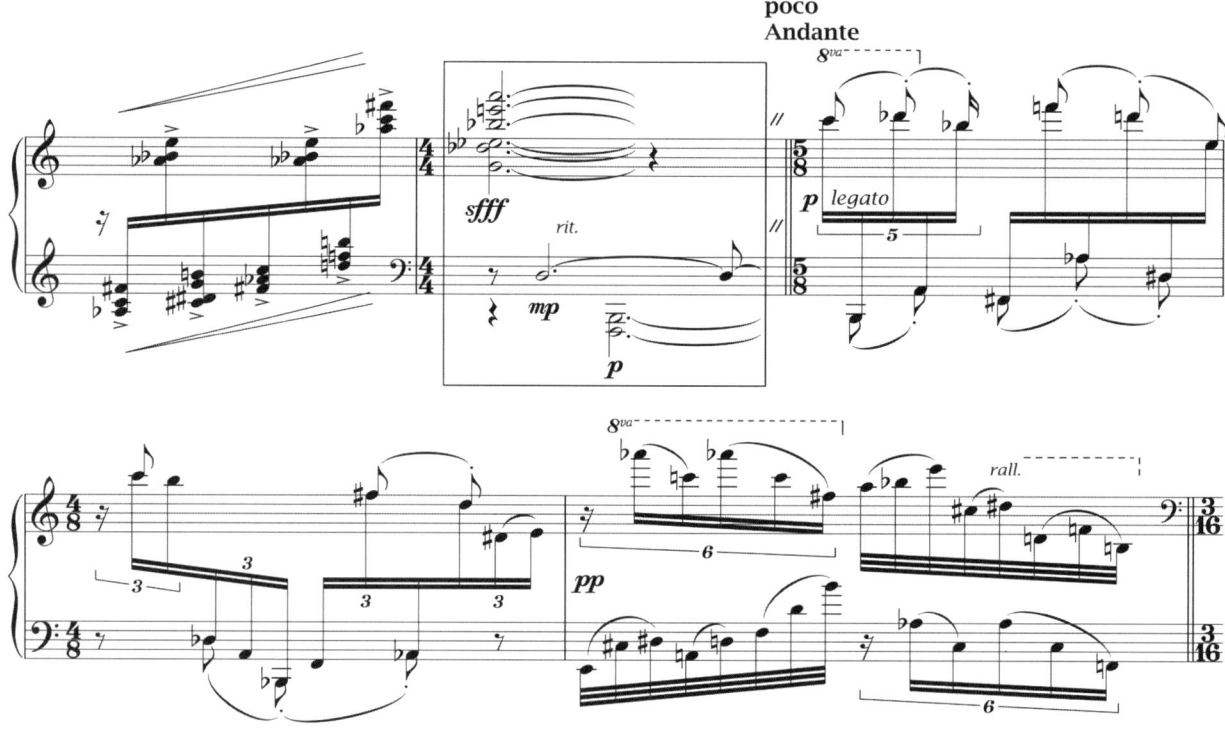

Figure 9.8.

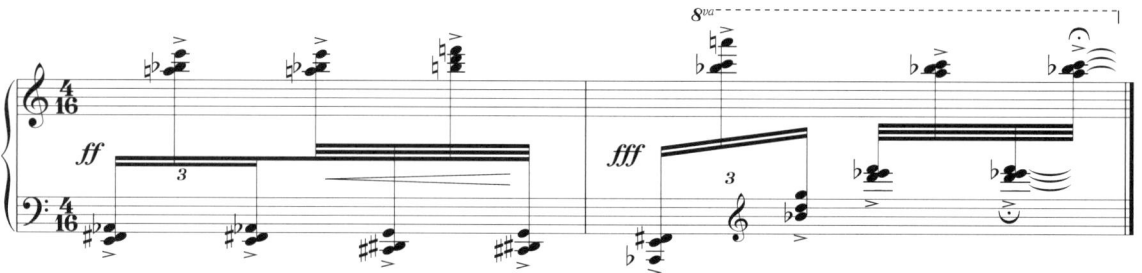

Figure 9.9.

In bar 2 of the third movement (shown in figure 9.7), Yun inserts an accelerando mark to increase the intensity of the rising gesture. In playing this, I have to consider what speed is suitable for this bar. I tend to play this passage increasing the speed of the last two beats, only hinting at the accelerando. Were I to rush this passage from the first beat, where the accelerando is marked, the rhythmic characteristics of the time signature $\frac{5}{8}$ would be missing. To me, from

222

my cultural understanding, this movement is reminiscent of Korean shamanic rituals, which engage with enthusiastic dance and music in an atmosphere of festivity or ecstasy in order to free people from suffering and heal them, connecting them to heaven and earth: I try to capture a moment of this feeling in the way I play these phrases.

In figure 9.8, the middle pillar (as shown in the box in bar 13) is located at the centre of the entire movement and functions as its climax, but also as the central moment of the complete set of five movements. Furthermore, the great distance between the interval across two hands signifies our arrival at the peak of the work. In Edward Park's view (2014, 38), this centre suggests "a wounded dragon," the title of Yun's autobiography, because the ending of the first section "gives the sense of letting out a sigh without reaching a proper conclusion." Similarly, Ko Eun Lee (2012, 66) notes that the extreme dynamic fall from *sforzatississimo* to *piano* in the climax might suggest Yun's bitter experience of developing his musical career in Korea and having lived through the Japanese occupation and the Korean War before relocating to Europe. For me, this moment in bar 13 suggests a shaman reaching a hyper-spiritual state and relieving the problem of human suffering. As noted above, Yun was exposed to shamanistic rituals during his youth in his hometown, Tongyeong. The middle pillar (bar 13) seems to embody aspects of Yun's social, cultural, and situational identities in this regard. Exploring Yun's encounters with Korean cultures via my memory and experience of Korean aesthetics has changed the way I perform this movement.

At first glance, the structure of pitches in much of this material appears almost random; however, on closer inspection, many elements are repeated. The andante section recalls the beginning of the movement by using the same tone row with fading dynamics (see figure 9.8). This cyclic system seems to echo the ways in which Yun tended to describe aspects of East Asian philosophy, particularly Taoism, where everything derives from nothingness and returns to it after travelling through change and variation, demonstrating how far a motion travels before returning to its original position (Yun and Sparrer 1994, 28–29).

In the fourth movement (see figure 9.10), the forceful allegro appears three times, altering with the soft moderato: this circular repetition of allegro and moderato signals Yun's penchant for yin and yang philosophy. As discussed by several scholars, such as Edward Park (2014, 43) and Ko Eun Lee (2012, 69), the tempo alteration between allegro and moderato conveys unity and diversity as a whole. The alternation of two different triads (A major and E♭ major for the left hand) relates to this philosophical balance. Gottfried Eberle also suggested that these two groups of triads involve complementary interaction, as they express the significance of the binary opposition of yin and yang forces (Yun and Sparrer 1994, 74).

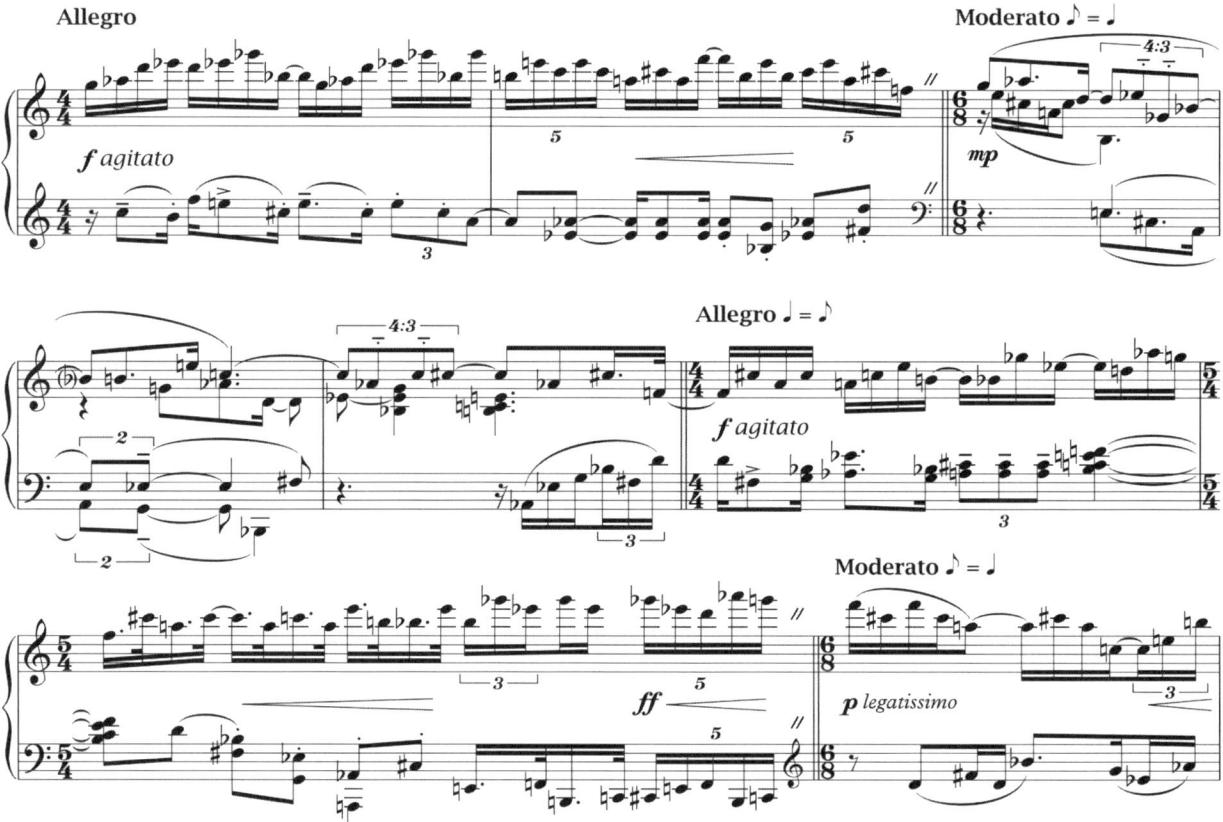

Figure 9.10.

Conclusion

The instances discussed above provide examples of how Yun's multiple identities are manifested in his first piano piece, and how the knowledge gained through my research has affected my performance decisions. The dramatic experiences Yun underwent positioned him in different social, cultural, and political contexts: his sense of identity underwent continuous transformation. However, aspects of Yun's "Koreanness" are ubiquitous in his music, manifested in all his works. Jeongmee Kim (2004, 171) considers Yun a typical diasporic immigrant, in that his "Koreanness" was formed not entirely in Korea but also in Europe, through his experience of transformation and difference. Geographical displacement gave Yun a particular perspective on his home country and its culture: he articulated his compositional philosophies by infusing Korean musical traditions into Western musical practices. This becomes far more apparent in his later works.

Of course, diasporic identity not only is embedded in artistic products (encoded) but also is discovered through reception (by performers and audi-

224

ences): it can, to an extent, be decoded. As I was born in Korea and lived the first half of my life there, I easily recognise features of Korean music in Yun's compositions, even when the soundworld is superficially that of Western modernism. As a performer, I then mediate Yun's "Koreanness" to the audience. Yayoi Uno Everett (2004, 10) notes: "Appreciation of contemporary art depends on such a dialogue between the maker and the observer/perceiver. Yet again, whether a musical element is perceived as 'Western' or 'Eastern' by an individual listener depends on the situated differences in cultural attitude—localized, embodied meaning and references we attribute to music." Ultimately, identity is distinguished by both differences and shared experiences. It is not a fixed or solid concept of being, but pertains to "becoming," constantly changing, plural, and in motion: it is a narrative of one's life. Identity is not only realised through cultural products—including musical works—but is discovered and reproduced in the processes of performance and reception in different contexts. When understanding and playing *Fünf Stücke für Klavier* using my knowledge and performative power, my performance is not an expression of the composer's idea. Rather—following Philip Thomas (2009, 78)—it is through my actions and decisions that I communicate with the audience: it is my way of living. In fact, my experience of examining, performing, and recording this piece theoretically, physically, and emotionally has shaped my identity and returned me to my imaginative cultural place, my homeland. Thus, in accordance with Laws and Auslander, performing *Fünf Stücke für Klavier* is akin to performing my ways of being as a pianist and as a musicologist.

References

Adorno, Theodor W. 1976. *Introduction to the Sociology of Music*. Translated by E. B. Ashton. New York: Seabury Press. First published 1962 as *Einleitung in die Musiksoziologie: Zwölf theoretische Vorlesungen* (Frankfurt am Main: Suhrkamp). This translation first published 1976 (New York: Seabury Press).

Aronowitz, Stanley. (1992) 1995. "Reflections on Identity." In *The Identity in Question*, edited by John Rajchman, 111–46. New York: Routledge. First published 1992 (*October* 61: 91–103).

Auslander, Philip. 2004. "Performance Analysis and Popular Music: A Manifesto." *Contemporary Theatre Review* 14 (1): 1–13.

———. 2006. "Musical Personae." *TDR: The Drama Review* 50 (1): 100–119.

Berger, Peter L., and Thomas Luckmann. (1966) 1991. *The Social Construction of Reality: A Treatise in the Sociology of Knowledge*. London: Penguin. First

published 1966 (Garden City, NY: Doubleday).

Boiger, Michael, and Batja Mesquita. 2012. "The Construction of Emotion in Interactions, Relationships, and Cultures." *Emotion Review* 4 (3): 221–29.

Born, Georgina, and David Hesmondhalgh. 2000. "Introduction: On Difference, Representation, and Appropriation in Music." In *Western Music and Its Others: Difference, Representation, and Appropriation in Music*, 1–58. Berkeley: University of California Press.

Byeon, Jiyeon. 2003. "The Wounded Dragon: An Annotated Translation of *Der verwundete Drache*, the Biography of Composer Isang Yun by Luise Rinser and Isang Yun." PhD thesis, Kent State University.

Chae, Sooah. 2003. "The Development of Isang Yun's Compositional Style through an Examination of His Piano Works." DMA thesis, University of Houston.

Cho, Joanne Miyang. 2018. "Luise Rinser's

Third-World Politics: Isang Yun and North Korea." In *Transnational Encounters between Germany and Korea: Affinity in Culture and Politics since the 1880s*, edited by Joanne Miyang Cho and Lee M. Roberts, 159–76. New York: Palgrave Macmillan.

Choi, Soo-yon. 2006. "Expression of Korean Identity through Music for Western Instruments." DMA thesis, Florida State University.

Choi, Yulee. 1992. "The Problem of Musical Style: Analysis of Selected Instrumental Music of the Korean-Born Composer, Isang Yun." PhD thesis: New York University.

Clifford, James. 1994. "Diasporas." *Cultural Anthropology* 9 (3): 302–38.

Cook, Nicholas. 2001. "Between Process and Product: Music and/as Performance." *Journal of the Society for Music Theory* 7 (2). Accessed 29 February 2020. http://www.mtosmt.org/issues/mto.01.7.2/mto.01.7.2.cook.html.

———. 2014. "Between Art and Science: Music as Performance." *Journal of the British Academy* 2: 1–25.

Cultural Properties Administration. 2000. *Korean Intangible Cultural Properties: Traditional Music and Dance*. Seoul: Hollym International.

DeNora, Tia. 2003. *After Adorno: Rethinking Music Sociology*. Cambridge: Cambridge University Press.

Everett, Yayoi Uno. 2004. "Intercultural Synthesis in Postwar Western Art Music: Historical Contexts, Perspective, and Taxonomy." In *Locating East Asia in Western Art Music*, edited by Yayoi Uno Everett and Frederick Lau, 1–21. Middletown, CT: Wesleyan University Press.

Eyerman, Ron. 2002. "Music in Movement: Cultural Politics and Old and New Social Movements." *Qualitative Sociology* 25 (3): 443–58.

Feliciano, Francisco. 1983. *Four Asian Contemporary Composers: The Influence of Tradition in Their Works*. Quezon City, Philippines: New Day Publishers.

Frith, Simon. 1996a. "Music and Identity." In *Questions of Cultural Identity*, edited by Stuart Hall and Paul du Gay, 108–27. London: Sage.

———. 1996b. *Performing Rites: On the Value of Popular Music*. Cambridge, MA: Harvard University Press.

Gilroy, Paul. 1997. "Diaspora and the Detours of Identity." In *Identity and Difference*, edited by Kathryn Woodward, 299–346. London: Sage; Milton Keynes: Open University.

Godlovitch, Stan. 1998. *Musical Performance: A Philosophical Study*. Abingdon, UK: Routledge.

Grossberg, Lawrence. 1996. "Identity and Cultural Studies: Is That All There Is?" In *Questions of Cultural Identities*, edited by Stuart Hall and Paul du Gay, 87–107. New York: Routledge.

Hall, Stuart. 1987. "Minimal Selves." In *Identity: The Real Me*, edited by Lisa Appignanesi, 44–46. London: Institute of Contemporary Arts.

———. 1990. "Cultural Identity and Diaspora." In *Identity: Community, Culture, Difference*, edited by Jonathan Rutherford, 222–37. London: Lawrence and Wishart.

———. 1996. "Introduction: Who Needs 'Identity'?" In *Questions of Cultural Identity*, edited by Stuart Hall and Paul de Gay, 1–17. London: Sage.

Hauser, Laura. 2009. "A Performer's Analysis of Isang Yun's *Monolog for Bassoon* with an Emphasis on the Role of Traditional Korean Influences." DMA thesis, Louisiana State University, 2009.

Henseler, Ute. 1992. "'Eine Musiksprache, die Humanität hat': Zu den Solokonzerten Isang Yuns." In *Isang Yun: Festschrift zum 75. Geburtstag*, edited by Hinrich Bergmeier, 58–80. Berlin: Bote & Bock.

Howard, Keith. 2006. *Creating Korean Music: Tradition, Innovation and the Discourse of Identity; Perspectives on Korean Music, Volume 2*. Aldershot, UK: Ashgate.

Kim, Jee-hyun. 2008. "East Meets West: Isang Yun's *Gagok* for Voice, Guitar, and Percussion." PhD thesis, Arizona State University.

Kim, Jeongmee. 2004. "Musical Syncretism in Isang Yun's *Gasa*." In *Locating East Asia in Western Art Music*, edited by Yayoi Uno Everett and Frederick Lau, 168–92. Middletown, CT: Wesleyan University Press.

Kim, Mi-ock. 2010. "한국 초기 작곡가들의 피아노음악" (Stylistic study of early Korean composers' piano works). *Journal of the Society for Korean Music* 40 (13): 47–90.

Kim, Sae Hee. 2004. "The Life and Music of Isang Yun with an Analysis of His Piano Works." DMA thesis, University of Hartford.

Kim, Taehyun. 2013. "The Korean Traditional Elements in Young-Ji Lee's Choral Works." DMA thesis: University of Northern Colorado.

Kim, Young Woon. 2015. 국악개론 (Introduction to Korean national music). Paju, South Korea: Eumakseagye.

Koizumi, Tetsunori. 1993. *Interdependence and Change in the Global System*. Lanham, MD: University Press of America.

Kwon, Donna Lee. 2012. *Music in Korea: Expressing Music, Expressing Culture*. New York: Oxford University Press.

Laws, Catherine. 2005. "Aspects of Form and Its Significance in Contemporary Music." *Performance Research* 10 (2), 135–46.

Lee, Dong-hoon. 2000. "A Study on the Narrative System of Agricultural Work Songs." MA dissertation, Dong-A University.

Lee, Ko Eun. 2012. "Isang Yun's Musical Bilingualism: Serial Technique and Korean Elements in *Fünf Stücke für Klavier* (1958) and His Later Piano Works." DMA thesis: University of North Carolina.

Lee, Suja. 1998. 내 남편 윤이상 (My husband, Isang Yun). 2 vols. Seoul: Changbi Publishers.

Lee, Young Ju. 2009. "Isang Yun's Musical World: A Guide to Two Songs and the Opera *Sim Tjong*." DMA thesis, Florida State University.

Lim, Jin Hyung. 2019. "Cultural and Political Overtones in Isang Yun's Works for Piano: Understanding Multiple Identity through Performance of *Fünf Stücke für Klaiver* (1958), *Duo für Viola und Klavier* (1976), and *Interludium A* (1982)." PhD thesis, University of York.

Liu, Yiming. 2005. *The Taoist I Ching*. Translated by Thomas Clearly. Boston, MA: Shambhala.

Mead, George Herbert. 1938. *The Philosophy of the Act*. Chicago: University of Chicago Press.

Noh, Dong Eun. 1994. "새로 발굴한 윤이상의 50년대 글과 노래" (Newly discovered 1950s writings and songs by Isang Yun). *Minjok Eumakei Ihae* 3: 325–41.

Oh, Da-mi. 1999. "A Study of Isang Yun's Two Piano Works—*Fünf stücke für Klavier* (1958), *Interludium A* (1982)." MA dissertation, Seoul National University.

Oha, Obododimma. 2008. "Language, Exile and the Burden of Undecidable Citizenship: Tenzin Tsundue and the Tibetan Experience." In *Exile Cultures, Misplaced Identities*, edited by Paul Allatson and Jo McCormack, 81–98. Amsterdam: Rodopi.

Oxford English Dictionary, 2020. "Emotion, n.3." Accessed 29 December 2019. https://www.oed.com.

Paddison, Max. 2004. "Performance, Reification, and Score: The Dialectics of Spatialization and Temporality in the Experience of Music." *Musicae Scientiae* 8 (1—Supplement: Discussion Forum 3): 157–79.

Park, Edward. 2014. "The Life and Music of Isang Yun." DMA thesis, University of Washington.

Park, MyeongSuk. 1990. "An Analysis of Isang Yun's Piano Works: A Meeting of Eastern and Western Traditions." DMA thesis, Arizona State University.

Park, Seon Wook. 2017. 윤이상 평전 (A critical biography of Isang Yun). Seoul: Samin.

Parker, Martin. 2007. "Identification: Organizations and Structuralisms." in *Exploring Identity: Concepts and Methods*, ed. Alison Pullen, Nic Beech, and David Sims, 61–82. Basingstoke, UK: Palgrave Macmillan.

Pullen, Alison, Nic Beech, and David Sims. 2007. "You, Me, Us and Identity: Introducing *Exploring Identity*." In *Exploring Identity: Concepts and Methods*, ed. Alison Pullen, Nic Beech, and David Sims, 1–10. Basingstoke, UK: Palgrave Macmillan.

Rutherford, Jonathan. 1990. "A Place Called Home: Identity and the Cultural Politics of Difference." In *Identity: Community, Culture, Difference*, edited by Jonathan Rutherford, 9–27. London: Lawrence and Wishart.

Safran, William. 1991. "Diasporas in Modern Societies: Myths of Homeland and Return." *Diaspora: A Journal of Transnational Studies* 1 (1): 83–99.

Said, Edward W. 1993. *Culture and Imperialism*. London: Vintage Books.

Sarup, Madan. 1994. "Home and Identity." In *Travellers' Tales: Narratives of Home and Displacement*, edited by George Robertson, Melinda Mash, Lisa Tickner, Jon Bird, Barry Curtis, and Tim Putnam, 89–101. London: Routledge.

———. 1996. *Identity, Culture, and the Postmodern World*. Edited by Tasneem Raja. Athens: University of Georgia Press.

Schmidt, Christian Martin. 1992. "Isang Yun—Mensch und Komponist." In *Isang Yun: Festschrift zum 75. Geburtstag*, edited by Hinrich Bergmeier, 11–17. Berlin: Bote & Bock.

Silverman, Marissa. 2007. "Musical Interpretation: Philosophical and Practical Issues." *International Journal of Music Education* 25 (2): 101–17.

Slobin, Mark. 1994. "Music in Diaspora: The View from Euro-America." *Diaspora: A Journal of Transnational Studies* 3 (3): 243–51.

Solomon, Thomas. 2015. "Theorizing Diaspora and Music." *Urban People/Lidé Města* 17 (2): 201–19.

Sonam, B. D. 2005. "Exile, Youth and Writings." *Tibetan Bulletin Online* 9 (3). Accessed 1 September 2016. http://www.tibet.net/tibbul/2005/focus2.html (page discontinued).

Song, Hye-jin. 2008. *Confucian Ritual Music of Korea: Tribute to Confucius and Royal Ancestors*. Translated by In-ok Paek. Seoul: Korea Foundation.

Sparrer, Walter-Wolfgang. 2008. "Virtuosity and Pathos, Beauty and Truth." Translated by Graham Lack. Liner note for *Yun/Beethoven: Pathétique*, performed by Kaya Han (piano). NEOS, 20803, 2008, compact disc.

Stevens, Richard. 1996. "Introduction: Making Sense of the Person in a Social World." In *Understanding the Self*, edited by Richard Stevens, 1–34. London: Sage; Milton Keynes: Open University.

Taruskin, Richard. 1982. "On Letting the Music Speak for Itself: Some Reflections on Musicology and Performance." *Journal of Musicology* 1 (3): 338–49.

Thomas, Philip. 2009. "A Prescription for Action." In *The Ashgate Research Companion to Experimental Music*, ed. James Saunders, 77–98. Farnham, UK: Ashgate.

Tölölyan, Khachig. 1991. "The Nation-State and Its Others: In Lieu of a Preface." *Diaspora: A Journal of Transnational Studies* 1 (1): 3–7.

Turner, J. W. 2013. "East/West Confluence in Isang Yun's *Glissées pour Violoncelle Seul*." *Virginia Review of Asian Studies* 2: 215–23.

Woodward, Kathryn. 1997. Introduction to *Identity and Difference*, edited by Kathryn Woodward, 1–6. London: Sage; Milton Keynes: Open University.

———. 2002. *Understanding Identity*. London: Hodder Education.

Yun, Isang. 1958. *Fünf Stücke für Klavier*. Berlin: Bote & Bock / Boosey & Hawkes.

———. 1991a. "드뷔시와 나" (Debussy and I). In *윤이상의 음악세계* (Isang Yun's musical world), edited by Eun-mi Hong and Seong-man Choi, 66–76. Paju, South Korea: Hangilsa.

———. 1991b. "정중동: 나의 음악예술의 바탕" (Jeong Jung Dong: the foundation of my musical art). In *윤이상의 음악세계* (Isang Yun's musical world), edited by Seong-man Choi and Eun-mi Hong, 41–52. Paju, South Korea: Hangilsa.

———. 1991c. "나의 조국, 나의 음악" (My country, my music). In *윤이상의 음악세계* (Isang Yun's musical world), edited by Seong-man Choi and Eun-mi Hong, 73–76. Paju, South Korea: Hangilsa.

Yun, Isang, and Walter-Wolfgang Sparrer. 1994. *나의 길, 나의 이상, 나의 음악* (My way, my ideal, my music). Translated from German to Korean by Kyochol Jeong and Injung Yang. Seoul: Hice.

Yun, Shin-hyang. 2005. "윤이상: 경계선상의 음악" (Yun Isang: music on the borderline). Paju, South Korea: Hangilsa.

Zheng, Su. 2010. *Claiming Diaspora: Music, Transnationalism, and Cultural Politics in Asian/Chinese America*. New York: Oxford University Press.

Steve Benford is Professor of Collaborative Computing in the Mixed Reality Laboratory at the University of Nottingham where he directs the Horizon "My Life in Data" Centre for Doctoral Training. He previously held an EPSRC Dream Fellowship, has been a Visiting Professor at the BBC and was elected to the CHI Academy in 2012. He has collaborated with many artists over the past thirty years to create, tour, and study interactive performances and installations with a view to gaining new insights into how humans can experience computers.

Richard Craig is a performer of contemporary music and an independent researcher based in Glasgow, Scotland. He has commissioned many new works for flute which he has performed around the world, and has been engaged by groups such as MusikFabrik and Klangforum Wien, as well as UK ensembles such as Explore Ensemble, the Riot Ensemble and Distractfold. His two discs of solo recordings (*Inward* and *Vale*) of works by Barrett, Croft, Ferneyhough, Pauset, and Sciarrino, among others, have received critical acclaim, and he continues to develop aspects of the flute and its technique in his collaborations and in his own compositions. As a teacher, he has given masterclasses and symposia across the UK and abroad on contemporary performance practice. From 2015 to 2019 he was a lecturer and Head of Performance at Bangor University, Wales. Craig was awarded a PhD from Middlesex University and was an honorary research fellow at the University of Huddersfield from 2014 to 2019. www.richardcraig.net.

David Gorton is a composer based in London. A winner of the Royal Philharmonic Society Composition Prize, his large-scale works include *The Fall of Babel* for the BBC Symphony Orchestra, *Oblique Prayers* for Claire Booth and the London Sinfonietta, and *Schmetterlingsspiel* for Christopher Redgate and Ensemble Exposé. Since 2010 three portrait albums have been released of his music on the Métier and Toccata Classics labels. The most recent, *Variations on John Dowland*, was featured on BBC Radio 3's Record Review, and contains two substantial pieces based on original material by Dowland: *Lachrymae Variations* for Longbow and violinist Peter Sheppard Skærved, and *Forlorn Hope* for guitarist Stefan Östersjö. David Gorton was a student at Durham University, King's College London, and the Royal Academy of Music, studying composition with Harrison Birtwistle and Simon Bainbridge. He has taught at the Royal Academy of Music since 2006, where he is an associate professor of the University of London. His music is published by Verlag Neue Musik, Berlin.

Chris Greenhalgh is a professor in the School of Computer Science at the University of Nottingham, where he is a co-leader of the Mixed Reality Laboratory and a member of the Horizon Digital Economy Research Institute. His research interests are at the intersection of human–computer interaction and distributed systems, including ubiquitous computing and mobile multi-user applications. His work is collaborative and multidisciplinary in nature and, in common with the Mixed Reality Laboratory as a whole, focuses on supporting everyday activities and situations, including home, work, leisure, and entertainment. He has a particular interest in creating platforms and tools that enable non-programmers to use emerging technologies and create engaging experiences.

Adrian Hazzard is a Research Fellow in the Mixed Reality Laboratory, School of Computer Science, University of Nottingham, who specialises in research at the intersection between human–computer interaction (HCI), music, and performance. Hazzard has a background in music performance and composition. He gained his PhD from Nottingham in 2015 on the subject of a compositional framework for locative music experiences. He has published and spoken widely at ACM conferences such as SIGCHI, DIS, MobileHCI, and Audio Mostly, alongside New Interfaces for Musical Expression (NIME). His research focuses on the creation and consumption of performance art, especially novel interactive musical experiences: charting how artists' approach their craft and the role digital tools play in both supporting and presenting new opportunities for their practice. Furthermore, he seeks to understand the audience experience of these new digitally enhanced performances.

Juliana Hodkinson is a composer, Associate Professor in Composition at the Grieg Academy, University of Bergen, Norway, and Visiting Lecturer in Classical and Electronic Composition at the Royal Academy of Music, Aarhus, Denmark. She has published on topics within sound art, contemporary music, and opera. Her current artistic work focuses on creating hybrid spatialised electro-acoustic formats for performance and listening, often in collaboration with other artists. She has received commissions from the BBC, Konzerthaus Berlin, Chamber Made Opera, the Darmstädter Ferienkurse, Haus der Kulturen der Welt, and others. Main recent works include the electronic chamber opera *Turbulence* (2013) to a libretto by Cynthia Troup, the instrumental- and object-theatre piece *Angel View* (2014), *Can modify completely / in this case / not that it will make any difference* (2016) for solo electric guitar and chamber orchestra, *All Around* (2019) for orchestra with spatialised ensemble and surround audio, and the hybrid ambient/binaural sound installation *On/Off* (2019) in collaboration with Ursula Andkjær Olsen.

Maria Kallionpää is an internationally active composer and pianist, currently working as an assistant professor at the Hong Kong Baptist University, and as a composer in residence of the Mixed Reality Laboratory at Nottingham University. Her research as a postdoctoral fellow (2016–2018) at the University of Aalborg, Denmark, focused on gamification as a composition technique (funded by Kone Foundation). Furthermore, as a winner of the Fabbrica Young Artist Development Program of Opera di Roma, Kallionpää was commissioned to compose an opera (first performed at Teatro Nazionale, Rome, October 2017). In collaboration with her colleague Markku Klami, Kallionpää also composed the first full-length puppet opera produced in the Nordic Countries (first performed in March 2018). Kallionpää was a laureate of Académie de France à Rome in 2016. She received her PhD in composition from the University of Oxford in 2015 and graduated from the Royal Academy of Music (2009) and Universität für Musik und Darstellende Kunst Wien (2010). In 2013 Kallionpää won the first prize of the OUPHIL composition competition.

Zubin Kanga is a pianist, composer, improviser, and technologist. His work in recent years has focused on new modes of interaction between a live musician and new technologies, including live electronics, film, AI, motion capture, live animation, and virtual reality. He has collaborated with many of the world's leading composers including Michael Finnissy, George Benjamin, Alexander Schubert, Nicole Lizée, Thomas Adès, and Liza Lim and has premiered more than 110 new works. Kanga has performed at many international festivals including the BBC Proms, London Contemporary Music Festival, Huddersfield Contemporary Music Festival (UK), Melbourne Festival (Australia), Festival Presénces (France), Klang Festival (Denmark), Podium Festival (Germany), Resonator Festival (Sweden), CUBE, Graz (Austria), and Borealis Festival (Norway). A Master's and PhD graduate of the Royal Academy of Music, London, Zubin was a post-doctoral researcher at the University of Nice and IRCAM (Paris) and is now a Leverhulme Early Career Fellow at Royal Holloway, University of London. www.zubinkanga.com.

Catherine Laws is Reader in Music at the University of York, UK, and a Senior Artistic Research Fellow at the Orpheus Institute, Ghent. As a pianist Catherine specialises in contemporary music, working collaboratively with composers and often drawing other artists, especially theatre and filmmakers, into her projects. Her artistic research is focused variously on processes of embodiment, subjectivity, and collaboration in contemporary performance practices. She currently leads the research cluster "Performance, Subjectivity, and Experimentation" at the Orpheus Institute, and her solo multimedia performance piece *Player Piano* is one outcome of that work, along with her substantial contributions to the book *Voices, Bodies, Practices: Performing Musical Subjectivities* (Leuven University Press, 2019). Recent recording projects include music by Annea Lockwood, Morton Feldman, and Martin Iddon, plus a series of "piano films": filmic versions of theatrical pieces for piano developed in collaboration with a number of composers, including Damien Harron, Juliana Hodkinson, Edward Jessen, Roger Marsh, and Paul Whitty, available at bit.ly/pianofilms. Catherine's research in the field of word-and-music studies examines the relationship between music, language, and meaning, focusing especially on Samuel Beckett and composers' responses to his work. Her book *Headaches among the Overtones: Music in Beckett/Beckett in Music* came out in 2013.

Jin Hyung Lim is Adjunct Professor of Music at Keimyung University, South Korea, where she also holds positions in piano performance. As an active pianist, she has performed in Asia, Europe, and North America, has broadcast on CBC and WPRB radio, and has been recorded by the Lemoine, Naxos, and CMRC labels. Recently, she completed a PhD in performance studies at the University of York, UK. Her research explores how political events and cultural and philosophical traditions influence music, focusing on Korean-German composer Isang Yun and his works. Her recent publications include the 2019 edition of the Tongyeong International Music Centre Journal "Understanding Isang Yun's Multiple Identities in performing *Duo für Viola und Klavier* (1976)."

Nguyễn Thanh Thủy is a leading *dàn tranh* player/improviser in both traditional and experimental music. She was born into a theatre family and was raised with traditional Vietnamese music from an early age in Hà Nội. She later studied at the Hanoi Conservatory of Music and at the Institute of Cultural Studies. Since 2000 she has held a teaching position at the Vietnam National Academy of Music. She has toured in Asia, Europe, and the United States, received many distinctions, recorded several CDs, and has collaborated extensively with choreographers, composers, and theatre directors on many interdisciplinary projects. Between 2009 and 2011, she was involved as an artistic researcher in the international research project "(Re)thinking Improvisation," a collaboration between the Vietnam National Academy of Music and the Malmö Academy of Music. In 2019 she received a PhD from the Malmö Academy of Music, Lund University, for an artistic doctoral project concerned with gesture in traditional Vietnamese music.

Stefan Östersjö is chaired professor of musical performance at Piteå School of Music, Luleå University of Technology. He is a leading classical guitarist specialising in the performance of contemporary music. Since his debut CD (Swedish Grammy, 1997) he has released twenty CDs and toured Europe, the USA, and Asia. He has collaborated extensively with composers and in the creation of works involving choreography, film, video, performance art, and music theatre. Since 2006 he has been developing inter-cultural artistic practices with the Vietnamese-Swedish group the Six Tones as a platform. As a member of the Landscape Quartet he has developed an articulated performative practice within ecological sound art. As a soloist he has worked with conductors such as Lothar Zagrosek, Péter Eötvös, Pierre-André Valade, Mario Venzago, and Andrew Manze.

Deniz Peters is Professor for Artistic Research in Music and Head of the Doctoral School for Artistic Research at the University of Music and Performing Arts Graz, and President of the Society for Artistic Research (SAR). His artistic research on interpersonal empathy combines phenomenological, conceptual, and interaction analyses with an experimental piano practice and improvisation with musicians and dancers including Simon Rose, Stevie Wishart, Ellen Waterman, Christopher Williams, Bennett Hogg, Stefan Östersjö, Magdalena Chowaniec, and Alexander Deutinger. Alongside rethinking musical expression in a philosophical-analytical research project, a third area of his activity is directed towards a fuller understanding of the methods, documentation, typology, and epistemology of artistic research through music. Peters has appeared as a speaker and performer at conferences in musicology, philosophy, and artistic research in Europe, Australia, and the USA, and has written on musical empathy, gesture, bodily listening, instrumentality, and rhythm. Publications include a collected edition *Bodily Expression in Electronic Music* (Routledge, 2012); articles in *Performance Research*, *Contemporary Music Review*, and *Empirical Musicology Review*; chapters in collections with Lexington, Springer, and Oxford University Press; and a CD of findings (Leo Records).

Eleanor Roberts specialises in histories of performance and visual art, and is currently based at University of Roehampton (London, UK). Her research focuses on feminist approaches to the archive, the 1960s and 1970s, contemporary live art, and practices of institutional critique. Previous collaborative projects include *Are We There Yet? A Study Room Guide on Live Art and Feminism* (2015), which was part of a wider initiative that involved bringing together a range of women artists across generations with Lois Weaver and Live Art Development Agency, and the Google Cultural Institute exhibition *Live Art and Feminism in the UK* (2015). Roberts's work has been published in *Art Monthly*, *Contemporary Theatre Review*, *Oxford Art Journal*, and the recent collection *Live Art in the UK: Contemporary Performances of Precarity* (Methuen Drama, 2020).

Anne Veinberg is an Australian pianist based in the Netherlands. She is passionate about music of and for today and regularly collaborates with other musicians, composers, actors, and technologists to develop new works and musical experiences. Veinberg is a member of Ensemble Scala for microtonal music and of Apituley's Locomotive Band for music theatre productions. Together with Felipe Ignacio Noriega, she forms the duo Off<>zz and is co-founder of the CodeKlavier—a system to live code with the piano. Through the docARTES programme, Veinberg is a doctoral candidate at Leiden University. Her research focuses on the intersection and interaction of pianistic and live coding performance practices.

Index

Editor
Catherine Laws

Authors
Steve Benford
Richard Craig
David Gorton
Chris Greenhalgh
Adrian Hazzard
Juliana Hodkinson
Maria Kallionpää
Zubin Kanga
Catherine Laws
Jin Hyung Lim
Nguyễn Thanh Thủy
Stefan Östersjö
Deniz Peters
Eleanor Roberts
Anne Veinberg

Production manager
Heike Vermeire

Managing editor
Edward Crooks

Series editor
William Brooks

Lay-out
Studio Luc Derycke

Cover design
Lucia D'Errico

Cover image
© Dimitris Doukas

Typesetting
Friedemann Vervoort

Printing
Wilco, Amersfoort
(The Netherlands)

© 2020 by Leuven University Press /
Universitaire Pers Leuven /
Presses Universitaires de Louvain.
Minderbroedersstraat 4
B-3000 Leuven (Belgium)

ISBN 978 94 6270 231 8
eISBN 978 94 6166 331 3

D/2020/1869/27
NUR: 664

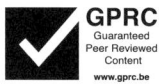

*This book is published in the Orpheus Institute
Series.*

https://doi.org/10.11116/9789461663313